D0909361

The Lucky Bastard Club

The Lucky Bastard Club

A B-17 Pilot in Training and in Combat, 1943–45

MISTER FLETCHER'S GANG

EUGENE FLETCHER

UNIVERSITY OF WASHINGTON PRESS

Published by arrangement with
University of Washington Press
P.O. Box 50096
Seattle, WA 98145-5096

ISBN 0-295-97232-7

Printed in the United States of America

Contents

MISTER

Contents

Foreword

Mister by Eugene Fletcher stirs up many memories—rough but fond memories of growing up in the depression days of the 1930s—jobs at $4.00 per week—the overrunning of Europe by Hitler's Germany—the breaking up of the football team as we went into the Army, Navy, Air Corps, and Marines —early marriages without thought, or doubt, about the future.

As individuals, we reflected all the indecisions, the complacencies even, of a nation reluctant to go to war. Reluctant, that is, until Pearl Harbor jolted us right into the middle of World War II. In this vigorous recounting of his cadet experience, in training to become an Army pilot, Fletcher captures singular voices and telling details. He brings to life a pivotal moment in American history.

Cadet training was right on target. There was no lack of grit and courage—that was a given. What we acquired were focus, skill, discipline, and resoluteness—honed through relentless hazing, toughened through basic and advanced training—creating the teamwork necessary for actual combat missions.

Fletcher takes us there from day one. His account is authentic and accurate. Arriving in civilian clothes at their first base, his reporting class had no idea that the caustic barrage—the belted commands: *Hit a brace, mister!*—were but the sniffles of a minor cold. Ahead lay a regular plague of hazing—chills and fever, flu and pneumonia!

Hazing during pre-flight training was delivered by the newly commissioned second lieutenants. Believe me, there was no ogre worse! In primary and basic, the upper classmen outdid one another in ways to degrade a person. In advanced flight training, hazing was still a threat, but it dropped off considerably as the upper classmen concentrated their efforts on winning those silver wings. Its point, of course, was to ensure battle-ready discipline—unquestioning, unquitting.

Fletcher tells of the many courses in preparation for combat flying. Instructors were both civilian and military, each dedicated to imparting knowledge essential to survival. They knew their subjects, and they knew how to cram a lot of information into a minimum of time.

Life Fletcher, I had previous experience and my private license. Unlike Fletcher, I flew the open cockpit PT-18 Stearmans in primary training at Sikeston, Missouri, in 20-degree December weather. At Randolph Field for basic training we flew night and day, formation, short cross-country, and instrument flights in the BT-9. At Kelly Field for advanced training we were assigned the AT-6 and the BC-1.

Finally, upon graduation, we received our wings. Although we had flown only single-engine aircraft, we had completed our training as bomber pilots. We were told to request where we would like to be stationed. I requested: first, the A-20 attack bomber at Oklahoma City; second, the A-20 school at Seattle, Washington; and third, A-20 flight training at Orlando, Florida. I received orders to report to the 56th Fighter Group at Bridgeport, Connecticut, to fly the Thunderbolt, the new P-47 fighter.

That's the military way. Hurry up and wait! Spin your wheels until they need bodies, and *then* you know. Fletcher does an excellent job of conveying the frustrations and quandaries of training and assignment as well as the indomitable spirit of flyers whose sights were set on being part of an Allied victory.

Rivalry existed among all pilots, especially between fighter and bomber pilots. This rivalry extended as we progressed to the combat theater, but on mission day it ceased to exist. A comradeship was forged as the "little friends," flying cover over the bomber stream, rallied to protect and escort home the crippled "big friends."

As we performed in the various theaters of World War II, in diverse aircraft and on multiple missions, the cadet experience was a vital link among us, a common bond. Fletcher recaptures those years of remarkable happiness, disappointment, courage—and the humor that sustained us all. *Mister* delivers a fitting and memorable salute to the cadets—a group of proud, eager, and determined young men. And, as a cadet of that period, I would say, in a loud and clear voice:

Aviation Cadet
Robert S. Johnson,
0661217, SIR!

[Publisher's note: Colonel Robert S. Johnson was the first American ace to exceed Eddie Rickenbacker's World War II record of twenty-six victories. When Johnson returned from the European Theater in 1944, he was the highest-scoring American ace of World War II, with twenty-eight confirmed aerial victories against the fighter pilots of the Luftwaffe.]

Author's Note

It is now June 1991. The undulating hills are green with the young growing wheat plants while the cattle patiently graze under the trees in the valley below. The tranquil sky overhead is a brilliant blue broken only by an occasional hawk or crow riding the thermals while watching the ground for prey.

Many years ago, as a boy, I watched this same picture unfold. One might have the impression that this pastoral, pacific scene had always been my way of life. But, like many others, I experienced an interruption of several tumultuous years during World War II, the greatest conflict ever waged. This was a war which required a countless number of machines on the ground, in the air, and on the seas. Millions of men and women were needed to build and operate these machines of destruction.

Because of changes in the concepts and the actual weapons of war, never again will we see this tremendous build-up of men and machines or the magnitude of training involved to provide crew members to all branches of the service. I will address, generally, only one phase of this build-up: the training of the aerial crew members needed for the U.S. Army Air Force and, in particular, the pilots needed to man these weapons.

Air power was gaining recognition as a viable weapon in conflict when our country launched a massive crash program to provide the thousands of pilots needed to fill this gap in our nation's human arsenal. This specialized training was not easy nor could it be accomplished in a matter of weeks.

This is the chronological story of the training of one pilot who enlisted as an aviation cadet. All of the incidents are true and I hope every cadet, service person, flyer, or reader can identify with some of the occurrences in this story.

Take a glimpse at the end product in the Introduction, then, keeping in mind the ultimate goal, travel with me from beginning to end through the process which molded the bulk of the pilots of the U.S. Army Air Force.

Acknowledgments

I would like to acknowledge and express sincere thanks and gratitude to Professors Maclyn Burg and Tom Pressly of the University of Washington History Department for their critique of the manuscript. May they know that their support and input were truly appreciated. A warm thank you to my good friends Ruth and Louis Kirk for their encouragement and suggestions after reading a very rough composition. And especially to Lane Morgan, who spent many hours skillfully preparing the manuscript for publication, my deep appreciation and heartfelt thanks.

Introduction

The B-17 was battered and war weary. The camouflage paint was blistered and peeling, the fuselage and wings held together by an assortment of patches of all shapes and sizes attesting to the accuracy of the German fighters and flak gunners. But the old queen was flying smoothly. The four Wright-Cyclone engines were purring in perfect synchronization, a tribute to the constant loving care she had received from the ground crew who had looked after her since her first combat mission and baptism of fire on March 27, 1944.

It was July 6, and again she was headed for battle against the Third Reich. While four months doesn't seem long, in combat it can be an eternity and, in this case, it would be the midpoint in her lifetime because she would not live to see the end of the year. Nor would the nine-man crew who perished with her on December 16, 1944.

Today she was carrying a new crew who were flying their first mission and who were secretly hoping and trusting that her experience would make up for their own inexperience. She wasn't a pretty sight. Her nose bore the name *Government Issue* and above the name was the ignominious caricature of a brown roll of paper with perforations about every four inches.

Her fuselage bore the large letters "QW" which, to the knowing eye, would identify her as a member of the 412th Squadron. Her high tail fin sported the serial number 297232, indicating the year and contract number under which she had been ordered from the Boeing Aircraft Company in Seattle, Washington. Both her pilot and copilot were also Washingtonians, and one lived only a few miles from where she was built.

Beneath the serial number and near the horizontal stabilizer was the letter "O," again a squadron identifier. Then in between was a huge black "B," indicating she was a part of the Ninety-fifth Bomb Group, superimposed on a white square, which was the emblem of the Third Bomb Division of the Eighth Air Force, stationed in England. Certainly the identifiers were the most noticeable things about the plane at first glance, but upon closer inspection the eleven manned 50-caliber machine guns commanded more respect from the attacking fighters of the Luftwaffe. Loaded in her belly were twelve 500-pound bombs bound for German installations in Abbeville, France.

It was a battle-hardened rule that a new crew would not be given a new airplane. Common knowledge had it that crews were more apt to be lost on their initial mission than at any other time, so it followed that you wouldn't risk a new airplane on a crew that lacked experience. The fact that our vehicle of war was far from new did not register even though we were surrounded by many more efficient aircraft. We would gladly have flown even a bucket of bolts to get this chance to prove our worth and satisfy our curiosity.

The new crew on board was a happy but apprehensive group. We did not know what to expect, but this was what we had been training for and now was the moment of truth. What would actual combat feel like? Would we be able to perform? Would we be scared? What would a battlefield in the sky look like? We did not have any answers. All we had was the exuberance of youth, the confidence of months of training, and a desire to inflict harm on an enemy we had not yet seen.

We had been warned not to underestimate the sheer numbers, zeal, and expertise of the enemy. But listening and doing are two different perspectives and only by doing would the reality be known. We would not have long to wait as the English Channel was disappearing behind us and the land of the enemy lay 21,000 feet below.

Our formation of fifty-four aircraft was well formed into a single combat wing. Ahead and behind us at three-minute intervals were other combat wings proceeding to the targets that had been preassigned. We knew that as we reached the target, each wing would separate into eighteen-ship groups, bomb the targets as individual groups, and then re-form and head for home. We also knew that some would not return, but in our innocence we knew it would be someone else.

Combat was a term which up to now had very little meaning to any of us. It sounded romantic and glamorous. Certainly the uniform of the United States Army Air Force, which we had donned at the beginning of our training, enhanced all of our looks and turned the heads of many of the opposite sex. We were a proud crew who showed little humility, but this was the day of reckoning we had all looked forward to.

I was jolted from my reverie by an announcement from the navigator that we were now approaching the Initial Point, at which separation would take place and the bomb run begin. We were lucky the Luftwaffe had not yet appeared, but the air was filled with our own P-47 escort fighters whose mission was to protect the bombers.

My role in this aerial drama was as first pilot or aircraft commander. This was the crew that I, with the help of many fine instructors, had trained for combat against the Axis Powers.

I looked in the distance as we were turning at the Initial Point and saw the beginning of the enemy resistance. There were a few scattered aerial artillery bursts, probably from 88-millimeter guns poised to defend the target area. Small black mushroom clouds emerged from the ball of fire as the shells exploded in the air.

There was a feeling of relief as the shells burst harmlessly in the air above and below the attacking force. We could certainly survive this type of inaccurate resistance. I smiled behind my oxygen mask as I naively thought this was the best the enemy could muster.

The next four mushroom clouds moved in a little closer.

There was no cause for alarm, but a pattern was developing. The guns were firing in batteries of four. As the next bursts appeared it dawned on me that some mushrooms are poisonous and that this might be one of those deadly varieties. In the next instant the whole airplane shook as the concussion waves enveloped us completely and the stench of the black smoke started coming through our masks. Several small holes appeared in the wings and then I heard the gunner call, "Tail gunner to pilot. Tail gunner to pilot. I've just been hit." There was only time to order the waist gunner to check on him when the bombardier called out, "Bombs Away!"

Immediately the radio operator reported that only half of the load had dropped. Six bombs were still hanging in the left-hand racks and the old airplane was still rolling and groaning from the initial impact. Knowing that I was asking her to respond to pressures that exceeded her original design limitations, I jammed the throttles to the fire wall.

The bombardier called again to say the bomb-bay doors would not close. The engineer called with the news that the bomb-bay motor was on fire and endangering the fuel transfer lines. Unless action was taken immediately the plane would blow apart. Was this to be the end of a gallant lady and her crew? Or was this all a nightmare that would go away on wakening?

Until this moment I had never questioned my ability to function as a pilot and crew member, and I certainly wasn't going to begin now. However, I would question my judgment and the decisions that had brought me voluntarily into a situation where we were all looking death in the face.

Where did it all start? It had to have a beginning before it could have an end.

1 Civilian Life

Walla Walla, Washington
June 2, 1942

It was approximately three o'clock in the afternoon. I had just gotten off work as an announcer for the local radio station and had returned home to rest and have dinner before going back to the station at seven-thirty to start the second session of my split shift.

Home was the apartment of my sister and brother-in-law, who had been generous enough to offer help that I might continue a college education which had started in the fall of 1940. The apartment complex was located on Park Street just across the street from the women's dormitory on the Whitman College campus.

I picked up the mail in the foyer and took it up to apartment nine. As I placed the mail on the dining room table I noticed an official-looking postcard bearing my name. It proclaimed to all who wished to read it that my 2-A (student deferment) classification would be changed to 1-A on July 1, 1942, when I would be subject to the draft and immediately inducted in order that my hometown Selective Service board might fill its quota of warm bodies for the month of July. In my own ego I had always known that I was A-1, but a rating of 1-A carried a different, ominous connotation. Though not un-expected since a war was in progress, the notice was still somewhat shocking. It was certainly a time for reflection, a time to review the events that had led to this occasion.

My mind drifted back to relive the events of my boyhood which were indelibly imprinted on my mind: the jobless facing starvation, soup lines, hobos, and extreme poverty everywhere. People would stop at our small family farm, which was off the beaten track from the town of Dayton, and ask to sleep in the barn. They would do any kind of labor for a place to stay and something to eat. These were people who knew my parents and it wasn't easy to say no, so it wasn't said. The length of the stay depended on the season and how close they were to the family. There were times when it was questionable what would be on the table, but our mother always found something. We six children were never at a loss for chores to do as we took care of the livestock, chopped wood, worked in the garden, and helped with field and housework. We weren't taught to work; we just had to.

Many people were hungry, but were too proud to ask for welfare or relief, had there been any available. Pride is a wonderful attribute. As long as you had pride you were a person who could hold your head high, who could accept almost any adverse condition and still prevail. People still cared and looked out for one another as best they could.

During this time we never thought of ourselves as poor; we just didn't have any money and no prospect of getting any. But we managed to get by from day to day.

As I entered high school the country was just starting to recover from the Great Depression. By 1938 and '39 jobs were beginning to open up and the country was starting to move ahead. But most six-day-a-week jobs, with nine- to ten-hour days, still paid under $100 a month, with many falling in the $65 range, and they were hard to come by. It was apparent that a college education would be a great plus. But how did you go to college when there was no money available and government loans were as yet unheard of?

There had to be some way. I dropped out of high school at the end of my sophomore year and went East to take a job as a jockey for a major stable. It was a career that I thought might lead to riches, but in slightly less than two years, after traveling

a good portion of the U.S. and riding at America's most presti-
gious tracks, I returned home with a pocketful of memories
and experiences, but no money.

So it was back to school and a chance to dream up new ways
of getting a college education. At five feet six and 123 pounds,
I had no chance at an athletic scholarship. Scholarships based
on grades were few in number and very meager in support
even if one could qualify as valedictorian or salutatorian. Since
this was also out of my league some other solution would have
to be found.

Since I was a little older than my new classmates and
through my travels felt a bit more worldly wise, I sought the
counsel of the superintendent of schools. He was a very kind
man and sympathetic with my desires to try to improve my lot.
He impressed upon me that I was attending a privately endowed public school and the first accredited high school in the
state of Washington. He brought out his master's thesis and
asked me to read it. The idea was to impress upon me the
work and time required to be an achiever. Did I have that
kind of dedication? The answer was that I would like to try.
He suggested that since I had a reasonably good speaking
voice and had appeared in school plays, perhaps I should
enter some oratorical contests. This might be one way to grab
the brass ring. I took his advice and the end result was that I
was offered a partial scholarship and a work grant at a local
college.

As I stood there with the draft notice in my hand the irony
of my position started to sink in. My mind zeroed in on my
senior year in high school as I recalled the title of a speech
which I had given to the local Kiwanis Club. And, as a re-
porter from the local paper reported, " 'Preparedness for the
Safety of Democracy' was the theme and Eugene dramatically
presented the case for cleaning up our internal affairs by revi-
sion of our espionage and deportation laws and preparing
externally by building up our defense system":

> Through our government we enjoy more liberties than
> the people of any other nation and as we see bankruptcy,
> starvation and panic causing the abandonment of democ-

racy in other nations we should take heed of the un-American activities in our own country. The Dies committee has found the existence of 800 un-American organizations and made a thorough study of 150 of these which are operating in the open and taking advantage of the very freedom we have built up by American democracy.

We have but thirty-eight hundredths of one percent of our population protecting over ninety-nine percent, he pointed out, and rank eighteenth as a military power. In case of invasion we couldn't mobilize rapidly enough to stop a second-rate army, he declared, and with our garrisons scattered to the four winds of political expediency we would find ourselves badly handicapped. Our armies lack training in large masses as common in modern war, he stated.

Further difficulties would arise from having to take the entire western fleet to the east coast to protect the heavily concentrated industries there.

Preparedness then, he concluded, would be our best insurance against war and gain the respect of all nations.

The speech was generally well-received as I accepted compliments from many who attended. But later that evening my sister told me that her boss (who managed a well-known chain store) and several others had said that the speech was well presented, but the subject matter was far too mature for a high school senior.

On September 14 of that year (1940), the first peacetime draft was approved by Congress. On December 7, 1941, the Japanese attacked Pearl Harbor, and on December 8, 1941, the United States declared war on Japan. Three days later, December 11, war was declared on Germany and Italy since these two had already declared war against the United States.

Now I stood staring at a notice that I would be a part of this nation's military buildup and a part of the subject matter which two years before was deemed too mature for my consideration. But since I had considered it, I had already set in motion a plan that was supposed to keep me from being drafted and yet allow me to serve my country's needs.

Whitman College, for the past year, had been sponsoring a Civilian Pilot Training (C.P.T.) program in conjunction with the Martin School of Flying. Ground school classes were held in the evening from seven to nine. The college professors volunteered their time and it was not an easy course because the instructors took this job just as seriously as any of the regular courses they taught. The flight training was provided by the Martin School of Flying under contract with the government. We did not receive college credit for this extracurricular activity, but tuition was free and it made it possible to acquire a skill which was in demand by the U.S. Armed Forces.

When I first enrolled in the program I had serious doubts that I could learn to fly. The air seemed to be a hostile and unnatural environment, and my nervousness seemed to cloud the decision-making process. My actions and reactions were too slow for the danger involved. But I was told that this problem affected everyone. Only by spending a lot of time in the air and becoming accustomed to this environment could I feel a part of this medium which seemed so alien.

My first flying instructor was a young man named Fred Campbell, and he could make that Piper J-3 Cub do anything that was in the range of its limited capabilities. After several hours in the air the feeling of insecurity did leave. All of a sudden I felt that I was a part of the airplane and making it do what I wanted it to do instead of riding and reacting to what the plane wanted to do. But then my new confidence was shaken by the fact that every time I set up a landing procedure the instructor would start to holler and jiggle the stick or kick a rudder pedal. I would have to recover from these gyrations in the few seconds before touchdown or else open the throttle, abort the landing, and go around the pattern again and set up a new landing approach. After several hours of these antics and nervous screaming by the instructor, I began thinking about giving up the program.

I finally decided that after my next flight I would sit down with the instructor and discuss dropping out since it was apparent that I was not pleasing him. When I reached the flight line for what I thought to be my last flight, the airplane was just taxiing in from the runway to the parking ramp. I waited at the assigned spot and as the airplane came to a stop the student pilot opened the door and climbed out of the back seat. The Piper J-3 Cub had two seats in tandem in an enclosed cabin. The instructor sat in the front seat with dual controls and instruments while the student sat in the rear seat with only the controls.

The airplane had a very small tail wheel as opposed to the tricycle gear of modern airplanes. That meant the student, because he was lower and behind, could only see the back of the instructor while on the ground. Since he couldn't see ahead he couldn't taxi in a straight line. He had to make a series of S-turns, weaving back and forth and looking out the side window to steer clear of any obstructions or other traffic.

As the previous student climbed out of the airplane with the engine still idling, the instructor gruffly shouted above the engine noise for me to get on board. Oh boy, it was obvious he was in a bad mood today. There was no friendly greeting. As soon as I had fastened my safety belt and closed the door he said that we would practice landings and would not leave the traffic pattern, so start taxiing immediately.

While I taxied to the runway he pelted me with an endless barrage of questions which required some concentration to answer. Meanwhile, I was also trying to locate other traffic, taxi the plane, and check the instruments. Eventually we reached the end of the runway and started the engine check. Since there were no radios in these planes and no tower for communication you waited at the end of the runway and watched until all was clear, and then taxied onto the runway and started the takeoff roll.

In the initial portion of the roll the student pilot's forward vision was blocked off, so I watched the edge of the runway for directional control. As the throttle was advanced and the speed accelerated the tail rose and I could look over the instructor's shoulder. The instructor had a rear view mirror located so he could see what I was doing.

On this takeoff we were playing a game of cat and mouse. If I looked over his right shoulder he immediately shifted his body in that direction to block my view. And the same way to the left. At the same time he was critical of everything I was doing. But in spite of all of this, we did get airborne, around the pattern, and back to the final approach.

I had a good approach set up and was over the end of the runway with about fifty feet of altitude when the instructor kicked full right rudder. Instantly I centered the control and applied full power for a couple of seconds to regain speed and directional control. As I pulled off the power the airplane roughly touched down onto the runway with the instructor still ranting and raving. I thought the landing was a good one in spite of everything that had taken place, but obviously my confidence was shaken as I really didn't know what I was doing wrong. Anyway, it appeared this was a good time to end the venture.

As the plane lost its speed I turned off the end of the runway and onto the taxi strip. The instructor became strangely quiet and motioned for me to head up the taxiway to the other end of the runway. As we were passing the parking area in front of the flight operations buildings he pulled the throttle back to the idle position and jammed on the brakes. The tail jumped about six inches in the air, then banged down on the ground. Immediately the door popped open and the instructor jumped out.

By now I was completely bewildered. He reached back in and fastened his safety belt across the empty seat. Then he said, "Fletcher, some day you're going to kill somebody and it's not going to be me. So take off on your own and make three landings." At this announcement I turned off the magneto switch and as the engine sputtered to a stop I crawled out too. "What do you think you're doing?" he growled.

"I've got news for you. If someone is going to be killed it's not going to be me either. I quit."

"Hey," he said, "you've got eight hours dual time, the minimum required for soloing, and you're probably the only student in my group who will solo at eight hours."

"Look, I can't be very good with all this hollering and grabbing the controls on landing. I must be doing something radically wrong; it must be time to stop."

"Fletch, you take this flying too seriously. Loosen up a bit. You've been doing too good a job on landing. I've been kidding you and kicking the airplane around to see how you would react in emergency situations, and frankly, you have come through with flying colors. Now get back in and solo."

I made one more protest and he said, "Come on, this was just a little ritual to keep you from becoming too cocky or overconfident and I wanted to see how you would react to stress. If I didn't think you could do it I wouldn't send you out alone. You don't think I would let you ruin my career and reputation as a flight instructor, do you?"

It seemed to make sense so I crawled into the back seat, fastened the safety belt, and closed the door. The Cub J-3 was always flown solo from the back seat in order to keep the C.G. (center of gravity) within its proper limits. I called, "Throttle cracked—switch on—brakes locked." My heels depressed the two awkward brake pedals, and immediately it was contact as Mr. Campbell swung the prop through and the hot engine sputtered to life. It was a good sound. Fred came around to the side of the airplane and with a big grin on his face gave me the thumbs up sign.

Still a little apprehensive and somewhat bewildered, I eased off the brakes, opened the throttle a little, and the plane began to move almost immediately. I was astonished how much easier it was to see without the instructor and that was a big plus. The engine was noisy and the fabric-covered aircraft vibrated incessantly, but somehow it seemed strangely quiet and maybe just a little lonesome too.

At the end of the runway I checked the magnetos, which supplied electrical current to the spark plugs, not just once as required but several times as I tried to gain confidence. It was November 4, 1941, and a cold day, but there was a drop of sweat on my forehead as I realized it was now or never.

The airspace was clear as I moved onto the runway and slowly but deliberately opened the throttle to its maximum. All sixty-five horses in the little Franklin engine were pulling together and the airplane literally leaped off the runway without the weight of the instructor on board. Before I even had time to miss the instructor's screaming it was time to pull on the carburetor heat as a precaution against icing in the carburetor, which could cut off the flow of air and gas to the engine. Then it dawned on me that in a matter of seconds I was going to have to land this craft by myself! Could I do that? I had better do it or someone was going to get hurt.

I was now passing over the airport boundary, then over the end of the runway. I kept moving the stick back, but the airplane kept floating. Would there be enough runway left? Without the instructor the airplane flew entirely differently. Finally the right wheel and tail wheel touched down—then the left wheel with a rocking motion. The crosswind correction had been kicked out too soon, allowing the left wing to rise slightly. Next time I would hold a little longer.

As the plane continued the roll-out I tried the awkward heel brakes; the airplane was under control and I was ready to try again. Exhilarated, I felt one with the airplane again, my confidence was running high and with the completion of the third landing my head was in the clouds. I knew then that I had to fly. It would be a long haul to master the art, but I would be a pilot and I would never let another instructor get under my skin again, or so I thought that day.

As I parked the airplane and shut off the mag switch, the instructor opened the door and said, "Congratulations, you've just been initiated into the realm of those who have the flying bug. Now the real work starts." But this time a big grin was on my face.

All too soon primary was over; I had received my private pilot's license. I was now enrolled in a secondary course flying a fully aerobatic light airplane, a bi-wing Meyers with a Warner 125 horsepower engine rigged to supply fuel for inverted flight. My new instructor was Vance Call, a perfectionist in aerobatics. He taught me every aerobatic maneuver he could think of, and it was breathtaking flying in the open cockpit airplane. Helmet, scarf, goggles, and the wind in your face: every pilot's dream. It was sheer pleasure to practice the aerobatic maneuvers: spins, loops, Immelmann turns, chandelles, Cuban eights, snap rolls, slow rolls, falling leaves, and so on. But it was also work as the instructor demanded a high level of competency in precision flying. The ground school continued and the college professors demanded more than just a passing level performance in Civil Air regulations, meteorology, navigation in all its forms, theory of flight, Morse code, map reading, aircraft structures, power plants, and on through the whole range of subjects pertaining to aviation.

With the flying and ground school phases passed with good ratings, I next applied for instructor school. The school was located in Belgrade, Montana, and the graduating instructors went directly to the military primary flight schools to instruct the aviation cadets in their first phase of flying. It too could be a dangerous occupation, but it was something that I wanted to do and it would be my contribution to the war effort.

It was at this point that I stood looking at the 1-A notice and realized that I had not heard from the instructor school. However, I had mailed my application only ten days previously. There appeared to be nothing I could do but wait.

In the meantime I continued with my job as a radio announcer and kept up my flying proficiency by taking anyone for a ride, including my parents, who would pay for the rental of the airplane. Many of my friends who were thinking of enlisting in the Army Air Force for flight training dropped by and asked me to take them for a ride so they could see if they liked flying.

Almost everyone insisted that he be given the full assortment of maneuvers that could be done in whatever plane we used. With my own experience in mind, I tried to explain that the first ride should be just a level, sight-seeing trip to get acclimated in the air. But most insisted they didn't have that much time and since they were paying the bill they wanted the whole works. Consequently, most became sick and lost interest in flying immediately. It wasn't a fair test and I knew it, although I have noted over the years that my flying seems to have that same effect on other people. Oh well, there wasn't a shortage of volunteers for air cadet training. It sounded glamorous.

By the weekend of June 20 I had received no word on my instructor application. This meant I had ten days left before induction. If I wanted to fly I had to make some decisions in a hurry because only volunteers were allowed into military flight training programs. I could already feel the weight of the backpack and the gun on my shoulder as visions of the infantry and foxholes went flashing through my mind.

On Monday, June 22, I drove to Geiger Field near Spokane, Washington, to enlist in the U.S. Army Air Force as an aviation cadet. One of the requirements at that time was two years of college. After a two-day examination including physical, mental, and psychological tests, I signed a contract specifying that if I successfully completed all of the training phases I would be commissioned a second lieutenant in the regular Army. My orders were to return to my home, which was now listed as Walla Walla, to await orders that would place me on active duty.

While at Geiger I decided to visit my cousin, Hallie Fletcher, whose outfit, the 845 Engineers Aviation Battalion, was temporarily stationed on the base. As I walked through their area looking for his tent, I became the recipient of many hoots, jeers, and catcalls from those in uniform. It seemed they didn't appreciate my civilian clothes. Even the fact that a member of my family was a part of their organization did nothing to mollify their attitude. Little did any of us realize that day that eventually I would fly off an airfield they had constructed.

I returned home the following day and on June 26 received a registered letter of acceptance for instructor training at the Civilian Flying School. The letter contained a notice that if I was now a part of any branch of the armed forces, the letter orders were without effect. The actions of the draft board and the events of the last three days had drastically altered my life. At least the uncertainty of where I would serve was gone: The military took precedence over the instructor school.

From here on I played a waiting game. True to their word the draft board ordered me to report for a preinduction physical on July 9. At this point the Army Air Force intervened by telegram stating that I was already a part of the military system, but the Dayton board could count my enlistment against their quota.

When it was late August and I still hadn't been called to active duty, I managed to talk a very lovely, vivacious young college co-ed, Evelyn (Sherry) Sherrod, into sharing a life with me, in a married status of course. I felt the knot must be tied immediately before either of us could have second thoughts. Because I was almost two months short of my twenty-first birthday it was necessary to have my father's approval in writing, a formality he was very happy to perform. Since active duty orders could arrive at any time we desired to be married that same day, so we had to find a Justice of the Peace who would waive the three-day waiting period. This accomplished, we asked our college Bible class instructor if he would perform the ceremony. So by 11 p.m. on August 25 in the presence of some family members, the ceremony was performed.

I was now a man of the world. I had a wife, a job that paid $80 a month, and a commitment to the Army Air Force. What more could one ask for? After a short honeymoon there were now four occupants in Apartment #9, all gainfully employed.

The vulnerability of our lives was brought to reality on Thanksgiving Day when my brother-in-law, Leonard Patton (Cap), received word that his younger brother, Malvern, was missing in action while flying over the Owen Stanley mountain range in New Guinea. We were in a state of shock since only six months had elapsed after his being drafted into the infantry.

Cap now felt it imperative that he enlist, although as a sole surviving son he could not be compelled to serve. But loyalty to family and the American way of life ran deep in those days. Everyone wanted to preserve this way. Even those who were physically unfit for military duty found ways they could share in this cause. Cap immediately tried to enlist in the Aviation Cadet Corps but was not accepted because of a minor eye problem. However, he was allowed to enlist in a glider training program. He too was ordered to return to Walla Walla to await the starting of his training classes.

With the exception of the family tragedy, life was beautiful for the four of us as we all had jobs and enjoyed one another's company. This happy, tranquil life came to an end on December 31 when I received a "War Department Official Air Mail Special Delivery" letter, short the required amount of postage. Apparently their franking privilege was good only for ordinary mail. It appeared that I was learning one of the first lessons of Army life—nothing is free, not even the orders to report to the recruiting station in Portland, Oregon, on Monday, January 4, 1943.

2 Preflight

Santa Ana, California

I checked into the Portland Hotel early Monday morning; the room rent was $3.50 per night and ham and eggs in the dining room $1.10. I had already spent $1.40 on taxi fare to get one-quarter mile from the train station to the hotel. At these prices I knew I had to get out of Portland quickly because I was already running over budget.

Fifty cadets reported in and when all were assembled we were given some more tests, a minor physical exam, and checked for any changes in status since our time of enlistment. In my case the only change was my marital status. It was deemed that the state of matrimony had not yet damaged my physical being so I was proclaimed fit to travel with the rest of the group by train on January 5 to the Army Air Force Classification Center at Santa Ana, California. The center was called the West Coast's "Little West Point," but any comparison to the Army's elite academy was certainly the figment of someone's warped imagination.

We arrived late in the evening on January 7. The center was a huge sprawling army air base and headquarters for the Army Air Force West Coast Training Command. It was estimated that 20,000 men were stationed here. This base combined the roles of reception center, classification center, and preflight training school for navigators, bombardiers, and pilots.

We were all overwhelmed with the size of the training facility. Everywhere you looked were two-story wooden barracks which served as housing for the cadets. There were countless other buildings whose purposes were not yet known to us. The whole base had a bleak appearance as there wasn't any grass to be seen. The area between the buildings looked like a well-pounded barnyard, but there was a huge hard-packed parade ground, larger than the south forty on many farms.

We appeared to be the only souls in civilian clothes and we certainly looked and felt out of place. In fact, we endured a few jeers and catcalls from several cadets as they sang out, "You'll be sorry." We were assigned to a holding area for the rest of the night and were told that our processing would begin the following morning.

On the morning of the eighth we were taken to a special mess hall for breakfast. We were told that we were assigned to Squadron 8 and were now in quarantine. We would be isolated for two weeks and if after that period no one had come down with a communicable disease we would be allowed to use the post exchange and other base facilities.

It was now time to receive our clothing issue and bunk assignments. Then we would assemble in uniform in front of the barracks for our official welcome from the squadron commander. Our clothing issue consisted of six pairs of olive drab (O.D.) boxer shorts and T-shirts, eleven pairs of socks, two ties, six pairs of pants, one blouse, one overcoat, one raincoat, two pairs of shoes (oxford dress and ankle top for work), six shirts, two zoot suits, one belt, four garrison caps, one service cap, several towels, a shaving kit, bedding, and other items which the military deemed necessary to our station in life.

This was more clothes than I had had at any one time in my life. Our civilian clothes were bundled up and sent home, for we would now wear a military uniform for the duration of the war. The zoot suits were really olive drab coveralls, which when issued were several sizes too large but once washed were always too small. They didn't look much like the wide-brimmed hat, broad-shouldered long coat, and key chain that inspired the name, but we felt just as ridiculous wearing them.

When it came time to assemble we stood around in front of the barracks like a band of sheep in our new uniforms. Some had perfect fits; those of us who needed alterations had to pay for them out of our own pockets. A sergeant arrived and tried desperately to get us into some semblance of formation. He was still working with us when a second lieutenant appeared and informed us that he was our squadron commander and couldn't understand why he had been chosen to receive the likes of us.

He said we weren't soldiers and it was against regulations to call us soldiers. We were officer material and would be spoken or referred to as *Mister* (usually in a very scornful and degrading manner). The commander impressed upon us that we were the lowest form of life standing on the earth. If we found anything lower it would probably be under a rock. We were not required to salute or to say "Sir" to the enlisted men or they to us. But to be on the safe side we had better say "Sir" or salute anything else that moved, because it would have more status than we did.

Squadron 8 had 240 men divided into four flights—A, B, C, and D—each containing 60 men. Most of us who had come down from Portland found ourselves in Flight D. We did everything by flights and always in formation. All duty details involved the whole flight. We were introduced to the world of the 3 Ws: walk, wait, and worry. In formation it was double time, "hurry up and wait." Any time three or more cadets were walking to the same destination a formation was mandatory. One cadet acted as the leader and the other two or more responded to his commands. If an officer was encountered the leader was the only one to salute. It didn't take us long to realize that being in cadets was the next (best/worst) thing to being in a nut house.

While in Squadron 8 we were introduced to a variety of tests. Although we didn't realize it at the time, this was the beginning of the winnowing process which followed us all through cadet training. First came the embarrassing physical examination which required the whole flight to line up without a stitch of clothing. Trying to hide behind a clipboard, which held our medical forms, was next to impossible as the doctors in front paraded up and down with stethoscopes, tongue depressors, and flashlights. The ones behind carried rubber gloves, vaseline, and blood pressure cuffs—each demanding the clipboard to scribble his findings. Bend over, stand up, say ah-h-h, stand on one leg. It was probably the most humiliating experience of our lives, but it wasn't the last.

Then came the drawing of blood and vaccinations. Some of the cadets actually fainted at the thought and sight of needles penetrating the flesh of those ahead of them in line. For me I thought both arms would fall off; I had the feeling I had been kicked by a mule. The following morning I was as sick as I had ever been. I knew I couldn't function, but I didn't want to go to sick call so I requested that I be assigned to duty as the barracks fire guard.

Then came the psychological, mental awareness (or ability to learn), and motor skills tests. The motor skills tests were used to measure manual dexterity and reaction time. They were fun because it was man against the machine or the mechanical elements, but the mental tests were a little scary. After all, who wants to tell some sinister stranger what he sees in ink blobs. How far do you stretch reality before you fall off the deep end? We all wanted to fly and we surely didn't want to lose this opportunity just because an ink blob might look like spilled ink, a naked lady, or some other screwy imagined image or hallucination. We found ourselves giving answers to questions we didn't even understand. No one knew how to respond to these strange people or why we had to. It was probably just as well we didn't know what their conclusions were because these results would follow us throughout our military career, if we were to have one.

By now we were following a regular routine. We answered a roll call formation at 5:20 a.m. in front of the barracks. Then we were dismissed to make our beds, sweep, mop, dust, and shine the barracks for inspection. And I do mean *shine*, for the inspecting officer always wore white gloves and his hands found every nook and cranny in the barracks.

The beds were tightly made. The inspecting officer would flip a quarter on the top blanket and it was supposed to bounce high enough for him to catch. If not, you were "gigged," given demerits. If something was wrong in your personal area you received the gig, but if it was something wrong in the barracks proper everyone was gigged. Inspections could come at any time, either before or after breakfast.

The barracks were never left unattended; one cadet was designated fire guard and remained in the empty building all day. This was strange because we did not have heat in the barracks, although there was a coal burning stove. Many cadets smoked but they were allowed to smoke only in the barracks. Gallon cans which had previously held canned fruit and vegetables were obtained from the mess halls and placed strategically throughout both floors of the building. The fire guard cleaned these cans, filled them half full of water, and returned them to their assigned places. He also made sure that a five-gallon bucket of sand and fire shovel were placed by the cold stove. He then remained in the building all day to watch for unauthorized entry or to escort the inspecting officer through the building, which occasionally was three or four times a day. The fire guard missed breakfast and lunch, but someone usually stood in for him at dinner time.

Unfortunately, one of our group came down with red measles at the end of the first week and our quarantine was extended for two more weeks. We remained in Squadron 8, which was the classification unit, for three weeks. This ended our twenty-one days in quarantine and coincided with announcing the results of the tests which would tell us whether we became eligible to continue as pilots, navigators, or bombardiers. These flying specialties would lead to commissions in the Army Air Force and all would be equal in pay and rank.

Those who were not chosen but had special educational qualifications could be classified for training as a ground officer in armament, photography, meteorology, engineering, communications, or a host of other specialties. These people would be sent to technical schools outside of our training center. Some who had failed the rigid physical exam for flying but were in otherwise good health could become ground mechanics or serve in some other enlisted capacity.

The permanent personnel of this classification unit from the highest ranking officers to the lowest private were all college graduates, or so we were told. There was supposedly a preponderance of M.A.s and a heavy sprinkling of Ph.D.s. We did not doubt this assessment but we were very curious as to the institutions from which these degrees were earned. But I suspect they also had reservations about us, the safety of democracy, and the United States in general as they surveyed our motley group.

It was with mixed emotions that I waited for the day the results would be announced. I may have been a licensed civilian pilot but I wasn't sure that I would even have a chance to be a military one. The tests and treatment we had received had destroyed the confidence and hopes we all had brought with us. Now it was up to the powers that be to render judgment and point us in the direction that our military careers would lie.

January 23 was a day we could never forget. It was pouring down rain with mud six inches deep and water running freely. At the morning formation it was announced that after breakfast we would receive tetanus, smallpox, and typhoid fever inoculations and before the end of the day we would be classified.

We had already lost several of our group but we were never told why. When the names were posted approximately fifteen were listed as potential navigators, about forty were on the bombardier list, over sixty were washed out, and about one hundred were eligible for pilot training. When I found my name on the pilot list I was so relieved and excited that I ran to a phone booth and spent four dollars on a long distance call so Sherry could share in the good news.

The heavens, as if in sympathy for the cadets who were washed out, retaliated with six inches of rain in twenty-four hours. The base was a sea of mud. The only solid ground was the hardened area of the parade grounds, the outdoor basketball courts, and the streets. The cadets of Squadron 8, already stressed by the quarantine, the events leading up to classification, and knowing we were losing one-fourth of our group were a time bomb ready to explode. The tension was mounting by the hour.

On the afternoon of the twenty-fourth, after returning from a rather torturous session of physical training, clad in T-shirts and shorts, we were dismissed from formation in front of the barracks by our cadet officers. Upon dismissal one cadet slipped and fell in the mud and in one spontaneous instant all of the cadets became embroiled in a pushing, shoving mud-wrestling contest.

There wasn't any animosity, but all the pent-up feelings of frustration were let loose as we pummeled one another and rolled in the mud. The cadet cadre and the more reserved cadets were immediately pounced upon and upended in the quagmire. Two officers in a jeep stopped at the intersection and watched the melee for a few minutes. They apparently had no desire to put a damper on the unseemly conduct for they quickly drove away.

The mud battle continued for about fifteen minutes and then everyone laughingly trooped into the showers and the cleanup began. Within thirty minutes the barracks were shining and the cadets were all in Class A uniforms ready for the evening meal formation. At this point two officers entered the barracks and a stand-by inspection was initiated without warning.

A stand-by inspection consists of each cadet standing by his bunk at attention with his footlocker open to view. All personal belongings must be in the proper order, all shoes and brass shined, and all buttons either on the person or on display had better be buttoned.

The inspecting officers left us all standing for five minutes in a brace before starting the inspection. Then they examined the barracks and each cadet with eye-piercing scrutiny. No demerits were given and not a word was uttered as they left; however, they were grinning from ear to ear as they pulled away in their jeep. We heaved a sigh of relief and fell into formation for the march to the mess hall.

The mess halls and their procedures are worthy of note. There were three cadet mess halls on the base. Each mess hall served three breakfasts, three lunches, and three dinners and could seat over 1,000 cadets at a time.

The cadets were seated twelve to a table which was presided over, in the beginning, by an upperclassman. He decided how and in what manner you would eat, the hazing being limited only by his imagination.

The food was served family style in huge dishes and brought to the table by cadet waiters who each served three tables. The food was not placed on the table until everyone was seated so it was served piping hot. All of the dishes could be refilled with the exception of the meat dish and desserts. Milk, water, and coffee were supplied in pitchers and the waiters ran constantly between the tables and the kitchen keeping up with the demands of the table host, who was the only one allowed to summon him. Eventually, when hazing by upperclassmen was prohibited, each cadet took his turn being the table host and enforced the rule of good table manners.

January 26 our quarantine expired and we were allowed to transfer from the classification squadron to Squadron 16 where we would undergo three weeks of Pre-Preflight training. Squadron 16 was made up entirely of potential pilot trainee cadets.

Moving consisted of placing all our belongings in two barrack bags and walking to our new area. The base was still a sea of mud so it was impossible to set our bags down to rest our arms. Some cadets slipped and fell and all of their belongings were covered with mud. The rain had not let up since it started on the twenty-third and all the surrounding towns and beaches were suffering tremendous property damage, according to the newspaper headlines. But our concerns were limited only to the base where we had firsthand knowledge. By now most of us had severe head colds and bronchitis. We still did not have any heat in the barracks and our clothes and blankets were very damp.

Our squadron was the first to move and we heaved a sigh of relief as we passed the guards leaving the quarantine area. Just as we reached our new squadron area we received word that the classification unit was again sealed off under quarantine as two cases of scarlet fever and several spinal meningitis cases had been diagnosed at sick call. We had beat the quarantine by about ten minutes. We knew the other squadrons would now be delayed at least a month or more, but we weren't entirely free either as we were still restricted to the base. The post exchange and other public facilities were off limits for at least twenty-one days.

As soon as we were settled in our new squadron commander, a second lieutenant, introduced himself and we gathered that he wasn't any happier to have us under his command than we were to have him. He explained that after our
partial quarantine was lifted we would be able to use the post
exchange twice a week for fifteen minutes, but as a unit only.
Eventually we could attend the post theater.

He explained that Pre-Preflight was a time when we would
learn basic military training. We would be subjected to rigor-
ous physical fitness training, our barracks were to be kept
spotless, and he would personally make men out of us, but he
certainly didn't see how any of us could expect to ever be
elevated to the rank of commissioned officers. He would do
his best but he held little hope for us. We would learn the
manual of arms and pull guard duty. We would also learn
mess management. As cadets we could not be ordered to do
K.P. (Kitchen Police). But if it was called "mess management"
we would be privileged to have the same opportunities to wait
on tables, wash dishes, and scrub the mess hall floors and garbage cans. He felt that was enough explanation for one day as
he did not want to tax our capacity to retain information by
overdoing it.

By now we had him pegged as a typical tactical officer. They
were called tactical officers not because they exhibited tact but
only because they were assigned to carry out a small-scale action which would serve a larger purpose, namely the production of air crew officers for the Army Air Force. These men
were known to us as ninety-day wonders. They were sent from
civilian life to Officer Candidate School for ninety days and
then commissioned second lieutenants. Some of them were so
enamored with their position they felt it necessary to make life
miserable for everyone else. However, for the time being we
would call them "Sir" and bow to their every wish to prove we
could take anything they could dish out. We had one purpose
in life now and that was to get to flying school and, should we
be so lucky as to endure nine months of training, win our
wings and receive a commission. These people would be
known to us as "ground pounders" or "gravel agitators."

The following day our partial quarantine was lifted. We

could now use more of the base facilities. We were notified that it would be two days before our schedule of activities would be posted, so we were kept busy by shoveling in the ditches caused by the heavy rains. We also maintained our calisthenics and drill schedules. Since we had two free evenings, several of the fellows went to one of the post theaters. They reported that it cost fifteen cents to attend the show, which was highway robbery for the type of movie shown.

After a day of filling in ditches and generally cleaning up the area most of us were sick with colds and other ailments and about half of the squadron reported for sick call. Several heavy applications of methyl violet took care of the cases of athlete's foot caused in part by the continuous wearing of wet shoes. Cold medicines were issued, but the real relief came when the medics requested that the barracks be heated. Within hours the stoves were lighted and this gave new meaning to the term "fire guard."

What a relief to have dry clothes and bedding. Our whole outlook on life was changed by this one simple act. It had never occurred to our squadron commanders who had warm offices and quarters that our health was threatened, and they certainly didn't appreciate being told by the medics how to run their squadrons by coddling the cadets.

The schedule was finally posted and we realized we were primarily in a holding pool waiting for an opening in Pre-flight. A few classes were scheduled which were brush-ups on math and physics. We were assigned work details, guard duty, and mess management in addition to calisthenics and basic military training. Our days began at 5:15 a.m. and ended at 8:00 p.m. with lights out at 10:00. However, we were allowed three hours for our three meals. The exceptions were guard duty and mess management. The whole idea was to keep us busy and uncomfortable. One day we changed uniforms five times just to please the squadron commander, who felt a little harassment would do us good. It did have the effect of solidifying the friendship of the cadets, creating an esprit de corps.

We came to depend on one another and offer encouragement during the rough times. We kept repeating to one another, "Praise the Lord and pass the commission. We will not be driven out. Give us your worst treatment and we will take it." We might not smile, but inside we knew we were better men than our tormentors and someday we would prove it. This gave us all a chance to see the mettle of our classmates and we were rarely disappointed with what we saw. The cadets came from all segments of our society from big city to farm and everything in between. We had students, teachers, and many occupations represented in these cadets. They were a sharp, elite group: the cream of our youthful society. They ranged in age from a high of twenty-seven years to about eighteen. The maximum age at the time of enlistment was twenty-six years. By now the two-year college requirement had been lifted and those right out of high school could qualify on merit tests.

Our cadet officers were either graduates of private military schools or those who had transferred with previous military training. I felt very lucky to be a part of this elite group and I knew pride alone would enable me to do my best to stay with them. By now several cadets had already resigned, stating that if this was what you had to go through to fly, forget it. To me this was the challenge and simply an augmented version of the hazing my primary C.P.T. instructor had given me a year before. Taking and following orders was not new to me since I had stood many times in the paddock area of the major race tracks receiving complete instructions from the owners and trainers on how to ride a particular horse. These directions and orders were given amicably on the basis of mutual respect, but they were followed explicitly since any deviation meant a loss of job. Now the orders were given in a condescending, insulting manner. This only strengthened my resolve: Degrade me all you want, I may be thrown out or washed out but I will never resign. It was a matter of pride. I was soon to realize that this was the prevailing attitude of practically everyone in the squadron. Occasionally we could even laugh at ourselves and poke fun at one another.

At our 5:15 morning roll call we were not required to be in full uniform. This was strictly roll call. As long as our heads and bodies were covered no one cared. After roll call we would immediately return to the barracks to shower, shave, and dress for the breakfast formation. Consequently, at reveille most everyone would jump out of bed, pull on shoes and tie a bow in the laces, grab a cap, wrap his O.D. raincoat around himself, and fall out. The standing joke was that we looked like 180 flashers in flights of 60 each, just waiting for a chance to perform. Luckily there weren't any WAACs (Women's Army Auxiliary Corps) in our area of the base or the Army Air Corps would have lost 180 fine men.

We were now being introduced to a whole new vocabulary on the drill field. We soon learned that FAHOD HOOETCH (FAHOD, the preparatory command, and the command of execution, HOOETCH) meant Forward March. HUT HUP HEEP HO was really a marching cadence count of One Two Three Four. ARTHRITE HOOETCH meant Column Right March. BREPP PAW meant Ready Front. This is only a sample of the many varied interpretations of the command as each individual had his own style and was not imitated by the others.

We had burly drill sergeants who dearly loved their jobs and really put us through the paces. All of this was done without a swear word being spoken. In fact, no one in command would have thought of using foul language. Sure, the cadets occasionally used raunchy language in their personal conversations, but these expressions were never used in public formation. According to *The Officers' Guide* a commander was cautioned never to swear at his troops as this would not be tolerated.

We often sang while marching in formation, or at least the others did after they realized I couldn't carry a tune. The command was "Everybody except Fletcher sing out!" The songs were *Dinah*, *I've Been Working on the Railroad*, *Count Off One Two Three Four*, and so on. This is quite a contrast to the foul-mouthed Hollywood-movie version of basic training of the 1980s.

But getting back to drill training: The drill sergeants showed us the maneuvers and led us through them, and then our cadet officers took over and drilled us until we could function as a single unit. The drill sergeants would grin or grimace as they observed our antics and offered suggestions as they were needed. But they let us know it was our show; we were the ones who would succeed or fail as they had already made their mark. The more we drilled the better we became and we made up our minds that we would be the best on the base. We were beginning to become a very close-knit, competitive unit.

Our calisthenics or physical training instructors were all either high school coaches or athletes who had been headliners on the sport pages. All were college graduates with postgraduate work in physical education plus extensive professional experience. These people knew how to get the most out of us and yet not endanger our health. They pushed us just a little more each day and when they thought we were ready they ran with us on the obstacle course. We had a lot of respect for these men because they participated in every exercise and challenged us to outdo them whenever we thought we could. At 118 pounds stripped, with strong arms developed from farm work, I could hold my own and excel at pushups and chinups, but when it came to running and many other activities I found myself in the lower echelons.

I had never played in organized sports so I stood in awe as I watched some of our group perform in basketball and baseball. I enjoyed contact sports but usually came out on the short end. However, this didn't dampen my enthusiasm. We left the physical training sessions filled with lots of aches, pains, and bruises but also with the good feeling that we were getting better each day. These instructors with their sense of humor, fair play, and dedication made a big impression on us and we forgave their "ninety-day wonder" status.

On Sunday, January 31, Captain Eddie Rickenbacker, former race-car driver and World War I flying ace credited with twenty-six kills, arrived at the base. His appearance was to coincide with the dedication of Theater 3, the newest and largest on the base. It was also the world premiere for the movie *Air Force*.

The cadets were admitted one thousand at a time with several showings. We were lined up in ranks in front of the theater. When our turn came it was dark, pouring down rain, with 999 voices singing the chorus of *Down by the Old Mill Stream*. Since there weren't any huge searchlights which were usually used in Los Angeles for a world premiere, G.I. trucks lined the streets by the theater with their headlights on bright. It was a poor substitute for the real thing but it added to the atmosphere and showed G.I. ingenuity.

At the conclusion of the movie the guest of honor was introduced. He told of his recent experience of being rescued from a life raft after drifting for twenty-two days in the Pacific Ocean when his observation plane was shot down. He also mentioned that he was envious of us because it would be our good fortune to be the ones to carry the bombs and destruction to Japan. He warned us that it would be our job "to kill, to have no pity, and to do the very best we could while here to learn this business of killing." He predicted the fall of Germany in 1944 and Japan six months to one year later.

It was all very sobering because up to this point we were only interested in flying and had not given any thought to killing anyone. In spite of this, he was given a standing ovation. The Hollywood big shots including the director of the movie and Warner Brothers executives were far overshadowed by the presence of this war hero, but they did receive attention from the newspaper reporters and photographers who were brought along to record this momentous occasion.

The following morning several measles cases were reported. If they were German measles everything would be fine. However, one case of the red variety was reported so we were restricted again for fourteen days. We were never quite able to understand why quarantine restrictions denied us all the privileges and pleasures on the base, including passes, but did not restrict our presence on work details, particularly guard duty or mess management which brought us into contact with other squadrons. Apparently we were contagious only in a social capacity.

On February 1 we were assigned to the mess management detail. We got up at 4:15 a.m., reported at 4:45, and worked until 9:30 p.m. We could volunteer for our choice of jobs: waiters, dishwashers, kitchen helpers, or garbage detail. I chose the garbage detail where there was less supervision. I felt I knew how to scrub a garbage can and did not want to run the risk of spilling a tray of food. Besides, I was running low on clean clothes as most were at the laundry. The garbage detail wore the zoot suit, or fatigues as they were later called.

The mess officer was very pleased with our performance and typed up a letter of commendation for us to give to our squadron commander. When we marched back to the barracks at 9:30 the squadron commander had just completed a tour of the living area and was waiting for us. He was given the letter from the mess officer and he proceeded to read it, with the help of a flashlight, out loud to the assembled detail. He seemed taken aback that we were praised instead of being censured. He took one long look at us and said, "If you're that good you can report for mess management again in the morning."

Our groans were suppressed until he was out of sight. Then some bright soul said, "Look at it this way, it's another day we don't have to work under the supervision of the S.O.B." This seemed to put everything in perspective. We had a good laugh and collapsed in our bunks so we could roll out again at 4:15 a.m.

None of us had any idea how many miles we had walked, marched, or run during our first month on the base, but on February 5 my G.I. work shoes had to be resoled.

By now our routine day, excepting mess management and guard duty, consisted of two hours of classes, two hours of calisthenics or athletics, four hours marching, and three hours off for breakfast, lunch, and dinner. The rest of the time was spent marching from one place to another and changing uniforms. Our day was seventeen hours long from reveille to lights out. The C.O. said that six hours of sleep was enough for anyone and we were getting seven, but he slept until seven each morning so it didn't bother him. Maybe he was right; people have been known to die in bed and we didn't want that to happen to anyone in our squadron.

When we were assigned guard duty it was for twenty-four hours at a stretch. If we used two details it was four hours on and four hours off, but occasionally we used three details with four hours on and eight hours off. On February 6 we drew guard duty and since our twenty-four hours fell on the weekend we were divided into three details. The first detail started at 6:00 p.m. I was placed in charge of the second detail which started at 10:00 p.m. We were relieved by the third detail at 2:00 a.m. and returned to the barracks at 3:00 a.m. We jumped into bed. Those of us on the second detail of the guard protested about getting up for the 5:15 formation, after only two hours of sleep, since we had to report again at 9:00 a.m. for the rest of our shift. The squadron commander very huffily said we could sleep in till 8:00 a.m., but the barracks had better be ready for inspection before we reported for guard duty at nine. We missed breakfast, but the barracks were shining and we reported to guard duty on time. While we were relaxing before guard assignment, everyone was griping about the harassment we had received from the squadron commander. Since he knew we would be relieved from guard duty again at 2:00 p.m. he had ordered us to report in formation for the full dress parade and review which was held every Sunday at 3:00.

The sergeant of the guard overheard us and immediately disappeared into the captain of the guard's office. We knew we were going to catch the devil for griping in public. In a few minutes a grim-faced captain appeared with the grinning sergeant. We were called to attention and answered roll call. Immediately we were gruffly given the general orders of the day, the password, a lecture about how lucky we were to serve our country and how appreciative we should be of this opportunity to be able to make individual sacrifices of time and energy. After his little speech, which put us in our place, he requested the sergeant of the guard to assign the details and post the guard. He then stormed back into his office leaving a group of bewildered cadets.

After the details were assigned, four of us found ourselves as supernumeraries, which meant we wouldn't be sent out on the first shift but would wait in the guard ready room until we were needed for relief. When the old guard had been relieved and the new guards posted we extras were still lounging in the ready room reading anything we could find.

The sergeant, his duties caught up for the moment, came over to us and whispered that the captain had said that if we were really officer material we had better start reading the cadet manual, especially a certain page, and abide by the manual. He then laid a copy on the table and went about his business. We grabbed the manual and on the page mentioned it stated that a cadet called for guard duty could not be called for any other duty until his twenty-four hours were up. We were to be released at 2:00 p.m. and the parade was at 3:00, but our twenty-four hours would not be up until 6:00 p.m.

As cadets we didn't know how we were going to use this newfound knowledge, but our problem was solved when we were dismissed from duty and in formation to be marched back to our barracks. The captain gave me a sealed envelope and requested that it be given to the commander of Squadron 16.

When we reached the barracks area the squadron was forming for the parade. With the guard detail still in formation and at attention, our squadron commander came over and requested that I dismiss the guard detail and fall into parade ranks. I saluted and presented the envelope to the commander. He opened it and his face grew livid as he read that we had performed well on guard duty and should be commended. It also stated that we were not relieved from duty and were to remain on stand-by status until 6:00 p.m., February 7, signed by the captain of the guard.

The 2nd Looey, a typical shavetail, was beside himself with rage and if looks could kill we would have all been dead. He looked at us with scorn and said, "*Misters*, thank your lucky stars that you are being transferred in the morning or I would make life hell for you." We thought he had done pretty well already. "Mister, dismiss your troops and get out of my sight." I was so weak I could barely mumble "dismissed." The mental depression set in as I realized how many more weeks were to come.

We heard that one squadron was summoned for a duty detail where the squadron commander asked all college graduates to step out and line up. Then he called for all who had two or three years of college to step forward. He requested that all the graduates take canvas bags and pick up the papers and cigarette butts in the squadron area. Those with some college time, but without a degree, were to start raking the area. Then he stated that the rest of the dumb clucks could stand around and watch those who were working and learn something.

We knew then that we were not the only ones who were being hazed. We just wished our squadron commander could have had an equally good sense of humor. By now we all had the impression that second lieutenant was a condition, not a rank.

On Monday, February 8, we moved to a new squadron which was just four barracks away. Here we joined another group of cadets to bring our pilot squadron up to a strength of 180 men. We brought our quarantine status with us so, consequently, the others were not overjoyed to see us since they had been released from quarantine only two days before. We had been on the base for a month with only three days out of quarantine. While in quarantine we could not leave the squadron area. This meant we could not go to the cleaners to get our clothes and couldn't go to the P.X. We could leave our barracks area only to go to class, drill, athletics, the mess hall, and work details.

Our moving day is best described by an excerpt from a letter I wrote to Sherry immediately after moving in:

> Today was the day of our big move. This is the last time we will move until Primary Flight School. That is, if I don't wash out in the meantime, which could happen. But I don't think so. Preflight is going to be okay. We now have upperclassmen on the top floor and we neophytes occupy the ground floor. Each of us has been assigned to an upperclassman, consequently we will experience some hazing.
>
> We will do mess management here every eighth day which isn't too bad. There are other work details plus guard duty. But I think we'll have a little time to study for a change, although as soon as we moved in I was appointed fire guard and will remain on duty for twenty-four hours. As fire guard you do not fall out for any formations, although they made an exception and allowed me a chance to pick up my books, sixteen of them in all, even though I will miss the start of our first four classes. We will progress through these books in six or nine weeks, depending on the

time we spend here. It hasn't been definitely settled yet, but I expect it will be nine weeks in Preflight. That's all right if it is because after you've been here so long you don't care when you're leaving or where you're going or what you're doing. It's just the old army spirit beginning to grow on us.

We had a swell day to move. For the past three or four days we've been enjoying California sunshine, then last night it started raining. So this morning we had to move in a sea of mud with more rain coming down and a cold wind blowing just to help matters along. Boy, this is the life. If you don't get the flu and die it will make a man out of you.

We have plenty of pet peeves and gripes too numerous to write about, but when we get together I'll explain army regulations and the reasons for many of them. Oh yes, another thing, our new squadron is also without heat. After everyone recovered from his cold in Squadron 16 heat was again shut off. If we ever feel heat again it will probably be too much for us and make us sick, but we would like to find out.

Classes begin in the morning at eight. This squadron is really on the ball.

While the squadron was in classes, as fire guard I was present for three inspections and watched demerits being handed out rather generously. But luckily my upperclassmate mentor and I were not recipients. Since I had free time I had given extra polish to our respective areas. We were allowed eight demerits per week. If you received more you had to forfeit your weekend pass and march a one-hour tour for every demerit over eight. Anyone receiving a total of over 100 demerits before commissioning would be automatically washed out. These records would follow us all through our cadet career.

After I was relieved from fire guard duty it was too late to participate in the activities of the squadron, which were mainly classes. Since I couldn't check in late I studied in the barracks until 4:30, at which time another cadet, Hunter by name, a former schoolteacher from southern Idaho, came by and suggested we go to the post office to purchase some airmail stamps. All cadets had franking privileges for regular mail, but for faster delivery most of us used the six-cent airmail. We knew if we hurried we would have time to get our stamps and still be back by five o'clock for our formal retreat formation. However, in our hurry we forgot to sign out, a procedure which was required when leaving the wing area.

Upon our return, when we were about four blocks from the barracks, we saw the squadron falling out the front door ten minutes early for the retreat formation. We started running but when we reached the rear door of the barracks the squadron was already in formation and being reviewed by a lieutenant. We couldn't break into the formation late and admit to being AWOL because we hadn't signed out, so we hid inside the back door and listened to roll call. Five cadets failed to answer, including us.

The lieutenant and first sergeant came in the front door looking for the absentees, but they made one mistake. They stopped to look at the sign-out sheet before proceeding into the barracks proper. This gave Hunter and me the opportunity to run out the back door and hide behind some other buildings. The other three cadets, who hadn't seen us, were caught in the stairway leading to the second floor which was occupied by our upperclassmen. They were tried and sentenced on the spot to three hours of marching every Sunday morning for the next three weekends. Since we were now AWOL for sure and didn't want to be caught in the squadron area, we took off for Squadron 16 which was still in the quarantine area. We rationalized the pretext that we would pick up the mail which had been delivered in the last two days for anyone who had mail in Squadron 58. We sorted the mail and picked it up for everyone we knew.

By then we figured it was safe to return to our area, but we also knew we would have to face the squadron commander in the morning to explain our absence. We were hoping to use the excuse that we had gone after the mail but had neglected to sign out. It was a flimsy story and we knew it wasn't an acceptable excuse, but we desperately needed something to enhance our story.

When we got back to the barracks with the mail we had some happy friends because letters were always the highlight of the day. We very innocently asked if we had been missed.

The cadet flight commander said, "Fletch, because of the way you handled the guard detail last Sunday and took the chewing out, we tried to cover for you guys. I told the lieutenant that Hunter and you were on a work detail. I think he bought the story. However, if he has suspicions and checks up, 'Katie, bar the door' because all hell will break loose and we'll all be walking tours." Such is the bond that forms when everyone faces adversity.

Nothing was mentioned the following morning when everyone responded to roll call and we realized we were home free. After dismissal the cadet flight commander whispered, "Fletch, never again." The warning wasn't needed because I wanted to fly and wouldn't make those stupid little mistakes again.

In Squadron 16 we used double bunk beds. I had the lower and the upper was assigned to Larry Luzader from Centralia, Washington. He was a good buddy and we became close friends. When we moved from Squadron 16 to Squadron 58 our unit was split between Squadrons 58 and 59. Larry was assigned to 59. Their barracks were adjacent to ours but by some strange reasoning our unit was in quarantine, yet 59 was not. However, this worked to my advantage in that Larry knew that I smoked and he also knew I was broke since I had only budgeted enough money for one month. I assumed we would be paid on the last day of January or the first day of February, but this did not happen. It was my first lesson on assuming anything in the Army.

After several days in the squadron one evening after dinner a cadet called and said that someone was waiting for me in front of the barracks. As I walked out of the door there was Larry standing in the middle of the street. He had just been to the P.X. He was carrying a small box which he placed on the ground and with a pleasant "Here's a present for you, Buddy," he hurried on. In the box were four packs of cigarettes and a ten-dollar bill. I thought this was very thoughtful for a new friend who didn't smoke and had known me for only a few weeks. He must have been psychic because I was out of cigarettes and about to have a nicotine fit.

This spontaneous action started a real trend as others in the squadron started contacting their friends in Squadron 59 requesting favors of such nature. This practice was short-lived as measles broke out in Squadron 59 and they too went into quarantine. However, these acts merely reinforced a bond that was rapidly drawing everyone together. There were a few personality conflicts among the cadets and several know-it-alls, but given the number of people in these units the individual conflicts were very few and we lived in a climate of mutual respect.

The welcome speech we received from our new squadron commander was in marked contrast to any we had received up to now. The C.O. was a second lieutenant, whom we again met with skepticism. He bade us welcome to the squadron and stated that he expected the very best from every man and if we gave our best we would find him fair and willing to help. If we were prone to goof off or disobey regulations we could expect no quarter and would be washed out immediately. There would be no second chances for disobedience and willful disregard of the rules. His job was to produce and bring out the best in us so we might be a credit to the Air Force, and to that end his career was dedicated.

He explained that the Air Force needed all the pilots it could get, but they had to be the best. From now on until we were commissioned probably 40 to 50 percent of us would fail. But he wanted us to realize that we were not in competition with one another. "Help one another if you can; encourage one another. If any of you have special skills use them to tutor those who need it. If you help one another you will be helping the military." Help, however, did not mean cheating. That would be grounds for immediate dismissal. He encouraged us to set up study groups and work as a unit.

He explained that Flights A, B, and C made up Squadron 58-J of the Third Wing on the base. The J, the tenth letter of the alphabet, corresponded to the tenth month. Those of us who survived all the training phases would be commissioned the last of October 1943. He wished that it could be all of us but knew it would not. Recognizing that most of us had spent all our time in quarantine, he said he would intervene to help us if it were to continue.

According to the C.O., Squadron 58 had been the top squadron on the base in the past and it was his job to make sure it remained that way. There was only one excuse for missing a scheduled formation and that was death. If we goofed and missed we had better have the certificate in hand. He also praised us for having the fortitude to enlist as cadets. Ours would not be an easy task but the goal, if attained, would certainly be worth our effort and any sacrifice we had to make. This was a man we could understand. It was the first time anyone had expressed confidence in us. We would give our all and hope for the best.

Our new routine was now established as we embarked on a highly intensive course of study in ground school. Our academic classes included such courses as: Army Organization, Customs and Etiquette, Naval and Aerial Recognition of Both Surface Vessels and Army and Navy Aircraft, Physics, Mathematics, Psychology, Radio Code, Photography, Meteorology, Theory of Flight, and Identification of Poison Gases. This constitutes a fair sampling but is not a complete list. The instructors for these classes were both civilians and military officers. They were outstanding in their field, the best the nation could offer. The military instructors were high school and college educators who were offered a commission upon completion of Officer Candidate School. They were in stark contrast to the ones we referred to as "ninety-day wonders." These were very dedicated, sincere men. Their job was to teach and they were not into hazing.

Classes were primarily lectures and demonstrations. Classroom participation was at a minimum and then only to ask a question. The cadets could respond every Saturday when the weekly tests were given. The cadets' grades were posted publicly on Monday starting with the highest down to the lowest. This provided additional incentive to do well, as no one wanted to be at the bottom.

In our unit we used the time from 8:00 in the evening to lights out at 10:00 studying or conducting study groups for those who felt they needed help. Our aim was to become the top academic squadron on the base as well as the top military unit. The latter we were quick to achieve.

Every Sunday all cadets on leave had to be back on the base at 2:00 for the 3:00 p.m. parade. Only those who were physically unable or on duty details were exempt. The units formed in their squadron areas in Class A uniform to be marched to the parade grounds where all units participated in the presentation of the colors and the grand review. During all of this the base military band played stirring marches. Each squadron marched past the reviewing stand, which usually contained all the visiting dignitaries and the highest ranking officers on the base. The base and wing commanders graded each unit on a variety of qualities all pertaining to military bearing. Each unit was formed with the tall men in the front ranks and working back to the shortest bringing up the rear.

After the judging, the top squadron in each of the bombardier, navigator, and pilot units was awarded a flag indicating they were tops in these specialties. Also a grand champion flag was awarded to the top unit on the base. This was a large blue flag with a red "E" for excellence inset in its center.

On Sunday, February 14, Squadron 58 was awarded not only the top pilot training flag but also the grand champion E flag. Our reputation was established, but we would have to work hard to keep these flags since they were re-awarded every week. All the other squadrons would now be out to beat us. Our upperclassmen and squadron commander were elated that we had not become the embarrassment they thought we might be. However, most of the credit should go to our cadet officers. These cadets had exemplary military training and were true leaders, well-liked by all of us.

On Monday four cadets, former Army men (two sergeants and two corporals), asked to be transferred back to their original infantry unit and reinstated with their original rank. They said that a commission was not worth all the grind and hassle that they had been subjected to. Their request was granted.

After our first week of classes the grades were posted and I heaved a big sigh of relief when I found my name listed in the top five. The squadron composite grade was very high and we were even more determined to become the top academic squadron in J-class.

While we were all under constant strain and knew we were

overworked, it was quite a surprise to find we were all gaining weight. In my case thirteen pounds had been added. I found it hard to reconcile this with the letters I had been writing home detailing all of the hardships and deprivations we were forced to endure.

February 17 the Army and Navy conducted a mock dogfight over the base, the Navy using Grumman Avengers and the Air Force P-38s. The cadet corps was really pumped up as we cheered the 38s on. This was an inspiration as we imagined ourselves in the pilot seats. It was positive proof of the goal we hoped to achieve. I received further encouragement when the next set of grades was posted. With a composite score of 97.5 percent my name was listed at the top of the academic list.

On the twentieth, after we had completed our ground school exams, we were ordered to remain in the barracks because the wing commander wanted to address the squadron. When the order came to fall into formation in front of the barracks we were pleasantly surprised to see our squadron commander wearing the silver bars of a first lieutenant. He introduced the Third Wing commander, who was a major. The major proceeded to tell us that he was very proud to have the grand champion red E flag and the top pilot training flag in his wing. He was also very pleased with the academic showing of both the upper- and lowerclassmen. He noted that our quarantine would expire on Sunday, but since no new cases of measles had broken out they were lifting the quarantine immediately. Also as a reward for our good showing, arrangements had been made for us to attend The Camel Caravan show, a nationally known radio show troupe with twenty singing and dancing stars. They would present two one-hour shows on the base at Theater #3, and we were scheduled for the 8:30 performance.

The major also told our upperclassmen that if our group could win the Big Red E again they could have their pick of any Primary flying field in California. This could range from the country club of the air at Oxnard to the dust bowl of Blythe. We were also informed that passes would be issued so we could leave the base Sunday morning, but we had to return by 2:00 p.m. for the parade. For our group this would be our first time off the base.

Before the passes were issued we had to pass personal inspection. The ranks were opened and the inspection party started down the ranks. At the end of the inspection 100 of us had failed. We needed haircuts so the lieutenant ordered the cadet officers to put us in formation and march us to the barber shop. He personally intervened and cleared the barber shop for us, using the quarantine clause. There were nine barbers on duty and in just fifty-five minutes the last cadet was sheared. Our hair was about one inch long, standing up on top and shaved on the sides. In formation we looked like 100 breathing scrub brushes.

The Camel Caravan show was a rousing success as the star-quality performers included comedians, singers, and dancers. Each cadet was given a pack of cigarettes. The smokers did okay as the nonsmokers handed over their packs. We all enjoyed the show and the cigarette company got their advertising.

As soon as the show was over at 9:30 we were hurriedly marched back to the barracks in order to beat the 10:00 p.m. lights out deadline. When we entered the barracks it was three minutes until ten. On Saturday we were required to strip our beds so the thin mattresses were folded in half and placed at the head of the bed. There was, of course, a certain procedure for folding the blankets, sheets, and mattress covers. The slip was removed from the pillow and all these items were displayed in neat piles in proper order on the end of the bunks. This process was not only designed to air the bed, which was certainly needed, but also to provide the inspecting officer with another chance to find something out of order and to give demerits.

Needless to say, lights out occurred before anyone had a chance to make his bed, so most gave up trying to put the mattress covers on in the dark. Sunday morning found most had simply crawled into the mattress covers and pulled the blankets over them. It was probably the funniest sight many of us had seen. Laughter broke out as each surveyed his own predicament as well as his neighbor's. An aura of irresponsibility pervaded the area and provided the first moment of complete abandonment of responsibility since the mud fight.

The following morning we caught the bus for the ten-minute ride to Santa Ana, a town with a population of about fifty thousand. Almost immediately the married men separated from the singles as we were concerned primarily with the availability of rooms or apartments just in case we could talk our wives into coming to join us.

The Army had written all wives that housing was critical and their presence would be frowned upon by the military, a policy which was in force all through cadet training. In the few hours available to us we sadly came to the conclusion that short-term housing was practically nonexistent and it was a poor place for a wife whose husband could only be there one night per week. A single bedroom was priced at five dollars a week. A room with eating facilities was about eight dollars, and some places had room and board for forty or forty-five dollars per month. Housing wasn't impossible but it wasn't desirable to bring a wife into this uncertain environment. For the present we knew they were safe at home with relatives, which eased some of the worry.

In our case my brother-in-law, Cap, had been called to active duty January 17. After reporting to a personnel pool at Hondo, Texas, he received his uniforms and orders to report to Okmulgee, Oklahoma, for the first phase of glider training. Sherry and my sister, Leora, were now war widows still occupying the apartment in Walla Walla. They both had jobs and there were relatives and friends near for help or visiting. Their biggest problem came when the landlord, realizing their husbands were gone, thought it would be a good time to raise the rent. Rents were frozen at this time but he apparently thought they weren't aware of this. He had underestimated these young women as his actions were reported to the rent control board. The raise was refunded immediately along with an apology stating he did not understand the rules.

I was amazed at the number of married men in our unit, almost 50 percent. Of course our biggest gripe and source of unhappiness was the separation from our loved ones. We lived for the letters and boxes of goodies which they sent although we knew they were using their sugar rations to make the candy and cookies to boost our morale. Without their support I don't believe we would have endured the separation. Perhaps the time of my worst loneliness came during the rainy weather when I received a package which contained an olive drab wool sweater knitted for me by Sherry. At the same time it was also a proud moment when I showed it off to the other cadets.

When we arrived back at the base at 2:00 it was pouring down rain and this time even the parade ground was a quagmire. The base commander called off the parade and we were allowed to retain possession of the honor flags for another week.

Tuesday brought the news that we were back in quarantine. Red measles was the culprit again. The upperclassmen were fit to be tied as they had just two weeks left before Primary and they didn't know what would happen if the quarantine wasn't lifted.

Our academic load continued to increase; the instructors were really pushing. We knew if we dropped our pencils that by the time we could pick them up we had just lost half a college semester in the course. Two cadets flunked out due to a poor showing on the exams and two others asked for voluntary relief. We finished a course in military hygiene and now knew how and where to dig latrine trenches. We just thought we were going to spend our time in the air; we had no idea that this would be a pilot's duty. We were also surprised to find out that the FBI wanted to know everything about our personal lives as well as our parents and ancestors. Some of them would have rolled over in their graves had they seen the questionnaire. All of this just to determine if we would be eligible to receive a commission.

Saturday night the wing commanding officer had one of the theaters cleared out so all of the quarantined squadrons in the Third Wing could see a movie. Squadron 59 was now back in quarantine so all the old buddies were able to see the movie together. It was a typical propaganda movie called *Hitler's Children,* designed to bring out anger in all of us and make us feel that it was our personal responsibility to exterminate all Nazis.

When we left the movie Squadron 59 collected ten cents from each of its members for a total of eighteen dollars. They wanted to bet that they would beat us out in the parade on Sunday and take possession of the prized flags. We couldn't let the opportunity pass so the bet was called and the squadron C.O. held the stakes. They also challenged us to a football and basketball game Sunday morning.

With all these challenges we felt we needed some divine guidance. With the quarantine we couldn't go to church so the C.O. notified the chaplain. Early Sunday morning church came to us. The chaplain packed up a portable organ and lectern and we had an outdoor service in front of the barracks. Squadron 59, sensing that we might be trying to gain the edge spiritually, immediately formed in front of their barracks where they could participate in the service and nullify any gain we might receive.

I cannot say enough about the quality of military chaplains. They are very sincere, dedicated men, good speakers who know what they're talking about. The chaplains know what they want to say and when it is said they quit. I've seen too many ministers in civilian life pass up many good opportunities to end their services.

With the close of the church service the football and basketball games started simultaneously. I was not a participant. Both squadrons claimed victory since no time limit or rules had been decided ahead of time and certainly no one was going to officiate at either contest. The competitors decided to finish the duel on the parade ground where impartial judges could render the decision.

We had just enough time for dinner, and then it was time to shine shoes, polish brass, break out the guidon and the winning flags, and march to the parade ground. We placed our three tallest men with impeccable military bearing in front of the squadron as flag bearers and guidon. It is impossible to describe the feeling of marching in a unit 180 strong with thousands of cadets participating, each hoping his unit will be chosen as the best. There was a lump in the throat as we passed the reviewing stand with eyes right, marching in cadence to a Sousa march. At the command of Steady Front a feeling of pride swept over us. Each person felt himself a part of the whole. We had plenty of confidence and pride so each one stood just a little taller and the bond that strengthened us all became tighter. As grand champions we were the leading squadron and we knew we had set a high level of performance for the thousands behind us.

When the judging was over we still had the best Pilot Training Squadron flag and the Grand Champion Red E as well. The squadron commander and the wing commander were elated with back-to-back wins. Squadron 59 placed second and had given us a run for their money.

Now the squadron commander wanted to know what we were going to do with the thirty-six dollars. Since we had been in quarantine for so long everyone wanted Coca-Cola, but we couldn't go get it. The commander disappeared and after a few minutes returned with the jeep loaded with cases of Coca-Cola. At five cents apiece each cadet had four bottles. We voted whether or not to share with 59. The vote was an overwhelming "no," so we went on a real Coke binge, drinking them as fast as we could and putting the empties in the jeep to be returned.

While we were enjoying our cold drink I started wondering how many cadets were in the parade. The exact number was probably confidential information, but I knew it was in the thousands. Was it ten thousand, twenty thousand, or somewhere in between? Then it dawned on me that this was just the West Coast Training Center. There was also the Gulf Coast and the East Coast Training Centers which were probably as large or maybe even larger than ours. I broke out of the reverie long enough to ask my upperclass mentor how many cadets he thought we had on the drill field. He said, "Look at it this way, Fletch, you were there and I was there so logically there was more than one." Big help! But I knew within two weeks he would be gone and we would be upperclassmen. Then someone else would have to do the sweeping and mopping and take the hazing that had been handed out to us. We could hardly wait.

Midweek came to pass and two more measles cases were reported so we started another fourteen-day extension of quarantine. We felt as though we were in prison and morale started to fall somewhat. Classes were getting tougher and there were no rewards, just more mess management, guard duty, and classes. We were developing cabin, or, more precisely, squadron fever. There was more griping than ever before. We all needed toilet articles from the P.X. but we couldn't go there. Also we had not been paid. I had broken my watch crystal but could not get to the repair shop to have it fixed; I couldn't have paid for it anyway. I had received seven demerits already that week, the most I had ever received. Any more and I would be walking tours. I was in a funk.

March 5 brought some good news. It started raining so hard again that drill and athletics had to be cancelled which meant we could use the time for studying. Someone started the rumor that we would be paid, and as far as I know that was the only rumor on the base that proved to be true. We all filed through the pay line and were paid in cash, although we received some surprises as some high ranking officials on the base had decided how we were to spend our money.

Cadets were paid $105 per month gross. Since we all had been ordered to active duty January 1, 1943, we had two months' pay coming. All cadets were charged one dollar per day for room and board and eight cents a day for laundry. These two charges could not be claimed for the first six days in January since we paid our expenses while en route to Santa Ana with the exception of transportation, which was paid for by the military. Each one of us by now had figured out how much we had coming. In my case this was two months' pay, $210 plus $10 reimbursement for travel expenses from Walla Walla to Portland to Santa Ana minus $53 for room and board and $4.24 for laundry equaled $162.76. However, as we went through the pay line the finance officer gave me $159.76 without justifying the $3 discrepancy in accounting.

Going through the pay line was a very formal affair. The finance officer was seated at a table with several armed guards behind him. The cadet marched to the table, executed a left face and saluted the paymaster. Since the paymaster was not required to return the salute, the cadet sounded off "Aviation Cadet Eugene R. Fletcher, 19033417, reporting for pay, Sir."

The paymaster scanned the pay list, checked off the name, reported the amount owed and counted the money out on the table.

The twenty-dollar bills were new and uncirculated with the serial numbers running in sequence. The cadet was then offered a pen, signed the payroll, picked up his money, saluted the paymaster who sort of waved his hand, did a right face, and proceeded to the next table. There he was informed that he was commanded to donate two dollars a month for grass seed for the base beautification fund, a project in which we should be happy to participate. Four dollars, please. At the next table we were told that we had to pay eight dollars for the gym suits we were issued (a pair of shorts, T-shirt, and tennis shoes). Eight dollars, please, even though they were government issue. Then on to the next table. There we were told the base commanding officer had decided that each cadet would voluntarily donate two dollars per month to the American Red Cross. Four dollars, please. Thank you.

It certainly was not going to be hard to spend our pay with this kind of help. Immediately I found the two cadets, Luzader and Hunter, and repaid the thirteen owed to them. After pay call, since we were in quarantine, the squadron commander offered to buy money orders for any of us who wanted to send money home. Most of the married men took him up on the offer and I was able to send $100 to Sherry. This left me with thirty dollars for the month. I knew I would spend $7.90 of this for a new pair of pants. After our initial issue of clothing, which was second- or third-hand, we were required to buy replacements as they wore out. The shoes issued were new, but we were expected to buy replacement shoes also as needed. We had to have a shoe ration coupon before we could buy them. These coupons were issued on an "as needed basis," but only after turning in the worn-out pair.

The next day two of our married cadets asked to be eliminated. I had a chance to talk to them before their request and they said they would rather be a part of the enlisted army and rejoin the human race where the pay was better, they could work eight hours a day and spend some time with their wives. These men had special clerical skills and felt they would not be a part of the shooting army, but would become permanent party personnel on a stateside base. They were tired of quarantine, tired of making love on paper in the form of letters to their wives, and tired of the constant hazing, put-downs, and the degrading cadet life. I knew how they felt. I, too, was lonesome but I still had dreams of silver wings and I would put up with anything to win them. We parted with mutual respect, but with each thinking the other was crazy. I hope their dreams were realized, but dreams were like rumors: not many of them came true in the army.

After we completed our weekly exams on Saturday, March 6, the squadron commander explained that more cases of measles had broken out and our quarantine was extended another fourteen days. Since we were virtual prisoners of the system he had appealed to the wing commander for one of the theaters to be cleared so all of the quarantined squadrons could have some social recreation. He knew morale was low and was doing what he could to help us, but it was an unusual situation over which no one had control. That evening we went to the movie *Amazing Mrs. Holliday* starring Deanna Durbin. It was a good try on our behalf by the lieutenant. I don't think it did much for morale, but at least we knew he was concerned about the welfare of his troops.

Sunday I again drew the fire guard detail so I was not able to participate in the parade ceremonies. When the squadron returned I learned that Squadron 61, another pilot training squadron, had taken all the honors. Squadron 58 had finished second and 59 was further down the list. Because of fire guard duties I also missed Monday classes but the fellows reported back that my cumulative grade average was back to 97.5 percent. It had fallen to 95 percent the week before. I knew this couldn't last long because one of the subjects coming up was Radio Code. This had been my poorest subject in Civilian Pilot Training where I had barely managed to pass. In high school I had problems with typing and Code required the same skill. It seemed that I was unable to acquire the rhythm necessary to do well. Maybe this all tied in with the inability to carry a tune or the rhythm for dancing.

The grade report was the only good news of the day. Our

upperclassmen received the field of their choice, Dos Palos Primary Flying School, and were in the process of moving. This should have been a cause of joy for us but our squadron commander informed us that he was being transferred for duty at West Point. The policy of having upper- and lower-classmen in the same barracks was being abolished. The crowning blow came when he stated that Squadron 58 was being disbanded. Most of us would move in with our counter-parts in Squadron 57 located three barracks away. Everyone felt a little sick when he realized that our squadron identity as well as the academic and military records we had established were now gone.

Squadron 57, which had been released from quarantine for two weeks, was not happy to receive us in our quarantine status and we weren't happy to be there so that placed us on equal footing. We didn't mind not having underclassmen as we didn't feel like hazing anyone. Besides, with our experi-ence we could sweep, scrub, and polish better than any under-classmen. At least we were in charge of our own demerits when we did the work.

Our Radio Code class started. At the first session the instruc-tor told us that anyone failing to make a grade of 70 would have to forfeit his weekend pass. The class erupted in a roar of laughter and the instructor was caught off guard. He was not used to anyone making a laughing matter out of his instruc-tions. Before he could chastise us some brave cadet explained that we were in quarantine. We had been off the base only six hours since we arrived the first week of January. Once the instructor realized we were not laughing at him but only at our own misfortune he registered disbelief. Upon reassurance that this was true he smiled and said, "Don't worry, I'll find another method of punishment," and we knew he would.

He also explained that we would be required to have a cu-mulative average of 85 percent in order to go to Primary. However, we could not fall below 70 in any one course. If that happened we would not be washed out but would be held back one class and allowed to go through Preflight again. By now they felt that they had such an investment in us that both we and the service could benefit. This was a relief to me because I now knew that if I failed Code I still would have another chance.

Another problem was that we wanted to let our wives and families know as quickly as possible that we had moved and changed addresses. This way our mail would be delivered directly to our squadron rather than coming to the old squadron and being rerouted, a procedure which took several days. There were pay phones in our quarantine area but they took only nickels, dimes, and quarters. We had just recently been paid and everyone had money, but it was paper money and no one had any change and we did not have access to any place where we could get change. Also the schedule called for us to pull mess management on the eleventh and guard duty on the twelfth. This meant missing two days of classes, then reporting for exams on Saturday.

These conditions did not make for a happy squadron. Everyone wore a long face and griped constantly. In fact, by now we could outgripe a five-stripe (five hitches) enlisted man in spite of his experience and longevity. We were quick learners.

Mess management went without incident, but guard duty was a little different. Up to now we had only learned the manual of arms and had not fired live ammo. Guard duty had been only an exercise. We were given guns without ammunition, posted at our stations of patrol, and told if we had problems with anyone who did not know the password or did not heed our commands after hearing the clicking of the rifle bolt to call out "Corporal of the Guard" for assistance. Most of the time was spent challenging members of the permanent guard who were constantly trying to catch us off guard and figuring out ways to get our weapons away from us. It was nerve-racking but also fun. It tended to break up a very boring job and was a learning situation in that you matched wits with some unidentified person or persons.

On earlier guard duty sessions we asked why we were not given ammunition. The answer was that earlier classes had been given ammo and several incidents of accidental discharge of weapons plus several close calls by challenging teams had led to an order to stop issuing live ammo.

I was placed on the detail that had the 10:00 p.m. to 2:00

a.m. shift. When we reported to the guard station it was a beehive of activity and we sensed an air of tension and urgency. We were immediately issued our weapons and flashlights and given live ammunition. The sergeant of the guard appeared to be nervous and explained this was not a drill. We would not be challenged by any of the permanent guard. This was for real; the base was under a red alert. We didn't even know what he was talking about but we understood that no one without the proper password and identification was to pass our position.

We were loaded into trucks and transported to our guard posts. I was stationed on foot patrol in a large warehouse unit. My surveillance area was about the length of a city block and how it was patrolled was left up to me. I was let out of the truck at the center point of my beat and admonished that if I had to fire my weapon the first shot was to be in the air unless my life was threatened. It sounded very romantic and intriguing until the truck pulled away. Suddenly it was pitch black and very lonely. I couldn't even see the ends of my patrol in the dark and it was cold. I tried to walk the beat, then realized my back was exposed. It didn't take long to discover that you can't walk in one direction and still protect your rear. The problem was: How do you protect your front, rear, and both flanks at the same time? No wonder they gave me that responsibility. Obviously they didn't know either.

I didn't have any idea where the other guards were stationed in relation to my location, so I tried side-stepping and walking in circles as it was too cold to stand still. Eventually my eyes adjusted somewhat to the darkness and that made it worse as the shadows took on shapes and my imagination willed them to move occasionally in synchronization with the night noises.

We didn't know if the base or the coast was being invaded, if saboteurs were reported in the vicinity, or whether the whole thing was a sham. It was the longest four hours I had ever spent in my life wandering around with a bullet in the chamber of my gun with the safety on. At one strange sound I wheeled around with the rifle at ready only to see the blinking blackout lights of the truck bringing my replacement. It was still terribly cold but my palms were sweaty. However, I suddenly became very brave as I crawled into the back of the truck. It was a quiet bunch of cadets who were transported back to the warmth of the guard headquarters. I knew then that I wasn't cut out for the infantry. I had to get to flying school.

Several days later rumors circulated that there had been submarine sightings off the coast and this had triggered our state of alert. All I knew was I had been asked to serve in a field which did not appeal to me.

With guard duty over and exams completed on Saturday we felt brave enough to ask our new squadron commander, Captain Wright, if there was any way we could have our money changed so we could use the telephones. Also, we all needed personal items from the Post Exchange. Our message fell on sympathetic ears. He went to the Third Wing commander and explained the problems of the men who had transferred in from Squadron 58. The wing commander, having a soft spot in his heart for us, requested that the P.X. be cleared and we were allowed thirty minutes to attend to our personal needs.

Once we were back in the squadron area we really burned up the telephone lines as we lined up at the booths. By limiting our calls to three minutes we could let everyone who wanted to call home. The change in morale was immediate. We were again civil to one another and the squadron commander's stock rose 100 percent. We knew we would never approach the esprit de corps of Squadron 58; we would still be a good unit but not a superior one.

Saturday night after Taps four cadets from the original Squadron 57 decided to sneak out of the barracks and go to town. Several of their friends tried to reason with them to forget it, but they were determined to go regardless of the consequences. They were tired of being cooped up in quarantine. We didn't know whether they got off of the base or not, but suspected they were apprehended at the gate. About 11:00 p.m. the O.D. (officer of the day) came to the barracks supposedly for inspection. The lights were turned on. He found the four empty bunks and left without saying a word to us. It was the first time the O.D. had ever come to our unit. We never saw the cadets again and their personal effects were picked up Sunday morning by the M.P.s.

Another strange thing about the Army was that the officer of the day always served at night. He was the stand-in for the base commander at night when he was home or off duty. The O.D. had many duties and carried a manual of duties and instructions, but his main duty was to relieve the commander after hours. He could solve all minor problems on his own and he kept a log of his activities. However, in an emergency he could call the base commander for instructions on major decisions.

Sunday afternoon I was one of the last to fall out of the barracks for the big parade. I fell into the last rank since this was where the shorter men were. Since there were only four of us in the last rank we were excused so the squadron would be uniform. They were a good looking group as they marched off but they didn't bring back any award flags. Our time in the limelight had passed, but this didn't mean we were giving up. Time was against us with two or three weeks left in Preflight. At this point survival was our main concern.

On Saturday, March 20, after exams we were told that our quarantine had been lifted. Captain Wright inspected the ranks and gave us all passes good until 2:00 p.m. Sunday. His order was to get off the base, loosen up, and have some fun. He noted we had been in quarantine so long that if we needed help finding the main gate he would be happy to escort us. Before he could dismiss us the whole squadron broke into the chorus "For He's a Jolly Good Fellow." He just smiled and said, "Don't forget, Misters, I'll be waiting when you return."

The cadets from Los Angeles and the surrounding area headed for home. The rest of us didn't really know what to do, but finally four of us decided to go to Long Beach. When we arrived there about seven in the evening we found the town packed with soldiers, sailors, and marines. It took us over an hour to find a hotel room for two so we flipped coins. Cadet Hunter and I won the tosses and took the room while the other two kept looking. The room was six dollars for the night. We felt the price was inflated because of the influx of service people and the shortage of rooms, but at three dollars apiece we splurged.

We wandered along the streets which were literally jammed with young sailors, more than I had seen in my life. Here a surprising thing happened which boosted our morale and made us feel like human beings. The cadet uniforms were very similar to the army officer uniform. We wore the round blue cadet shoulder patch with gold wings and prop on the left shoulder. We also wore the U.S. brass insignia and the combination brass propeller and wings on our blouses. The visored cap had the wings and propeller insignia in place of the American Eagle on the officer's cap.

The young seamen and army privates looked somewhat perplexed when they saw us, but immediately saluted. The first several times this happened we looked behind us to see who they were saluting. Finally it dawned on us we were being accorded the honor. We immediately returned the salutes until we felt our arms would fall off. It is impossible to describe the feeling of rising from the lowest thing on earth to a position of respect in one hour. It didn't matter that it was a case of mistaken identity.

We found the huge Long Beach amusement pier and tried all of the rides including the roller coaster. There was also a small lake so we rented electric powered boats and drifted in the moonlight dreaming dreams of home and our loved ones until 2:00 a.m. closing time. It was interesting to note that practically all the young ladies, who were few in number, were always escorted by a group of sailors. It must have been the white bell-bottomed trousers.

We piled into bed at 3:00 a.m. dog-tired but with a feeling of satisfaction that would last a lifetime. By the time we got up for breakfast it was time to catch the bus back to Santa Ana. Our little escapade had cost fifteen dollars apiece, but never again would therapy be so cheap.

When we arrived back at the base the single cadets were talking and bragging about their evening on the town. One said he met a young lady who accused him of being AWOL. There was no doubt in my mind that he was a wolf on the loose and my sympathy was with the young lady. After hearing all sorts of amorous tales we felt there couldn't be a virtuous female left in Southern California, but we knew it was mostly hot air designed for the benefit of the married cadets. Squadron 57 was a sorry lot at the Sunday review, but luckily we placed higher than I thought we deserved.

When classes started on Monday I checked the grade list. My Code grade was 70 percent, barely passing, and it had pulled my aggregate down to 95 percent. However, good news came when the Code instructor announced that he would gladly donate his time for an evening class for any of us who wanted to participate. All we had to do was sign the sheet and show up at 8:00. My name headed the list because I could surely use the practice.

The rest of the week passed very quickly; every spare minute was spent studying. Several of us spent our evening hour in remedial Code classes. The instructor and several sharp cadets were doing all they could to help us. We were concentrating on receiving. The code messages were on tape and we used headsets to receive the sound. The tape was played at a speed which would enable the slower of us to copy. Someone finally experimented with speeding up the tape to a point where we were pushed and didn't have time to think but only record our first impression. Then things started to fall in place. The instructor seemed pleased with our progress and stated he would give us three final tests over a three-day period, then take the highest grade of the three. This gave me cause for renewed hope that I would depart for Primary with J-class.

During the week we were informed that no longer would top squadrons be allowed to choose their Primary field. In fact, we would leave the base under classified orders without any advance notice. This seemed to dispel all the rumors we had heard, but it was also a cause for more griping and complaining since this would mean another lengthy interruption of our mail service.

After the exams on Saturday we picked up our passes and seven of us went to Long Beach again. This time hotel rooms were readily available. The four of us who were married spent most of the evening trying to call our wives. Everyone was successful except myself. Since we did not have a telephone at home it was necessary to reach Sherry at work, but by the time I was able to get a circuit she had gone home.

We wandered around the streets for a while looking for someone to visit with but saw only two other cadets from the squadron and they had other things on their minds rather than visiting with us. Next we found a photo booth and for ten cents had our pictures taken to send home since this was the first time in uniform. We found an all-night movie house and watched movies until 2:00 a.m., then found an all-night restaurant and had breakfast. We turned in and didn't get up until time to return to the base the next day.

When we reached the barracks everyone was upset. It seemed that another case of red measles was reported Saturday and the unit immediately went back into quarantine and the passes were revoked. The guards at the gate were notified to refuse exit and pick up the passes of any Squadron 57 cadets. Apparently about twenty of us had beaten the order by twenty minutes. It was a great homecoming: just like old times, back in the slammer. We had very little hope of getting off the base again before we left for Primary.

We grudgingly participated in the parade and our attitude was reflected in our placement which I do not care to reveal, but it wasn't good.

On Wednesday, the last day of March, Captain Wright, the squadron C.O., gave us a real pep talk. He knew we were disgruntled, especially the guys who had not been able to get off the base on Saturday. Captain Wright, in our eyes, was the perfect example of an Army officer. His very presence commanded respect. He was a handsome man whose military bearing and uniform were impeccable. He let us know he was disappointed with our showing and felt that we were now underachievers. He knew we had fallen from the best to the mediocre. Our morale was low and he knew why, but what we were experiencing now was probably child's play compared to what we would face when we were commissioned and reached combat. It was imperative that we shape up and he was willing to help. He knew that the original members of Squadron 57 were in quarantine and had not seen the movie *Air Force*, which had premiered on the base in conjunction with the appearance of Captain Eddie Rickenbacker, so he felt that now was a good time to see the movie and reevaluate our goals in the light of what we would see in the movie. Perhaps we would show more dedication to a greater cause. He cancelled our drill and calisthenics classes for the afternoon and we were marched to one of the theaters for a special matinee showing. The movie made more of an impression on me this time since I could now see what we were training for and view it in that context.

This was our last week of classes and his lecture couldn't have come at a better time. We didn't need sympathy, we just thought we did. We needed the boot applied to where it would do the most good.

By the week's end our classes and exams were over and the scores posted Saturday morning. I had finally managed to get an 80 in Code and my final average or aggregate was 95 percent out of a possible 100. It wasn't the top but it was a long ways from the bottom. At Sunday's parade we made a decent showing but certainly were not contenders for the big E flag.

The new week started with our old nemesis drill, calisthenics, and instructional training films. All of our academic classes were over and we knew we were now going to Primary. The attitude of the unit was one of relief. There should have been cause for joy, but the strain and hustle of the last three months had taken its toll. It was just one big let-down. We had a little more free time but quarantine was still in effect so we couldn't use the time for anything constructive. What it meant was that we had more time to gripe. The C.O. felt we had reached a point where we would still gripe even if we knew we were going to be hung with a new rope. His theory was everything had a bright side and we should find it. Stress the positive.

This sounded good but at our first calisthenics session after Preflight we were informed that we still had to participate in a calisthenics physical test. It seems that on our first session after arriving on the base someone had recorded all our performance statistics: number of chinups, pushups, time over the obstacle course, and on through every exercise. We were now put through these tests again. Then these scores were compared with our beginning ones to measure our performance improvements. Everyone did compete to his limit but only to work off the feelings of frustration. When it was over we were so tired and sore we couldn't even gripe.

The following day we were introduced to the world of chemical warfare. We had studied this in the classroom, but we now experienced it in the field under actual conditions. We were placed in shacks where tear gas was released so we had to immediately don our masks and get out of the building. There were enlisted personnel standing by to help if anyone should experience trouble or panic. Then in the open field we were exposed to all of the poisonous gases we had studied about including lewisite, phosgene, mustard, and chloropicrin. As each one was released we opened our masks, took a quick short breath, closed the mask and identified by smell which gas had been released. I was glad to see this day end as the only way you could flunk this test was to croak. That evening some of the cadets had slight headaches, but that was the worst that happened.

Wednesday morning dawned hot and cloudless. The squadron commander announced that we would be going to the gunnery range. Since we would no longer be drawing guard duty the Army in its infinite wisdom had decided to teach us how to fire our weapons. The commander stated that we might want to bring our shorts and T-shirts and perhaps make a small contribution to the squadron fund. Each cadet put in fifty cents and wondered if we were buying our own ammunition. We loaded into army 6 × 6 trucks and were transported to the firing range which was located near the beach. We spent three hours of fun shooting 30-caliber machine guns at moving targets, firing shotguns on the skeet range, and then firing at fixed targets with 45-caliber Thompson machine guns.

My scores were terrible. The gunnery sergeant had a little talk with me but I told him he had no reason to complain since I had not ruined any of his targets. He should be getting after the cadets who were blowing them full of holes. His final statement was, "Let's you and I both hope you or no one else has to rely on your shooting for survival. I certainly wouldn't recommend you for infantry training." It proved to me there were some very bright enlisted men on the base. There was one ray of light. I did qualify with the 45-caliber handgun, which was the only score that mattered.

When we left the firing range the truck drivers took a very poor road on down the beach to a secluded cove right on the ocean. When we unloaded we were met by Captain Wright who explained that the cove was a safe place for swimming. We could have a swim if we wanted, and then we should gather driftwood for a fire. His vehicle was loaded down with soft drinks, a keg of beer, wieners, and buns. Our squadron fund had been transformed into a picnic. We didn't know how he was able to get the wieners since meat was rationed but he said that was his secret, to forget it and have a good time. We did and it was my first chance to ride the breast of a WAVE (Women Accepted for Volunteer Emergency Service—a woman serving in the Navy). Taking no chances, I explained this joke to Sherry in my next letter.

It was a tired but happy squadron that returned to the base. We knew we would miss the captain. He had taught us a very valuable lesson in the humanities: be tough, be demanding, be fair, be concerned, be interested in the welfare of the people in your command. It was a lesson I would never forget.

At noon Saturday our quarantine ended and since this was our last weekend here everyone except the fire guard was given a twenty-four hour pass. I polished my shoes and shined my brass. I didn't know where I was going but I was getting off the base. The fellow who drew the fire guard detail was a married cadet from the Los Angeles area. He tried desperately to get someone to take his place so he could visit his wife and family before we shipped out. All of his close friends turned him down even though he offered several twenty dollars to trade places. They were sorry but it was the luck of the draw. I was secretly hoping he would have some luck, but when it was apparent that he was stuck I told him I would trade places with him. He immediately opened his billfold. I said, "No, I won't take your place for money." As his face fell I explained that I knew how he felt as I would like to see my wife too, but since that was impossible I certainly wouldn't be the one to ignore his entreaty. It was with very misty eyes that he thanked me and said maybe some day he could repay the favor. "Let's hope you don't have to. Get moving, Buddy. Time's a-wasting." I settled down to twenty-four hours of peace and quiet with a good feeling.

I wrote a long letter to Sherry explaining what a nut she had married, but I suspect she was secretly happy that I had been confined for most of my stay at Santa Ana. That was one sure way to resist temptation. This was also the last letter that I was allowed to write from Santa Ana. Orders to leave were in the mill. Troop movements, times, and placements were classified. We would be able to write again when we reached our new base.

Several days earlier I had received a letter from Cap informing me that the glider training program had folded. With his flying experience documented he was immediately transferred into cadet class 43-J. Apparently his eye problem had improved over the last few months, or else the brass had now come to the conclusion that anyone who could fly a glider could fly an airplane. He was now at Muskogee, Oklahoma, a Gulf Coast Flying Training Command base for Primary training. Soon he would be flying a Fairchild PT-19 Cornell, a low-wing monoplane. Cap had managed to escape all of the Pre-Preflight hassle we had to endure and Sis would be able to join him before long.

On Friday, April 16, about ten of us stood around and watched the rest of Squadron 57 move out. We were confused and were not told anything. I looked around and realized I was in good company regardless of what happened because included in the ten were the top academic cadets. We were placed in a convoy for some destination wholly unspecified, but obviously to the north. Of the ten most of us were acquainted but not close friends. However, in this new group there was a cadet named Gene Jones, who was a classmate and friend at Pietrzyski High School in Dayton, Washington. I didn't even know he was on the base at Santa Ana. While there I had met two college classmates and one fraternity brother, but these were only chance meetings. This was different: two cadets from a small town in Eastern Washington headed for the same flying school.

3 Primary Flying School

Oxnard, California

The Primary Flying Schools were all civilian contract schools directed by a small cadre of military officers and enlisted men. The flying training was conducted by civilian flight instructors, whose ranks I might have joined had the draft board not forced my enlistment. All of the ground school classes also were taught by civilian instructors. Classes in military discipline were conducted by the officers, but their primary function was administration. They must have been overstaffed, for we soon learned they had plenty of free time to make life miserable for the cadet corps.

As the convoy rumbled along it was a quiet group in the truck in which I was riding. Occasionally someone would mention the name of the town we were passing through. Because of the canvas covering which enveloped the bed of the truck, only the cadets on the side benches at the rear could get a glimpse of the countryside. Now and then someone would speculate on our destination only to be greeted with dead silence. We were happy to be out of Santa Ana and on our way to Primary, but as yet we were practically a group of strangers.

The convoy eventually ground to a halt and we were ordered out of the truck by a group of cadets who referred to us as "dodos." As such we were ordered into formation complete with barrack bags containing our extra clothes and toilet articles which were slung over our shoulders. As we were forming according to their commands I could see a sign over the main gate which read Mira Loma Flight Academy, Oxnard, California.

We were marched onto the field parade ground and here were drilled with our packs until I thought we would drop. The cadet cadre from Class 43-I finally wearied of their ignoble hazing and we were ordered to remove all wing and propeller combinations from our caps and uniforms. As dodos instead of cadets we were ordered to stow the brass and only when we had soloed would we be allowed to restore the combination wings to our uniform. We were informed that our military unit consisted of sixteen officers, six of whom were rated pilots, and thirteen enlisted men. The Base Commanding Officer was Major J. S. Fouche, Jr. The director of training and adjutant were both captains, the rest were lieutenants. Lt. W. S. Powell was introduced as the commandant of cadets. He explained that the Class of 43-I, the upperclassmen, was divided into four squadrons numbered 1, 2, 5, and 6. Our hazing by I-class was now over. They were allowed to welcome us but that was the end.

The upperclassmen occupied one half of the housing area which was arranged in three concentric circles separated at one end by the headquarters building and the other by an entry arch. The round parade ground with the flag pole in the center constituted the inner open circle. We would occupy the other half of the housing area. The two classes would have very little contact since our schedules were designed so that only one class would be on the flight line at a time. We would alternate between morning and afternoon flying. J-class would be divided into two groups of two squadrons each. Group 1 contained squadrons 3 and 4, Group 2 received squadrons 7 and 8.

He now demonstrated how we would be picked for squadron assignment. In the past we were assigned alphabetically, but here we saw something different as we lined up according to height. Squadron 3 became the big gun group since their average height was six feet two inches. Squadron 4 had an average height of five feet ten inches and soon became known as the raunchiest squadron. Squadron 7 became the odd-ball squadron since these people didn't fit anywhere. Squadron 8 was tagged the 8-ball outfit, the short end of 43-J, because we were all under five feet nine inches. I thought it an odd way to make assignments, but since we were all strangers and no one asked my opinion that was the way it was.

We were ordered into formations by squadrons, each squadron with approximately fifty men. We opened ranks and Lieutenant Powell and the first sergeant started down the line. The first three cadets were asked their names and the first sergeant wrote down the names and gave them a cottage assignment. This continued until everyone was assigned. This is how our roommates were decided. After our room assignments we were given a smattering of do's and don'ts including an admonition that we were in quarantine for fourteen days, a procedure that would be followed after every move. So what else is new? In the sixteen weeks I had been in the military service I had received only one twelve-hour and two twenty-four-hour passes.

My reaction to our new base can best be described in an excerpt from a letter sent to Sherry dated April 18, 1943, two days after our arrival:

> At long last we've finally reached Primary. We are now at Mira Loma Flight Academy, Oxnard, California. The day for which all of us here have been waiting has finally arrived. We will now be *flying*, believe me it is really a happy day because we've been building up to this for quite some time.
>
> The type of ship we will fly here is called a Stearman and looks very much like the Meyers I used to fly in Secondary Civilian Pilot Training except this one is quite a bit bigger as it has a 220 horsepower engine.
>
> This is one of the best Primary fields in the country and known as the Country Club of the Air. It is run by civilians. I was really fortunate to be sent up here as my old squadron at Santa Ana was either sent to Blythe or Hemet which is just as bad. About ten of us were picked out and we joined a convoy and were sent here. Maybe our Preflight grades had something to do with it.

This place is really beautiful and for once we're living like
civilians again. Instead of barracks we live in little cottages
with private bathrooms, three men to the cottage. All the
woodwork is done in pine paneling and believe me we keep
the place shining. Another thing, we sleep in real beds with
inner spring mattresses, none of this G.I. issue army cots
and iron bunks like Santa Ana.

K.P. and guard duty are things of the past. We are now
going to be flyers so all our work will be in that direction.
This is really a dream place and I know I'm going to like it.
I feel very lucky to be here.

On the morning of the seventeenth we marched to the flight
line and were introduced to the civilian flight instructors.
These men wore the uniforms and A-2 jackets of commissioned officers, but lacking military insignia. They wore a set
of wings on their caps. Before the assignments were made
Herman Asmus (pronounced *Ace Mus*), who was the squadron
commander, asked for all men with previous flying time to
drop out of the formation and wait in his office. Two of us
from Squadron 8 entered the office. Asmus asked the first
cadet how many flying hours he had and the cadet replied,
"Five hours, Sir." He was then told to rejoin the squadron
where assignments were being made. Then he turned to me
and asked what my qualifications were. I said I was a licensed
single-engine civilian pilot rated to fly aircraft from 0 to 330
horsepower. After I recounted my flying experience a big
smile lit up his face and he stated that he would be my instructor. As squadron commander he had many duties, so he took
two or three students and chose only those with considerable
flying experience. We would begin flying together Monday.

Ordinarily an instructor had five students, but since there
was a shortage of instructors on the base some had six. These
men were really overloaded. I knew then that only the quickest to learn would pass and the instructor load would be
brought back to normal.

After the assignments we were welcomed to the academy by
Major C. C. Moseley, who owned the flying school. It turned
out that he also owned Cal-Aero at Ontario and Polaris Flight

Academy at Lancaster. We were given this background information before his speech:

Major Moseley was a World War I veteran who had been a
pursuit pilot with the Twenty-seventh Squadron of the First
Pursuit Group and was credited with the destruction of enemy
aircraft. After the war he was a test pilot for the Air Corps
Engineering Division at Dayton, Ohio, and won the first Pul-
itzer Prize for the High Speed Trophy Race in the International Air Races in 1920. From then until his retirement from
the Army he was involved in a number of Air Corps training
programs and also organized, commanded, and trained the
California National Guard Air Forces. In civilian life he was a
director for several commercial airlines.

As novices we were quite impressed with Major Moseley. He
spoke to us as though we were pilots. He did not mention his
administrative accomplishments but gave us a hearty welcome
and then reminisced about his flying experiences. He made us
feel that we had to succeed, not only for ourselves but for the
Air Force and for our country. He left us pumped up and
ready to emulate his accomplishments and ideals. But perhaps
most important, he left us with a sense of pride in ourselves
and a feeling that we could control our destiny.

Monday morning the nineteenth we again met our instructors in the ready room at the flight line. Each instructor took
his students to a private area where the first half hour was
spent visiting. I suspect they wanted to learn a little more
about our personalities and goals before risking their lives in
the cockpit with strangers. I am not sure what our instructor
learned from us, but we found out that he had been a Navy
carrier pilot before becoming an instructor. In addition to being the squadron commander he was also one of the senior
pilots on the field, and because of his many ratings, he wasn't
sure how much longer he would continue to be an instructor.

Since all of the instructors were civilians they were referred
to as Mister. By now most of the cadets were sick of this title.
Because it had been used in a derogatory manner most of the
time we felt it didn't convey the measure of respect to which
he was entitled. He was a thin-faced man with very sharp,
piercing eyes. He fixed us in a frozen gaze for a moment, then

after ascertaining we were sincere, gave a tight smile and stated we could call him Captain Asmus. We immediately came to attention and saluted. This rather embarrassed him and he reminded us that it was not necessary to salute the civilian instructors. We told him we were aware of this, but since we had to salute the military officers, it would be good training for us. He conceded that it would be okay to salute at our first and last meeting of the day. He would cheerfully return the salute as a matter of courtesy and recognition.

Next we proceeded to the flight line where there were about 150 primary trainers, all Stearman PT-13Bs, biplanes produced by the Boeing Company under Stearman patents. We were given a thorough briefing on the physical characteristics and instrumentation of the aircraft. The wingspan was approximately thirty-two feet and the length about twenty-five feet with a height of a little more than nine feet. The instructor sat in the front cockpit and the dodo in the rear.

I was impressed with the size and the 220-horsepower engine, but two features caught my attention. One was the engine starting device. In all the aircraft I had flown the engine was started by pulling the propeller through by hand, but here we had an inertia starter which consisted of a geared flywheel and counterbalanced weights. Two cadets would crawl up on the lower wing, insert an iron crank into an opening in the engine compartment, and then turn the crank until the flywheel reached a howling speed. There wasn't a tachometer to measure the speed so the two cadets cranked until it sounded right, which was usually when they were sweating and out of breath. Then they stowed the crank, crawled down from the wing, and moved clear of the plane. The pilot then called Contact, turned on the ignition switch, engaged the weighted flywheel to the engine, and hoped the inertia was great enough to spin the engine and propeller fast enough to start. Occasionally the engine fired on the first cranking, but more often not. The cadets cheerfully performed this act when an instructor was around, but woe be to the solo cadet whose engine wouldn't start on the first try. He was subject to ridicule and verbal abuse as though he alone were responsible for the extra work of cranking.

The other system was a method of communication. In the past my instructor had always used hand signals and dirty looks to convey what he wanted done, a crude but effective method which thoroughly intimidated a student. But this airplane was equipped with a more confusing system. It was called the gosport system by the more respectable persons. However, it had many more less reputable names applied to it by cadets who had just been chewed out by a screaming instructor.

The device was very simple. The instructor spoke into a funnel which was attached to a rubber hose that ran to the rear cockpit. The hose was divided by a metal fitting into a "Y" of two smaller hoses; these hoses were then slipped over a metal tube which protruded from the ears of the cadet's flying helmet. This system worked well on the ground before the engine was started, but in the air the engine noise and howling wind of the slipstream rendered communication almost impossible. It didn't take the cadets long to appreciate the noise, however, as it partially and sometimes completely drowned out the invectives directed at them by the instructor. This was strictly a one-way system, instructor to cadet. It worked the best for the first two cadets who flew with the instructor. By the time the last three or four students had their turn the instructor was so hoarse he could barely whisper. He would stick the funnel out in the slipstream and let the cold blast of air and engine noise be directed to the cadet's ears to get his attention. At this point he reverted back to hand signals. The result of all this was that by the day's end the instructor had lost his voice and could only whisper while the cadet was stone deaf and couldn't hear.

In the beginning two factors had to be considered before determining whether this was a plus or a minus. First, the mood of the instructor, and secondly, the type of ride the cadet had given the instructor. Later a third factor entered in, the condition of the airplane on completion of the landing roll. The instructors' job was not an easy one and I'm sure they questioned their own sanity for applying for the job on more than one occasion.

After our briefing and familiarization session Captain Asmus asked who wanted to receive the first lesson. I immediately volunteered and crawled into the rear cockpit. My motivation to be first stemmed more from the fact that I did not want to crank the engine than from the genuine desire to fly. However, the good captain interpreted it to think I was an eager beaver. My first dual flight lasted forty-two minutes; I was almost overwhelmed. I had been idle for so long that it appeared I was starting from the beginning. I had lost the feel that goes with good piloting, but the desire was still there. I was bewildered by all of the aircraft in the air, in the landing pattern, and on the ground. Previously a half dozen airplanes in the air seemed like a lot, but here there were over a hundred. We had three runways side by side, and consequently there were three aircraft landing or taking off simultaneously. I was so busy watching out for the other planes I hardly had time to concentrate on flying. When the forty-two minutes were up I was in a daze. The instructor was not displeased with my efforts, but I knew enough about flying to know that it was far from a stellar performance and I had a lot of work cut out for me if I were to graduate.

We were able to fly for three consecutive days: another forty-minute session plus a sixty-five-minute one. Then we were grounded for two days because of morning fog. In between classes we all engaged in hangar flying, which amounted to everyone telling tall stories. This is a ritual in which most pilots perform their best flying feats. We never tired of boring one another, but occasionally the truth came out and we could profit by someone else's mistake. Certainly we couldn't learn from our own.

It became apparent that I would have to learn to fly all over again. Most of the maneuvers were performed differently in the military than I had been taught in civilian flying. The changeover was not that great, but I had to be careful not to revert back to my old ways. While my mind should have been concentrating on my problem, here I was usually thinking of home and trying to figure out how to get Sherry from Walla Walla to Oxnard. I wasn't overjoyed with my two roommates. They were good fellows but hard to get acquainted with.

After five flights with Captain Asmus, which amounted to

just under four hours of flying time, I was summoned into his office where he explained that I was being assigned to another instructor who had just arrived at the base. When he saw my crestfallen look he was quick to explain that it had nothing to do with my flying. On the contrary, it was just the opposite. He would no longer be an instructor but would be a check pilot and ride with the students as they progressed through the various stages. He would decide who was passed through the stages and he would also give the final check flights for the cadets of Squadron 8 and some of the other squadrons to determine who went on to Basic.

I was immediately relieved and my morale soared. Every cadet hated and feared check rides because these determined your future in flying. Now I knew that I had started with the best and had pleased him, so every check ride from now on would be just the same as taking my instructor for a ride. There would be anxiety to do well, but not the fear and uncertainty of riding with a stranger.

The incident gave me even greater reason to be happy as I described the aftermath in a letter to Sherry:

> Changing instructors is never pleasant, but this change appears to have a plus side. One of the cadets told me that he overheard Captain Asmus' conversation with my new instructor and this was his version of what took place. It seems that he really built me up to the new instructor, not only because of my flying ability but because of personality and military bearing. He gave compliments like I've never heard in the army. While this has bolstered my morale and makes me feel good it has also caused a lot of ribbing from the other cadets and brought forth hot pilot innuendos all of which are done in the spirit of fun.
>
> Now that I've started off on the right foot I only hope I can stay that way. The first impression means a lot here and I know if I can just keep improving on my flying I'm going to stay here because it looks like the big boy is on my side.
>
> When I heard this it made me feel good because I was just about disgusted with flying, the army and everything that goes with it. But this made it different. It let me see that I was getting someplace and that all my time here and at

Santa Ana wasn't being wasted. . . . It makes little difference whether the cadet was pulling my leg or actually telling the truth. . . .

By now we've settled into a regular routine. Our first call is at 6 a.m., reveille at 6:15. Then we begin cleaning the cottages until 6:45 breakfast time. Immediately after breakfast we finish cleaning our rooms and living area for a white glove inspection. These inspections are just as thorough as those at Santa Ana, but here our college campus-style semi-private living quarters give us greater incentive. We are proud of our units and this provides the motivation to keep them spotless. It is also possible that this short poem posted on the bulletin board provides some stimulus:

> One drop of water, one grain of dust,
> Makes inspecting officers raise an awful fuss.
> One fuss a day, seven days a week,
> God, how those ramp hours wear upon my feet.

Seven-forty finds us marching to the flight line where we remain until 1:10 p.m. The time on the line is spent flying, receiving ground instruction, studying or flying a no-name static monstrosity, a contraption which is a modified version of the Link trainer. At 1:15 we change from flight clothes to the uniform of the day for dinner at 1:30. At 2:00 we go to classes which last until 4:00. At that time we change clothes again and go to physical training where a lieutenant tries to whip us into shape. A better name would probably be physical torture. This lasts until 5:10, then we shower and change to our olive drab uniforms and are ready for drill at 5:30. We drill for an hour and then stand in formation for the retreat ceremonies which take place at 6:35. From there we are marched directly to the mess hall which is now called the restaurant since we are on a civilian field. Evening chow is over by 7:15 when we proceed back to the living area. If we don't have evening classes we're free from then on until 9:30. But at least two or three nights a week we have classes from 7:30 to 9:30.

But if we don't have classes then we have exactly two hours and fifteen minutes to do our studying for the next day, shave, write letters, shine shoes, carry out missions assigned to us, look out for the rest of our personal things and then possibly ten whole minutes with absolutely nothing to do but loaf before lights out at 10:00.

I'm not overdoing this a bit for that is our actual schedule and it is followed to the letter. If you're more than 45 seconds late for any one of these formations it is a gigable offense and the usual sentence is three demerits. Again the rules are the same as at Santa Ana; eight demerits and you start walking tours. So you see we spend most of the day double-timing. People say that idle hands create trouble, but we cadets are living proof that even the busiest of people can also get into trouble.

What I wouldn't give just to sit down once in the middle of the day for ten minutes with absolutely nothing to do. It must be a wonderful feeling.

The food here is good but I believe I'm losing weight. My clothes are beginning to fit loose again so that's a good indication. This running all day is taking all the fat off that I put on in Santa Ana.

My new instructor was just out of flying school and a swell guy. We immediately developed a good rapport. He did not have the flying experience of Captain Asmus, but he was determined to prove that he was a good instructor, just as I was trying to prove that I could be a good student. On our first flight together we flew out to an auxiliary flying field where we practiced landings, then finally up into the blue where I had to demonstrate all of the maneuvers that were required for soloing. He was attempting to determine my level of competence.

When the flight was over he stated that I was capable of soloing immediately. However, there was a rule that a cadet could not solo before receiving six hours of dual instruction regardless of how much previous time he had. (My first solo under civilian flight rules required a minimum of eight hours dual instruction.) That was all right with me for I was still scaring myself to death on landings even though they were good. At least the instructor hadn't detected a lack of confidence, for which I was very grateful. I knew my flying was improving and that in another few days I probably wouldn't even mind riding with myself. These feelings were transmitted to Sherry in my letter for the day. I hate to admit it but there was more truth than humor in the letter.

That evening the base went on blue alert at about 10:30 p.m. The entire cadet corps was routed out of bed in a blackout and rushed to the flight line to manually disperse 150 aircraft. It was almost daylight when we finished and a short time later the alert was lifted.

This was a regular occurrence at Santa Ana, too, but there we did not have aircraft to push around. Here at the flying field it meant a lot of hard work. These alerts were prompted any time a coastal aircraft strayed off course and remained in effect until the plane was identified either by radio or aerial interception. All of the towns in the coastal western states had organized a twenty-four-hour-a-day sky watch under the auspices of the Ground Observation Corps, an agency of the Office of Civil Defense. People volunteered their time to man these lookout points and they called in every aircraft sighting they could not identify in the daytime. At night every aircraft was reported to a central point where flight plans were matched with the reported sightings. Thus an aircraft off course or unidentified was reported immediately to the military, triggering an alert.

While those of us who were pushing airplanes around were not overjoyed with these reports, we certainly appreciated the fact that people were volunteering their time to help protect us. In fact my father-in-law, a farmer near the little town of Tekoa, Washington, gave generously of his time even during his heavy work season. Apparently most of the people involved gave a minimum of three hours one day a week, and all they received for this vital contribution was a pair of silver wings. In the center of these wings was a large letter "O" (U.S. Air Observer). In the center of the "O" were the letters GOC (Ground Observation Corps). They were well trained in aircraft identification and knew what they saw in the skies. This was a group that never lacked for volunteers since everyone in the communities had friends or relatives who were actively involved in the military service. This was just another way they could show their loyalty and support.

It was a sleepy group that reported to the flight line on the morning of the twenty-sixth, but at least the instructors were wide awake. Since they lived away from the base their sleep was not interrupted. Because it was impossible for Oxnard to handle all of the air traffic, several auxiliary fields were set up. These were just grass fields without any accommodations. As the dispatcher assigned the airplane to the instructor he was also told which auxiliary field the squadron would operate from. The instructor and one cadet would board the aircraft and fly to the auxiliary field, receiving his lesson on the way out. The rest of the students, along with the dispatcher, went by bus to the same auxiliary field. By the time the first student had completed his lesson the rest were already waiting.

The first student crawled out of the cockpit and the second student climbed aboard for his lesson. While this was going on the idle students were studying their ground school textbooks. All students received sixty-five hours of flying time, including dual and solo time, in the Primary School. These figures were not estimates but accurate right to the minute.

Another purpose of the auxiliary field was to provide a place with less traffic for the student's initial solo flight. This was pressure cooker time and the cadet did not need the distraction of having the whole field watching as he performed his maiden flight. A pilot never forgets his first solo flight. He can always recall his feeling of uncertainty before and during as well as the joy of a successful conclusion. It is the major event in a lifetime of flying.

On Friday, April 30, the instructor said I would receive the first lesson so I was to check in with the dispatcher, get our aircraft number, and find out which auxiliary field Squadron 8 was using. On our way to the airplane he explained that he had checked my log book and I had exactly six hours; today would be my big day. So far no one from our four squadrons of 43-J had soloed. I was excited and could hardly wait to get to the auxiliary field. We climbed into the plane and two cadets performed the starting ritual. The engine fired on the first go-round and while the engine was warming up at idle speed the instructor quietly stated into the gosport, "Mr. Fletcher, I want you to take off on the left-hand runway and make three full-stop landings. On the third, come back to the ramp and pick me up, then we will go to the auxiliary field. By the way, don't make me regret my decision." He slowly crawled out of the cockpit and when he cleared the wing he turned, grinned, and gave me a thumbs-up gesture.

The two cadets who had cranked the plane were bug-eyed and in a state of shock, but I knew they weren't any more surprised than I was. As soon as the initial shock of being told to solo on the home field had worn off a feeling of exhilaration swept over me. I slowly started taxiing toward the end of the runway. I pulled over, ran the engine check and, satisfied that everything was okay, inched toward the runway. Suddenly I was almost blinded as the green light from the tower operator's Aldis lamp hit me in the face. I was now cleared for takeoff. Go man, go. I slowly opened the throttle, gently applying rudder pressure to counteract engine torque. Then I was suddenly in the air. I made the left-hand turn as I passed the end of the runway onto the crosswind leg, another left-hand turn and I was on the downwind leg at traffic altitude. Two-thirds of the way down the downwind leg I retarded the throttle and set up my landing pattern. One more descending left turn and I was on the base leg. Starting the descending left turn of the final approach leg I was hit again with the green light which meant I was cleared to land. Without having to apply any more power the plane settled on the end of the runway and I turned off at the first taxi strip to repeat the same procedure again. On the third landing, turning final, I got the red light which meant pull up and go around. The runway was occupied with a ship on takeoff. I immediately cut across to the downwind leg while climbing to pattern altitude and resumed the same procedure. This time the green light was forthcoming and again I settled onto the runway and taxied to the ramp to pick up my instructor. He was grinning from ear to ear, but he wasn't nearly as happy as I was. I had spent my first thirty-four minutes of solo military time in the air. The instructor and I spent another hour and twenty minutes practicing maneuvers before we landed at the auxiliary field.

The news of my solo flight had already been reported to the waiting cadets by the two who had cranked the engine. I was hazed and kidded as the cadets of Squadron 8 realized that one of their members was the first on the flight line to solo and had beaten out the other squadrons. It was with great humility that I explained to them what it was like to pilot an airplane without an instructor on board and that I was reasonably sure that some of them would be able to follow in my footsteps. I'm positive it was only the presence of the dispatcher and the bus driver that allowed me to return to the base unharmed.

As we marched to the restaurant for dinner I was on cloud nine for I now had all the brass back on my uniform, which placed me in the same category as the upperclassmen. I was no longer a dodo.

The afternoon brought another surprise. Since this was the last day of the month we were informed that it was payday. The flight school issued the following explanation about our pay. It was a different procedure and did not create the controversy and surprises which happened at Santa Ana.

About Pay Day . . .

So that you will understand "what it's all about" when pay day comes around, the following explains Army practice in this regard.

When Army personnel live on an Army post, they receive their regular rate of pay and the Army supplies housing facilities and food.

When, for any reason, Army personnel such as yourself must live off the post for either a temporary or an extended period, they are given an additional allowance to cover housing and food . . . a total of $64.50 for "room and board."

Therefore on pay day, Army paymasters will give you a total of $139.50—your $75 salary plus the $64.50 explained above—and representatives of the commissary and housing organizations will, in turn, collect from you for these costs, leaving you the full $75 pay of your rank.

So—when you draw $139.50 on pay day instead of the $75 you were promised, don't think you've had a raise in pay! When you live on an Army post, the expenses of food and housing are taken care of by the government "behind the scenes." But when you're on detached service, as you now are, you do this yourself and the government supplies you the additional funds with which to do it.

On Saturday, May 1, I received forty-five minutes of dual instruction. It was a case of the instructor trying to out-fly the cadet. We had a ball. The session ended with the instructor flying over the fair-weather cumulus clouds floating in from the ocean. He dropped down into the valley of a cloud and we flew below the peaks, banking the plane very steeply to remain in the valley and, on occasion, applying full power and maximum climb to retain visual contact and stay out of the cloud proper. Finally the instructor said we had better stop before we met two other nuts who might be coming in our direction and doing the same thing. We pulled up over the top and found a large hole between clouds to make a let-down for landing. The instructor said we had had our fun, but if I ever attempted to do this on a solo flight and he heard about it I would be washed out immediately. It was a bumpy, fun ride that I'll never forget, but I took his warning seriously and never attempted it on my own, at least not where there was any chance of being seen.

When we returned from the flight line we were told quarantine had been lifted and we would receive our first pass after supper. Since the threat of an invasion was always present, all coastal bases were required to have 50 percent of their personnel on the base at all times. Thus leave time had to be scheduled between the two classes. During the time we were in quarantine the upperclassmen were allowed longer passes, a privilege which would be granted us when our time came. My pass was good from 7:00 p.m. Saturday until noon Sunday.

Sherry and I had discussed the possibility of her joining me at Oxnard. Up to now everything had been based on speculation. The feasibility of her coming now depended on the conditions I would find in the local area. As soon as I got back from my first visit I wrote to her:

> Here it is Sunday and I've just returned to the post after enjoying a few hours of liberty. I was quite surprised by the town of Oxnard. It's much smaller than I had imagined. Most of the buildings are wood-frame structures and quite old. But then again I guess a town of 8,000 wouldn't be very large or too modern.

The town is divided into two sections. One part is very run down and its population consists almost entirely of people of Mexican descent. The other part is much nicer and it is where the permanent residents of the village live along with the wives of sailors and soldiers. About one-fourth of the population is service wives. This is really a navy town as you will see when you get here.

Last night I stayed at Oxnard's most luxurious hotel, the Hotel Oxnard. It is quite a place to say the least. It is a three-floor wooden structure built probably in the 1800s and has never been remodeled because of its value as an antique. At least that's the way I figure it. The rooms could be worse but only if they took the beds out. It reminded me of the hotel at Tekoa, but Tekoa has the edge I think. The hotel is inhabited with mostly wives whose husbands are in the service.

The lady who runs the hotel said her husband was in the South Pacific so she was interested when I told her I was expecting my wife here and would be interested in obtaining a room for a while until we could find an apartment. At the present all the rooms with bath were filled, but she says she will have one for me by the time you get here. She is to call me as soon as one is vacant and I will make a reservation and pay for the room from then on until you get here so you will have a place when you arrive. There are several auto courts here and if I haven't a room by next weekend I will get you a tourist cabin there. I will make this definite by next weekend and then wire you where to come before you leave on the 11th.

Another thing, I want you to try to plan your arrival here before evening because I don't want you to try to find your way around in a strange sailor town after dark. In the evening all coastal towns are in a partial blackout and it isn't any place to be chasing around without an escort unless you know where you're going.

Conditions here are far from being good but even at that it is much better than lots of the towns I've seen so far. Now then, you wanted to know about the work situation. Well, I don't know much about it, but I met a sailor and his wife at the hotel last night and she said finding work was no problem at all. She had been here three days and had already found a job. She also said wages were good. That's about all

I know about that, but we won't worry about jobs because we know we can make everything work out okay.

I went to church this morning. By the way, I don't think there's a Christian Church in Oxnard. The one I went to was the Baptist Church. It was quite nice and they have a wonderful minister and he had a good sermon. I didn't get acquainted, nor was I able to stay for communion as my pass was almost up so I had to leave right after the sermon. I was quite impressed by the cordiality and willingness of the congregation to want to help wives and girlfriends of service men. In fact, the sermon was built around this theme and was very good. If all else fails we can probably contact the church for help in finding a place to stay.

By May 5 it was time for two-stage checks. I left the home field a little after 10:00 and flew solo to auxiliary field #3. There Captain Asmus climbed in and proceeded to give me the tests. At the conclusion he stated that he was happy with my progress, but that I should work a little harder on some of my acrobatic maneuvers and spend some time practicing forced landing approaches. He was certainly justified in criticizing my acrobatics and I was disappointed in the Stearman as an aerobatic airplane. It was heavy with a maximum gross weight of 2,700 pounds, very stable and easy to fly, but underpowered I thought for a good acrobatic plane. The little Meyers I had flown previously had less horsepower but was also considerably lighter. Consequently, all aerobatic maneuvers could be made from level flight; all that was necessary was to open the throttle and you had the power and speed to do whatever you wanted. You could also roll it upside down and fly inverted as long as you wanted. The only things you could do with the Stearman from level flight were spins, stalls, and falling leaves. In other words, anything that allowed you to lose altitude. All other maneuvers such as loops, chandelles, Immelmann turns, snap rolls, slow rolls, and the like required lowering the nose and opening the throttle to build up airspeed in order to do the maneuver. If there was any hesitation at the top of a loop or Immelmann turn the engine would cough and sputter and airspeed was lost immediately. Once the plane was back in its normal position and gas could flow to the carburetor the engine would cut in and the plane resumed flying. If the gas tank had had another outlet on top and plumbed into the fuel pump the problem could have been solved. The engine would have kept running in any position, which would have made it easier to fly, but this was a training airplane and no one wanted to make anything easier for a cadet.

I soon tired of aerial maneuvers and decided to practice forced landing approaches until I had to return to the home field at 1:00 p.m. Practicing forced landing approaches is very simple: you just retard the throttle and with the engine idling pretend you had an engine failure and pick out the best field or open space where you think you can land, supposedly into the wind. Of course it has to be within gliding distance of where your supposed emergency occurred. The main idea is to learn the gliding capabilities of the airplane so you don't over or undershoot the field you have chosen. Some time during every dual flight when you least expected it the instructor would retard the throttle, scream "Forced landing," and then you immediately set up a gliding landing pattern. He would hold the throttle closed so you couldn't cheat with power. Then the instructor judged you on your choice of fields, how well you executed, and whether or not you were able to reach your chosen objective. When the plane had descended to within 200 feet of the ground you opened the throttle and abandoned the approach. At this altitude it had already been determined whether you were successful.

This day there was no wind and as long as you stayed away from buildings almost any field in the practice area could be used for an emergency landing. I made three or four approaches from different altitudes and felt that I had made good choices. I decided to try one more before heading home so at 2,500 feet I pulled back on the throttle and spotted a flat, beautiful barley field directly under the airplane. This was great because I could start a descending spiral right over the field and this would give me practice in losing excess altitude and choosing the right time to start the landing pattern which would lead to the final approach. Everything had to be perfectly timed. Trying to stretch the glide would decrease the airspeed and create a stall, causing the airplane to crash. Too much airspeed and you would overshoot the field with the same dire consequences. At 800 feet I broke out of the spiral and established a base leg and at 400 feet turned onto a final approach. The barley field was as flat as a tabletop and not a breath of wind. At 200 feet I knew I had the field made, but for some reason I decided that I would wait until 100 feet to apply power. As I passed through 100 feet I was almost hypnotized by the green field coming up and by the time I reached for the throttle it was too late. The wheels were already turning in the crop and the drag caused the plane to touch down.

It was a beautiful landing; the barley was just starting to head out. The farmer had a bountiful crop and there I was sitting in the middle of it. The ground was quite firm so I taxied to the far end of the field and with full power was able to make a 180 degree turn and get back into my original tracks to decrease the ground drag. The airplane accelerated very slowly at first, but finally I was able to get the tail up and the speed increased immediately. I was airborne long before I reached the point of touch down.

I heaved a sigh of relief and headed home. It was a crazy, stupid thing to have done and certainly a good way to wreck an airplane. I kept scanning the skies but there weren't any airplanes in sight so I felt reasonably sure no one had seen me go down. The plane was okay and only the farmer would notice strange tracks in the field. No one would ever know except the farmer and me.

When I reached the base I was the last plane in the landing pattern and the old Stearman settled onto the runway without a bounce. I taxied to the flight line, parked the plane, and as I was crawling out of the cockpit my instructor came down the line and stopped by the tail waiting for me to fasten the seat belt around the stick, a procedure that was done to keep the controls from moving in case the wind came up. As I stepped down from the wing he said that he had talked with Captain Asmus. He was pleased that I had passed my two-stage checks and the captain had told him what areas I needed to work on to be a better pilot. We would concentrate on them at our next dual session. Then he walked around to the front of the plane, stopped, and I thought he was having trouble breathing. He motioned for me to come forward where he was looking at the plane. By now he had recovered his voice and said, "Where have you been? What happened?" I looked and saw that the landing struts had turned green. The front of the plane and the leading edge of the lower wing were covered with juice from the barley plants. The silver fabric was now olive drab. It looked funny, but it wasn't a laughing matter. "I'm waiting for your story," he fumed. I thought about saying maybe somebody should mow the grass on the auxiliary field, but I knew that wouldn't fly. I was caught red-handed so there was only one thing to do and that was tell the truth. While I was explaining he kept saying, "No, no, oh my god."

I kept saying, "Yes."

"Oh no, I'm gonna be fired from my first instructing job because of some nitwit cadet." He looked tired and somewhat resigned to his fate.

I told him I would go to the squadron commander and tell him the truth and he wouldn't be responsible for anything. I would accept the consequences of my actions whether it was punishment or wash out. I was filled with remorse but couldn't undo what had happened. I would just have to live with it. At this he bristled and said, "Don't you dare tell anyone. I don't want anybody to know that I had a student dumb enough to pull such a trick. You're not going to make me the laughing stock of the instructor corps. Check in your parachute and meet me in the ready room on the double and forget about chow, Mister. You're in trouble." I was busy "yes sirring" and he was busy shaking his head and muttering "I don't believe it."

When we met in the ready room he had a bucket of warm water complete with suds and the chamois from his car. We did not draw any undo attention as we proceeded down the line to the airplane carrying the bucket. Since many cadets experienced air sickness it was standard procedure for them to wash out their planes. Although it didn't take very long to wash off the green juice, he kept repeating that it was students like me who gave instructors gray hair long before their time.

He couldn't figure out what he had done in life that would cause him to be punished by being assigned such a student. I couldn't answer his question but only scrubbed harder.

Finally he said, "Well, it looks okay. You had better get going so you aren't late for classes. If you mention this to anybody you're asking for trouble. Believe me, you better not screw up again 'cause I'll be watching you like a hawk going for a chicken."

The following day I spent two hours in the air demonstrating every flying maneuver I had been taught while my ears were ringing to the innuendos of an inhuman screaming demon who now occupied the front seat of the airplane. It was hard to believe that this was the same kind gentleman who had been my instructor two days before. It was apparent to me that he had a split personality. I had heard that traumatic experiences sometimes affected people that way. Before landing there was a request to fly over the barley field at 1,500 feet. When the tracks became visible the inside of my knees took a terrific beating as the demon threw the control stick from side to side. Frustrations finally vented, he requested we land at auxiliary field #4 and then I could proceed with an hour of solo time. As I taxied away the spent shell of a man was still shaking his head, and I quietly gave thanks to the Dayton draft board that had saved me from a similar fate.

By now most of the men in the other squadrons with previous time had soloed. To the best of my knowledge there were four of us. Over the next few days the men without previous time started joining our elite ranks. Cadet Jim House, our cadet wing adjutant, became the first from Squadron 8, followed closely by our cadet squadron commander M. J. Dumont. I was particularly happy to see them do well on the flight line since they excelled as cadet officers. Their military knowledge and expertise commanded respect from all of us. A little more brass was starting to appear on uniforms so there was hope that we would soon look like a military unit again.

Saturday, May 8, I received a call from Mrs. Frank Eastwood, the manager of Hotel Oxnard, stating that Sunday she would have a vacant room with bath available. I managed to get a short pass and paid thirty-six dollars for two weeks in advance. Sherry arranged to take the Union Pacific stage, arriving the fourteenth. I left a note in the room asking her to come to the base after 7:30 p.m. that night.

On May 12 Squadron 8 was assigned to fly out of auxiliary #3. The instructors departed with their students and I was assigned my solo lesson, which was one hour in length, after which I was to land at auxiliary #3 and pick up Captain Asmus for another stage check. The stage check took forty minutes. Then I was to practice landings at the auxiliary field for thirty minutes after which the airplane would be assigned to someone else and I would return on the bus.

Everything went as scheduled. The newly soloed cadet was told to go up and do several stalls, get a good feel of the airplane, and then come back and practice landings. When the student returned for landing practice the white flag was flying. This was a signal for everyone to land. The cadet made a good landing in spite of the wind which was just beginning to come up. In short order all of Squadron 8 aircraft were on the ground. The instructors were in a huddle while the students were sitting in the airplanes with engines idling and full brakes applied. The wind was really picking up and the western sky was black.

Oxnard was only two or three miles from the ocean with an elevation of thirty-three feet. Our auxiliary field was slightly north and east of the home field. A squall line was rolling in from the ocean; moisture was not a problem, but the wind represented a real hazard for it meant a crosswind landing at the home base. While the Stearman was a stable airplane, it was jokingly known to have a built-in ground loop. This was attributed to the fact that it had a narrow landing gear. For the uninitiated, a ground loop is an accident which occurs on landing by inexperienced pilots. The pilot loses control of the plane after touch down and it does a very sharp 180 degree turn. The resulting sharp turn causes a wing to drag the ground as the airplane pivots in a tight circle. The pilot, because of inexperience, has allowed the airplane to get ahead of him and by the time he reacts a wing has been damaged and the pilot has suffered considerable humiliation to his pride and reputation. Wind in extreme cases could be a cause, but usually it was the inattention of pilots.

The instructors finished their consultations, boarded their aircraft, and started taxiing for takeoff. At this point Captain Asmus motioned for me to join him. He explained the white flag meant that all solo flights were cancelled; only dual aircraft were to be in the air and they were headed for Oxnard. There was one problem. We had one more plane than instructors so he was requesting that I fly the extra airplane back. I must have had a questioning look for he immediately said, "I know you are capable. Will you do it?"

"Yes, Sir."

"Okay. What I want you to do is fly over the base 500 feet above traffic altitude, check the severity of the crosswind and if you don't feel you want to make a crosswind landing, circle the field until the traffic slows down. Then forget about the runways, head into the wind and make your landing directly into the wind crossing the runway at an angle. You won't have any trouble so give me a head start and I will notify the tower to watch for you and they will hold up traffic until you get down."

By now the wind was becoming more severe and it was necessary for the captain to crawl in the front seat of my airplane and hold the brakes so the solo cadet could get out and give me his parachute. As soon as I was buckled in and had control, the captain climbed out and boarded his own plane while the cadet boarded the bus. Captain Asmus circled the field once to make sure I got off the ground okay, then he headed home.

As I came over the home field I saw that they were using only one runway, the same one I had soloed on. The reason for this was that the wind was so strong they had cadets stationed about two-thirds of the way down the runway. As each plane turned off the blacktop runway four cadets, two on each side, immediately grabbed the wings to stabilize the aircraft while the instructor slowly taxied to the tie-down area. I circled the field twice then decided I would land on the runway the same as the others. Pride would not let me land across the field into the wind. I would do it right or wreck the plane trying.

I entered the traffic pattern making sure I had good separation behind the lead aircraft. When I turned final I carried
power to help counteract the crosswind. When I set up the
crab (nosing the airplane sufficiently into the wind to counteract wind drift) and lowered the wing into the wind, it dawned
on me how hard the wind was blowing, but I wouldn't back
down. It was now or never. I wasn't about to make a full stall
landing allowing the wind to get under the wing. I passed
over the end of the runway still carrying slight power; at the
last second I kicked out the crab and leveled the wings. The
old Stearman behaved perfectly as I applied slight forward
pressure on the stick and greased a wheel landing. Still maintaining slight pressure on the stick I slowly retarded the throttle to idle, allowing the tail to drop gently onto the runway
and then applied full back pressure on the stick. It was so early
in our training that the cadets had not yet been taught how to
make a power-on landing, but it was a procedure I had
learned in civilian flying. I let the airplane decelerate on its
own and applied brakes only to turn off the runway and allow
the cadets to grab the wings. I taxied back very slowly savoring
every minute.

When we reached the tie-down area I remained in the cockpit until the ground ropes were attached to the wings. After
shutting down the engine I slowly got out of the cockpit, realizing that the mental strain had left me weak. Walking down
the line I heard one instructor, who was still sitting in his
airplane, ask his student, "Who the hell is that hot rod?" The
answer was inaudible but it brought on a real high. I was now
walking at just about traffic altitude.

About that time a voice from below was heard to proclaim,
"That's my student." Through the film in my eyes I could
faintly see my instructor appearing from nowhere. No one will
ever know the feeling I had at that moment and I certainly
couldn't describe it.

Two days later for some unexplained reason Mr. Fletcher
was transferred to another instructor, a Mr. Pulici, who had
just arrived from Hawaii. Mira Loma was his first instructor
assignment and it appeared to me that the instructors hazed
one another the same as the cadet corps.

When I was notified of the change of instructors Captain Asmus remarked, "Fletch, I don't think I did you a favor by having you return the plane the other day. Every military pilot on the field knows about it and they are just waiting for an excuse to get you on a check ride. Whatever you do, don't make even a little mistake. You've now been warned. They won't wash you out, but they can sure make a flight miserable for you."

The role of the six military pilots on the base was to see that all of the instructors taught the students in the same manner. It was a matter of standardization. There may be many ways to perform a maneuver, but, in the eyes of the military, there was only one correct way and that was the army way. It was their job to ensure that not only were we taught the army way but also practiced it. It was possible, however, to graduate from Primary without ever having ridden with a military pilot since the senior civilian pilots had the responsibility for the final checks.

Another task of the military pilots was to give check rides to students who were having trouble with their flying. After a check ride they would decide whether the student had the potential to continue in the program or was to be eliminated. This relieved the civilian instructor of this responsibility. The instructor and the check pilot worked closely together comparing notes and discussing the student's progress and potential, but in the end the military had the final say.

Some of the students who were washed out might have been good pilots had they been able to have a little extra time, but this was wartime and pilots were needed immediately. Those who learned the quickest would succeed. Occasionally a student was held back one class, but these were students who had demonstrated good flying ability and had fallen behind for some reason, maybe a case of measles, a sprained ankle or some other mild health problem. The reason had to be related to something other than flying or ground school.

At Mira Loma we also had eight student officers in class 43-J: one captain, three first lieutenants, and four second lieutenants. These officers from the infantry, cavalry, and other branches had applied for flying duty and were now undergoing the same training as the cadets. Assigned to Squadron 8 were second lieutenants George Kinnon and Dale Miller. They attended class with us and always sat in the back of the room. During class breaks they left the room first and stayed away from us. These men were good officers and had no desire to inhibit us by their presence. They were always cheerful and they sympathized with some of our problems, but we knew they had already experienced most of what we were going through. We also found out that they had other duties including officer of the day, which they rotated among their group. These student officers did not live on the base, although they took their meals there. While we weren't always aware of it, these men were pulling for us to succeed and provided help whenever they could, always behind the scenes. One of these student officers would eventually provide a worthy service for me.

As more of the cadets started soloing, more goofs were committed. Ground loops, airplanes standing on their noses because the brakes were applied too harshly, and damaged wings from either parking or taxiing too close together became a routine sight. The cadets who committed these blunders were awarded red stars on the squadron progress report sheet. It wasn't long until the squadron had collected enough red stars to make a Russian general's heart pound with pride.

For a small infraction the cadet had to wear a red arm band for whatever length of time the instructor prescribed—two days, a week, or whatever. This was to notify everyone that he was an accident ready to happen, so beware. A cadet who had a major infraction had to wear a cowbell around his neck while on the flight line. This was known as belling the goat, but this farm boy knew the difference between a goatbell and a cowbell. This bell, without a clapper, was worn until the next incident occurred, when it was passed on to another culprit. There were times when it changed hands two or three times a day. It was my good fortune not to wear either the bell or an arm band, but I felt sorry for those who were thusly humiliated. Eventually the cadets were able to see the humor of their mistakes and the stars, arm bands, and bell became badges of honor and were worn with pride, albeit false. Once they adopted the attitude of "don't fight it, join it," things became a lot easier.

There were times when the auxiliary fields resembled a three-ring circus. One of the incidents involved a student on his first solo. He made a good takeoff and flew a perfect pattern. The final approach was right on, but just before touchdown he applied full power and went around. We all had the feeling that he wasn't satisfied with the approach and we anxiously awaited his second try. Again it was the same thing. Before touchdown the power went on and the plane climbed to pattern altitude. We were beginning to suspect the cadet was experiencing a lack of confidence.

After the third go-around his instructor was becoming very nervous and concerned. The other instructors weren't helping by suggesting that he might have to be shot down. On the fourth go-around all the levity was gone. Up to now we had not had a personal injury or major accident, but it now appeared we had one in the making.

On the fifth approach everyone was frozen in place, eyes riveted on the airplane, following every move. More than one silent prayer was riding with the cadet as each one of us was willing him the courage and confidence to make a successful landing. As he came over the end of the grass strip the nose elevated in a perfect flare-out and the Stearman settled on the ground in a perfect three-point landing. The grim-faced cadets broke into a rousing cheer as the airplane rolled to a stop and a misty-eyed instructor ran to congratulate the cadet. It was obvious that the instructors cared more about the welfare of the students than they were willing to admit.

It was a nervous, smiling cadet who crawled out of the cockpit exclaiming, "I did it. I did it." It was a relieved, jubilant group of cadets who pounded him on the back while the instructor was explaining that was enough for one day. There would be a tomorrow. This was the most celebrated solo in Squadron 8, but it was not a cause for punishment.

By now flying was the furthermost thing from my mind. Sherry was coming. After a separation of four and a half months we would actually see one another again. My spirits were so buoyed that Friday afternoon I summoned the courage to call on the base commander after classes to request a long weekend pass. I had polished my brass, shined my shoes, and put on my best military manners in hopes that my request would be well received. It was very important to me.

When I entered headquarters the first sergeant asked what was the nature of my business. I told him I wished to see the commander in order to request a long weekend pass. He gave a faint smile and disappeared into the commander's office. Upon his return he stated that the major would see me now and held the door open. I marched into the major's office and up to the desk while the first sergeant closed the door. I stood at attention and held a salute until the major looked up from his papers and returned it. The major ordered, "At ease, Mr. Fletcher. State your business." I proceeded to tell him that my wife had arrived early that morning and since we had not seen each other for four and a half months I was requesting, if possible, a long weekend pass.

He answered, "Request denied, Mr. Fletcher."

I immediately responded, "Thank you, Sir," saluted, did an about face, and left the room. On the way out the first sergeant stopped me and said he was sorry that I had not been successful but the major was only following the policy in regard to the number of people required on the base. I told him I understood and thanked him for allowing me to see the major. To say that I was disappointed was a lie; I was crushed. Anyway, I would see her for two hours that evening and we would have Saturday night together. Even that would be heaven. I was just hoping for more.

That evening just after 7:30 the cadet runner came to the cottage and said I had a visitor at the gate. He handed me a pass and explained it was good only for a two-hour visit in the visiting area just outside of the main gate. He also presented me with a copy of the rules in regard to a female visitor. It would be wise to give the copy to my spouse that she might know the rules before starting divorce proceedings. I knew the rules but it dawned on me that I had not prepared Sherry.

The rules were essentially this: We were required to remain in the visiting area under the supervision of the guard at the gate. The visiting area was a small barbed wire enclosure with two benches facing each other about five feet apart as we were not to touch each other. If we sat on the same bench there had to be eighteen inches between us. An embrace or even a handshake was out of the question. This arrangement reminded me of the prison visits I had seen in the movies. The whole environment was very embarrassing. The barbed wire enclosure, the guard watching our every move, the wooden benches and dirt floor all gave the appearance of a prisoner of war camp. Rules were in place to make men of us, but certainly not fathers. The hard part was telling Sherry to stop where she was and read the rules before we greeted each other. But in spite of all of this our spirits were not dampened and she promised not to divorce me until we had one night together.

While we were visiting, a couple came to the gate and requested to visit Cadet Jim House. The lady was a real beauty; she was accompanied by a huge man with a full red beard. It was very unusual to see a man with a beard in those times. They arrived in separate cars: the lady in a new red convertible and the man in a new sedan. When Cadet House arrived we moved to the far end of the compound to allow them some privacy, but we did overhear enough of their conversation to realize that the young lady was Jim's sister. Her husband was Andy Devine, the movie star, and the reason for the beard was they were filming *Ali Baba and the Forty Thieves*. Here we were in the presence of a movie star and his family who were being accorded the same indignities.

When our time was up Jim's family left first, driving away in the sedan and leaving the convertible for him. Jim was a very pleasant, low-key person and this was the first time I realized he was close to members of the film industry. I chose not to tell any of the cadets what I had seen since I felt this was a private matter.

It was impossible to sleep that night. Mixed emotions kept nagging me awake. I was very happy that Sherry was there, but I was also miserable because of the way she and the other guests had to be treated. I could only hope that those who wrote and directed the policies of war exhibited more compassion and intelligence than those who were directing the cadet corps. I could not envision any situation where warmth, love, and pride of family could be construed to be a detriment to the service and me in particular. If a handshake or a quick embrace were to determine the outcome of the war we were in deep trouble. But as a cadet who wanted to fly you pocketed your pride and continued the farce of, "Yes, Sir. No excuse, Sir."

The next day, Saturday, I flew two hours and fifteen minutes. When I explained to Mr. Pulici that my wife was in town he suggested we fly the first hour dual because he needed to be sure my mind was on flying instead of something else. We spent most of the hour on aerial work, and then we proceeded to the auxiliary field to shoot landings. Traffic at the field was nonexistent as everyone was in the air practicing. Only the bus driver, dispatcher, and a few cadets were present. We practically had the field to ourselves.

We entered the pattern on the downwind leg. Visible to us about 400 feet inside the field boundary was an exceptionally green area about 100 feet in diameter. Just after passing the green spot Mr. Pulici jerked the throttle closed hollering, "Forced landing." I lowered the nose and set up a glide for the field. Through the gosport I heard Mr. Pulici say, "I hear you are pretty good at forced landings so let's see you hit that green spot." I nodded my head in agreement. I knew in a flash what I was going to do. Rather than risk going out too far and landing short of the green spot I would play it safe, come in high on the final approach then side-slip the airplane, a cross control procedure designed to lose altitude quickly, thereby avoiding any miscalculation. It was a recognized procedure taught in civilian flying just for this sort of emergency.

When I turned final Mr. Pulici gloated, "You blew it. You're way too high. You'll be lucky to hit the field, let alone the spot. Poor judgment, Mister. For this you get the bell." At that instant I lowered the left wing while applying pressure on the right top rudder to maintain directional control, elevating the nose slightly to keep from gaining excess speed. The Stearman was now in a slide-slip. The altimeter needle was unwinding at a highly accelerated pace. At 100 feet of altitude I released the pressure on the controls and resumed a normal glide, crossing over the airport boundary at seventy-five feet. Mr. Pulici, completely taken by surprise, let loose a barrage of screeches which I interpreted to mean "What do you think you are doing?" The airplane floated to the edge of the green and when the flare-out was completed the ship settled right in the center of the spot.

As I pulled over to taxi back Mr. Pulici gave me an earful. "Where did you learn that? Don't ever do that again. That is never done in the army and is not taught." I tried to explain it was a safe procedure designed for such an emergency. "Yes, in light planes it is okay, but in the heavy military aircraft you will eventually fly, NEVER. You can kill yourself. Because of the weight you can't recover fast enough. That's why we don't teach it."

"Okay, okay. I thought you wanted to see if I could do it."

"Not that way. Now don't ever do that again for me or any other instructor."

When he finished chewing me out he wearily climbed out of the airplane and said, "Since you are going to see your wife tonight I know it won't do any good to give you lessons to practice because you're going up to celebrate and have a good time. But please don't do any more side-slips or tear the wings off the plane and, above all, don't forget to return to the base on time. I will ride back with another student." I spent one hour and fifteen minutes doing every fun thing I knew and the instructor didn't have to worry about my losing the wings. The Stearman was a very sturdy airplane built more like a boxcar than a plane. It had withstood the stresses of pilots far better than me and even those who were worse.

On our way to dinner after flying I could tell that my roommate, whom I will now call Lester, was very moody and unhappy. I knew he lived in the Los Angeles area and had just become a father which should have been a reason for joy. His problem was that on our short pass he could not get to where he lived, visit his wife and daughter at the hospital, and still get back before his pass expired. This meant he wouldn't be able to see them until we got to be upperclassmen. I suggested that he explain his dilemma to the major and perhaps he might be more sympathetic to his plight than mine. He snapped back that he had already tried that and had been turned down. Lester was a good cadet but very moody, with light red hair and a temper with a hair trigger. While we were roomies we didn't become good friends. My other roommate was just plain withdrawn so the three of us never became close friends; each did his share of the communal chores and that was it.

When we returned from dinner we had thirty-five minutes before personal inspection. If we passed inspection we were then given our passes. I felt sorry for Lester and wanted to help him. An idea dawned on me. Every Saturday at inspection one cadet was selected out of each squadron in class 43-J and given a long pass, a gimmick to inspire us to look our best. The one chosen was known as the best-dressed cadet in the squadron. I told Lester that I would shine his shoes and brass, he could wear my new tie and maybe he would win, but we had to hurry as there wasn't much time. He said, "Do you really think so?"

"Why not? Somebody has to win." He got into the spirit of the competition and with five minutes left we had him shining and looking good. I was impressed. I had five minutes to get dressed and get into formation.

I lined up behind Lester. We had to stare straight ahead and not move a muscle during inspection, but in this position I could see Lester and the inspecting officer. I was surprised to see that this day the major was inspecting our squadron. After we opened ranks the major started down the front rank, trailed by the first sergeant who carried a clipboard with the squadron roster of names. The cadets wore name tags at all times so the inspecting officer could call your name and report violations to the first sergeant.

At the end of the first rank no demerits were given, but two cadets were ordered to remain in place when the squadron was dismissed. At the end of the second rank inspection one cadet was given a demerit for some infraction and another was ordered to stand fast. Then came the third rank: two were given demerits and when the major reached Lester he gave him a good look over and then ordered him to stay in place. I was elated. Lester was in the top four; he had a chance and I felt good about helping him. Now if his good luck could just hold he would have the long pass.

Coming down the fourth and final rank the major was speeding up. When he came to me I was frozen in place, my eyes glued straight ahead. The major gave me the once over, then seemed to be concentrating on something, maybe I had missed a button in my hurry. As he stood looking I knew I was going to be gigged so I couldn't believe my ears when I heard, "Stand fast, Mr. Fletcher."

The inspection over, the squadron closed ranks and was dismissed. The five of us remaining were ordered into a single line and the inspection commenced again. This time three cadets were dismissed; Lester and I stood side by side. I knew he was going to win. There we were, the two cadets who had both requested long passes now the finalists. Coincidence? Maybe, who knows. Anyway, Lester was a cinch. The major looked us over very carefully then commented to the first sergeant that it was certainly a tough decision and he didn't know how he was going to resolve it. He would try one more test. "Misters, let me see your dog tags." Since they were always worn on a chain around our necks, I immediately unbuttoned the next to the top button on my shirt and flipped out the tags. I couldn't see Lester since my eyes were still focused to the front. I assumed he was displaying his, but then I heard him utter, "Damn, I left them hanging on the bedpost."

We were dismissed as the first sergeant penned my name on the pass. As we walked into the cottage Lester looked at me with contempt, muttering, "You didn't even shine your shoes." But his remarks fell on deaf ears as I was heading for the Hotel Oxnard.

I ran over to tell a good friend, Don Bell, that I was ready to go as we were going to walk to the hotel together. Don was from southern Idaho, a little older than myself, having worked his way up to become a trainman in civilian life. He was a level-headed cadet and would have made a good roommate. His girlfriend was a school teacher from southern Idaho and had arrived in Oxnard on Friday to spend the weekend. Don had managed to reserve two rooms at the hotel, one for his girlfriend for Friday and Saturday nights and one for himself for Saturday night.

When we reached the hotel we found that his girlfriend had been assigned a room on the first floor and Don on the third floor. The four of us had supper together and then Sherry and I returned to her room to spend some time, which in today's vernacular would be called "quality time." She had room 62, a corner room on the ground floor. Don's girlfriend had room 60 and the headboards of our beds were back to back on the adjoining wall.

Upon returning to the room the suspense of the sleepless night, the stress of flying, and the surprise ending of the inspection were beginning to take their toll. A tired, relaxed, peaceful mood set in and I suddenly realized that in order to reach our goals all of us in the cadet corps had been running on nerve alone. We had long exceeded our own potential and stamina. Sherry and I were now reunited; I would start with renewed vigor, but only after my long pass had expired. For now I was happy and contented. My life was whole again and the entire cadet experience was pushed into the background.

It was hot in the room so I raised a window and put a stick in place so it wouldn't fall. We were visiting like there would be no tomorrow; so many things to catch up on. We could hear Don and his girlfriend laughing next door. In spite of the war we still lived in a wonderful world.

Our light went out early before Taps. As I prepared for bed I realized the room did not have a closet so I very painstakingly folded my clothes and laid them on a straight-back chair, with my shirt and blouse hung over the chair back and my service cap on top of the pile on the chair seat. My pajamas consisted of a T-shirt and O.D. boxer shorts. In my hurry to get to town I had even forgotten my shaving kit. Sherry remarked that she would probably be scared if she woke up and saw a man's clothes hanging in the room after all these months. I assured her that any clothes she saw in the room tonight would be mine. Not to worry.

Exhausted, I fell asleep. I thought I might be dreaming, but I finally realized Sherry was poking me in the ribs and whispering that someone was in the room with us. Half asleep I muttered that it was my clothes on the chair. Go back to sleep. Again she whispered, "Do something. There is someone in the room." Before I could answer something like a felt glove passed across my face. For a second I felt sharp terror. She was right, I had to do something.

It was pitch black in the room. I needed to turn the light on but the only one in the room was a ceiling light and the switch was by the entry door at the far end of the room. I jumped out of bed and bounded toward the door. Someone tripped me and as I fell I hit the footboard on the bed, jamming the headboard against the wall with a bang. I wasn't sure whether I was hurt or not but this was no place for a coward. As I jumped up I immediately flipped the light switch. Blinded by the light it took a second or two to realize I had fallen over the chair where I had placed my clothes. There did not appear to be anyone else in the room, but obviously something was wrong. At that moment a large bat dropped from the ceiling and made a pursuit pass over my head. I dropped to the floor and grabbed my shirt with the idea I would throw it over him on the next pass.

When Sherry saw the bat she screamed and immediately pulled the covers over her long blonde hair. Completely covered, she issued the muffled command, "Put on your cap. Bats can get tangled in your hair." By now I was so used to obeying commands that without even thinking I clutched the leather bill of my service cap and jammed it on my head. The bat would have had a problem since my G.I. haircut was so short even a marine would have been embarrassed. I jerked open the door leading to the hallway hoping to shoo the bat out, but for some reason he or she kept dive-bombing me. I was running around in my boxer shorts, T-shirt, and service cap, flagging the bat through on every pass.

Sherry, although completely huddled under the covers, was experiencing stark terror. Bats were never her favorite mammals. She was screaming, "Get that thing out of here." I was trying to reassure her that everything was okay even though I knew it wasn't since I wasn't having any luck chasing the bat by waving my shirt and doing a war dance. She took one more peek and screamed, "I can't stand that thing any longer.

Please get it out of here." I renewed my efforts of running around the room waving the shirt and ducking out of the way as the bat was now upset too. One more "I can't stand it" echoed from the bed as I crashed against the wall running out of breath.

Just as I was getting ready for another pass there was a slight knock on the wall and a reticent voice whispered, "Fletch, is everything okay?"

I hollered back, "No."

Again a very reluctant, half-hearted voice said, "Is there any way I can help?" Before I could answer, the bat made another pass. I jumped over the fallen chair, grabbed my shoe, and threw it. Sherry responded with another "Get that thing out of here" in a trembling voice while I shouted at Bell that I needed help.

Within seconds Don appeared in the doorway in full uniform. He took one look in the room just as I was performing another "pase de pecho" with my shirt. As the bat went by he hollered "Olé" and doubled up with laughter. In between fits of guffawing he managed to gasp, "Thank God it wasn't what I thought." I didn't know what he thought but I suggested he could be a little more helpful. There was something about a camera and then, still laughing like a hyena, he gasped, "Why don't you put on your pants and I will go see if I can find a broom." I took his advice and pulled on my pants and shoes, still swinging the shirt. I suggested to Sherry that she go next door until the room was clear but she wasn't about to come out from under the covers.

Bell quickly returned with a straw house broom. The high ceiling gave the bat the advantage over us but we eventually chased it into the hall. When we went to return the broom the desk clerk, who was a young lady, announced that we were not going to leave the bat in the hall which led to the reception area. She wasn't about to have it in her domain so we opened the two large French doors that sealed off the dining area, while she hid under the front desk. After another long chase the bat flew into the dining room and we hurriedly closed the doors. The desk clerk, now mollified, thanked us profusely.

It was 11:30 and Bell, still laughing, headed up the stairway to his room. I surely wasn't going to thank him for his efforts after essentially providing the evening's entertainment. As I passed his girlfriend's door I did apologize to her for ruining her evening. She gave me a strange look and icily said they would still have some time in the morning since Don didn't have to report until noon, but I left with the impression she wasn't overjoyed with Don's choice of friends.

When I finally got back to our room Sherry was sitting up in bed pondering what Bell had said. When the meaning of his remarks eventually dawned on us we were able to have a good laugh at our perceived predicament. After finding a large hole in the screen I closed the window, rationalizing that not too much mental acumen was expected from a cadet.

We spent most of Sunday visiting, planning, and speculating what Sherry could do since she was on her own for the first time in a strange military environment. She was sure that Hotel Oxnard would not play a role in her future plans; the hotel had lost its romantic intrigue and the town fared no better.

Ventura sounded more attractive, but that was a decision she would have to make. My decisions were always made for me with a simple "Yes, Sir," but hers would not be made that easily. The responsibility for finding a place to live and a job rested on her shoulders as there wasn't any way I could help. Since we were married adults we would not be humiliated again by the army's bullpen visiting policy. We would see one another only on weekends. However, if an emergency arose or if something transpired that I should know about, she could come any evening.

Left with her dilemma, we embraced in the room out of sight of the all-seeing military eye. Then I hurriedly headed for the base, arriving in my room just as Taps was sounding. At the breakfast formation I was greeted with some strange all-knowing looks and grins from close friends. Bell managed to stay clear of me, but I would have given anything to have heard the concocted, titillative, licentious stories he must have related to the others upon his return.

My two roommates were scheduled for a check ride that morning and both were in a foul mood. By midweek they were gone and I was the sole occupant of the cottage. Word quickly spread that the best way to wash out was to have Fletcher as a roommate. It was rumored that he drove his roommates batty.

The strict rules under which the cadet corps operated can best be conveyed by excerpts from a letter Sherry wrote to her parents:

> Gene was in some big parade Wednesday on the public school lawn but he didn't find out what it was for unless it was for publicity or better community relations. All he knew was he got hot—too hot in the sun.
>
> One of his roommates flunked out and had to leave Wednesday. The other one is on the verge but he doesn't know either way yet.
>
> Gene is going to get night flying while he is here so he is thrilled about that. All the instructors are practicing now so you hear them at all hours. He has a new instructor, his third one since he has been here. He hated to lose his old one as they were good friends and had so much fun together. He had about the same number of hours Gene has as he was a student instructor.
>
> I've been meaning to tell you that the cadets only sleep in their beds one night a week and that's Thursday night. You see it takes a compass, protractor, ruler and two fellows about an hour to make one bed. They don't have that much time each morning so they sleep on top of them. Fridays they have to change the sheets so that's why they sleep in their beds Thursday nights. Isn't that something?
>
> The scenery is beautiful here and the weather warm but not hot because of the breeze from the ocean. I've seen so many new sights. Barrage balloons are flying everywhere along the coast, everyone is raising victory gardens and just outside of town there are huge truck gardens of cabbage and lettuce.
>
> Thursday a cadet wife came from Georgia, also a girl from Nebraska who is marrying a cadet today. There are wives here from nearly every state in the union—Washington sounds as if it's just in the backyard.

On Friday I was summoned to Captain Asmus's office on the flight line. He told me that he had coordinated with the commandant of cadets and that I was being assigned two room-mates. Both had demonstrated good potential as pilots but were victims of minor accidents—a ground loop and a minor wing brush. He felt the cadets were experiencing a lack of confidence in their abilities, but they were men he did not want to lose. If I could inspire them and raise their morale, perhaps the army would gain two good pilots.

I knew the two men he was talking about. Both had a good sense of humor and I was pleased to have them as roommates. I could only hope the feeling would be reciprocated. This was how John D. Bride, Jr., became one of my roommates. Captain Asmus did not need to worry about J.D.'s morale. He was the second cadet in Squadron 8 to do a medium bank 180 degree turn on the runway: a ground loop. This was not a spectacular feat in itself, in fact it was rather commonplace, but what made it noteworthy was the fact that J.D. was able to accomplish this with an instructor on board. John thought the instructor was flying and the instructor was positive J.D. was in control. One thing was certain, the airplane was out of control.

Anyway, J.D. was taking it all in stride and I wasn't about to tell him how to fly an airplane since he outweighed me by about forty pounds. He always wore a pleasant smile and was a master of one-liners. When the need arose he could become very serious and you knew he was thinking all of the time. We did as much hangar flying as time allowed and I don't know if it was a help to him, but I certainly enjoyed and profited from our sessions.

J.D. had earned the nickname of the "Light Duty Kid," which simply meant he had learned how to manipulate the system. Whenever any project or physical fitness tests were scheduled he always showed up with a slip from the medics restricting his participation to light duty. Not everyone could do this. It took brains and a certain amount of wiliness to do this correctly and not cross the fine line of being a goldbricker (those who did absolutely nothing).

By now many of our instructors had acquired nicknames, all of them printable but never used in their presence. I'm sure the instructors had pet names for the cadets also, although we had no desire to learn what they were.

Our roomie had drawn an instructor we called Laughing Boy. This man wore a perpetual frown combined with a slight sneer. He had a sharp, shrill voice and was continually needling his students. It was said that he had whipped many a cadet into shape for a check ride: it was easier to pass it than to face Laughing Boy if you failed. Our roomie was complaining about him constantly. One day I remarked that he shouldn't complain, he should feel sorry for the man's wife since she had to live with him and put up with him longer than he ever would. His response was that his wife lived with him because she wanted to, otherwise she could get a divorce and leave, whereas he was stuck with him until he graduated or washed out. Unfortunately the latter came first.

Our next roommate was the victim of a nose-over, which was apparently the result of applying the brakes too harshly. His story was that the brakes locked, causing the longitudinal axis to rotate over the lateral axis while the plane was still in a three-point position. He was able to walk away so it must have been a good landing. It was his good fortune to be awarded the cowbell for several days.

In the meantime Sherry was busy scouring the rental ads in the local newspaper. By Thursday she had run out of leads and decided to try in Ventura, a small town located on the ocean about eight miles away. Ventura was a navy town and a bedroom community for Port Hueneme (pronounced *y Knee me*). There was transportation service between Oxnard, Ventura, and Port Hueneme with buses leaving Oxnard about every half hour.

She spent most of the day Thursday looking in Ventura. It was a disappointing day but she decided to try again on Friday. While on her way from the bus stop to a place where she could buy a newspaper she thought she heard someone call her name, something she knew was impossible since she was 1,500 miles from home and friends. Again a lady said, "Evelyn Sherrod, is that you?" and to her surprise she was staring at a good friend who had taught school with her older sister, Mildred, in the small town of Fairfield, Washington. Lorraine Littleton. It was a pleasant shock and surprise for both of them. Lorraine was now married to Howard McNew, who also was a teacher in civilian life but was serving as a pharmacist mate assigned to a ship stationed at Port Hueneme. Lorraine took Sherry under her protective wing and brought her to the Hoover Hotel where Lorraine and Howard had a room. Since Lorraine was acquainted with the lady manager, she felt something could be worked out. The manager said she had a room that was available immediately. The cost was seven dollars a week, but on the nights when I stayed over there would be an extra one dollar charge to cover the cost of extra towels, water, and the like. Sherry paid for the room and caught the bus back to Oxnard to pick up her belongings. Just seeing a friend and knowing that she would have the company of someone she knew during the week gave her a sense of security along with a boost in morale that was sorely needed. She called the base and left the message that she had moved and if Cadet Fletcher received a pass on Saturday to catch the bus for Ventura.

During midweek 43-I class finished flying training. They were now just marking time until orders were received which would transfer them to Basic training. It was rumored they would leave during the last week in May. The weather had been very cooperative and we were now ahead of schedule in flying time; most of us had about forty hours. In my case I had logged forty-one hours total time including twenty-one hours of solo time.

Saturday, after flying, I received a short pass and was able to catch the bus for Ventura. Cadet Bell had no desire to accompany me this time. Arriving at the Hoover Hotel, I met the McNews for the first time. I was very impressed with this handsome couple. Both exuded warmth and kindness and were the type of people you would want for lifetime friends. Lorraine was a beautiful, no-nonsense lady. I knew she would be the perfect companion and big sister for Sherry. It was a great feeling of relief to know she was in such good company in the heart of a sailor town.

We didn't have a lot of time together since I had to return at noon Sunday, but at least Saturday night was not interrupted by another bat chase. When we parted Sunday morning

Sherry was very happy with her situation and excited over the prospect of job hunting.

I-class departed on schedule and 43-J became the top dogs. Their legacy to us came in story form but without title or author:

IT SAYETH HERE . . .

Now, verily, I say there liveth among the many of the mighty land a tribe of barbarians whose ways are passing strange. Themselves they calleth Air Cadets and woe be unto those who joineth their ranks. When they goeth to sup, their meal they speaketh of as mess. Though they consumeth the meal, the mess they leaveth behind.

Their raiment doth bewilder the eye. Of color and of texture each garment looketh alike one unto the other. But, verily, the tall among them sticketh out like four brooms in a flour sack, while the short among them becometh lost in billowing folds. Upon their heads they wear dull brown hats which doth have ear flaps and small tin horns thereon; while crost the top two bulging eyes protrudeth, which the supply room doth term goggles.

Early each morn, sure as the sun riseth unto the heavens, behold, a group of these creatures marcheth forth from their stronghold; each one singeth with lust his war chant. Rock ye not in terror, brethren, for the tale hath just begun. For these barbarians, all clad in their strange raiment, mount unto strange winged crates and soar about the heavens like birds, each one seeking to drive the other from the sky. Now, hark ye, a strange thing. While some mount crates behind the stalwart figure who graceth the front seat, there are others who go unto the sky alone, there to fly crazily about, describing great and awkward eights throughout the heavens. It is these, brethren, that righteous men fear; for in their haste and zest, they calleth unto the Being for the wrath to beat about their heads, and many times doth their engines conk out and leave they and the world in fear and trembling. Then, as the strange tale goeth, they descend from the heavens and enter again unto their stronghold, lustily trying once more their war chant.

Truly, brethren, if one doth peep about in the late afternoon, one doth see them all unto a line, dressed now in gray, sack-like apparel, describing great arcs in the air and while some bendeth on hands and knees and kicketh about their legs, others about them stand and goldbrick. Verily, these are strange men, and wise men would shun them for truly, they seem to use their heads only to keep their two ears from slapping.

Friday, finishing a solo practice session, I flew over auxiliary field #3 five hundred feet above traffic altitude to determine the direction of traffic. Our direction indicator on the auxiliary field was not too sophisticated. It consisted of two 1-by-12 boards about ten feet long, painted white. The two unattached boards were placed to form a T with the top of the T pointing to the direction in which to land. As I looked down the T was pointing to the west and I noticed two cadets walking toward the area where the T was located. I set up a landing pattern in accordance with the T and proceeded to concentrate on the landing procedure while daydreaming about my upcoming Saturday pass.

About halfway down the final approach another airplane appeared on final from the opposite direction. A quick look down showed the T now pointing east and the two cadets sauntering back toward the bus, their mission accomplished. I immediately applied full throttle, climbing and turning away to the right, which was the correct emergency procedure, at the same time quietly hurling invectives at the cadets for changing traffic with an airplane in the pattern.

I wasn't particularly worried because the complete airfield lay between the two landing aircraft. There wasn't any danger of a collision as I had yielded right-of-way in the proper manner before reaching the airport boundary. With the new pattern set up I landed and taxied to the parking area to exchange with another student. After crawling out of the cockpit I started to remove my parachute when the cadet from the plane which had landed ahead of me came running over and said to leave my parachute on as Captain Wells, the senior military check pilot, was requesting that I report to him immediately at the airplane. The cadet was agitated and nervous so it was safe to assume that I was in trouble since this was the plane I had given way to on final approach.

Captain Asmus's warning now came surging back: "Don't make even the appearance of a mistake because they're waiting for you." I had now goofed and would have to pay the price. While there wasn't any danger involved, the least I could have done was rechecked the T while on the base leg since I had seen the cadets moving in that direction and knew their purpose.

I hurried to the airplane and saluted the grim-faced captain on board while standing in the breeze of the idling prop. He waved back a salute and motioned me into the rear cockpit. As soon as I was buckled up and had placed the gosport tubes on the metal connectors on my helmet the captain let loose with, "Mister, I want you to take off and perform the following maneuvers in the exact sequence that I will now give you." With pencil in hand I started making scratches on my knee pad indicating the maneuvers: sideways u for an Immelmann turn, o for a loop, slash for a stall, squiggle for a snap roll, squiggle with a minus for a slow roll, z for a falling leaf, and 8 minus for a lazy eight. After several minutes I ran out of symbols and could only hope that he couldn't remember the order either. Finally he ran out of maneuvers and breath and motioned for me to taxi.

This could be my last ride, but if it was it would be my best because he had a very determined cadet in the rear seat who would not wash out without a protest. Upon reaching altitude I rolled the airplane from right to left to make sure there wasn't anyone below us on either side. Then after checking above I lowered the nose, applied full power to gather airspeed, and pulled up into an Immelmann turn. Again checking to make sure we were clear of other airplanes I performed a tight loop, retarding the throttle on the downward side as we pulled out in level flight. The captain had the controls in a firm grip and the rudder locked in neutral with pressure from his feet. I wasn't sure whether I was supposed to break his control or what.

Before I could respond he shouted into the gosport, "I've got it." I relaxed my grip on the controls and throttle, but kept them in place to follow through with his motions. For about twenty minutes he put the Stearman through the paces, then made a straight-in approach to the auxiliary field and landed without entering the pattern. It dawned on me that this was the same thing he had done when I was forced to leave the pattern. Had he flown a pattern I would have seen him across from me on the downwind leg.

Upon landing he taxied back to the staging area with a speed far in excess of what the cadets were allowed to use. When the airplane came to a full stop I was prepared for an earful, but instead he motioned for me to get out. I crawled out of the cockpit, stepped back three paces and saluted him. He gave me a stern look, returned the salute and taxied off. It was a strange flight. The only words spoken in the air were, "I've got it." Those were the only and last words I heard and no one ever mentioned anything about it: the military, Mr. Pulici, or Captain Asmus. It was just as if it had never happened and I certainly didn't bring up the subject to anyone.

Saturday evening found me back in Ventura. Sherry was in a happy mood for she had found a job as a clerk in the local store of a large chain. She and Lorraine were enjoying each other's company and they found many things to do to fill their spare time. When I left Sunday morning to return to the base, Sherry decided she would sunbathe on the sandy beach which was just about two blocks from the hotel.

Back at the base everything was routine flying and classes, both punctuated by the usual harangue of the instructor. The cadet corps had now been weeded down. We were working on more precise flying skills which included spot landings, landing after passing over a rope hurdle, and various other tactics which required more expertise. It was a challenge the cadets enjoyed, each attempting to outdo the others. The flight instructors were starting to relax a bit and enjoy watching the fruits of their labor perform.

The week passed very quickly but not nearly as fast as the weekend pass. Sherry had been promoted to cashier and was now working in the office. She had been assistant cashier in the branch store at Walla Walla and consequently knew the procedures and duties.

On her trip to the beach the preceding Sunday, she, not being used to the effect of California sun on her fair skin, received a very severe sunburn. The hotel manager, seeing her return to the lobby, advised her to get olive oil and vinegar, mix them half and half, and keep her body saturated until nature could provide healing. I don't know how successful the treatment was but she thought it worked wonders. However, the blisters and red peeling skin certainly altered the appearance of the young lady I had bid good-bye. She jokingly insisted that she was promoted into the office to keep her out of sight of the viewing public.

As we continued our flying the advantage between previous-time men and the newly soloed men continued to shrink. The cadets who were flying for the first time were now demonstrating a proficiency to be envied because of the rapid pace in which they mastered the art of flying. As their abilities increased so did their level of confidence. We knew we were watching men who would some day make aviation history. And while we all laughed and joked about the cadet/teacher relationship, we knew a bond had been forged between the student and his mentor. The cadets would later relate with pride and admiration the stories of learning to fly and the impact these Primary instructors had on their lives. If nothing else, the immense load that these instructors carried flying six days a week with as many as five or six students, risking their lives to impart knowledge and expertise, commanded admiration.

The last two weeks of flying passed in a very routine manner as we passed stage checks and flew dual and solo cross-country flights. The name is somewhat misleading since we did not actually fly across the country but flew to a neighboring town and returned without landing, testing navigational skills. For me the dual flight lasted one hour and ten minutes as we flew from Oxnard to Newhall and returned. My solo flight was to Moorpark and return, a total of forty-five minutes in the air and never out of sight of either destination. I felt it was a very trivial flight and not a test. However, the half-dozen cadets who got lost and spent more time in the air did not agree with my analysis. To me the real test was back in Civilian Pilot Training. There, to qualify for a private pilot license, the solo cross-country was a triangular flight with each leg over an hour in length with a landing at the end of each leg to have your log book signed by the airport manager. Refueling was also required, so this all resulted in more than four hours flying time plus the time spent on the ground at the end of the two vectors. That was a test.

On June 11 I received my final check ride. I was requested to take off, spend thirty minutes getting used to the flying characteristics of the airplane, and then land and pick up Captain Asmus for the final test. Even though I had flown many times with my former instructor I was slightly nervous. I wanted to perform at my best to show him that I had made considerable improvement. A check ride with anyone always creates some anxieties as you question your abilities to perform any test under stress.

The test was going along smoothly, although I had the feeling that I could have done better on some of the maneuvers. Finally it came time to do a slow roll to the right. As I lowered the nose to pick up flying speed I picked out a point on the horizon on which I could center the nose of the aircraft and hold it there while the craft rotated through 360 degrees in the horizontal position. As the plane moved to the inverted position I felt myself falling out of the aircraft. It was a feeling of sheer terror. In the same instant the falling sensation stopped; the friction catch on the buckle had allowed the safety belt to slip about two inches. My body was hanging on the belt with the seat parachute not touching the seat in the airplane, but with my feet still on the rudder pedals. With deliberate precision I made a quick shift from full right rudder to full left rudder hoping to speed up the roll so centrifugal force would overcome gravity and push me back into the seat. To the end of my life I will always remember the leg movements that were made by a frantic pilot. I got the desired results and as the roll was finished I realized that the nose had stayed glued to my check point on the horizon. It was a sober, ashen-faced cadet who finished a ride that lasted forty-five minutes. I dreaded the critique to come; I didn't want to hear about the slow roll fiasco. This was a mental block as it could be the one thing that would cause real trouble.

On the ground Captain Asmus pulled out his checklist and we started going through the flight step by step as he explained my performance on each maneuver: Snap roll, not bad, but the nose went a little too wide around the point. Learn to tighten it up. On the next: Entry speed a little too slow. Loop could have been a little tighter, and so on. Nothing too bad, just a little more refinement. Finally the dreaded slow roll. He stopped and thought a minute. By his hesitation I knew he was choosing his words and my heart started to sink. Here it comes. In slow, measured tones he said, "Fletch, I've flown with a lot of experienced pilots as well as hundreds of cadets and I must tell you that no one has ever demonstrated a slow roll such as yours." Oh, no, it was worse than I thought. "The entry was perfect. The timing on the rudder pedals and the recovery was exact. The nose never wavered. I would have to say it was the best slow roll I have ever ridden through."

I was dumbfounded but I managed to mumble, "Captain Asmus, when I started that slow roll my seat belt slipped and I thought I was a goner. All I was trying to do was stay in the airplane. It was a survival roll as far as I was concerned. If it turned out good I can assure you it was accidental, not intentional." He smiled and said, "Well, let's hope you continue to fly accidentally. You have just completed all the check requirements to go on to Basic. You will have one more flight. That will be Monday night when you will experience your first night landing. I have decided that I want to be the one to demonstrate that. Have a good weekend. I know you have a long pass and I will see you Monday."

Even though it was Friday afternoon I could hardly wait for Saturday to get to Ventura to tell Sherry the good news. We celebrated with the McNews and they were just as happy as I was that I had passed the second hurdle in the cadet program, even though we knew this meant we would be parting company after one more weekend.

Monday evening was a real event on the flight line. The runway was not lighted, consequently the cadets and the instructors worked together to place kerosene burning pot flares about a hundred feet apart down both sides of the left-hand runway. The Stearman did not have landing or cockpit lights.

The instructors carried flashlights on board but this was only to check oil pressure, altitude, and airspeed. This was known as blind flying in its most elementary sense.

After every flare was in place we waited for complete darkness. Then the flares were lighted and the whine of the inertia starter on the engines filled the air, along with a few wracking coughs as the starters were engaged and the engines sputtered to life. The atmosphere resembled that of a pep rally. Everybody was excited, including the instructors, since these demonstration rides were only given once, at the end of every class. They really looked forward to this event. I was never sure whether it was the thrill of night flying or the fact that it was the last time they had to ride with us that was the cause for joy.

When I crawled in with Captain Asmus he said, "Prepare yourself for the thrill of a lifetime." We made two night landings, never leaving the pattern. At the conclusion I now had fourteen minutes of dual night flying in my log book. The entry didn't amount to much on paper, but the thrill of being in the night air, the wind whistling by the open cockpit, the scarves around our necks snapping in the slipstream, the lights of the town sparkling in the clear night, the lighted flares marking the runway all combined to produce a feeling you don't forget. And for us it was even more momentous since we knew this was our last ride in a Stearman. What a way to end Primary training and say good-bye to the men who had brought us through sixty-five hours of arduous and dangerous training.

As I crawled out and shook hands with Captain Asmus there was a feeling of warmth and a bond. All I could say was, "Thank you for everything, Sir." That was all that needed to be said as the look in his eyes showed he understood.

The next day we started finishing up our ground school and physical fitness tests, but I received a surprise in the afternoon when I was pulled from a formation and ordered to report to the flight line in flying gear. What had gone wrong? Had the military pilot raised some doubts? Uncertainty. That was what cadet training was all about. I went on the double to Captain Asmus's office as I was sure I had completed every-

As a jockey, Detroit, 1938

Open ranks inspection

Mud fight after a rainstorm

Cadet demonstrating a "brace"

First picture in cadet uniform. The photo-booth camera reversed the U.S. insignia on the uniform, but what could you expect for ten cents?

A segment of Squadron 57. (Front row center) Captain Wright; *(second row standing, third from left)* Cadet Fletcher

Flagpole in center of courtyard, Mira Loma Flight Academy

Class 43-J, Squadron 8, Flight 1. (Front row, left to right) *DuMont, House, Durnal, Clay;* (second row) *Algranti, Bostford, Riggs, Hornbeck, Boldi, Pulaski;* (third row) *Pollack, Emery, Powell, Hammond, Bell;* (rear row) *Wilson, Bride, Turner, Fletcher, Kelly* (Flight 2 not shown)

Flight instructors, Class 43-J, Squadron 8. (Front row, left to right)
J. E. McLean (Laughing Boy), W. L. Martin, H. A. Asmus, E. H. Busch,
A. W. Soare, M. J. Mabry (dispatcher); (rear row) I. Miller, P. A. West,
L. Pulici, A. A. Gabardi, P. E. Reed

Stearman PT-13Bs

Instrument training class

Stearman PT-13

War Eagle Field, Polaris Flight Academy

D. C. Bell

With Sherry

(Left) With Gene Bowen in front of the BT-13A Vultee Valiant, nicknamed the "Vultee Vibrator." Note our dress shoes. (Right) In the "Vultee Vibrator"

In front of a BT-13A

The "igloo," where pilots waited their turn to fly

BT-13As in formation

The tower at War Eagle Field

In the BT-13, calling the tower for permission to take off

With Gene Bowen under the wing of the BT-13A "Vultee Vibrator"

Ordering the massed formation to pass in review

Graduation day parade

AT-17 Bobcat, advanced training plane, Douglas, Arizona

Sherry in front of the house where she was rooming

Cadets marching to class

Students of Lt. J. H. Connell and Lt. K. R. Dye. (Standing, left to right)
Feuerstein, Fisher, Fall, Ferry, Folsom; (kneeling) *Foley, Fletcher*

The obstacle course

Douglas – Rodeo
Rodeo – Columbus
Columbus – Deming
Deming – Hardsburg
Hardsburg – Rodeo
RODEO – DOUGLAS
VIA LIGHT LINE

Cross-country briefing

B-17F cockpit and instrument panel

B-17 trainer

The crew. (Bottom row, left to right) *Eugene Fletcher, Myron Doxon (with daughter Kimmie on his lap), Robert Work, Frank Dimit;* (top row) *Kenneth McQuitty, Robert Lynch, Martin Smith, Joseph Firszt, Edward Brown, George Hinman*

thing, but in the military you run on doubts and rumors so this should have been routine.

When I reached his office he looked up, smiled, and said, "Mr. Fletcher, I have just been going over your log book and find that you are eleven minutes short of sixty-five hours. Mr. Pulici is on the line with an aircraft. Run out, jump in, and fly around the pattern, make one or two landings, log eleven minutes, and report back to the cadet compound."

As soon as I crawled in Mr. Pulici jumped out, insisting that I was trying to leave without finishing the course. I hollered back, "No, sir. How about letting me fly the crate to Basic?"

With a big grin he replied, "Fly your eleven minutes and get out of here. Give my condolences to your next instructor because he will surely need them."

When I was done, the log book showed sixty-five hours total: thirty-six hours solo time, twenty-nine hours of dual instruction including fourteen minutes of night flying.

With our Primary flying time completed everyone was looking forward to Basic Training. At Santa Ana, secrecy had surrounded our next destination. But here, since we were on a civilian field, we were immediately told where we were going. All four squadrons were heading for Lancaster, California.

We got our passes early Saturday morning so upon reaching Ventura I was able to tell Sherry where we were going. We knew that Lancaster was a very small town and places to stay would be in short supply or nonexistent. As we mulled over the situation we hit upon a plan that might work. If we could get to Lancaster before we were transferred we might beat the rush and find something, so we rented a car.

Once there we started asking people if they knew of any place where lodging was available. We really didn't receive any encouragement since most of the available places were already rented to the spouses of H and I classes. Finally we started knocking on doors in the residential area, introducing ourselves and asking the residents if they rented rooms or knew of anyone who did who might have a vacancy. It was the same story. When the wives of H class left we might be able to find something, but it would be on a first-come basis.

We decided to try one more home before returning to Oxnard. The door was answered by a motherly middle-aged woman. We told the lady who we were and explained our predicament. She invited us into her home for a cool drink while she thought about how to help us. After a short visit she explained that her daughter was a WAAC serving on a distant military base, consequently her room was not occupied. She was sure her husband wouldn't object to renting the room to Sherry, even though it had not been rented before, providing Sherry felt the room was large enough and was interested. We explained that any room would be large enough since we did not have any other prospects. Sherry closed the deal immediately, with Mrs. Story apologizing for the four dollar a week rent for a room without a cooler, especially with the heat of summer coming on.

It was a happy drive back to Oxnard. The mission had been a success. When I returned to Mira Loma on Sunday I knew that Sherry would be leaving on Monday for Lancaster.

In a letter from Sis received two days before, she had mentioned they were thrilled that Cap had finished Primary and they were heading to Coffeyville, Kansas, a BT-13 school for Basic Training.

That night as Taps was sounded it was the sweetest sound anyone could expect to hear. Our bugler was Cadet Boldi, a master of the trumpet. He was the first in Squadron 8 to commit a ground loop, followed two days later by J. D. Bride. Boldi could have committed any sin he wished and not been washed out. He was irreplaceable. His prominence as a bugler was well known at Santa Ana and his reputation preceded him to Oxnard. One evening during the first week at Oxnard immediately after Taps, he played two popular songs of the day. Everyone in the cadet corps thought it was great. He rendered music with such dignity, grace, and clarity of tone that we were mesmerized. We wondered what would happen as this was a total departure from tradition. If it meant tours every cadet would have walked with him. Our worries were put at ease two days later when he said that the officers were also impressed and as long as we were on a civilian field this could be a nightly occurrence.

With Taps over and lights out, the sweet sound of the trum-

pet permeated every nook and cranny on the base. The familiar sounds cast a spell over a life filled with responsibility and
we listened in awe, each with his own memories and dreams of
the future. It became a ritual that we all anticipated: a security
blanket, or at least a momentary escape from reality.

Our departure date was set for June 22. Bus transportation
had been arranged for the corps of cadets. We had arrived in
army 6 × 6s but we were to leave in style. There were three
exceptions: Cadet Jim House and two others were allowed to
drive their personal autos. Just before boarding the bus I was
presented a leather billfold. This same memento might have
been awarded to all members, but I'm not sure. Mine contained a citation stating:

> E. R. Fletcher is hereby granted this school's Gold Star
> Merit Award and his name has been inscribed in the Acad-
> emy's Hall of Fame in recognition of having completed the
> course of flying training with distinction and without acci-
> dent of any kind.
>
> Signed C. C. Moseley, President
> Mira Loma Flight Academy

As we boarded the bus I noticed that Gene Jones, my classmate from Dayton who had been assigned to Squadron 7, was
still with us. We had spent nine weeks at Primary and still had
not had a chance to visit.

We had come to Mira Loma over 200 strong; we left with a
head count of 176, plus our eight student officers. Our ranks
had been thinned by more than twenty-five cadets.

4 Basic Flying School

Lancaster, California

We arrived at Polaris Flight Academy, War Eagle Field, in the afternoon of June 22. We were somewhere in or near the Mojave Desert, too far to walk to civilization. The buses parked by the main gate and the drivers started unloading our bags. There was no welcoming committee; it must have been siesta time. The heat was stifling, putting a damper on any activity that required physical exertion.

While the bags were being unloaded several of us walked over to a large flatbed trailer parked not far from the front gate. The trailer appeared to be loaded with scrap aluminum and junk. It didn't take us long to realize that we were looking at the mangled components of one or possibly two Basic trainers. Upon closer inspection we saw small flecks of bone and shreds of material that might have once been a flying suit. I turned away with a sick feeling having seen enough to remind me that not all flying was fun and games. Sometime, somewhere, someone was paying the ultimate price to provide our nation with pilots and air crewmen. I will never know why this spectacle was allowed to greet us. Maybe it was meant to be a reminder that we were training in a hazardous occupation, but more likely it was just an oversight. We had already found out that two former members of Squadron 58 had perished in a head-on collision and a third in a spin. But those were letter statistics. This was grim reality, a sight that could not be pushed to the farthest recesses of the mind. For that reason I suspect I unconsciously became a more cautious, conservative cadet.

Filing into the central compound through the main gate, we realized that Polaris Flight Academy was almost a complete replica of Mira Loma, only on a grander scale. The same style: cottages in circles enclosing a courtyard with a flag pole in the center. There was green grass and all the buildings were bathed in a new coat of paint. There was only one drawback immediately apparent and that was the burning sun. Later we would find others.

We had been told that all Basic flying schools were completely militarized. But here we were on a civilian field also owned by Major C. C. Moseley: another Country Club of the Air. We suspected this was the only civilian Basic school in the country.

We were eventually told that the base had been built to train English cadets for the Royal Air Force. The European conflict had made it difficult to train cadets in England, and the RAF had sought a safer haven to pursue this endeavor. British cadets had been arriving since 1941. Their last class of pilots had departed Number 2 British Flying Training School, Lancaster, California, about February 1943. All British trappings had been removed, but many letters of commendation from the British government were framed and hanging in the headquarters building. Apparently a new name and a fresh paint job was all that was necessary to convert to an Army Air Force Basic Flying School.

As we filed into the courtyard we were met by a contingent of military officers. We were assigned cottages and told to report in formation at 0900 the next morning wearing fatigue uniforms. At this time we would be briefed on our schedule and the rules of the post. We were then dismissed to settle in.

The cottages were slightly different from those at Mira Loma in that four cadets were assigned to a unit. A unit consisted of two rooms separated by a common latrine and a hallway. Don Bell and I were assigned as roommates. He said that this was his choice. Since he had to look after me at Primary we might as well be roomies and make the job easier for him. He had already received a Dear John letter from his girlfriend, for which he thought I was responsible. Once he made up his mind whether this was good or bad he would be able to make life miserable for me or thank me on a twenty-four-hour basis. But I had the feeling he already counted it as a blessing.

At supper that evening we learned that both classes shared the common dining hall but each was assigned a designated area. The regular military officers and student officers had a separate dining facility in another building which housed the small post exchange, a facility which was deemed necessary due to the remoteness of War Eagle Field.

After Taps we were again treated to the melodious sounds of George Boldi's trumpet. So what had changed? We were still on a campus-style civilian field; our flying and ground instructors were all civilians; we still had a military cadre only slightly larger than Primary; Sherry was already in Lancaster. What more could a cadet ask? When I was explaining all of this to Don Bell he exclaimed, "Fletch, if you think you've died and gone to heaven take a look at the thermometer over there. We're probably nearer to shoveling coal than growing wings, possibly closer than either one of us would care to admit."

"Knock it off and let's see what tomorrow brings."

At 0900 we assembled in the inner court and received our usual welcome including all the threats and no-nos. We would retain our cadet officers who had served us so well at Mira Loma, but apparently there were several rule differences here. One: There were many female employees on the base and there would be no fraternizing. Two: We would not fly on Saturdays. Three: We were not placed under quarantine as we had been led to believe. It was obvious the hot sun had sterilized everything including the cadets. We received the usual pep talk and an announcement that we would meet our ground school instructors Friday and our flying instructors on Monday. The ensuing time would be spent on orientation. We were then introduced to our first orientation instructor, a second lieutenant who was in charge of the physical training unit.

We were greeted by a ninety-day ground-pounding wonder who had just reported to the base a few days before. It was his first assignment from Officer Candidate School. He was formerly a high school coach and he would not be satisfied until all of us were as physically hardy as himself. To show us how he was going to accomplish this we were to fill our canteens and he would personally lead us on a ten-mile forced march along the desert roads.

We marched off the base in formation singing the Air Force Song with the temperature well over 100 degrees, but once out of sight of the base we were allowed to break formation and continue at our own pace. One mile down the black-topped highway we turned off onto a sandy desert road.

The desert sun was cruel. Trailing us by about fifty yards was an ambulance. The instructor smirkingly stated that if anyone could not keep up he could show his true colors and ride in the ambulance. However, he was challenging the wrong group of people. We had been in training for six months compared to his ninety days.

We were in top physical condition, but none of us was used to the searing heat. We made regular rest stops and visited while resting. Eventually we gave up the visiting and merely tried to convince those who were suffering from heat and blisters on their feet to get in and ride a ways, advising them that they were more valuable as pilots than desert rats. But pride kept most of them on their feet. Eventually two cadets fainted from sunstroke and were placed in the ambulance.

It was sheer torture. Some of the cadets were picking up sunburn and showing signs of heat exhaustion. Those of us with darker skin were spared the sunburns but we still suffered from the heat. The lieutenant was slowing down and he started limping, a sure sign of blisters. When the instructor showed signs of stress the cadets pushed harder and became more determined. We were finally able to convince several cadets to ride a short distance to recuperate. We did not want to see anyone's health or flying career ruined because of some misguided nut who happened to be wearing gold bars.

At the next stop it was evident that the lieutenant was in trouble with blistered feet. We implored him to ride in the ambulance; it was ridiculous to continue in his condition. We made it clear that no one would think any less of him. No one doubted his stamina or resolve, but it was foolish to continue with swollen feet and blisters. He let us know that he would not get in the ambulance. His pride was just as great as ours; he started out leading and he would continue to lead until we reached the field.

We had been following roads which formed sort of a rectangular pattern around the field. There was no question that everyone had had enough by the time we reached the blacktop. One last rest, and then we would go the final mile. We used the last of our water from the supply on the ambulance. The driver was willing to drive to the base and bring back more, but we all felt we could make it.

During the rest the lieutenant removed his shoes. His feet were so swollen and blistered that he could not put them back on so he tied the strings together and draped them around his neck and started down the hot blacktop highway in his stocking feet. We felt sorry for him but it was his decision to push ahead. At this point we just wanted it to end. We didn't believe in martyrs or miracles; we just wanted to fly.

When we entered the base it was a sad lot that silently passed through the gate, a direct contradiction to the marching, singing group that left. As we headed for the showers we were advised that the medics were standing by to treat blisters, sunburn, and any other problems we might have. We did not see the lieutenant for at least a week and to my knowledge no one asked about him. The four of us in our unit could hardly wait to get the two coolers turned on and the shower running. It was a day we could not easily forget.

All of the cottages were cooled by swamp coolers, a primitive form of air conditioning. The unit was mounted in the wall so that air could be pulled in from the outside by an electric fan mounted in the back. Water was allowed to drip down through excelsior-type filters and the air was cooled as it was forced through the saturated filters. As water built up in a sump in the bottom pan it was pumped back up to trickle down again. These units were quite effective in the desert climate and most of the cadets left them on all night in order to sleep more comfortably.

We soon found we had a problem with the cooler in our room. The room had been freshly calcimined in a strange green color but, unfortunately, the painter had decided to calcimine the inside of the cooler and had also spilled some in the sump. Just as soon as the water was turned on and the unit started, the smell became unbearable. We decided it was easier to sweat than to put up with the stench. We tried several times to clean it but without success, so we decided to leave it off and hopefully gain some relief from the cooler in the other room.

We received a short pass on Sunday and were assured that our regular permanent passes would be available before the next weekend. I caught the bus into Lancaster and headed for the Story residence to check on Sherry. She had arrived Monday on the Pacific Greyhound Lines bus and was the only passenger to get off at Lancaster. Upon stepping to the ground she turned around to wait for the driver to open the side hatch so she could claim her suitcase, but instead he closed the door and drove off. She had only the clothes on her back, the lingerie on her bottom, and her purse. She notified the station agent who advised her not to worry, they would track down her luggage and it would arrive in three or four days. Mrs. Story provided her with a dressing gown so she could wash her clothes every evening. The hot, dry air of a Lancaster night provided a perfect dryer so she was able to have clean clothes every day; however, the choice was limited.

Mrs. Story told Sherry that many young ladies were employed at Polaris Flight Academy, and perhaps she could put her name on the list. Consequently, Tuesday morning she caught the local bus for War Eagle Field and proceeded to the employment office. The man she needed to talk to was on the telephone. When he finished his conversation, she told him she would like to place her name on the list to be notified if they had a vacancy. His response was, "Can you start to work right now?" She assured him that she could. He explained that the phone call was from the manager of the officers' dining hall. They were short a waitress and needed one immediately. The paperwork could be taken care of later. She received two meals a day and worked through the dinner and supper hours.

She had seen us arrive and at this point she knew our schedule better than we did. The job was a blessing for her since her work area was air cooled and she was there during the hottest part of the day. It sounded great to me even though I knew I would never see her on the base.

I was able to meet Mr. Story, but it would be another week before we really became acquainted. My few hours were up; it was time to return. Sherry's suitcase had been found and returned on Friday, so she now could change clothes.

Monday we reported to the flight line for instructor assignments. Bell and I wound up with different instructors. Four of us were assigned to Eugene Bowen, a fine looking man endowed with a pleasant, outgoing personality with the right blend of sternness and humor to command respect and at the same time make you feel at ease. I could sense that my usual luck on the instructor draw was holding; our personalities meshed on the first handshake. Now if I could just fly and make progress, Basic would be fun. Mr. Bowen said we would spend all morning on the line but we would not fly. There was an instructor's meeting he had to attend which probably would last two hours. In the meantime we were to go out on the flight line and inspect the basic trainers, crawl into the cockpit, familiarize ourselves with the location of controls, and then report back. We would go over everything we had seen and he would explain the function, location, and operation of everything in the cockpit.

"Pay attention to what you see and what I tell you. Before you solo you will be placed in the cockpit and blindfolded, then as I call off each control, gauge, or lever you must instantaneously touch or grasp the object. You will not be allowed to grope. In an emergency you have to react on instinct, you won't have time to look for something. Now it will be best if you work in pairs. Eventually you will perform buddy rides so let's start right off that way. Mr. Fletcher and Mr. Hoffman will work together. Mr. Littlefield and Mr. Marchant will function as a unit starting as of now. Mr. Fletcher, do not report to the flight line again in your work shoes."

I stupidly suggested that I thought the uppers on the work shoes would give ankle support in case of a bail out. He smiled and said, "My students are trained to fly, not to bail out. Wear the thinnest soled shoes you have so you can actually feel the amount of pressure you are placing on the rudder controls. Report back in two hours. Dismissed."

It was a pleasure to be assigned to learn and fly with Cadet Robert Hoffman. He was known and liked by all in the cadet corps. He was a good-looking cadet with a deep bass voice, a pleasant grin, a heavy suntan, and a sense of humor which worked overtime. Every morning as he greeted his fellow cadets it was always the same. In my case it was, "Mornin' Fletch." Then dropping his deep voice one octave lower he always growled, "How you doin', old dawg?" It was a greeting that was pleasant to hear and always brought a laugh from the recipient, but it also led to his being nicknamed "Old Dawg" since the response was always, "Fine, Old Dawg, how are you doing?"

It didn't take Old Dawg long to find us an unoccupied BT-13A, a low wing monoplane manufactured by the Vultee Company and known as the Vultee Valiant. However, previous cadet classes had already nicknamed it the Vultee Vibrator. It was equipped with a 450-horsepower nine-cylinder radial Pratt Whitney engine. It had a maximum gross weight of 4,490 pounds, a wingspan of 42 feet 2 inches, length 28 feet 10 inches, height of 12 feet 5 inches, and a top speed of 156 miles per hour, along with a service ceiling of 16,500 feet plus a range of 516 miles.

As he climbed up the wing he called, "Fletch, I'll take the front cockpit, you get in the rear and we'll compare notes." The glass canopies were open to keep the heat from building up inside, but it was still hot. We climbed aboard, each exclaiming to the other all of the new things we would learn about. We knew we were in an airplane with a complete electrical system including a self-starter plus cockpit, wing, tail, and landing lights. With electricity we had two-way radios and an intercom system to communicate, complete with headsets. We had a plane with a two-position propeller as well as navigational and flight instruments necessary for blind flying. There were toggle switches everywhere, trim tab controls, and, above all, wing flaps to be lowered to slow the aircraft down and provide additional lift to make landing easier. There were so many goodies we did not find them all and some we did find we did not know their purpose.

Here were two cadets who were having a ball, just like two kids turned loose in a candy store. This was an AIRPLANE, not a box kite with an engine, an airplane completely wrapped in aluminum and glass, or so we thought then. It was going to be a challenge to fly. We could hardly wait to get started. Old Dawg commented, "Now, Fletch, you know what it is like to be in hawg heaven. Say, did you notice this airplane is equipped with a gosport system? I'll bet it's a back-up system, in case of an electrical failure."

"Well, Old Dawg, I don't see any tubes back here and I don't know how you would hook them to the headset anyway."

"If you don't have electricity the headset wouldn't do any good so you'd take them off and stick the hoses in your ears."

"Whatever, but I haven't found the hoses yet."

"Well, while you're looking I'll speak into the funnel and you see if you can hear me. Fletch, old dawg, I'm speaking into the funnel. Can you hear me?"

"Yes, but since the engine isn't running I can hear you without the hoses."

"Then I'll speak a little lower to see if you can hear it come out the end of the hose. Maybe that will help you find them."

After a few minutes it dawned on us that our time was about up so we had better report. We joined Littlefield and Marchant on the way back and found they were just as enthusiastic as we were. We sat down with Mr. Bowen and he started explaining many of the things we saw in the cockpit, telling us the procedures we would use and some of the flying characteristics of the airplane. He talked to us for over an hour, then said that we would receive a short orientation ride the next day, probably only a takeoff and landing. From then on we would fly full periods.

Did anyone have questions or remarks? Littlefield said he would like to know something about the gruesome sight of mangled metal that we had seen when we arrived. Mr. Bowen said all he knew was that the accident involved one airplane. It had crashed head-on into the dry lake bed, killing two cadets on a buddy ride. He did not know whether there was a mechanical problem or pilot error involved and no one would ever know. He stressed that the BT-13 was a good, safe airplane but it was not a toy. Treat it with respect, fly it properly, and you won't have any trouble. The plane was not known to have any chronic mechanical problems, so forget it and concentrate on the positive.

Were there other questions? Old Dawg replied, "I don't have a question but I think it's neat that the designers put a gosport system in as a back-up in case of failure of the electrical intercom."

Mr. Bowen looked quite puzzled and said, "Mr. Hoffman, I'm not aware of a gosport system in the BT."

"Well, there is one. It is a black synthetic funnel hooked onto a tube that leads down into the fuselage. The funnel is shaped a little different than in the Stearman, but otherwise it looks the same."

"Where was it located?"

"On the right-hand side of the fuselage just about in line with the front of the seat. The hose could have been a little longer but I could lean over and talk in the funnel."

Mr. Bowen started to smile. "You talked to Mr. Fletcher?"

"Yes, Sir."

"Did he hear you and talk back?"

"Yes, Sir, he said he could hear me, but he couldn't find the hoses in the rear cockpit."

"Well, Mr. Hoffman, if Mr. Fletcher had been more observant he would also have found the hose and funnel slightly to the right and below his seat. This tells me you men have to be more alert and be able to spot these things."

By now Mr. Bowen had a huge grin and was obviously trying to suppress an urge to laugh. "Mr. Hoffman, I don't know how to tell you this, but the BT does not have a gosport system. It has a longer range than the Stearman and, consequently, some provision must be made to afford pilot comfort on a long-range flight. Now if you had traced the hose through the fuselage you would have noticed it was vented to the outside. Speaking in the funnel only vented your voice outside and that really isn't its purpose. That little gadget is known as a pilot's relief tube and its purpose is to relieve the pilot's discomfiture. Do you understand what I'm talking about?" Old Dawg, with a look of horror on his face, started gagging and requesting that he be excused to look for a water fountain. The instructor could not contain his laughter any longer and dismissed the four of us with, "This is just the beginning. Wait till they start to fly."

The following day when we reported to the flight line, Old Dawg told the instructor he was quite embarrassed over the gosport incident. Mr. Bowen praised his inquisitiveness and ingenuity, saying these were qualities of a good student. He said he was sorry he had laughed in Hoffman's presence but the incident was so funny he couldn't help himself. Besides, very few students provided an instructor with an opportunity to laugh. He said, "I was laughing with you, not at you. This incident should be one which we can both look back on in fun and not embarrassment." We knew we had a diplomat and a gentleman for an instructor and that he would bring out the best in us, an ability which was sometimes lacking in others.

Mr. Bowen then placed the four of us in a circle on either side of him and proceeded to explain the functions of all the "new to us" equipment on the airplane. After a lengthy session we went out to the flight line and each of us received a ten-minute ride which consisted of a takeoff and landing with the cadet following through on the controls. It was a real thrill and we could hardly wait to experience more, especially when we found out the cadet now rode in front with the instructor in the rear cockpit.

We soon settled into a routine reminiscent of Primary: one-half day on the flight line with the rest of the day spent in ground school, physical training, and the usual drill. A few night classes were also thrown in once or twice a week. The classes became more advanced and the magnitude of the new material piled on every day boggled the mind, so again the cadets set up study groups in the evening led by those who excelled in a particular subject.

On June 29 all of the cadets received their permanent passes. The passes authorized us "to be absent from this post (within a radius of 150 miles) at all times when not on duty."

Of course the catch was all cadets were considered to be on duty twenty-four hours a day seven days a week, so this required another pass to be issued stating you were not on duty. This was the procedure that allowed us to receive Saturday nights off. There were no procedures set up to allow the cadets to receive visitors on the base, which was okay since we didn't have time to visit anyway.

My first overnight pass came on Saturday, July 3. Mr. and Mrs. Story were salt-of-the-earth people and insisted that we have our meals with them. We were a family and they enjoyed having young people in their home again. Sharing meals was for them more than a courtesy, it represented a sacrifice on their part because this was a time of rationing.

Since I was a part of the military I did not have a food ration book, but Sherry contributed her food coupons to the family since she was taking her meals on the base and had no need for them. Meat especially was in short supply with only twenty-eight ounces per week allowed each person. All butter went to the military while the civilians made do with butter substitutes.

Things weren't too rosy on the home front. People were contending with ration books for food, shoes, gas, and tires. Ladies' skirts were shortened and the cuffs removed from men's trousers to save fabric. Silk and nylon stockings were replaced by leg make-up, which was just as well since there wouldn't have been anything to hold up the stockings. Garters, girdles, and anything containing rubber had already been turned in to help in the war effort and substitutes were not available.

A permit to buy replacement tires was obtained through the local rationing board and was not easy to come by. Gas coupons allowed essential travel only, with the speed limit set at 35 miles per hour to save wear and tear on cars and tires. All kitchen fat and meat drippings were saved to make soap, and tinfoil was collected and balled. The local Boy Scouts and Camp Fire Girls took on the project of collecting and turning them over to the government receiving stations.

Price controls were in effect on all consumer items including rents. Wages were frozen and this allowed the economy to function without inflation. Consequently, windfall profits and profiteering were virtually eliminated. Some bartering occurred, but this was minuscule given the size of the big picture.

Mr. Story was the local butcher and also a Technocrat, a believer in a theory in which government and our social system should be controlled by scientific technicians. Every Saturday night we discussed technocracy while Mrs. Story and Sherry did the dishes. Once the dishes were over I would lose interest in the conversation, since I was more interested in other subjects and activities. Mrs. Story could always sense when my patience was wearing thin and would intervene with, "Come on, Dad, you can continue this conversation some other time. We must allow these young people some privacy." Thank you, Mrs. Story.

Sherry's room was quite small, containing only a closet, bureau, and a single bed. It was a corner room with cross-ventilation which only meant the hot night air was allowed to enter from two directions. I will not address the size of the bed except to say that it created a feeling of togetherness.

The local churches were practically filled every Sunday morning with the influx of the cadet corps of both classes. My roommates and some close friends usually joined Sherry and me for Sunday services and we would spend part of the day visiting together. The small town afforded few opportunities for dates for the single men, so most who wanted to talk to someone other than another cadet had to settle for a short visit with the wives. Sometimes it would be for suggestions of gifts to send home to family or girlfriends. Since the stores weren't open on Sundays, many times it was a request to make a purchase in town or mail a package. Other times it was just a desire to hear a female voice.

The first full week in July was spent learning all we could about the BT-13. Not all the aircraft were the same. Some had better instrumentation and excellent radios. These planes were to be used for instrument and cross-country flying. Others with poorer instrumentation were to be used for aerobatics, and still others had a plywood empennage and were not to be used for aerobatics. Aircraft were assigned on the basis of the mission, but it was up to us to make sure that the right airplane type was used for the proper purpose.

After six hours of dual instruction, I was allowed to solo on July 12, and during that week most of the other cadets soloed. After that it was a wonder we had any airplanes left for instrument flying. The field looked more like a rodeo grounds than an airfield because the landings were like riding a bucking bronco with the cadets cheering "Ride 'em cowboy" as the trainers bounced and bucked. Two or three landings were made with a single approach. No one was hurt but the aircraft took a beating. At night the cadets shared their stories of close calls and an occasional incident showing surprising expertise.

We had one incident that really caught our attention. The heat was terrible. In fact, we used gloves to keep from burning our hands when we touched the metal on the airframes. The heat also attracted rattlesnakes and we were told to watch out for them. Most of us took this as a joke but on this day an instructor and cadet were seen to jump from the plane on the flight line screaming "SNAKE." A rattler had curled up for his siesta on the fuselage and it seems they had disturbed him when they attempted to climb aboard. We all took this pretty seriously except for one cadet who had had Laughing Boy as an instructor at Oxnard. He couldn't see what the fuss was all about, insisting it would have been a pleasure to ride with the rattler after putting up with Laughing Boy.

Again we were flying as in Primary using auxiliary fields and buses. The auxiliary fields were on Muroc Dry Lake. It was possible to land anywhere on the lake but certain areas were designated and marked only with a strip of oil sprayed on the ground to indicate a runway. In addition to the buses a jeep with radio receiver and transmitter was driven to the auxiliary field to serve as a portable tower. We were now initiating all takeoffs and landings using radio communications.

Going out to the auxiliary fields on the bus was quite an experience. You could see what looked like a lake in the distance but you never came to the water. At one particular place the silhouette of a battleship always appeared, but it was never visible from the air. The bus driver once said the battleship was a wooden mock-up used by the Navy for gunnery practice, but because of the other wild tales he had told us his credibility factor with the cadets was zero. The reports of mirages became a full-time conversation topic. We cussed, discussed, and speculated but we never arrived at a conclusion on how these visions were formed.

Mr. Bowen was on my tail constantly trying to get me to practice more aerobatics and spins. I kept asking him to spend more time demonstrating some of the things he wanted me to work on, but it seemed we were always in the wrong type of airplane when I made the request. He kept insisting that his making the maneuver wouldn't help me. Only by practice could I really learn how to do it. "You know the procedure so practice on your solo time."

Finally it got to the point where he would ask me every time I returned from a solo flight what aerobatics I had done and how many times. I always told him the truth even though I wasn't doing as many as he thought I should. He kept inquiring about spins and I would honestly tell him that I wasn't practicing them. He had demonstrated one sloppy spin and I didn't feel comfortable with what I had seen. The spin is probably the easiest of all maneuvers to do in an airplane but, for some reason, maybe it was what we saw when we came on the base, I had a built-in resistance. Finally I told him, "If I ever get up to 10,000 feet with nothing to do I'll try it, but right now I'm working on other things."

His response was, "If you're going to fly, either master all the arts of flying or forget it." I knew he was right but there was something about his reluctance and lack of demonstration that held me back.

The time finally arrived when I felt it absolutely necessary to practice spins. Mr. Bowen probably took my 10,000 feet of altitude stipulation as an attempt at humor, but in this regard I was definitely serious. Since the elevation at Lancaster was about 2,300 feet I set the altimeter at zero on the field. This procedure allowed me to read my actual height above the ground directly from the altimeter. I then flew out over Muroc Dry Lake to a deserted practice area as I did not want an audience or, for that matter, any airborne traffic. On the way to the practice area I maintained a constant climb but at

8,200 feet the plane was not climbing as fast as I desired. In ignorance I decided to manually crank down about fifteen degrees of flaps and hopefully get more lift to speed up the climb. This act did not speed up the climb but I slowly reached 10,000 feet.

I do not wish to bore the nonflyers with a long, drawn-out flying lesson, but I will tell you the control of an airplane is maintained by a smooth flow of air over the wings and tail surfaces. As the control surfaces such as the rudder, elevators, or ailerons are moved, they extend into the smooth airstream and cause a reaction. An example: If the control stick is pulled back the elevators are extended upward into the airstream; the tail is forced down and the nose rises. The same principle applies to every control surface. In this manner the pilot exercises control over the airplane and, theoretically, it flies where he wants to go instead of just wallowing around in the sky. As I said earlier, the spin is probably the easiest maneuver to enter and the easiest to recover from, especially in the trainers which I had flown.

Upon reaching 10,000 feet I picked out a reference point on the horizon while sliding the front canopy open. I'm not sure why except that in case of a bail-out the hatch would be open. I repeated to myself "Here goes nothing" and retarded the throttle while slowly applying back pressure on the stick. When the stick finally reached its limit of travel the aircraft had lost its airspeed and was completely stalled. At this point the aircraft is out of control and can only nose over and fall off on a wing. In this case I had determined to spin to the right so I applied full right rudder causing the plane to fall off on the right wing.

The airplane fell over into a vertical dive and was now in a spin to the right. As the plane spun around my eyes focused on the reference point and I knew I had completed one complete revolution. This is how orientation is maintained and the number of revolutions determined. I had decided to do a two-turn spin. This meant that spinning would be stopped by the exact time the nose reached the reference point for the second time. To stop the spinning, full left, or opposite rudder, is applied before reaching the pull-out point, in this case about ninety degrees before the reference point is reached.

Once the spin has stopped the back pressure on the stick is released. The stick is returned forward to the midpoint of its travel; the controls are now neutralized and the control surfaces are streamlined, putting the aircraft in a dive. The smooth, steady flow of air is again crossing the control surfaces. All that remains is to slowly ease back on the stick and the nose returns to level flight as power is added to maintain normal airspeed.

Three-fourths of the way around the second revolution I applied full left rudder and felt the spin slowing down. I realized that I was overshooting the check point but I wasn't concerned about accuracy. I just wanted a recovery this time, I could work on precision later. The spin slowed down but did not stop, in fact, it suddenly became tighter and faster. No problem. I neutralized the rudder pedals and started the recovery again. As before, the spin slowed but would not stop. The nose dropped lower and again took to a tighter spin with increased speed. By now I wasn't concerned with recovering on the point; I would recover any place I could around the circle. After four unsuccessful recoveries it became apparent that I had a problem. The airspeed was far greater than I wanted it to be and was approaching the red line. There wasn't time to panic, the ground was rushing up, but for some reason I could not stop the spin. I made a decision: Two more attempts at recovery, if nothing happened I would bail out. Those two attempts were made very hurriedly, but again with no success.

Since the canopy was open it was only a matter of getting out of the airplane. Before unfastening the safety belt I looked over the side to establish how I was going out when I noticed that the flaps were still in the down position. I had failed to retract them before starting the spin. In that instant I knew the flaps were disturbing the airflow, making recovery impossible. As I immediately cranked up the flaps with my right hand and stood on the left rudder the spin stopped. The airspeed indicator was past the red line and the altimeter was passing through 1,500 feet, the plane still in a vertical dive.

It took every ounce of willpower to keep from jerking the stick back. A quick movement would have created either a high-speed stall with no response from the airplane or if the plane did respond it could have lost a wing or tail section and disintegrated. I bit my tongue and slowly eased back on the stick. The nose started to raise ever so slowly and finally returned to level flight with the altimeter reading 700 feet. As the airspeed finally settled down, the power was eventually restored. My supposed two-turn spin had consumed 9,300 feet of altitude.

My flight suit was wringing wet with sweat, but still in better shape than my nerves. As I flew around trying to regain my composure and flying confidence I kept thinking of the poor judgment I had exhibited. The dangerous predicament was precipitated simply by my own stupidity. I thought of the trailer at the gate and wondered if the two cadets had pulled something similar. After flying around for approximately fifteen minutes I knew what I had to do: either fly back to the base and quit flying or go back upstairs and practice spins in the proper manner.

I climbed back up and flew the aircraft through three more two-turn spins. This time all three hit the reference point right on the nose. Flying back to the base I knew I had conquered a self-imposed adversity. If I didn't kill myself some day I would be a pilot and a good one at that.

Sitting on the ramp after landing I started filling out the Form One, in which the pilot notes anything that is inoperative or anything unusual that he has observed about the aircraft. The ground crew then has to check and repair any abnormalities before the airplane can be flown again, unless the next pilot signs that he has read the notation and accepts the aircraft in its "as is" condition. While filling out the form I walked around the airplane to examine the exterior and realized I was flying an airplane with a plywood tail, one which was not authorized for aerobatics. Again it was decision-making time: Do I ignore what has happened since no one would know or do I tell what happened and face the wrath of the instructor and squadron commander and probably a military check ride? Knowing that other people would fly this airplane, my conscience dictated only one course. Among other things the entry in the Form One read: "Aircraft was flown at a speed in excess of the red line and was spun several times. Check for undue stress. Signed, Cadet Fletcher." It sounded better than Stupid Cadet Dodo.

At critique Mr. Bowen inquired about my flying activities to place in the record. I was able to report that I had practiced spins, which seemed to make him happy. I went on to say, "but in an aircraft with a plywood tail."

"So? Do you think you're the only cadet that has ever done that?"

"Well, I don't know but I also exceeded the red line. However, I have written that up in the Form One."

"Every airplane on this field has had the red line exceeded but we don't make a practice of it. So what else is new?"

"I guess that's about it, Sir, but I can assure you at the next stage check I will be able to recover a spin on the point." By now I had learned that there was no need to overburden an instructor with graphic details. They were already aging prematurely from the stress of their occupation.

A perfect example occurred a few days later. I had finished my lesson and landed at one of the auxiliary fields. Old Dawg took over and would land back at War Eagle Field while I returned on the bus. Most of the auxiliary fields had a shelter resembling an igloo to provide a place for the cadets to study out of the desert sun. On this field a crew was building an igloo. I walked over to see how these shelters were built. They had constructed a frame of narrow mesh chicken wire, and then they proceeded to blow, from a large tank truck, a mixture of water, sand, pea gravel, and cement into the frame. The mixture set up very quickly in the daytime heat. It was a fascinating procedure but the heat compelled me to seek the shade by the side of the bus.

While walking back I noticed a parachute blossom quite high in the sky. I ran to the jeep where radio traffic was being controlled by a sergeant and a lieutenant. I explained that I had seen a parachute open in the sky in the direction of the morning sun. Since it was not visible at the moment in the brilliant sunlight they thought I was reporting a mirage or hallucination. They were sure if someone had trouble there would have been a radio transmission or a distress signal.

Finally the sergeant also saw the chute, and started calling on the radio to alert the planes to watch for it. A very meek voice came on the radio and asked if they were inquiring about a man in a parachute. The controller answered that he was. The meek voice replied, "That's my instructor."

"Please repeat your transmission."

"That's my instructor."

"What happened?"

"I don't know. He just asked me if I had control of the airplane and when I said yes, he opened the back canopy and bailed out."

The cadet was ordered to return to War Eagle Field. "Should I finish my lesson first?" the voice inquired.

The lieutenant shouted into the mike, "Return immediately."

"Yes, Sir."

The lieutenant made one more transmission notifying everyone that the auxiliary field was closed since radio communications were suspended. The jeep took off in the direction of the parachute, leaving a trail of dust on the lake bed.

The bus driver requested the cadets board the bus for home since the auxiliary was closed. By the time we reached the base the incident had been reported. Mr. Bowen told us that because of occupational fatigue the instructor had decided to quit teaching and since he had always wanted to make a parachute jump he had achieved both goals that morning.

I would like to say that all my problems were confined to the flight line but that would not be entirely true. The physical fitness instructor who had taken us on the forced march was now back making life miserable for us in the 120-degree temperature. Pushups, chinups, situps, side straddle hops, running, anything to produce a sweat seemed to give him great satisfaction.

There was a huge swimming pool in front of the unit where Bell and I lived. The pool was officially off limits and was used only when the instructor scheduled a class. Recreational swimming was not allowed even on time off or during weekends.

This didn't particularly bother me since I couldn't swim anyway. But one day he announced that one phase of our final fitness test would be to swim two lengths of the swimming pool. Anyone incapable would be failed. I had never been around a pool or lake and had never learned how to swim, in fact, I couldn't even float. In the several classes we had in the pool I had been able to dog paddle about twenty feet and that was it. Finally two close friends who were Eagle Scouts and expert swimmers decided they would teach me how to swim, but the time in the pool was limited so we were not making much headway. I would battle the water with my arms until I was worn out, then the two cadets would swim alongside and grasp hands under my chest using a modified side stroke. That way they would keep me afloat until we were at the end or at least out of deep water. They decided I had to have more time in the pool if I was going to succeed. Consequently, they decided that since I had helped them with ground school during our evening study sessions they would now reciprocate by helping me.

Since the pool was right in front of my cottage they met at my unit just after dark. We would put on our bathing suits and quietly slip into the pool. Several other cadets served as lookouts. If anyone besides a cadet left headquarters and started around the large housing circle a flashlight would be turned on, a signal to get out or hide. We had had several sessions and were making some progress, but I had the feeling they were placing themselves at risk simply to help me. Their attitude was, "What are friends for? This is not cheating, we're just breaking the rules by being in the pool."

Friday night after our session I had just returned to the unit and was standing still dripping in the shower removing my bathing trunks when there was a knock at the door. Bell responded and the cadet runner informed him that Cadet Fletcher was to report to the officer of the day at headquarters on the double.

Bell delivered the message that I had already heard. I knew then that someone had seen me in the pool and it was time to report and face the music. I could only hope the other two cadets had not been seen. Several of the cadets rallied around

shining my shoes and polishing the brass on my uniform while
I finished my shower. As soon as I dried off, my uniform was
hastily laid out spic-and-span. I hurriedly dressed among
words of encouragement from the cadets, but I was beyond
cheering up. I had obviously been caught; now it was suffer
the consequence. A better solution might have been to drown
while taking the test. I thanked the guys for their help with my
clothes and their moral support and started off on the double
for headquarters.

I was very relieved not to see the other two cadets on the
way. Maybe they hadn't been seen or maybe I would be asked
to identify them. Who knows what a fertile imagination is capable of? Wash out, walk tours; the answer was just several
steps away. I marched into the commander's office, came to
attention, saluted, and stated, "Cadet Fletcher reporting as
directed, Sir."

The O.D. was one of the student officers. He returned the
salute, hesitated for a few seconds, long enough for some
more unpleasant thoughts to come and go, then stated, "Mr.
Fletcher, how would you like a pass?"

I couldn't answer. I wasn't even sure I had heard the question correctly. My mouth was dry but our military discipline
kept me from shaking. Again he asked, "How would you like a
pass?"

This time I responded, "I would like that very much, Sir."
He immediately handed me the white slip that activated our
permanent pass. I stepped forward, took the slip, backed up
two paces, "Thank you, Sir," and saluted.

He returned the salute with, "Be back on the base before
Taps Sunday evening." I did an about-face and hurried from
the office. I ran all the way back to the unit to get my shaving
kit as the bus would be leaving for Lancaster in fifteen minutes.

As I entered the cottage I realized that the place was
crammed with cadets all waiting to see what punishment had
been meted out. All I could do was exclaim, "I got a two-night
pass."

"What for?"

"I dunno, but I'm getting out of here before somebody

changes his mind. See you Sunday night." I grabbed my shaving kit and as I started out the door I told the two cadets who were helping me to forget the nighttime lessons. I would rather drown than go through that again. I caught the bus still wondering what had happened, but I certainly wasn't going to look the gift horse in the mouth.

It was almost 10:00 when I greeted Sherry at the Story residence. I told her I had just received a two-night pass but I had no idea why. She explained that at dinner that day one of the lieutenants wanted seconds on dessert. She told him she couldn't do that but he insisted, saying he would do a favor for her in exchange. She asked him what kind of favor and he asked her what she would like. She said that what she'd like would be for her husband to have extra time off the base. He said that he was O.D. for the weekend and he could make it possible. Against the rules she served the extra dessert but with no anticipation that I would really get the pass as the officers were always kidding those who worked in the dining room. So for a paltry piece of apricot pie I was given an extra night off.

Saturday night I was just about ready to convert to Technocracy when Mrs. Story intervened. Sunday morning Bell and several cadets came by and we went to church together. On the way I told him the story Sherry had told me. "I am glad," he replied, "because after Friday night half the cadet corps thinks you're crazy."

"How about the other half?"

"They know you are."

I-class finished on schedule and were to ship out the next day. By the time we joined them at dinner in the restaurant they were having a good time laughing and joking within their own group. There was one staple that we were always served at dinner and it was always prepared in the same manner. "Case hardened potatoes" was the name used by the cadets, although the cook probably used a more appetizing terminology. The potatoes were small, ranging in size from a large marble to a golf ball. They were peeled, boiled, and then placed in a greased pan and fried as they rolled around in the hot grease. The outside of the potato became very hard, hence the name "case hardened." The potatoes tasted good and were served piping hot, but the problem was trying to cut through the hardened shell to make them bite size and allow the inside to cool. Most attempts to fork or cut them caused them to jump off the plate, roll around the table, or even onto the floor.

The door to the restaurant was always open during mealtime but a screen door functioned to keep the flies out. As one of the J-class cadets opened the screen door to come in, an upperclassman seated just beyond our table picked up one of his potatoes from the floor and with the exclamation, "I've chased these potatoes for the last time," proceeded to toss it out the open screen door. Unfortunately a captain chose that moment to enter the dining hall. The potato hit him on the forehead. The only damage was to the captain's pride.

It was an act which was done in jest and the cadet had not deliberately thrown at the officer, but it was an indiscretion that could not be overlooked. Some form of punishment was not only expected but required. However, none of us anticipated or were even prepared for the harsh sentence that was meted out. The cadet was removed from the shipping roster. He was told that if he desired to remain in the cadet corps he could join J-class but since his flying was completed he would be required to walk an eight-hour tour every day in Class A uniform, which meant wool blouse, trousers, and visored cap. He would carry a rifle and constantly march between the headquarters building and the flag pole. Upon reaching the flag pole he would present arms, shoulder arms, do an about-face, march back to headquarters, and repeat the procedure. He was allowed to rest five minutes out of each hour in the headquarters latrine.

The cadet was confined to the post and denied any visiting privileges for the rest of the time J-class would be on the base. His wife and two small daughters lived in Lancaster. Further, he was not allowed to converse with any of the cadets and was assigned to an isolated unit. If he could not accept these conditions or failed to perform properly he would be washed out immediately.

He refused to quit and accepted the challenge. It was obvious that the military had underestimated his desire to be a pilot. Every cadet on the base knew that we were witnessing cruel and inhuman punishment as the temperature on the base was now reaching 120 degrees every day. The unfortunate cadet had the support of all of us but we could not vocally express this support; we could only give a veiled thumbs up sign at a chance meeting. The military took the attitude that he could quit anytime he wanted to and, therefore, they felt no responsibility.

At the end of two weeks the cadet could hardly walk because of blistered feet. He was called before the commanding officer and asked what he desired more than anything else. The cadet replied that he would like to see his wife and daughters. The commander expected him to respond that he wanted to fly. Consequently, he was ordered to complete the punishment or quit. The cadet went back to marching. It was obvious that as long as he could move he would not give up. We groused to every civilian instructor on the base about the type of punishment and the contest of wills that was going on, but their reply was that they did not have any influence with the military.

We also had to exhibit a very low profile since any display on our part would also affect our own flying careers. Even so, it did have an impact, which surfaced when we eventually reached a position of command. It could be seen in the humanitarian manner in which we tried to exercise this authority.

The incident was eventually resolved after nearly three weeks. The cadet had withstood the ravages of the desert sun with his head held high. His feet were giving out but he still hobbled his rounds. At this point the medics intervened, stating that his health was being endangered and the humiliating public display had to stop. They insisted that his family be allowed to visit him in the infirmary and that the incident had to be resolved: Either eliminate him from cadet training or honor his commitment to duty and his attempt to comply.

While this human drama was being played out, J-class was busy learning formation, instrument, and night flying. Formation flying was a real challenge but was enjoyed by all of the cadets. The BT-13 was perfect for this. It was a heavy airplane but very stable in flight as it responded immediately to power changes and control movements which made it ideal for flying in formation. Old Dawg and I liked nothing better than to fly formation on Mr. Bowen's wings, each trying to see who could consistently fly the closest without being warned by radio to back off. We finally reached a level of expertise where we could change wings with one crossing over the top while the other crossed underneath, all without causing the instructor undue alarm.

At this point Mr. Bowen decided we were ready for formation takeoffs and landings, a procedure in which the students watched only the wing of the lead aircraft and by imitating its every movement would become airborne, circle the field, and come in for the landing. As the flaps came down on the wing of the lead ship we immediately cranked ours down, perhaps five degrees lower. The leader then brought us over the runway and again, with our eyes glued only to the wing, we would execute a perfect landing without ever realizing where we were in relation to the ground. It was fantastic and gave a feeling of elation I have never forgotten.

On instrument rides a hood was placed over the pilot's head, blocking off the windows, and he learned to fly by using only the instruments for orientation. Since the pilot was flying blind, a cadet rode in the rear cockpit to serve as an observer, keeping the aircraft away from other airborne traffic. These were known as buddy rides. Only the pilot logged the flying time; consequently, we spent more time in the air than the log books showed. We gained valuable flying experience by observing and evaluating the actions of the pilot under the hood.

Old Dawg and I flew most of the buddy rides together, each being more critical than an instructor would ever be. We spent hours in the Link trainer (a static flight simulator) practicing all phases of instrument flying and navigation, trying to keep ahead of the operator who could simulate all forms of conditions, hazardous or otherwise, that we might encounter on any flight. Needless to say, many times we heard the operator's voice saying, "Sorry, you just crashed. Let's start over again."

As long as these mishaps were confined to the ground trainer everything was okay, but eventually there came a time when I had to face an emergency in the air.

Most of the airplanes had taken off. Mr. Bowen and Old Dawg had taken off on a stage check and I was assigned an aircraft for a one-hour solo flight and was to land at an auxiliary field where the aircraft was to be used in other stage checks. I taxied to the end of the runway and proceeded with the engine ground check. The magnetos checked okay, well within the 100 rpm loss that was allowed. All gauges were in the green and the engine responded well to a full power check.

Confident that everything was okay I called the tower and received permission to take off. The takeoff went perfectly; I was airborne with one-third of the runway left. At 300 feet, still climbing and just passing over the airport boundary, the engine coughed and sputtered. I lowered the nose and remembered a cardinal rule: With engine failure on takeoff you keep the airplane under control and land straight ahead. There was one problem: The area around the field was filled with Joshua trees. An emergency landing under these conditions meant you would probably not walk away.

As the engine sputtered I suspected the engine fuel pump had failed. I took my left hand off the throttle, leaving it in the wide open position, grabbed the control stick and using my right hand activated the wobble stick, a hand operated back-up fuel pump. Rocking it back and forth did not produce the desired result as the engine continued to cough and sputter. The altimeter fell to 150 feet and the little Joshua trees looked like huge telephone poles with outstretched arms. I switched techniques. This time I used my left hand to pump the throttle back and forth, hoping that some fuel remained in the accelerating well that could be discharged to the engine.

The engine responded and I was able to regain a little altitude before the engine started acting up again. Something must have worked but I wasn't sure which, the wobble pump or pumping the throttle. As the engine sputtered the second time I held the rudder pedals in neutral by applying an equal amount of pressure on each. Then with the control stick clasped between my knees I started pumping both the throttle and the wobble stick. The engine responded with intermittent power but it was impossible to gain altitude. By leaning my knees slightly to the right I could execute a slight bank and by more pressure on the right rudder I was able to make a skidding turn to the right.

I desperately wanted to call the tower but I only had two hands, two feet, and two knees and they were already all occupied. The engine continued to sporadically respond and then quit. By now I had one hope and that was to circle the base to the right, staying outside the boundaries, and with good luck maybe I could reach the same runway that I had used for takeoff. There was one frantic cadet in the cockpit flying with his knees, pumping with both arms, and shouting obscenities at a balky engine.

Each time the engine responded I gained a few feet of altitude only to lose an equal amount on the cut-out. The altitude fluctuated from 200 to 250 feet, while the Joshua trees kept providing the impetus to pump and wobble faster. I heaved a sigh of relief as I turned onto the base leg. In two or three hundreds yards I would be past the trees.

As I skidded onto the final approach I was almost blinded by the green light from the Aldis lamp in the tower. The color made no difference to me; I was committed to land whether I reached the runway or not. I placed the throttle half open and grabbed the stick with my left hand while still pumping like crazy. The engine settled down and began running smoothly. Passing over the boundary I quit pumping, switched hands on the stick, and closed the throttle. The engine idled perfectly and the landing, under the circumstances, by my standards was a success. I slowly taxied back to the flight line with the engine running as smoothly as a sewing machine.

I was completely baffled. I didn't know what was wrong. How could an engine run so smoothly on the ground and refuse to run in the air? One thing was certain, I did not have time to think or worry about my safety while in the air, but now taxiing on the ground the gravity of the situation was starting to register. I considered myself very lucky to be able to land with the airplane intact and my body in one piece. Little did I know as I shut off the engine and crawled out of the cockpit that there was even more trouble to come.

I looked up to see an instructor advancing toward me. I waited by the airplane wondering if he had seen my flight or if maybe I would be assigned a different airplane. Instead he sneeringly demanded to know why I had not taken the aircraft to the auxiliary field as I had been told. I explained that I had taken off, had engine trouble, and returned. The instructor cynically replied, "Look, if you're scared to fly your lesson, at least take the airplane out to the auxiliary field where someone can use it. We are very short of planes and we need them all in the air." I protested that the airplane was mechanically unsound and I had no desire to fly it again until someone from maintenance had checked it. His next reply burned me to the core. "You cadets are all alike. Forty hours of pilot time and you are all expert pilots and mechanics. Now get that airplane in the air and deliver it."

I tried to explain that my not flying the airplane had nothing to do with hours of flying time but involved mechanical problems. If he was giving me a direct order to fly it I would have to refuse because I considered the airplane unsafe. In a very arrogant, scornful, and condescending manner he asked, "If I fly it once around the pattern will you deliver it?"

"Yes, Sir, but I don't think it is wise. The plane performs perfectly during the ground check but it will not run in the air."

"Give me your parachute, get out of the way, and let a pilot on board."

As he donned the parachute I tried to explain the procedure of opening and closing the throttle and using the wobble pump to stay airborne. "Mister, when I want your advice I'll ask for it."

"Yes, Sir, I'll be waiting when you return."

He taxied off and I watched as he went through the ground check. The airplane appeared to function in a normal manner as he proceeded into position for takeoff. I was suddenly hit with the dilemma of what to do if the airplane performed satisfactorily. I hadn't imagined what had happened, it was real, but now if it performed okay I would look like the idiot he had portrayed me to be. No one likes to be humiliated, but at the same time there is only one life to live and I didn't want to end mine because of some overconfident, insulting instructor. But it was possible that this time it might fly okay. Then what?

Straight as an arrow in flight the aircraft went down the runway and lifted toward the sky out across the field boundary. It was a beautiful sight. Then in an instant the engine sputtered and coughed, and the plane started a nose down descent. I was sure that a crash was imminent, then the engine caught again and I hoped the instructor's ride would be as successful as mine. I watched intently as the airplane went out of sight behind the buildings which obstructed my view. I could hear the engine sporadically cut in and out and finally realized the instructor was using the same pattern to return to the airfield that I had. I don't believe he was ever able to get over 200 feet above the ground but he eventually made it down.

I waited for him to taxi over but it appeared that he was avoiding me. He would not look in my direction but kept on taxiing down the line. I was mad. I knew we would have one more encounter if I had to chase that airplane all around the field. Finally it dawned on me that he was taxiing to the maintenance hangar so I headed for it on the double. By the time I got there the instructor was out of the airplane talking to a mechanic.

When he finished I walked over not caring whether I flew again and remarked, "Do you still want me to fly that crate over to the auxiliary field?"

With wide eyes and a grim face he looked me over from head to foot then said, "She was one sick son of a gun."

Spinning on my heel I replied, "I guess you'll return the parachute since you used it last." Without waiting for an answer I took off on the double for the Link trainer building, hoping to find a trainer not in use. At least I could practice instrument flying from the safety of the ground while waiting for the airplanes to return from the auxiliary field.

The following day Mr. Bowen and I sat down to discuss the incident. He had heard that engine trouble had prevented me from reaching the auxiliary field. I related what had happened from my point of view and said that while I didn't know the name of the instructor I had tangled with, he was certainly the most arrogant, stupid individual I had ever met in the flying community. Mr. Bowen said that he was aware of part of the story and the man in question, who was from a different squadron, was not the most popular person on the base. He thought a moment then said, "Fletch, there is one thing you cadets have to realize and that is you're probably being trained to shoot down, in some instances, better people than you are being trained to protect."

It was several days before I could get back to the maintenance hangar to find out what was wrong with the airplane. The fellow who worked on it was gone for several days, but he had told someone that the problem was in the carburetor. Something was loose. At full throttle with the engine drawing maximum power it would run for about three minutes or until the fuel supply in the carburetor was exhausted. Then whatever was loose, it could have been the butterfly valve, caused the engine to starve for fuel. He said that working the wobble pump did not help since the engine fuel pump was okay. Moving the throttle to off and then advancing it was the procedure that kept it trying to run. In fact, the engine would have run perfectly for any length of time if no more than two-thirds throttle had been applied once it was in the air. Since the full power ground check lasted only a few seconds, the problem wasn't detected. At full power on takeoff the two and a half to three minutes was just enough to get airborne before the engine was starved for fuel. "But," he hastened to add, "these are not problems a pilot can diagnose or correct ahead of time. It is only something you can react to. Luckily you both reacted in the right manner; however, the second flight was probably superfluous."

With perfect weather we were flying every day, but the schedule was very tight since we were experiencing a constant shortage of airplanes. It seems that the wash-out rate was not as high as had been anticipated so we were overloading the system.

Our graduation day had been set for Saturday, August 28.

This meant that a lot of us would have to fly on Friday in order to finish on time. Our ground school courses were completed and the final tests were administered with everyone receiving a passing grade. The potato cadet from I-class was brought to the flight line and allowed several hours of refresher flying. This gave us all a good feeling when we learned he would be allowed to graduate with us. Thursday all that remained was the completion of our physical fitness test, including swimming two lengths of the pool. Then Friday night we would have to complete the last phase of flying which was a night solo cross-country flight.

I dreaded the swimming test. In my own mind I wasn't even sure they could wash me out if I failed, though that threat was made by the physical fitness instructor. But I had learned one thing by now: Anything can happen in cadet training and most threats were carried out as a matter of principle.

We were divided into groups. One group at a time was allowed in the pool while the others completed different phases of the test. Finally our turn came for the swimming test. It was not a speed event, only a requirement to swim two lengths without a break. As the cadets dove into the water my two cadet swimming instructors dove off one on each side of me. They had cautioned me ahead of time not to panic or try to swim too fast, just take it easy and keep up a slow easygoing rhythm. They would swim beside me to instill confidence and if I should flounder there was a promise of rescue.

About halfway through the first length we met most of the others on the return lap. When I turned around at the end of the first lap three-fourths of the group had already finished and were clinging to the edge of the swimming pool. Several others circled back and joined us. I wasn't sure I could finish the last half length. I was getting very tired and not making too much headway but I could hear the reassuring voices of the two cadets repeating, "Come on, you can do it." They had more hope than I did. Finally I closed my eyes so I couldn't see how far it was to the end.

Eventually I felt my hand hit the end of the pool. Opening my eyes I grabbed the edge and wasn't even sure I could pull myself out. Then I realized that all of the group was still in the water. Immediately hands grabbed my legs and waist as I was shoved up and out of the pool. Gasping for breath I saw the instructor making a checkmark on the roster as the other cadets crawled out. I might have been the last to finish but I was the first one out of the pool. No one in the group said a word as we went on to other tests.

The following night at briefing we learned that our solo night cross-country would entail flying from Lancaster to Mojave to Daggett to Palmdale and back to Lancaster. Mr. Bowen stated that Littlefield would take off first, followed by Marchant five minutes later at an altitude 500 feet lower than Littlefield. Hoffman would take off five minutes later climbing to the same altitude that was assigned Littlefield. I would take off last, five minutes after Old Dawg, and fly 500 feet below him. In this manner everyone had a five-minute, 500-feet separation.

Several other routes had been established and other groups were also taking off at the same time. We were using two parallel runways with both right- and left-hand traffic and were to return and land on the same runway from which we had started. From the time I took off it would be at least another twenty minutes before anyone else would take off using our route. The purpose of this procedure was two-fold: First was safety; second, it would be impossible to just follow the lights of another airplane instead of navigating on your own.

We were assigned to the right-hand runway, the same one on which I had made the emergency landing. Everything went as scheduled. It was a typical desert night—not a cloud in the sky and the stars were sparkling bright. As I approached Mojave from the south the engine was running smoothly. It was a peaceful flight as the radio traffic from War Eagle Field had slowly faded out. I made the turn over Mojave heading east by southeast, and in due time the lights of Barstow appeared just slightly left of my course. Everything was proceeding according to plan, on course and on time, with the lights of Daggett slightly south and east of Barstow.

In the vicinity of Barstow the radio crackled to life with the message, "Fletcher, this is Hoffman. Do you read?"

"Roger, Hoffman, receive you loud and clear. Transmit your message."

"This is to inform you that I inadvertently spiraled down below your altitude and am now climbing back up through your airspace and request that you watch for me."

"Roger. Will keep watching for you. Do you have mechanical problems?"

"Negative. Just wanted to warn you that I'm passing through your altitude."

"Roger. Thank you."

Within a few minutes I made the turn over Daggett and headed west toward Palmdale. The compass headings were right on, an indication there wasn't any wind. Passing over Palmdale I turned north and could see the airport beacon at War Eagle Field only a few miles away. When I reached the airfield there was lots of air traffic as other units were also returning. Finding a break in the traffic I entered the pattern for the right-hand runway. While making the right-hand turn onto the final approach I flipped on the landing lights and was suddenly struck by the beauty of the lighted runway ahead of me. There was a feeling of nostalgia as I realized that I was landing at War Eagle for the last time. I retarded the throttle and the aircraft floated over the airport boundary and down the center of the runway while I executed the perfect flare-out. The aircraft stalled and in the instant that followed, before the plane hit the ground, I realized I had leveled off too high. It was the hardest landing I had ever made. The airplane just dropped about ten feet to the runway in the three-point position.

Turning off the runway I taxied to the line and hurried to the ready room. Littlefield, Marchant, and Mr. Bowen were in critique when I joined them. Mr. Bowen inquired how the flight had gone. I explained that everything had gone fine. Every checkpoint was reached right on time and the ETA (estimated time of arrival) at the field was off about five minutes, but some of that time was spent entering the pattern. The only problem was the landing. I thought I was making a good one but leveled off too high and was just lucky the airplane held together. Mr. Bowen laughed and asked if I knew what happened. I said I suspected since there was so much traffic and absolutely no breeze there must have been a dust cloud hanging just above the runway. "You're right," he interjected, "and your landing lights reflected off of the dust layer. You made a perfect landing on the haze and so has everyone else. Luckily so far the only damage has been to the pilots' pride. While we are waiting for Hoffman I want you guys to tell me what you thought of the course and the instruction you received. This is your chance to tell me what you think. I want you to be as honest with me as I have been with you throughout the course. So let's have it, good or bad."

At first we were a little timid, but he assured us that he really wanted to know, and since we were through flying we should level with him. Surely we could find something to criticize. He was sure he wasn't a perfect instructor and while we were good our flying wasn't perfect either. "We'll start with Marchant, then Littlefield, then you, Fletch, and Hoffman when he shows up."

Each one expressed his opinion. We were all very happy to have had him as an instructor. We felt he was more than just an instructor, he was a person we had come to like. He was someone who understood our problems and was never found lacking when we needed advice. He was certainly a gentleman at all times and we hoped that we would be able to emulate his example. I did suggest that in the beginning there was a time when I felt I could have used a little instruction on spins and aerobatics. He smiled and said that yes, he felt we were shorted in this regard. There were times when he felt a little inadequate in this situation, but remember, he was learning too. Then came the surprise remark, "Besides, Fletch, I thought the hot pilot from Mira Loma could figure out a few things on his own."

"Wait a minute. What have these guys told you?"

"Nothing. I was on the field at Mira Loma and watched you bring the Stearman home one windy day not too long after J-class arrived." He explained that he was an instructor in another squadron at Mira Loma while we were there. He had applied to become a Basic instructor and when our class finished he was transferred to Polaris. He had arrived three days before us. When we received our orientation rides he had only five hours and thirty minutes flying time in the BT-13. We were his first Basic students. "Does that answer any of your questions?" It certainly did and it only increased our admiration of the man and his flying ability.

By now I had been on the ground for over forty minutes and Old Dawg had not arrived. If he had been on schedule he should have been down before me. Mr. Bowen was showing some signs of concern that maybe he got lost. After another five minutes I felt compelled to tell him about the radio contact that I had with Old Dawg near Barstow. I didn't know whether it was relevant or not, but I knew he was okay then even though I did not see his lights and felt he must still have been ahead of me. Only an occasional plane was landing now and most of the instructors and cadets had already left the line. I was sure something had happened but I didn't know what. Mr. Bowen assured us that it was too soon to start worrying as the BT carried plenty of fuel and he would probably show up in a little while.

Sure enough within a few minutes, to the relief of everyone, Old Dawg walked in with a big smile on his face. Mr. Bowen exclaimed, "Well, we're all down. Let's go home. It's getting late and tomorrow is your big day." He shook our hands, wished us well, and hoped his next class would be as much fun as his first.

On our way back to the cottages, when no one else could hear, I asked Old Dawg what had happened. What took him so long? Did he get lost? "No," he said, "I was on the ground and saw your sloppy landing and watched you park two airplanes away from me."

"What were you doing? I was really worried about you, especially after your radio transmission and then not showing up at the ready room."

"Well, it's like this. Since this was our last flight I decided to use that relief tube to see if it worked. I had just passed Daggett with all systems go when I realized the tube was plugged. In the excitement I fell off into a spiral. That's when I called you. You can guess the rest. When I got to Polaris I stood outside by the airplane for about an hour waiting for things to dry. Do you think I was going to walk into that ready room with a wet flying suit? No way."

The graduation ceremonies were set for 10:00 a.m. Saturday. We had received a new commanding officer and he, along with Major Moseley, put forth considerable time and energy planning a major publicity event. Several representatives from three states, all members of the House Subcommittee on Appropriations, were present along with the Army Air Force Commandant of Cadets as well as the head of Basic Training for the West Coast Training Command. In a spirit of cooperation and a show of solidarity high ranking members of the Navy, Army, and Coast Guard participated in the review of the cadet corps.

The citizens of Lancaster were also invited to attend the open house and ceremonies. The Muroc Army Band was bused in to provide martial music. A feeling of euphoria returned as the colors were posted and the cadets passed in review. We were then allowed to watch as a test pilot from Lockheed Aviation roared a few feet above the runway in a high speed fly-by in a P-38 Lightning pursuit plane. On his second pass over the runway at 500 feet with one prop feathered he proceeded to do a slow roll, then pulled up into a victory roll while restarting the dead engine. At that moment I knew I wanted to be a P-38 pilot. Any airplane that could perform like that certainly could make a pilot out of the likes of me.

The cadet corps performed with precision complete with new white gloves, the gift of Mr. and Mrs. Herman Gold of Lancaster who donated 700 pair. It was a proud, confident, happy group who marched into the huge hangar for ceremonies commensurate with the elite guest list. Lieutenant Rudy Vallee, resplendent in the white uniform of the Coast Guard, acted as master of ceremonies and sang several songs, including *Mad Dogs and Englishmen,* to the delight of everyone present. At the conclusion of the festivities the wives were allowed to join their husbands and received a complete tour of the base. We were given the orders transferring us to Advanced flying school, the last school in the cadet program. If we could survive this last hurdle we would win our wings and become commissioned officers in the Army Air Force.

That evening as George Boldi sounded Taps, we eagerly awaited the two selections he would choose to play at the conclusion. We were treated to the euphonious sounds of *Stardust* and *Till We Meet Again*. When the last note sounded I was swept up in a feeling of nostalgia as I realized this was the last day we would enjoy his company and hear the trumpet sounds that had become so much a part of our lives. Before I fell asleep the events of the day filtered through my mind.

Twenty-two of us were selected to go to the twin-engine Advanced Training School at Douglas, Arizona, which in my fantasy was the first step to the P-38. This made up for the fact that all of my close friends were being sent in small groups to other fields throughout the Southwest. Lieutenant Scott, one of the student officers, would drive Sherry and two other wives to Douglas with only the stipulation that they share the expense of the gasoline.

My log book showed 36 hours and 20 minutes of dual instruction and 43 hours and 40 minutes of solo time, added to the 65 hours of Primary. I now had 145 hours of military flight time, not counting time flying as an observer on buddy rides.

I was not sure what the future would hold, but I could tell Mr. Pulici that the BT-13 could perform both forward and side-slips just as easily as the Stearman.

5 Advanced Flying School

Douglas, Arizona

After a bus ride to Los Angeles and a long train trip we finally arrived at Douglas Army Airfield on August 31, 1943. Douglas, located in the extreme southeast corner of Arizona, was right on the Mexican border with an elevation of over 4,000 feet. It was a thriving modern city with a population of 14,000, the third largest city in Arizona. The climate was warm and sunny with very low humidity. The annual rainfall, around fourteen inches, created a more scenic locale than Muroc Dry Lake. The temperature was quite pleasant compared to the Mojave Desert.

As our group entered the base we were immediately subjected to cultural shock. Most of the buildings were wrapped in black tarpaper held in place with a few wood strips for batten. We were truly on a military base: back to barracks style living. Everything that moved on the base wore the insignia of the Army Air Force. The beauty of the bases, the privacy and frills of Mira Loma and Polaris, faded into the past and were only a dream which had suddenly turned into a nightmare.

As others reported in we were suddenly a squadron of approximately 250 J-class cadets. The cadet corps consisted of an equal number from I-class. There was also a contingent of Nationalist Chinese cadets on the field. It was a sprawling unsightly base whose only redeeming feature was the flight line and the endless rows of AT-17 Cessna "Bobcats," twin-engine fabric-covered airplanes powered by two radial seven-cylinder Jacobs air-cooled engines generating 245 horsepower each. The aircraft had a wingspan of 41 feet 11 inches, length 32 feet 9 inches, height 9 feet 11 inches, gross weight 5,700 pounds, top speed 176 mph with a range of 750 miles and a service ceiling of 22,000 feet.

There were dual controls with side-by-side configuration for a pilot and copilot. All of the flight instruments were located in front of the pilot on the left-hand side of the instrument panel. The engine instruments were on the right side of the panel in front of the copilot. There was a bench seat in the rear of the cabin which could comfortably accommodate two passengers or a crowded three in an emergency. Being as observant as possible I was unable to locate either a gosport system or relief tube.

We could hardly wait to start flying this rather strange looking aircraft. We had hoped to find an airplane of metal construction and much more streamlined, but it had controls, wings, and engines. What more could a pilot ask for?

Our first trip to the mess hall confirmed the fact we had indeed been pampered while attending two civilian flying fields. We knew that some of the finest cooks and chefs in the country were serving in the army, it was just unfortunate they were assigned to the motor pool.

As we received our barracks assignments we realized it was being done in the true army tradition: alphabetical order. It meant that all close associates would now have surnames starting with E, F, or G. The list of twenty-two cadets coming in from Lancaster did not contain any E's, only one F and one G, then jumped to M. Cadet Gajda and I found it relatively easy to make new friends since all of us shared a common bond. Somewhere at sometime we had all been chewed out and maligned by some individual who felt it his duty to return us to our proper mental status in the cadet community.

Monday we reported to the flight line and were given our instructor assignments. With my good luck still holding I was assigned to Second Lieutenant Kenneth Dye. Lieutenant Dye was a gentle, good-natured, humorous individual who felt that it was easier to talk a person into doing a good job in the beginning rather than having to resort to verbal abuse to correct a mistake already made. He was small in stature with light blond hair, blue eyes, and an infectious grin. His physical size was obscured by an overabundant knowledge of flying, expertise, and good common sense. It was my first experience of being able to stand flat-footed and look directly into the eyes of an instructor, an attribute which could only enhance a feeling of competence.

He explained that it was not his responsibility to teach us how to fly. We were here because we had already demonstrated this capability and were now considered to be pilots who needed only to hone our skills and learn more advanced techniques. He would show us how to take off and land a twin-engine aircraft and acquaint us with all the emergency procedures pertaining to the aircraft. Once we mastered these techniques we would begin flying as teams of pilots and copilots. New techniques would be demonstrated, our progress would be monitored, and help would be given on an "as needed" basis. He would talk, explain, and demonstrate, but the execution of the maneuvers was left to the student. The first two weeks of the course he would be an active flyer in the right seat, but from then on his position would be one of an observer, adviser, and monitor. We were cautioned to do our best and stay out of trouble because we had the meanest squadron commander on the field along with several other disagreeable persons.

On our first flight three cadets were put on board, one in the left-hand pilot seat and the other two cadets in the bench seat at the rear of the cabin. I had the privilege of being the first in the pilot's seat, and with the others watching, we received a lengthy cockpit check and explanation of the controls. We were shown a toggle switch located under a red plastic cover along with the admonition to never touch it while on the ground since this was the landing gear retraction switch.

While taxiing out for takeoff I mentioned to Lieutenant Dye that this would be only the second time since I had joined the military that I had been accorded the privilege of flying with an army pilot. He feigned shock and dismay that I had been denied the opportunity of such a pleasant experience and said he would certainly try to make up for this deficiency in my training program. I wasn't sure whether this offer was good or bad but I suspected with his sense of humor and dedication that things would turn out okay.

We received our first open post on Saturday, September 11. Sherry had already written me that Lieutenant Scott had dropped them off at the Gadsen Hotel August 30. The three young ladies, Mrs. Saling, Mrs. Meeks, and Sherry, spent the night at the Gadsen where they rented a room for three at six dollars. This was a luxury hotel built in 1906. The lobby was impressive with a leaded stained-glass mural and a curved marble staircase leading to the second floor. The next day they were all able to rent rooms in private homes at a more modest rate.

Sherry found a room with an outside entrance in a very lovely stone house. The room was much larger and nicer than the one at Lancaster; it even contained a double bed. The lady who owned the home was very nice and quite friendly, but this could not match the close family relationship which had developed with the Storys. On several weekends when the lady was gone, Sherry was granted kitchen privileges in exchange for looking after the house and a pet cat.

She had no trouble finding a job and was working six days a week in the mail order department of a major chain store. Because of the proximity to the border a large percentage of the customers were of Mexican origin and most did not speak English. Sherry's two years of high school Latin and two years of French at Whitman College did not help much, but since it was a catalog department they could point to pictures and guess at sizes.

She had also become close friends with the family who lived across the street. They had several teenage daughters and had welcomed her into their home. Since Sherry was a music major they spent many evenings together playing the piano, singing, and visiting. Here she was introduced to her first Mexican food. I was greatly relieved to find that she had such nice friends including several cadet wives. It was a pleasant way for her to fill the time between our short overnight weekend passes.

As time went on I became more impressed with Lieutenant Dye. The AT-17 was an easy airplane to fly and land and everyone caught on very quickly. When I asked when we would start doing something other than just flying level Lieutenant Dye laughed and said in a joking manner that was all we were going to do. This wasn't a P-38, it was a wood-and-fabric "bamboo bomber." Our greatest thrill would probably be a stall; forget the aerobatics. Here the emphasis would be on instrument flying, formation day and night, and navigation in all its forms. The fighter pilots had already been weeded out and we had been selected for a different role in the flying military, but at this point no one knew what that was.

I wasn't very happy with this analysis. In fact, I was downright disappointed. However, I would play the game. The important thing was to win the silver wings and then, as an officer, again make a bid for the P-38.

Our schedule now was very similar to the other schools. We still had our half day on the flight line, ground school, physical training, and drill. The ground school courses were more advanced and new courses were introduced, many of which pertained to leadership, customs and courtesies of the military, the responsibility of command, and the need for censorship and military security. Everywhere we looked there were signs: "Loose lips sink ships," "Button your lips," "Don't spread rumors," "Remember the enemy is listening," "The life you save may be your own." But the one that brought a hearty laugh to the cadet corps was an anonymous verse tacked to the bulletin board entitled *A Military Secret:*

> Absolute knowledge have I none,
> But my aunt's washerwoman's son
> Heard a policeman on his beat
> Say to a laborer on the street,
> That he had a letter just last week
> Written in the finest Greek,
> From a Chinese coolie in Timbuctoo,
> Who said the negroes in Cuba knew

Of another man in a Texas town
Who got it straight from a circus clown
That a man in Klondyke heard the news
From a gang of South American Jews
About somebody in Borneo,
Who heard of a man who claimed to know
Of a swell society female rake
Whose mother-in-law will undertake
To prove that her husband's sister's niece
Has stated in a printed piece
That she has a son who has a friend
Who knows when the war is going to end.

As we settled into our flying routine the tempo picked up because we were spending more time in the air. The flights were longer and we still used auxiliary fields but they were much farther from the home field. Buses were no longer practical and weren't needed since we could carry the instructors and two or three cadets with us. This eliminated the study time we used to have at the auxiliary field as we now spent all our time in the airplane.

Every Monday morning we followed a little ritual as we saluted and reported to Lieutenant Dye. His response was always the same, "Please, gentlemen, don't salute so loud. Woe is me. Poor little Kenny has had a rough weekend and now you expect me to touch my aching head to acknowledge your presence. Misters, please show a little respect for your superior who has to spend all weekend with a jug and some female company in order to forget your errors of last week and work up nerve enough to fly with you again this week." We assumed that it was all a charade, but only he knew the truth. He was a good looking single lieutenant in his early twenties. This verbal exchange was always done on the ground for once in the air everything was business and no foolishness. I'm sure this relaxed approach resulted in a better flying performance by the cadets.

There was only one exception of light-heartedness in the air and that I suspect was to keep our minds from dwelling on what could have been a rather frightening experience. During our second week of flying Lieutenant Dye was giving two of us a stage check. The other cadet had received the first check and had done well. I was now in the left seat with the instructor in the right seat and the other cadet belted in on the bench seat. My check had just been completed and all of my mistakes pointed out. I was told to head back to Douglas and land as our time was up.

Navigating back to the field was no problem. Douglas was the site of a large copper smelter which contained four tall smoke stacks of which at least one was always spewing forth tons of yellow smoke. The active stacks were visible for miles during the daylight hours. We didn't need a compass heading; we just flew toward the stacks.

Approaching the field I called for landing instructions and upon entering the pattern we started the landing checklist. Lieutenant Dye flipped the gear switch to the down position and nothing happened. He immediately called the tower and explained we were leaving the pattern since we were experiencing landing gear problems. While he was making the radio call I moved the landing gear switch to up then back to down, but still no response. The instructor then turned to the other cadet and told him to crank the gear down manually.

He located the crank and placed it in the emergency slot to start the long process of manually cranking the gear down. In a few minutes he reported he could not turn the crank, which was now connected to the long screw which lowered the gear. Lieutenant Dye told him to turn it clockwise since he was probably trying to crank it up instead of down, but the cadet said, "Sir, I am trying to turn it clockwise, but it won't budge."

"Can't you guys do anything right? Mr. Fletcher can't flip the switch correctly and now you can't crank the gear down."

I interjected, "But, Sir, you flipped the switch down."

"I did?"

"Yes, Sir."

"Well, jeez, that's the trouble. I have to do everything: flip the switch, crank the gear down, next I suppose I'll have to do the flying too. Now, Fletcher, climb up another 500 feet and keep circling the field while I show your buddy how to put the

gear down and please don't run into anyone while my back is
turned."

"Yes, Sir."

After a few more minutes of grunting and griping I finally
gathered that the screw had loosened up and the gear was
very slowly going down. After another five minutes they announced the screw wouldn't turn any more so the gear must
be down. I reported that the red light was on indicating that
the gear was not down and locked. "Take off your sunglasses
and look again."

"It's still red, Sir."

"Well, maybe we hit a hard spot on the screw. We will try
some more."

Another couple of minutes of grunting and it was decided
that the gear had to be down because the screw wouldn't
move. Whether it was locked or not was another question.
Lieutenant Dye slipped back into the right seat exclaiming,
"Oh, my aching back. I flip the switch, I crank the gear down.
Fletcher, the least you could do is turn out the red light."

"I can unscrew the cover and remove the globe if the red
light is too bright."

"Forget it. Call the tower and let's go in. We've done all we
can up here."

I notified the tower that we were reentering the pattern,
that we had cranked the gear down manually, but still had a
red light indicating that the gear was not down and locked,
but suspected the light was not functioning properly. The
tower recognized we had an emergency and responded by
sending out the fire trucks and an ambulance. Lieutenant Dye
watched the activity on the ground then turned and said,
"Fletch, you had better make the best landing you've ever
made because if you mess up my Saturday night they won't
need that meat wagon."

"Are you sure you want me to land it, Sir?"

"Yes, I want you to make the landing. You're the one who
needs the experience and I feel more comfortable following
you through on the controls since that is my job. Besides, if
anything happens I can lay the blame on you."

With his constant bantering there wasn't any time to think

about the consequences, but I did notice my buddy was white knuckled even though he wore a slight grin. As we settled onto the runway we all held our breath for a few moments until we were sure the gear was not going to collapse. Then we all exhaled at the same moment.

As we turned off the runway we had quite a caravan following us: two fire engines, the ambulance, and the fire chief's control vehicle. Lieutenant Dye, grinning from ear to ear as he watched the parade, broke the ice exclaiming, "Men, it looks like we disappointed the vultures this time."

As we taxied on down to the line the emergency vehicles left us. Before we reached our parking area we passed an AT-17 sitting on the ramp with the gear up and the wooden props splintered. After we crawled out of the airplane we proceeded to give the crew chief a bad time about the gear switch. Then Lieutenant Dye gave the Form One to the other cadet saying, "Fletcher made the landing and since you got to crank the gear down you get to fill out the form. To vent your feelings make it good and I will sign it in the spirit of a cooperative endeavor."

We then asked the crew chief about the AT-17 sitting on the ramp sans wheels. He grinned and said one of the Chinese cadets had somehow managed to flip the gear switch to the up position and apparently that switch had worked better than ours. Maybe they wouldn't even repair our switch, but just assign the airplane to the international group.

The following weekend the four alphabetic couples, Ellsworth, Fisher, Fletcher, and Foley, decided to spend Sunday in Douglas' sister city, Agua Prieta, Mexico. It was just a short walk to the immigration and customs building where by showing identification we were allowed to cross the border.

Agua Prieta was a small, sleepy border town. The shops contained many of the things that were in short supply in the U.S. The four ladies had fun trying on shoes which were plentiful, but they knew they couldn't buy them since we had been told by the customs officials that anything that was rationed in the U.S., if purchased in Mexico, would still require giving up a ration coupon when we came back across the border. Somehow the regulation did not make much sense. Things were rationed because they were in short supply. It appeared that something bought in Mexico would extend U.S. supplies. But after ten months in the cadet corps we were well aware of the fact that rules do not have to make sense, they were only made to be obeyed.

The following Monday we were scheduled for a solo night flight. Lieutenant Dye was going through his usual Monday ritual and in his perceived condition he was glad he did not have to fly with us since our rough landings would only jar his head and prolong the ache. Feeling rather brave I suggested that if he were married he would not have these problems since the state of matrimony outlawed most of his indiscretions. "Mr. Fletcher, please do not resort to blasphemy. I've washed out cadets for just thinking about this word which you have found it necessary to utter. If you wish to keep flying never mention *that word* again. Why would you deny all of these young southern belles the pleasure of my company? Have you no compassion? You must seek forgiveness."

"Yes, Sir. I'll speak to the chaplain, Sir."

"Okay, but when you do don't mention my name.

"Now let's get on with the flight that has been planned. It's not a true cross-country flight but a rat race cross-country to give you experience in night landings and takeoffs from strange fields. You will take off from here in trail at thirty-second intervals, then proceed to the auxiliary field at Rodeo, land and join the line for takeoff, head for the auxiliary field at Cochise, then to Fort Huachuca and back to Douglas. You will fly two cadets to a plane, pilot and copilot, but at Cochise you will change seats and split the time in each position. Now plot your courses and keep in mind that you're flying between mountain peaks that range in height from 8,500 feet to almost 10,000.

"There will be an instructor parked in an AT-17 at each field who will act as the tower for radio communications. All of these fields are well lighted with flare pots but there is always the possibility that some will blow out so use caution. You will transmit on one frequency and receive on another. This way you will not be able to block out the tower ship with your transmission. It also means that you will not have airplane-to-airplane communication. All communications will be conducted through the control ship."

It was a beautiful moonlit night when we took off from Douglas. I flew as pilot for the first leg, making the landings at Rodeo and Cochise. We were in the middle of the pack and by the time we reached the auxiliary fields they were enveloped in a haze of dust. These were grass fields without runway markings. In the daytime we just landed near the center of the field after passing over the boundary, but at night the flare pots outlined a runway in the landing area. The dust did not create the problem which I had encountered at Lancaster; we had learned how to land without completely stalling the aircraft and could feel our way through the haze until the wheels actually touched down.

As soon as we cleared the landing runway we changed places in the cockpit and taxied back toward the takeoff point. Since I was now in the copilot's seat it was my duty to initiate the radio calls and free the pilot of this chore. With this routine he could devote his full attention to the hazards of night taxiing and the location of other aircraft. Since there weren't any defined taxi strips everyone left on his landing lights. Upon turning toward the runway I called the control ship and requested permission for takeoff. The answer came back to hold our position as there was an aircraft on final. We could now see the other aircraft coming down the final approach. Just before he reached us at about 100 feet of altitude the other cadet remarked that the landing craft didn't look right. At this instant I realized what was wrong and immediately called the control ship reporting the airplane landing did not have its gear down.

Instantly the control ship requested the ship landing to pull up immediately, go around, and check the landing gear. The pilot responded by pulling up and exiting the traffic pattern. By this time there were two more ships in the pattern and we had to hold for about five minutes before receiving takeoff clearance.

In the meantime my partner wondered why the airplane left the pattern. I speculated that he was hoping they hadn't copied his call number. Since we couldn't hear his call number we didn't know what it was either. He could delay and come in later and no one would know his identity. If this was the purpose it obviously worked since the incident was not mentioned at critique after we completed the rat race.

The next day I was telling a good friend about the airplane that had tried to land with the gear up and if we hadn't noticed it some dumb cluck would have smeared a trainer across the Cochise countryside. His reply was, "Fletch, I resent you talking like that."

"What do you mean?"

"Your calling me a dumb cluck just because I overlooked the small matter of flipping the gear switch to down."

"I'm sorry. I didn't realize it was you."

"That's okay because no one else does either, but thanks anyway."

Our training continued on schedule. The physical fitness instructor was a little more humane than the one at Lancaster and allowed time for recreational swimming at the cadet pool. He did not feel it necessary to make swimming a part of the final test; he was more interested in the obstacle course that he had designed. The impediments were rough and varied but the cadets seemed to enjoy the rugged course. It was a good place to vent frustrations. For ten months we had been climbing mental walls trying to remain in the corps. Now it felt good to be climbing and jumping physical ones, especially in the more temperate climate.

The ground school instructors were shoving us through the courses at top speed. It was still reading, lectures, and testing. There was no time for classroom discussion, only an occasional question. The only way we could possibly keep up was to assume that retention equalled survival and this provided the incentive to absorb all that was given.

I was still having problems in radio code. We were using the international Morse system. I could maintain a minimum passing grade but felt I should be doing better. It was so easy for some of the cadets that they couldn't imagine anyone having difficulties. One day the opportunity arose to explain my problem to the instructor. He thought that I had reached a plateau and the lack of rhythm was preventing me from improving. He suggested we try an experiment. "What do you hear when I say dah dah dit dah?"

"Well, I hear two dashes, a dot and another dash which is the letter Q."

"All right, you repeat it back to me."

"Okay, dah dah dit dah."

"I heard payday today, Q. Repeat it over and over, pick up the rhythm, dah dah dit dah, payday today, Q. Pretty soon you will only hear the jingle that you know means Q." At this point he proceeded to give me a whole group of jingles that corresponded to the letters in the alphabet. It did make code more fun and there was a little improvement, but not the breakthrough for which I had hoped.

In the meantime, all the cadet wives were attending, once a week, classes on the base sponsored by the Officers Wives Club. Most of the classes were supervised and led by the commanding officer's wife. The wives were instructed in the art of military protocol as it pertained to an officer's wife. They were expected to provide a wholesome, warm, family home atmosphere whether they lived in humble or luxurious quarters. The wives were instructed to establish a simple but gracious, hospitable style of living. They must be prepared for any emergency and were expected to devote some of their free time to worthy causes sponsored by the base. There were certain functions which a wife was obligated to attend, only one of which was to be present when her husband presented his card to call on the commander, at his home, at each new base.

The classes also included these suggestions: Their husbands, who would soon be commissioned as officers, were not to carry packages, children, or babies in public. A wife should always walk on the left side of her husband, leaving his right arm free to salute, draw weapons, or whatever. Hand-holding in public was outlawed as well as taking hold of an officer's arm. In addition to making a good home it was their duty to be good hostesses and support their husbands at all times. They must always keep in mind the rank of their husband and defer to those whose spouses were of a higher rank. Above all, they must do nothing to embarrass their husbands. A wife's conduct reflected upon the husband's character and had great influence on his progression in the chain of command.

As Sherry related these new positive suggestions to me it seemed best to remain noncommittal. I could only smile and nod inwardly. After all, I still wished to maintain a marriage and there might come a time when I would be a civilian again.

On the flight line the only thrills generated were in recovering from unusual positions, a procedure in which the student closed his eyes and bent over until his head was parallel with his lap. At this point the instructor would make several turns and pull-ups to disorient the student, then he would place the airplane in an unusual position and tell the student to recover and return to level flight by using only the flight instruments for orientation. One of the favorites was to go into a dive, pick up excessive speed, and then put the airplane into a climbing turn and holler "RECOVER." When the student saw the excessive airspeed he would think he was in a dive and pull back on the stick, or yoke as it was now called in the AT-17, which only exaggerated the climb into a stall and the plane would fall off in the direction of the lowered wing.

Eventually we learned to read all the flight instruments in one glance: the artificial horizon, airspeed indicator, turn and bank instrument, and rate of climb or descent indicator. This would give us the attitude of the airplane and we could apply the correct recovery procedures immediately.

Lieutenant Dye was right, the stall and the unusual positions were the only self-imposed thrills that we could experience. Any others came as a result of something unexpected: mechanical malfunction, a near aerial miss, just plain poor piloting technique or judgment on the part of the student.

Unlike Basic where buddy rides were almost always with the same cadet, here we found ourselves flying with a different cadet almost every time. In my case the situation was exaggerated because one of Lieutenant Dye's students was eliminated, and that left three of us with me becoming the odd man. The advantage of this was that I was exposed to the flying abilities and temperaments of a great many more students. Standardization in flying and procedures was still required and adhered to, but personalities varied from student to student and this was a true lesson in human attitudes and individualism in a regimented society. It also kept everyone on his toes, alert, thinking, and ready to react since we were not lulled into complacency because of familiarity.

After days of the humdrum of routine flying our interest was greatly enhanced by an announcement that we would be taking a long cross-country trip to Santa Ana where we would all undergo tests in a static high-altitude chamber. We would leave on Monday morning, spend Tuesday and Wednesday at Santa Ana, and then fly back to Douglas Thursday night. The outgoing flight was a daytime cross-country while the return flight would be at night.

Eventually all of J-class would make the trip, but we were in the first group. Our twenty airplanes were divided into two groups, and a flight commander in a separate airplane was assigned to each flight of ten.

The two flight commanders were pilots who were involved with administration rather than flight instructors, and we weren't familiar with them. We were buddied up two cadets to an airplane and I was not acquainted with the cadet who was paired up with me. I had never seen him before and was sure he was not in our squadron. On the outbound trip I was assigned as copilot and navigator.

The airfield at Blythe, California, was designated as our refueling stop. There was a Green westbound airway that ran from Cochise to Tucson to Phoenix to Blythe to Riverside, just northeast of Santa Ana. I didn't like the idea of flying the airway since it took us through areas of very heavy air traffic so I plotted a course from Douglas direct to Tucson. This was one traffic area I could not avoid and still have a highly visible checkpoint. From there we would fly to Casa Grande, then to Tonopah where we would pick up the airway and head due west to Blythe for refueling. From Blythe we would fly to Indio and then direct to Santa Ana.

There were two mountains on the route. Old Baldy at 9,500 feet, was approximately thirty miles south of Tucson on our first leg. Then after Indio, there was San Jacinto, a peak of 11,000 feet north of the course on the final leg. Since it was a daylight flight the peaks would not be a hazard but actually would make good landmarks.

The flight commander went over the plan thoroughly, and then he asked what I would do if I missed Casa Grande. I answered that we would tune in the Phoenix radio and home in, then pick up the airway to Blythe. We chose an altitude of 8,500 feet since all visual westbound traffic flew at even thousands plus 500 feet.

The course was approved and we took off on a fun flight. After passing Tucson we picked up the outline of a dry river bed and followed it to Casa Grande which appeared right on time. Continuing on we crossed the Gila River near Buckeye which was twenty miles south and east of Tonopah. From there it was just 100 miles due west to Blythe.

Landing at Blythe we realized we were the talk and envy of the cadets. Here we were advanced cadets flying in from some unknown place in twin-engine aircraft heading on west for some purpose which was beyond their imagination. We did our best to ignore them and perpetuate the myth that we were probably gods from the heavens merely pausing for a brief moment in the span of perpetual life.

After refueling we had lunch and took off for Santa Ana, 200 miles distant. After passing south of Hemet we let down to 6,500 feet and kept a sharp lookout for other traffic, which we knew would be heavy in the Santa Ana area. I was just starting to question our course as we reached our ETA and the airfield was not in sight. I wondered if we could be slightly north of course. Then I saw the tall mooring masts and the large quonset-shaped hangars that housed the lighter-than-air craft that were stationed in the area. In a matter of minutes we were in the traffic pattern at Santa Ana. The cadet made another good landing while I was busy congratulating myself on a good job of navigation. I just hoped my counterpart would do as well on the way back, but that was two days away.

Within the space of the next hour all of our ten aircraft had landed. The flight commander had already made arrangements for our billeting and messing. It seemed strange to wander around our Preflight base not in formation or wondering whether someone was going to chew us out. It had been a long trip out so we turned in early.

Before entering the chamber the following morning we were given a lecture explaining the effects of anoxia or hypoxia and how this condition would alter our personalities, but nothing could prepare us for the actual test that we were going to experience. The chamber was a huge metal tube with extra thick walls and hatches. We entered through a very small hatch at one end into a small chamber which would accommodate three or four people. This was the outer chamber. Then we crawled through another hatch into a larger cylinder. The sides were lined with long benches separated by a narrow aisle. These benches seated ten people on a side and there was barely headroom to stand up in the aisle. Since I was one of the first to enter I was literally shoved to the end of the tube-like chamber.

When all twenty of us were seated, three enlisted instructors entered the chamber and explained how to use the oxygen masks which were located at each station. Once everyone demonstrated that he could use the mask the instructors ordered the inner hatch closed. As it clanged shut I experienced a feeling of claustrophobia and only the presence of the others kept me glued to the seat. The attendant in the outer chamber turned the huge wheel which locked the hatch in place. From the looks of the eyes surrounding me I realized that I was not the only one who was having trouble adjusting to the enclosed area.

As soon as the inner chamber was sealed the attendant exited and closed the hatch which led into the outer chamber. Again we knew the huge wheel was being turned although we could not see it since the hatches were solid. We donned our masks again and hooked up our headsets to the intercom system so we could receive instructions from the three attendants. There was an altimeter which started to measure the lessening pressure as soon as the pumps were started. We were told that we would be elevated to a pressure of 25,000 feet.

In the meantime we would be given tests to prove to us that we could not function without oxygen. Several candles were lit so we could see the effect of a lack of oxygen on the flame. At 10,000 feet two cadets began exhibiting signs of claustrophobia. An outside attendant was ordered to enter the outer chamber and when the pressure in the two chambers had equalized, the inner door was opened and the two cadets were removed to the outer chamber. With the sealing of the inner door we continued our ascent into lessening pressure while the attendant and the two cadets in the outer chamber started their descent to ground pressure.

The flames on the candles shrunk to a slight glow. They were eventually extinguished. In the meantime each cadet, one at a time, removed his oxygen mask under the supervision of an instructor, and was asked to write his name and state how he felt. Most of the transmissions made little sense and the signatures were illegible. In my case there was a false feeling of well-being, but the signature didn't prove much since mine was illegible even when I was on the ground.

We all realized that we could not on our own recognize the danger of anoxia since in most cases it was preceded by a carefree feeling and a sense that all was okay. We felt we were functioning normally when, in fact, we weren't functioning at all. When everyone had completed the individual test we were warned to be ready for an explosive change in pressure. The hatch in the inner door contained a round window which was sealed with a thick layer of a red cardboard-type material. A large mechanical knife was attached to a spring on a lever just inches away from the cardboard barrier. The pressure was increased in the outer chamber to where it greatly exceeded ours. At a signal from the instructor the mechanical restraint was removed allowing the spring to plunge the knife into the cardboard barrier. The result was an immediate explosion from the outer chamber as the pressure neutralized in both chambers.

Recovering from the shock, we realized the cardboard was now confetti settling to the floor of the chamber. The on-rushing pressure created a vapor which looked like smoke and it was a few seconds, which seemed like minutes, before we could see. This ended the demonstration. Our pressure was slowly increased to ground level and then the hatches were opened and we were allowed to stumble out. It wasn't something that you wanted to do every day. In fact, I had the feeling that one time was once too many; I should have joined the two cadets who had to be removed. They were not washed out since this was not a test, only a demonstration. Their problem was not related to high-altitude pressure but only to being enclosed in a cramped space, a phobia which affects many people. We now had renewed respect for the sailors who manned our submarines.

The rest of the day was spent attending lectures relating to the dangers of high-altitude flying and a demonstration of various types of equipment used in this endeavor. The lectures were given by flight surgeons and we took them seriously since we were all aware that the atmosphere represented an even greater danger to us than that posed by an enemy.

The next day we had free run of the base until our late afternoon briefing at the flight line. Since our return flight was at night, our course was laid out for us. We would fly from Santa Ana to Riverside and pick up the Green east airway, proceed on over Blythe, and eventually break away just before Phoenix with ten planes landing and refueling at Luke Field. The other ten would proceed to Williams Field. After refueling we would continue on the airway south and east to Tucson and Cochise, then leave the airway and proceed on to Douglas.

I was in the group landing at Williams. I knew some cadets at Williams, but our arrival time was around midnight, so it would be impossible to visit anyone.

As we buckled ourselves into the seats I mentioned to the other cadet that I hoped he had as much fun navigating back as I did on the outbound trip. We knew his course would be longer since we were following the airway and he would not be able to take the shortcuts that I had used on the way out. We also knew the night course would keep us away from all the high peaks en route, including San Jacinto and Old Baldy, and was the safer of the two routes.

We fired up the engines and took off just after dark. We knew we were flying a gas guzzler as we compared the fuel used on the way out with some of the other pilots, but we didn't feel this would be a problem. We were assigned an altitude of 9,500 feet on the return flight. This corresponded with eastbound traffic rules on the airway of odd thousands plus 500 feet under visual flight rules. Once on the airway at Riverside we flew on the right side of the civil airway which was deemed to be ten miles wide with a light line running down the center.

We were over halfway to Blythe before we picked up the light line. Wartime regulations prohibited the beacons from being lighted within 150 miles of the coast. The lights were spaced about fifteen miles apart depending on terrain, with each one flashing a code number when viewed from above. The numbers ran from one though nine to zero, each one coded to the nearest ten-mile increment. The first beacon we could identify flashed a number eight which we knew was number eighteen on the airway since the course lights flashed only the last digit of the beacon number.

The airway started at Los Angeles so we knew we were 180 miles from there. All of the beacons were numbered from west to east on the line. Thus the signal would be the same for 80, 180, or 280 miles. Beacons having the same signal would be approximately 100 miles apart. This was a good system as long as you knew which 100-mile segment you were in. Its main drawback was that it was only usable in periods of good weather since it relied on visual contact.

This was a perfect night, not a cloud in the sky with a forecast to remain that way all over the Southwest. We continued to check off the beacons. The other cadet remarked this was so simple it was just like shooting ducks in a rain barrel, and he was right. Only a fool could get lost on a night as beautiful as this. Eventually the lights of Phoenix came into view and there was no reason to identify the beacons any longer.

We chattered about the chamber experience and were glad it was over. The city lights still well ahead in the distance became a sight of beauty, a view which always brought a thrill to a pilot. We decided we would fly toward them until we could see the beacon at Sky Harbor airport, the civilian airport at Phoenix.

All civilian airports were marked by a rotating white and

green beacon. The beacon, which was shaped like a barrel, had a white lens in one end and a green lens in the other. As it rotated through 360 degrees you saw two flashes of light, one green and one white, 180 degrees apart. The military fields were marked with the same kind of beacon but had a white lens in each end and showed two split white beams. Thus it was possible from a long distance to differentiate between civilian and military airports at night.

As we continued on I asked the other cadet how many miles we were from Phoenix. He replied, "I dunno. We can see it so what difference does it make? We'll just fly till we get close, then head for Williams."

"I think you should be keeping a log."

"What for? You kept one on the way out and nobody asked to see it. It's a lot of work for nothing."

"Well, we got there."

"Yeah, and we're going to get to Williams too."

All of a sudden there was a horrendous noise drowning out not only our conversation but the noise from our two engines also. Our airplane was pushed downward by a cushion of air, then started rocking and rolling while I fought to keep it flying straight and level. In the same instant I saw four flaming exhausts which had just passed at an angle overhead and were now streaking away at a tremendous speed. I realized that we were floundering in the prop wash of this huge airplane.

We did not panic but were shocked beyond belief by the sudden appearance of the monolithic craft and its deafening noise. We actually became weak as we realized what could have happened had we been even inches higher. The beautiful night sky, a dwelling place of angels, had suddenly become a black sinister home to the demons and spirits associated with fear and horror. We only wanted to break loose from this inhospitable environment.

How we escaped a midair collision I will never know. This airplane had come at a forty-five degree angle from behind us on the left side of the ship, passing over us so close the distance could not be measured. It was obvious they never saw us as we were overtaken on the airway at the same altitude. The other cadet suggested that maybe we should get off the airway while we were still alive; one near miss was enough. The traffic could only increase as we continued on course. I readily agreed and altered our course to a more southerly direction.

In a few minutes, with the lights of Phoenix still ahead, my partner spotted a military beacon south and east of our course. He immediately exclaimed, "There. That's Williams Field right over there." I responded that I was sure that we were not far enough east yet since I could now see the green and white beacon of Sky Harbor airport still ahead. But his reply was, "That beacon is farther east than you think. Besides there aren't any other airfields in the vicinity except Luke, Sky Harbor, and Williams. That has to be it." With that he threw the maps in the back seat. I altered the course to fly to the airfield but it didn't look right. I still had apprehensions, but since he was the navigator I didn't make any big fuss.

The lights of Phoenix disappeared before we reached the military field. It was farther away than I thought. Eventually we came over the field and I started circling while the copilot called Williams Field for landing instructions. After three attempts and no answer I was sure that either the radio didn't work or we were not where we were supposed to be, or possibly both. On his fourth try the radio crackled to life with the response, "Ship calling Williams tower, this is Gila Bend tower. We hear you loud and clear and believe you are in our pattern. Do you wish landing instructions?"

The copilot asked me if I wanted landing instructions and I asked if he knew where Gila Bend was. He said, "No."

"Well, I don't either. The maps are in the back seat so we had better land and find out where we are."

In just a few minutes we were on the runway. I turned off at the first taxi-strip and headed in the direction of the control tower. As we braked to a stop near the tower a staff car pulled up and an officer with an O.D. (officer of the day) arm band on jumped out, crawled up on the wing and opened the door to the cabin. His first words were, "Welcome to Gila Bend Army Airfield."

We both gasped, "Where's that?"

Remembering the events of the night we weren't surprised

when he said, "Right at the crossroads of hell where the devil bid the owl good-bye."

"Thanks. We suspected as much but we still don't know where that is."

He flipped his flashlight on and picked up our map as I turned on the cabin lights. He took one look at us and said, "Well, look what we've got here: two RONs." This was a reference to a military order which stated that any time a cadet landed at night at a strange field which was not on his itinerary he had to "remain over night" and finish his flight during daylight hours.

We acknowledged that we understood the rules. We explained that we were on our way back to Douglas from Santa Ana and were supposed to land at Williams to refuel. He showed us where Gila Bend was located and said that we had turned off course too early. We were thirty-five miles south of course. It was seventy miles northeast to Williams.

We could now see that he was a first lieutenant. "Look fellows," he said, "I don't want to cause you any trouble. If you want to take off and head for Williams I'll pretend I never saw you and won't make a report."

This was an offer we should have accepted, but after checking the fuel supply, which was low, I wasn't sure I wanted to take the chance. I thanked him but said we had already made one mistake. We could probably make Williams okay but we wouldn't have any reserve and this could be another mistake. Two in one night might be too much.

"You're probably making the right decision, but if I have to refuel you then I have to report you as a matter of record to cover the transaction."

"That's okay. I don't feel we have much choice. Common sense tells me to refuel, spend the night, and proceed in the morning."

"Sounds like a reasonable decision and I don't think anyone can find fault with it."

The other cadet replied, "Sir, you don't know our flight commander."

Giving us a funny look he requested us to shut down the engines and head for the mess hall. I grabbed my pilot's briefcase, crawled out, and joined the other two in the command car. On the way to the mess hall the lieutenant was doing his best to put us at ease. He seemed to enjoy having someone to visit with even though it was only two lowly, lost cadets.

By the time we reached the mess hall he had raised our confidence level 100 percent and we were actually starting to see some humor in our predicament. Once in the mess hall the O.D. shouted to the cook to bring coffee and rustle up some chow for the two hungry fliers. The cook brought the coffee and wanted to know if some Spam, toast, and eggs would be all right. At this point we weren't too hungry, but anything he wanted to fix would be fine. We weren't used to being asked ahead of time whether something would be okay.

As soon as the coffee was poured I asked the lieutenant if he could notify the O.D. at our base at Douglas where we were, assure him everything was all right including the aircraft, and that we would fly out in the morning. He said that he could do that but he had a better idea. He explained that since our flight commander was at Williams maybe it would be better to call there since he would be waiting for us. If he could locate him he undoubtedly would give permission for us to take off and join the group at Williams. Sounded good to us; anything was worth a try. The lieutenant left to make the telephone call while the cook brought out four plates filled with Spam and eggs along with a plateful of toast. The cook joined us at the table expressing an interest in our flight.

Upon the lieutenant's return the four of us pitched in and made quick work of the chow. He explained that he had reached Williams and they were trying to locate the flight commander. In a few minutes a sergeant poked his head in the door and said that the lieutenant had a telephone call. He excused himself saying that he would probably have us airborne in a few minutes. We couldn't get over the relaxed atmosphere, courtesy, and treatment we were receiving. As cadets we just weren't used to being treated like people.

Soon the lieutenant returned and apologetically explained that the flight commander had refused to give permission for us to take off. Instead we were to wait where we were and he would fly down and deal with us personally. It seemed that he had aircraft scattered all over the Southwest. Right now he knew where three airplanes were including ours.

The cook brought out more coffee and we all decided to wait at the mess hall for the flight commander. The lieutenant said he couldn't understand why the captain was so upset. After all, we could be at Williams in a little over half an hour, which would make more sense than having us sit around while we were waiting for him to fly down.

"Lieutenant, we don't know the captain very well as he is not one of our instructors. He is a Flight Operations Officer in administration."

"Well, whatever he is he sounds as if he has a cocklebur under his blanket."

While we were visiting I opened my flight case, spread out the map, and started plotting a course from Gila Bend direct to Douglas. I wanted to make sure that going direct wouldn't force us to fly into Old Baldy in the Tucson area. It turned out to be twenty-five miles south of the course so it didn't appear to be a problem.

I asked the lieutenant if he had been to Douglas. "No," he said. "All of our flying here is out on the gunnery range or towing some darn target sleeve around. Occasionally we get a break and fly to Los Angeles or up to Phoenix, but I guess we're stuck here for the rest of the war. Maybe you fellows will have better luck and get to see some action."

We kept on visiting and drinking coffee for about an hour when a sergeant came in and told the lieutenant there was an airplane in the traffic pattern. The lieutenant told him to take a vehicle down to the flight line, pick up the pilot, and bring him to the mess hall. In just a few minutes the captain made his presence known by banging through the door and asking where the two knuckleheads were. The lieutenant jumped up to meet him and I heard him say, "Hey, take it easy. We have a lot of planes land here thinking it is Williams."

The captain looked at him with contempt and said, "Lieutenant, nobody in his right mind would mistake Gila Bend for Williams. Nobody lands here. This is probably the first transient aircraft that you've seen in six months so don't give me that malarkey."

As he strode over to the table I rose to attention amid a query of, "What do you think you're doing, MISTER Fletcher?"

"I've just finished plotting the course to Douglas, Sir."

"Put your maps away. You don't need a course. Get your tail end in that AT-17 and I'll show you the way home."

"Yes, Sir."

He completely ignored the other cadet and was still sputtering as he went back out and crawled in the jeep with the sergeant. The lieutenant looked at us and said, "The timing just didn't seem right to offer him a cup of coffee. You can count yourselves lucky that you don't have to fly back in the same airplane with him."

With that he proceeded to take us back to the line in the staff car. The refueling crew had just finished with our airplane. As we got out of the staff car one of the crew asked the lieutenant if they were supposed to refuel the AT-17 that had just landed. "No," he dryly responded. "The captain has all the gas he needs."

We thanked the lieutenant for all that he had done for us, saluted, and started to climb aboard. The lieutenant waved and hollered, "Feel free to drop in again anytime." We couldn't think of a pleasant reply because we weren't even sure if we would still be flying after the events of the night were reviewed.

While we were starting up the engines we heard the captain call the tower requesting permission for two AT-17s to taxi to the takeoff position. Permission was granted with the notation that there wasn't any other ground or air activity in the local area. As the captain taxied by he called on the radio for us to follow him. On takeoff he would circle the field and "Mister Fletcher, I want you on my right wing before the circle is completed. If you get more than ten feet away from my wing on the way back to Douglas your flying career is over."

We didn't bother to acknowledge, we just started taxiing behind him. Once we were airborne we swung around to join up in formation and the earphones pulsated with, "Mister Fletcher, what is your position or are you lost again." I radioed back that I was approaching him from behind on the inside of the circle, would pass underneath and pull up on his wing in a couple of minutes. He radioed back, "Mister Fletcher, I hope you are better at formation flying than navigating."

The other cadet remarked, "I think he's just trying to humiliate you." I was doing a slow burn because the other cadet didn't exist in the captain's mind and I was catching all the blame. But I did point out to the other cadet that the captain wasn't trying, he had already succeeded. The more I thought about it the madder I got and kept easing in a little closer. In fact, I had learned that one of the best ways to work off frustration was to fly tight formation. The closer you get to the other ship the more concentration is required. Consequently, you block everything else out of your mind except the navigation light on the wing of the lead aircraft.

The other cadet finally started to fidget and squirm in his seat remarking, "What are you trying to do, Fletch, stick the left wing in his window?" I thought to myself, neither you nor the captain have been much help on this leg so you both can squirm. I'll keep pushing in till someone cries "Uncle."

The closer I got the better I felt and the easier it became to maintain position. In fact, I was just starting to enjoy the cadet's uneasiness when the captain called and said, "Mister Fletcher, do you think you could move out a little bit? The red wing light is blinding my copilot."

The cadet grabbed the mike and with relief in his voice answered, "Yes, Sir." I eased off a little and the other cadet yelled, "You heard his transmission, didn't you?"

"Yeah, but remember he said ten feet and he didn't say which ten feet so I'll use the inside ten."

Eventually the lights of Douglas came into view. As we passed over the airfield the captain came on the radio and in a very sarcastic voice intoned, "Mister Fletcher, do you see those lights beneath us?"

"Yes, Sir."

"Well, that's Douglas Army Airfield. Do you think you can possibly land there without getting lost?"

I jerked the throttles to idle and fell away calling the tower for landing instructions. The other cadet said, "Thank the Lord. I thought you were going to kill us."

"Shut up and quit whining. I have taken the heat on this flight and the first guy that calls me Mister in civilian life is going to have a fight on his hands. In your case it might happen sooner."

Before we could touch down the captain was back on the air proclaiming to anyone within receiving distance of Douglas Army Airfield that the two cadets will report to the squadron commander's office at 10:00 a.m. today. It was now well past 2:00 a.m., but I knew I probably wouldn't sleep too much in the next few hours. I also knew that if by some miracle I finished the course and received a commission I would never ridicule, discipline, or humiliate another person in my command in public or within earshot of someone else. This individual certainly was not my ideal of a commissioned officer, but he had the bars and rank which I could respect, if not the person.

By 8:00 a.m. I was at the flight line where I asked Lieutenant Dye if he could spare some time for a private conversation. He obliged and I told him the whole story including the near miss on the light line, only it was impossible to describe, it had to be experienced before you could relate to the events that followed. I explained that it appeared that I was being held responsible for the whole flight. I didn't know whether I would be around much longer, and I wasn't sure where they dug up the cadet who had been assigned to fly with me.

"Let me give you some advice. First, keep your cool. At this point the Army has too much money invested in your flying career to wash you out on one incident which did not endanger an airplane or personnel. Now be prepared to receive another chewing out. Accept it as coming from a squadron commander who, just like the squadron operations officer, is envious of you because you're probably going on to combat and he is stuck in the training command."

"Maybe they should request a transfer."

"They say they have, but I think if it were granted both would certainly look at their hole cards a long time before they made a bet. Now about the cadet that went with you. He is a holdover from I-class who had some problems with navigation and this was his chance to get back on schedule and graduate with J-class. That information you can use if you want to, but remember this: As your instructor my input would be needed before anyone could wash you out for something that involves flying. Insubordination or discipline problems are a different matter—I wouldn't be consulted. So go get your chewing out and then we'll get on with your flying."

"I hope you're right. Anyway, I feel better about the meeting."

At 10:00 I reported to the squadron commander's office. The other cadet was already waiting when I arrived. The first sergeant informed us that the squadron commander would see us one at a time. I was first and he ushered me into the commander's office. After salutes were exchanged I was ordered to stand at ease. The commander stated that he understood that I had had some problems on the cross-country which probably involved some errors in judgment and a demonstrated lack of knowledge in navigation. Did I care to recount what happened?

I explained that in briefing for the trip out I was assigned the position of copilot and navigator. We had flown the course making every checkpoint on time. Our positions were switched on the return trip. We hit our checkpoints on schedule and eventually we saw the lights of Phoenix. I had no intention of telling about the near collision and the part it played in our leaving the airway. I had explained it to Lieutenant Dye and he was the only person who would hear the story. Maybe it was tantamount to admitting fear, but you had to experience it to fully appreciate what happened. Words would only fall on deaf ears and true feelings could never be transmitted.

At the mention of the lights the captain interjected, "I know exactly what happened. I can see the two of you right now in the cockpit. You saw the lights of Phoenix and thought you had it made so you tossed the maps in the back seat and flew to the nearest military beacon."

His insight unnerved me somewhat but I managed to say, "Well, that's not quite the way it happened. The other cadet chose the beacon and we flew there. It was my understanding that I was responsible for the navigation to Santa Ana and he was responsible for the trip home."

That was as far as I got before he exploded with, "Mister Fletcher, the pilot in the left seat is always responsible for anything that happens on an airplane or where it flies and is held accountable for every action. Now I gather you are trying to shift the blame on the copilot."

"No, Sir. This is the first time anyone has ever mentioned this accountability. It has never been mentioned before at briefing or any other time. This was described as a lesson in navigation in which each one of us was assigned a certain area of responsibility. I am not trying to shift the blame, I'm only telling you what happened as you requested."

"You have just violated the cardinal rule of navigation: how to get from here to there without going somewhere else. Now go ahead with your version."

At this point I knew any further discussion was impossible, I was already pegged the loser. I relied on the one thing that everyone in the military understood. I came to attention, fixed my gaze on the wall just above the commander's head and replied, "Sir, in the light of what you have just told me about accountability I have nothing further to add. I accept full responsibility for what happened and the consequence that goes with it. I have no excuse, Sir."

This brought on a seemingly endless, vehement lecture on responsibility and leadership, but the only part that really registered was "dismissed." I saluted and got out before my ears burned off. Before I reached the headquarters door I heard the first sergeant tell the other cadet he was free to go as the squadron commander had no desire to speak to him.

When I got back to the ready room Lieutenant Dye inquired how the confrontation had gone. I explained that he was looking at one well chewed-out cadet who probably wouldn't be able to sit down for a week. "Did he mention any disciplinary measures?"

"I don't think so. The mind can only retain so much abuse before it blocks everything out, but I did hear him say dismissed. Beyond that I'm not sure what happened."

"Well, it's obvious that is the end of it because the captain has a way of making sure that you not only know but understand any further consequences. The incident is closed. The choice you have now is do you want to go tell it to the chaplain or fly the Link trainer?"

"I'll take the Link. The chaplain probably has enough trouble of his own."

The Santa Ana trip was the last major event before graduation. We were soon informed that upon graduation we would receive a $250 clothing allowance. It would take time to order and alter uniforms for a class the size of ours. Since the base clothing store had a very limited selection and rather poor quality, most of us chose to use Levy's Military Shop in the town of Douglas. These people offered good service and carried a top line of military apparel for both officers and enlisted men. They also had a monopoly and were assured a good business with a new class graduating every four and a half weeks. Two weeks before graduation my uniforms arrived and were altered to a perfect fit. Now all that remained was to make sure I didn't foul up and get the axe before graduation since these uniforms were sold on the basis of no returns or refunds after alteration.

Graduation day was set for Wednesday, November 3, 1943. A cadet graduation party was scheduled for the evening of November 2 at the base officer's club. Wives and girlfriends were invited to attend a buffet dinner and an evening of dancing. The end was in sight; the brass ring was within reach. Most of us were amazed that we had survived and were now just days away from the goal which we had hoped to attain: the winning of the coveted silver pilot wings of the U.S. Army Air Force.

My last flight was set for the day of the cadet party. It was an instrument cross-country. I had practiced the flight several times in the Link trainer so was quite familiar with the procedure involved. All I had to do now was actually fly the course under the hood and all my training requirements would be met.

Reporting to the flight line I was assigned an airplane and Lieutenant Dye wanted to know if I understood the mission. I told him that upon takeoff from Douglas I would fly to Cochise, let down on the auxiliary field there, pull up and go to Rodeo, let down on the field there, again pull up and come back to Douglas utilizing all three radio ranges. Upon arrival over the Douglas range I could come out from under the hood and land. My flying would be done and I would get ready for the graduation party.

"You've got it. Get going."

I was flying with another cadet I did not know who was the observer. After takeoff I went under the hood and the observer flew around for a little while. I shielded my eyes so I couldn't see either the compass or the directional gyro. When the observer felt that he had flown long enough to confuse me in regard to location I took over, tuned in the Cochise radio range, then turned to an average bisector heading corresponding to the N quadrant, which was the signal I heard. Using the following procedure I switched off the automatic volume control, flying the chosen bisector until I could determine whether the signal grew stronger or weaker. If it was stronger I would know that I was headed in the direction of the beam and the station. But it turned out the signal was fading so I knew I was flying away from the station and proceeded to make a 180 degree turn.

Once on the beam I flew to the station and entered the cone of silence which is directly over the station. At this point I turned to the heading leading to the auxiliary field at Cochise, at the same time setting up a rate of descent which would place me in a position to land if I had worked the problem correctly. At 500 feet above the ground the observer took over, added full power, and we climbed back up to altitude. At this point I removed the hood to see how successful I had been. We were right over the field. I went back under the hood, tuned in the Rodeo range and, since my position was now known, flew east on the west leg to Rodeo. Once over the station, I took the southbound heading to the airfield. As we descended to 500 feet the observer opened the throttles screaming, "Get out from under the hood. We just lost the number two engine."

I jerked down the curtain that separated us in the cockpit as

well as those covering the windows and tossed them back behind us. We were at 400 feet, just short of the field but too
high to land straight ahead. The nose was high and the airspeed dangerously low. I grabbed the yoke, lowered the nose
to gain airspeed, then standing on the rudder rolled in rudder
trim to counteract the loss of the right engine. The number
one engine was at full throttle. The wooden butter paddles
which served as a propeller on the number one engine were
churning the air while the number two propeller was windmilling, creating considerable drag. Both were very inefficient
airfoils. I realized we could not maintain our altitude but only
stretch the glide. Immediately I decided to make a 360 degree
turn to the left into the good engine which, if successful, was
the shortest way to set up a landing approach. I asked the
other cadet if he had seen any aircraft in the vicinity. He answered that the field was deserted. He had seen only one aircraft in the air but it was well beyond the airfield.

Then he queried, "Do you want to make the landing just
coming out from under the hood?"

"You better believe it. I have it on good authority that the
left seat is responsible for the airplane. Don't worry, if we
don't make it you won't be held accountable."

By now we were halfway around the turn and still had 300
feet of altitude left. We continued flying the wide almost flat
turn which provided the best lift possible with the airspeed
below cruise speed, but well above stalling speed. As we finished the turn we had 200 feet between us and the hard
ground. I hollered at the other cadet to make sure his safety
belt was cinched tight just in case we didn't make the field.
The ground was level enough if we had to land short, but
there was a six-foot fence which served as the airport boundary and kept range livestock off the landing area.

I kept holding pressure on the throttle to keep it wide open
and hopefully eke just a little more power out of the engine.
In a few seconds I was positive if we didn't hit a down draft we
would make the field. I asked the other cadet to roll out the
trim when I gave him the signal which would be just as I
started to reduce power, but I wanted to get over the fence

first. We were now below 100 feet and the fence posts looked like trees.

Before we reached the boundary the other cadet hollered, "Fletch, there's another plane landing from the opposite direction."

I yelled back, "I see him, but the field is wide enough for both of us. I'll hold as close as I can to the right fence. Roll out the trim now. We're over the fence." I hauled the throttle closed and we touched down, a good 300 feet inside the field. On the roll-out we were about 100 feet from the right fence. As the other airplane rolled past on our left we waved to two surprised pilots.

As we braked to a stop I decided to taxi a little closer to the fence so as not to pose a hazard to anyone else landing. This proved to be wishful thinking as the airplane would not taxi on the grass field. It would only pivot in a circle. I tried holding the outside brake, then it wouldn't move at all. The old butter paddles just blew dust while the engine made noise. It was obvious we were trapped where we were. We shut down the engine and crawled out.

The other cadet said, "Fletch, I was sorta worried there for a few minutes. I wasn't sure whether the Bobcat would make it or not."

"That was sort of foolish, you know, worrying about it."

"What do you mean?"

"Well, I was worrying enough for both of us. Our Polecat turned out to be a real stinker. What a way to finish our last flight."

By now the other airplane had taxied up to us and the instructor was crawling out. We felt good because we could see that there was only one other person in the airplane which meant there was room for us to fly home. The instructor came over, commenting, "Fellas, looks like you've got problems."

"Yes, Sir, we just lost the number two engine and would sure appreciate a ride home."

Our hopes were dashed as he answered, "No, you guys stay with the airplane and when I get back to Douglas I will send somebody back for you."

I interjected, "Hey, wait a minute. Nobody is going to steal this airplane with an engine out. It won't even taxi, let alone fly."

"MISTER, you heard what I said. Stay with your airplane."

Again it was, "Yes, Sir" verbally, but if he knew what we were thinking we would have been court-martialed on the spot.

He proceeded to take off and left us in a cloud of dust. It was almost 3:00 and we had hoped to be back at Douglas by 4:00. Happy Hour preceding the party was scheduled to begin at 6:30. Sherry had already made arrangements to ride out to the field with Mrs. Foley. They were one of the few who had a car. In fact, she was bringing a carload including Mrs. Ellsworth, Mrs. Fisher, and Mrs. Gassman.

We sat around hoping another plane would land with a more charitable pilot on board, but there didn't appear to be any air traffic at all. As far as we knew, with the exception of ourselves, only K-class was scheduled for flying. We knew we were only forty-five miles from Douglas so it wouldn't take long for somebody to fly up and pick us up. In the meantime, we kicked the tires and spun the prop on the number two engine. It moved easily with grinding sounds; obviously it was no longer connected to the crankshaft.

Five o'clock came and passed and still no ride home. We were sitting on a deserted field feeling sorry for ourselves when the other cadet piped up with, "What if that blankety blank instructor forgot to notify anyone about us?"

A few minutes before 6:00 we could hear an airplane in the distance. We grabbed our pilot cases, slammed the door shut on our crippled plane and watched as the AT-17 settled onto the field. The airplane braked to a stop a few feet away from us. We clambered on board and buckled into the back seat. The plane was piloted by two stern looking lieutenants, strangers to both of us. There was no sign of greeting. Finally over the roar of the engines the other cadet remarked that we weren't sure after waiting three hours that anyone was coming to pick us up. He didn't get an answer so we flew back to the base in silence. I didn't care whether they spoke or not but was surprised they didn't ask about the airplane or express some interest in what had happened. This was just one of the many times in cadet training that nothing made sense.

As we crawled out of the plane at Douglas one of the lieutenants said, "Mister Fletcher, you're to report to the squadron commander at 8:00 in the morning."

"Yes, Sir."

That was the total conversation. But who cares, this is party night. I ran all the way to the barracks, which were deserted as everyone was at Happy Hour. I quickly showered, shaved, and donned my new uniform.

It was 7:30 when I walked in the door at the Officers Club. There were cadets, wives, and girlfriends everywhere. Everyone seemed to be talking in whispers. I thought I was going to a party, but the atmosphere was more fitting of a mortuary. I looked for Sherry and our friends, but they were obviously obscured in the crowd. I finally decided that there must be some officers present and that was putting a damper on the crowd. They had told us the club was reserved strictly for graduating cadets and their guests, but the usual exuberance of the cadet corps was missing. Oh well, the thing to do was locate my friends and get the party rolling.

As I started walking through the area I received some startled, questioning looks. The same kind that would greet you walking into a party with your fly unzipped. I had dressed in a hurry but I knew I was safe on that count. There was no reason to check. I spotted Sherry and the others seated at a round table in a far corner of the club. Then I saw Larry Gassman leaving the punch bowl carrying drinks to the table. I hurried over and asked if I could help. He turned around and his grim expression mirrored surprise, then a big grin. "You better believe it, Buddy. Where in the hell have you been?"

"Well, all afternoon and early evening I've been sitting in the cow pasture called Rodeo auxiliary field with an engine out waiting for someone to come and pick me up."

"Then you haven't heard?"

"Heard what?"

"We lost an AT-17 this afternoon and two cadets were killed, but nobody knows who they are because the names have not been released. When you didn't show up people were starting to jump to conclusions. Get over to the table and make your presence known. Sherry and the rest are worried sick."

In that instant all of the unusual actions of the afternoon fell into place. Further discussion brought out the fact that most people knew two airplanes were missing, one from J-class and the other from K-class. With my arrival all J-class planes were accounted for. This meant the missing aircraft carried two underclassmen. The party continued on a lighter note, but was far from the lively celebration we had all anticipated.

The following morning at 8:00 I reported to the squadron commander and his demeanor was still adversarial, consistent with our last confrontation over the Gila Bend blunder. But this time I was not the scared cadet who had previously been cowed in his presence. In three hours I would be a commissioned officer. This time my eyes locked on his in the stare down.

He started off with a barrage of questions regarding the engine instruments, namely oil pressure and other readings before engine failure. I could only give one answer. "I don't know, Sir. I was under the hood and all engine instruments are located on the right-hand side of the panel, unavailable to me. I don't know what the readings were. I can only tell you what they were after the engine malfunctioned."

"In other words you let ice build up in the carburetor until the engine, starved for fuel and air, conked out."

"Sir, I learned about carburetor ice long before I joined the cadet corps. How many cases of carburetor ice have you seen in seventy-degree temperature? We reported a mechanical malfunction and that is what we had. We also know the propeller is not connected to the crankshaft, a fact which can be verified by pulling the propeller through several revolutions."

He lowered his eyes, rattled the papers on his desk and harshly ordered, "MISTER Fletcher, you are dismissed."

There wasn't time to go back to the barracks as all graduating cadets were scheduled to pass in review at nine. I headed for the parade ground, but on the way I couldn't help but think about the egotistical captain and his carburetor ice bluster. There wasn't anything in his personality that could let him believe that a cadet could do anything right. I felt we had done a good job making the emergency landing. The airplane was intact sitting on an airfield and would fly again, but the captain could not bring himself to acknowledge that something must have been done right. It was a good lesson for me as I made another mental note: If you are going to criticize and chastise a poor performance then you have the obligation to recognize and compliment that which is out of the ordinary.

At 9:00 sharp we passed in review and then were arranged alphabetically in a single line on the parade grounds. It was explained that we would walk by several tables. At the first we would sign our resignation from the cadet corps. At the second table we would receive orders showing our appointment as officers, sign the oath of office, then at the next table receive orders which placed us on flying status with the rating of pilot. At the last table we would receive our new assignment orders.

As the front of the line moved past the tables a controversy started to develop. Word was quickly passed down the line that we were not receiving the Regular Army commission which was promised in our original enlistment papers. I asked some of the fellows what that meant and why we were being denied that which was promised. One cadet replied, "It means we are the bastard sons. They need us but no one wants to accept responsibility for us so they have created a temporary army in which we receive temporary appointments for the duration plus six months."

There was a little acrimony as the cadets realized they were being short-changed and stated their objections as they passed the tables, but no one was refusing. Then all of a sudden the line was halted. Apparently one of the administrative officers, fearing the worst, decided that the first two tables should be switched.

The table order now was: You signed the oath of office, received your appointment, and then signed your resignation from the cadet corps. This was an apparent violation since you were not allowed to hold two offices at one time, but it also meant that you couldn't sign a resignation from cadets and walk away without accepting the commission that was offered. This official certainly didn't understand the aviation cadet when he panicked and switched tables. We were there because we wanted the silver wings which allowed us to fly. We had a legitimate gripe, but we would have signed anything that granted us the privilege of flying. This was our primary goal; everything else was secondary.

The line started to move again and when I finally reached the first table I read the paper placed before me. It stated that I was appointed a temporary second lieutenant in the Army of the United States (Air Force). The line above, which read second lieutenant Air Corps in the Officers Reserve Corps, was crossed out, as well as the line below which read Flight Officer Army of the United States (Air Corps). The officer remarked, "Come on, sign the paper and keep the line moving."

My answer was, "I've learned to read everything before I sign and even that doesn't mean anything."

After every one of our group, which was now 237 in number, had progressed through the line we gathered at 11:00 in the Post Theater where we were presented our wings. After the oath of office was administered, the graduating class sang the Air Corps Song (which was only a different version of the one the cadet wives had been singing for months):

> Off we go leaving our homes back yonder
> Into the lands we never knew
> Joining those who we love and cherish
> And we're both loyal and true.
> We have known plenty of joy and sadness
> And we'll stay ready for more
> We have no dough but still we know
> We'll always follow the Army Air Corps.

> With such pay there's no way
> For us to lead a happy normal life
> And you'll find there's no kind
> Of work to get when you're a cadet wife
> There's never any rooms within the town
> The Army looks upon us with a frown
> Still we go, cause we know our husbands are
> The Army Air Corps.

Silver pilot wings were presented to 239 members. The increase represented the two student officers who were a part of the class. It was a moment of sincere pride when Sherry pinned the silver wings and gold bars on my blouse. She was a popular lady as several of our single friends asked that she do the same for them. During this little ritual I was amazed to see Larry Luzader, my friend during Preflight, cross the stage and receive his wings. I had not seen him since Santa Ana and did not realize he was on the field. He disappeared in the crowd and, unfortunately, we were not able to meet.

It was a real melee as everyone hurried to clear the theater and get off the base. We were authorized a ten-day delay en route and every minute that ticked by at Douglas was one less we would have at home. We bolted from the theater with the speed of a bride and a groom leaving the altar and heading for the honeymoon.

Outside the theater many of the top ranking NCOs (noncommissioned officers) were waiting. They were well aware of the old custom that a newly commissioned officer would present a dollar bill to the first man to salute him after commissioning. As Sherry and I ran out the door the sergeants were saluting as fast as the right arm could move while the left held a sheaf of bills. Not wishing to patronize the money grabbers we ducked our heads and kept on moving in the crowd, ignoring the flapping arms.

We finally disengaged from the group and within a block from the theater a young corporal rendered a salute as I responded, "Corporal, do you know what happens to a soldier when a commissioned officer is saluted for the first time?"

Startled, he froze in place with eyes as large as saucers, "No, Sir, I do not."

"Well, custom dictates that the officer is required to present him with a dollar bill." With that I handed him the bill. He looked very perplexed but took the dollar and saluted again. "Hey, no seconds. On your way, soldier." He broke into a grin and continued on his way. I wondered what his story would sound like as he would surely recount this strange encounter to his friends.

We had known about the delay en route after graduation

for several weeks. Sherry had managed to purchase two train tickets to Salt Lake City, where we had made arrangements to meet Cap and Sis. From there we would continue on in their car to visit our families in southeast Washington. Cap, who had also been flying AT-17s, graduated at Altus, Oklahoma, in the Gulf Coast Flying Training Command and we received our commissions and wings the same day. We had lots to be thankful for as well as to celebrate as it was a milestone passed for the four of us.

Our Texas friends, the Foleys, accommodated by transporting us and our baggage to the train station for a late afternoon departure before they headed for Corpus Christi. The Army had issued me a new watch, a pilot's briefcase filled with navigation computers and other pilot aids along with a fleece-lined flying suit complete with boots, a backpack parachute, oxygen mask, helmet, goggles, and other related flying articles. Not knowing what to do with all this equipment, which was packed in a large bag, I finally decided to have it shipped by Railway Express to Sherry's parents' home in Tekoa.

We boarded the dirtiest coach car that I had ever seen in service in the railroad system. The coaches were filled to overflowing with a raunchy-looking group of individuals. All were wearing dingy, civilian clothes. Sprawled over the seats and in the aisles, they looked and acted like refugees from a chain gang. They were slovenly and raucous. Since there weren't any seats available we moved to the end of the coach, plunked our suitcases down, and used them for seats. The group pretty much ignored us but we weren't entirely comfortable in their presence. They weren't the kind of people who would offer a lady their seat and I wasn't about to suggest it.

After about an hour of bumping along the rails a sergeant entered the car. Seeing the two of us he hurried over and said, "Sir, why are you sitting in the aisle?"

"Well, Sergeant, the train appears to be overloaded and this seems to be the only space available."

"I'll fix that in a hurry." With that he moved to the end seat in the coach and the occupants immediately disappeared into the next car. He returned and helped us move our bags to the vacant seat. As we moved in he leaned over and in a low voice stated, "I'm sorry, Sir, that you had to sit in the aisle. We just ran these draftees out of the bayou and we're headed for boot camp in California. By the time I get them in uniform and I've had them for two weeks they'll not only be broke to lead but will have enough manners to offer a lady a seat as well as show respect for an officer."

We were a little overwhelmed with the encounter, but I was sure the tech sergeant knew what he was talking about, and if these young men even suspected what the next few weeks held in store for them they would probably jump train.

As we settled back in the seat I opened my briefcase and sorted through the papers as well as my thoughts about the past few days. It dawned on me that I had not been able to say good-bye or thank you to a very fine instructor, Lieutenant Dye. The realization that I would no longer be scurrilously referred to as MISTER started to register. By an Act of Congress and an order by the President I was now an officer and a gentleman. I made a solemn vow never to violate this trust. I would find a way to carry out my duties in a manner consistent with the characterization of both. I had seen examples of the best and the worst. I knew which I would emulate.

Going through the orders I was surprised at some of the assignments. Ninety-four members were ordered to report to the Eighteenth Replacement Wing at Salt Lake City. These men were destined to become copilots. The list included my friend Lieutenant Luzader and the student officers, plus three officers who were already stationed at Douglas. The cadet who had flown to Santa Ana with me received a Flight Officer's commission and was also on the list. In all, thirteen out of the twenty-two who came from Lancaster, including Lieutenant Gadga, were subject to this order.

Five lieutenants were sent to Del Rio, Texas, for B-26 training, twelve were ordered to the Central Instructor School at Randolph Field, Texas. Lieutenant Ellsworth, the only other person from our Portland days, was in this group.

Four went to Selman Field, Louisiana, for unspecified duties. Seven were sent to Albuquerque, New Mexico, for B-24 Transition and twenty to Mather Field, California, for B-25 Transition. Seventeen stayed on the base at Douglas to be trained as instructors or whatever. Forty-seven were sent to Hobbs, New Mexico, for B-17 Transition.

Thirty-six of us were ordered to report to Roswell, New Mexico, for B-17 Transition training. All of the assignees for transition training knew they were being trained as first pilots in their respective aircraft. Our friends Lieutenants Foley, Fisher, and Gassman were included in this list, so the wives could look forward to another nine weeks of shared company.

I had received 26 hours and 30 minutes dual time, 52 hours and 20 minutes solo pilot time, plus 48 hours of copilot time for a total of 126 hours and 50 minutes in the AT-17. I had now flown 271 hours and 50 minutes in military aircraft.

Oh yes, Mr. Pulici, you can perform both forward and side-slips in the AT-17. In fact, it responds to these maneuvers very well.

6 B-17 Transition and Crew Assignment

The dirty coal-burning train chugged into Los Angeles station about 9:00 a.m. The train was behind schedule which was probably normal, but it meant we had missed our connection and nothing else was scheduled until the following day. I ran to a phone booth and called the bus station, hoping that we could avert the long delay and continue on by bus. The station agent said the bus to Salt Lake City was due to leave in five minutes and only one seat was available. I immediately replied that I was a military flyer traveling on government orders and was accompanied by my wife. He stammered a bit and then said they would hold the bus for fifteen minutes and there would be two seats.

We hailed a cab and in a few minutes were at the bus station. I paid for the tickets while the driver loaded our two bags. Boarding the bus we found two seats, one in the middle and the other near the back. Within an hour after leaving the station the person sitting next to Sherry offered to change seats with me so we could sit together. Maybe the bars and wings brought some compassion from the bus load of civilians.

It was a long overnight drive to Salt Lake City. We arrived in the afternoon and were to meet Cap and Sis at Sherry's brother's home. He was an Army Air Force captain with the supply department stationed at one of the bases in the area. In civilian life he was a food broker but now he was a purchasing agent buying for the military. We had never met, so I wanted to make a good first impression. As we got off the bus we realized we were a mess. I was still in tan summer uniform which had changed color with smoke and coal dust from the train, and a two-day growth of beard did not enhance my military profile. I was out of uniform for the area, cold, shivering, and dirty. The snow was about six inches deep.

We decided it would be best to rent a hotel room and clean up. That would also allow me to get into the proper uniform before being picked up by the military police. We tried two hotels but there were no rooms available. At the third I was sure we were in luck because a man was filling out a guest card at the front desk. When he finished I told the clerk we would like to register for a room but his reply was that the gentleman ahead of us had rented their last vacant room. Then I asked if it was possible to rent a room they might be holding for someone just long enough for us to bathe, clean up, and change into winter uniform. The clerk was sorry but he could not help us.

The gentleman who had just rented the room heard the conversation, stepped up to the desk, laid his key on the counter, and asked the clerk to let us use his room long enough to clean up. I offered to pay for towels and whatever was necessary. The clerk smiled and said the arrangement was all right with the management and they would have the housemaid clean up after us and supply the gentleman with clean towels at no charge to either of us. It was the least they could do for a military flyer and his wife.

We used the room and upon leaving thanked both the gentleman and the clerk for their hospitality. They seemed pleased to have helped. The silver wings employed magic qualities which were now becoming apparent. Anyway, before the day was over, clean-shaven and dressed in the proper winter uniform, I was able to meet Sherry's brother and his lovely wife and daughter. Cap and Sis arrived shortly after 6:30. We were all treated to a delicious dinner. Then the four of us loaded into a Champion Studebaker and started a nonstop, rotating drivers drive to Dayton.

On the way home I read Cap's orders. He had been assigned to the Central Instructor's School at Randolph Field,

San Antonio, Texas. We both had the same reporting date, 15 November 1943. His orders read that "dependents will not accompany or later join the officer at this station."

During our time with Sherry's folks in Tekoa I went to the train depot and reshipped all of my flying gear back to Roswell. We had several days of visiting friends and relatives, then all too soon it was time to travel again.

Since Sis could not return with us the three of us started our around-the-clock drive south. We entered Roswell about 4:00 p.m. November 14 in the middle of a snowstorm. We stopped at the first motel in sight and by good fortune they had one vacancy. We very hurriedly removed our bags from Cap's Studebaker and bid him good-bye and good luck. He was due at Randolph Field the following day.

While we were moving our bags in, Lieutenant Norment Foley and his wife, whose nickname was Bill, pulled in looking for a place to stay. The motel was now filled so they drove off to continue their search. About nine that evening there was a knock on the door; the Foleys were back. They had not been able to find lodging and it was too cold and late to continue looking. Luckily we had two double beds separated by a wall divider so they could spend the night with us. It was an invitation they could not refuse.

The next morning Sherry and Bill toured the town looking for a home for the Foleys while Norment and I caught the bus for Roswell Army Airfield. After signing in we went down to the flight line to inspect the airplanes which we had now been assigned to fly. We were very impressed by the four-engine "Flying Fortress." It seemed almost too large to fly.

While we looked in disbelief at this aluminum-covered flying machine we were approached by a very proud crew chief who offered to guide us through his airplane. We accepted his offer and crawled into the largest cockpit we had ever seen. The crew chief very patiently explained in great detail the many mechanical features of the plane. His hands caressed the controls and his soft voice conveyed a sense of pride and love as he explained the various controls and their functions.

It didn't take him long to overload our minds as he related the specifications of the B-17F: gross weight 55,000 pounds, a

crew of ten men, wingspan of almost 104 feet and a length of
approximately 75 feet, powered by four Wright-Cyclone engines each capable of producing 1,200 horsepower and a top
speed of 310 miles per hour. These numbers were beyond
comprehension compared to the twin-engine AT-17. The
jump in horsepower from 490 to 4,800 was almost ten times
and every feature seemed to correspond to this same ratio. It
was truly a mechanical marvel. To say we were overwhelmed
would be a gross understatement. Here was an airplane that
could fly for over ten hours, but there was no pilot's relief
tube.

We could hardly wait to get home to tell Bill and Sherry
what we had seen. When we finally exhausted their listening
span and they were allowed to converse they explained that
no housing could be found, so the spare bedroom invitation
was again extended. It turned out to be an arrangement
which lasted nine weeks.

The next day we turned in all of the flying equipment we
had shipped from Douglas. In classic army tradition it was the
wrong issue.

Classes got underway immediately and we found that we
had very little time for socializing even though we lived off the
base. Drill and physical training were dropped, but new
classes were added as we continued to learn about airframes,
power plants, and all the mechanical marvels installed on the
"17." A working knowledge was required of every system: mechanical, electrical, and hydraulic.

We met our flying instructors and again I was assigned to
one of the finest flight instructors on the field. He was a very
patient man who understood human nature just as well as he
understood the mechanics of the airplane. He could teach
anyone to fly the airplane whether they wanted to or not. In
my case that was a plus since I was not happy looking forward
to being responsible for nine other men. We had been told in
cadet schools that the small men would become fighter pilots
due in part to the small size of the cockpit. Wanting to be
responsible for only myself, I was still dreaming of a twin-
engine P-38 and its crew of one.

I started griping and suggesting that maybe a transfer was

possible from the first moment we met. He took it all in stride and told me I was sent there because they thought I had leadership qualities and would make a good first pilot. But I didn't want flattery. I wanted a transfer to a P-38 fighter school and I kept on griping. Finally he told me that he would reluctantly sign my request for a transfer but that I would be making a big mistake. Most people wanted a command and here I was trying to turn one down, even though I was making good progress flying an airplane which many pilots would love to fly.

Together we filled out the request for a transfer, both signed it, and sent it to the squadron commander for approval. The next day as I was going down a deserted hall in Squadron Operations, I had just passed the Instructors' Room when I heard someone call "Lieutenant Fletcher." I turned around and saw a major standing in the doorway with a paper in his hand. He was just about my height and build, certainly not any bigger.

I immediately came to attention and held the salute. In a very nasty manner he stated, "Don't bother to salute me." Then he said, "I understand you can't fly the B-17."

I answered, "What do you mean I can't fly the B-17?"

Then he waved the request for transfer under my nose. "This paper means you can't. When you asked for a transfer it told me you can't do the job and are trying to shirk your responsibilities."

By now I was red-faced and trying to explain that I would like to fly fighters and it had nothing to do with my lack of ability to pilot a bomber. He kept on needling me to the point that if I hadn't been outranked I would have taken a swing at him. After a few more exchanges I lost my temper, looked him in the eye, and said, "You learned to fly the B-17, didn't you?"

He said, "Yes."

Completely out of control, I stated that I felt I was every bit the man that he was and if he could do it I could do it. Probably even better.

At this point, with a cynical smile, he tore the transfer in half, handed it to me, and said, "Good, now we will see whether you can." Then he spun on his heel and disappeared, leaving me shocked as I looked at the two pieces of paper. At this instant my instructor appeared and asked what happened.

Very sheepishly I said, "I think I just flunked Psychology 101."

With a smile he answered, "I know. I heard. And I'll tell you one thing, we better get busy because you are going to fly a check ride with him before you leave here." A note was made for the mental file as I learned another valuable lesson which I hoped would help me through a flying career and perhaps stay with me the rest of my life. It was essentially this: No matter how mad you get, don't let it affect your judgment. In other words, if you're going to race your motor, keep your brain working and take your mouth out of gear.

While the bar and wings seemed to hold magical qualities in the civilian sector, on the airfield we were still low man on the totem pole. The rank of second lieutenant was not a solution as we had hoped, it was only the beginning of the problem. With no recourse and the blunder of the day clearly in focus, I knew I had to exert every effort to become the best that my physical and mental limitations would allow. The old challenge of competition in the air, on the ground, and in the classroom returned. If I had to be a commander, those who would eventually fly with me were certainly entitled to the best that I could muster.

Learning to fly the "17" was hard work. We practiced emergency engine-out procedures which required maximum physical stamina to fly without trim control and manhandle a huge airplane whose controls were only aided somewhat by using natural opposing forces. The instructor worked our tails off but in a positive, constructive manner. We were challenged on every flight and in a matter of days I realized that the squadron commander was a very shrewd, knowing individual who knew how to motivate.

It wasn't long until I could relate to the attachment that the crew chief had shown for his big bird. The airplane captured our imagination and affection. We soon realized its capabilities far exceeded our imaginations. Its forgiving ways with student pilots brought admiration and a sense of security which no other airplane could match.

Lieutenant Foley and I had a ball as we tried to out-fly one another on our numerous buddy rides. Each demanded more and more of the other as we rotated from left to right seat. We picked the brain of every person who flew with us, including the instructor flight engineers whose total mechanical knowledge was tested on more than one occasion.

The second lieutenant syndrome vanished as we realized that it was the silver wings which provided us the opportunity to fly this "Queen of the Skies." Flying the left seat of the airplane elevated our status in our own eyes far beyond the meager rank pinned upon our shoulders.

As our flying progressed the group commander stated that we would not receive any leave time before reporting to our next station. But if everyone would cooperate and we fulfilled our requirements ahead of time we would be allowed to leave early and perhaps have two or three days extra travel time. This incentive caused everyone in Group Two to push to the limits.

Eventually it was time to fly the final check ride with the squadron commander. By this time we had both overcome the emotions of our first confrontation. It was a clear victory for him for he had kept his command intact. It was also a victory for me in that I was now flying an airplane in which I could exhibit pride and affection. Much of this confidence came from the fact that I could lose two engines and still be able to fly. Certainly there had to be safety in numbers.

The major had also demonstrated that he was too much of a gentleman to allow a petty squabble to affect his personality and judgment. But this is not to say that I got off easy on the check ride. In fact, my check lasted an hour longer than the others.

Yes, Mr. Pulici, I even demonstrated a forward slip in the B-17 and it responded perfectly. The major's only comment was, "We don't usually use or teach that maneuver, but you're going to a combat theater where you will have to use every maneuver you know in order to survive. That is the sole purpose of your training."

We were scheduled to finish on January 19 so it was a happy group that assembled in the base theater January 16 with all requirements satisfied. We knew we were going to hear the magic words "Well done. You have finished early and have earned two extra days."

The group commander was a major who enjoyed the respect of all present. He mounted the stage and explained that we had met our goal, but he was not able to deliver the promise that he had made earlier. In fact, we were going to be delayed one day longer than our original departure date. The base was to be inspected by a general from Headquarters Training Command, and a formation fly-over was to be performed by the members of the graduating class so the general could judge the quality of the training we had received. He knew he had raised our expectations and was proud of our performance but now he was forced to renege. He hoped we would understand and accept his apologies and recognize that he was subject to orders just the same as we were.

Everyone was disappointed and groaning, but one individual could not contain himself and yelled "bull shit!" which rang out like a bomb going off. Well, this was a definite lack of taste on the part of the second lieutenant and it was too much for the major. He called us all to attention and told us we would remain that way until the guilty party identified himself. After about ten minutes at attention the major said he was prepared to keep us all night if necessary, but he did hate to punish everyone just to get at the guilty party.

In a matter of a few minutes a fellow lieutenant and good friend stepped forward and confessed that he was the one who uttered the profanity in the heat of the moment. He said he was sorry, but he didn't want to see anyone else punished for his indiscretions. "Besides," he said, "I only said out loud what everyone else was thinking," which was, in essence, the truth.

The major requested that all be seated, with the exception of the guilty lieutenant, and he proceeded to give him the lecture and tongue lashing he had coming. When it appeared that everything was going to be resolved by another public apology to the major as well as to all present, another major from out of the crowd came up on the stage and told the commander that he should court-martial the culprit. A lively argument ensued while we were all sitting there with our mouths agape wondering what was going to happen. It was bad enough to be embarrassed by a member of our own group, but to be subjected to this verbal exchange by our superiors was more than we anticipated or wanted to hear. It had never occurred to us that there could be dissension above the level of a lieutenant.

Finally the group commander had enough. He turned to the second and replied that he understood why we were upset; he had made a promise which he couldn't deliver and he was sorry too. But he had orders and we would fly the formation. This we thought would end the controversy but, as usual, we guessed wrong.

The second major started to bug him again and at this point the commander turned and said, "Look, this is my command and my problem. I will solve it in my own way. This man said B.S. to me and I say B.S. to you. Now court-martial me!"

There was a stunned silence. Then came the order "Dismissed."

As we were leaving the room there were several lieutenants muttering that we would fly since we were ordered to, but the formation probably wouldn't look too good. This must have been overheard by the staff because the day the flight orders were given we were told at briefing that instructors would be on board to fly the aircraft.

After briefing when I had completed the ground check and was in the cockpit in the left seat, the instructor showed up. We were to fly in the lead unit of the big formation in the #2 slot, flying somebody's right wing. I was glad because the #2 slot was easier to fly from the left seat than the #3. The instructor who came to my airplane was not my regular one but an individual I had flown with several times. He told me to get my tail end out of the pilot's seat and get in the right seat. Grudgingly I got up and moved, asking him if as well as he knew me, he really thought I would try to screw up the formation. He replied he didn't know and didn't care. He was going to fly the airplane and to keep my hands off the controls.

I was doing a slow burn, but my answer was a prompt "Yes, Sir."

We finally got off the ground and had the formation formed

when we were notified that the general's plane was an hour late and that we should clear the area. The formation flew around for over two hours before the general arrived.

The instructor was getting fairly tired and said I could fly the plane while he took a break. I replied that if he couldn't trust me when we started out and since his orders were to fly the airplane, he could keep on flying. A little later the order came that everything was "go" and we should proceed with the fly-over.

It was a beautiful tight formation that crossed the field. The general was impressed with the training we had received. The instructors flew their best and I'm sure the general was never told who was in the pilot seats.

When we landed the instructor told me to thank the good Lord that our training had been completed before this last flight, and it would be better if this incident would just remain on the field. For me I was happy to go since all of us were caught in a situation where there were no winners. But I still knew my instructors were the best and they had taught me more than enough to compensate for one embittered day.

Unbeknownst to us the group commander, during our lay-over, had worked out a plan whereby we could depart Roswell in the early evening on the day of the flight. The announcement was made while we were turning in our flying gear. We were to proceed to the railroad station and travel to the Eighteenth Replacement Wing, Salt Lake City, Utah, reporting there no later than midnight on January 22. Wives of the married men could accompany them on the train for a fee. The officers with autos were allowed to travel on their own. There were 153 first pilots on the order, including those with cars.

It was a mad scramble as we all rushed to clear the base, at the same time calling our wives to pack everything, check out, and meet us at the railroad station. We loaded aboard several coach cars whose run-down condition was a disgrace to the American railroad industry. It was apparent that anything that could roll had been placed in service; round wheels were not a necessary requirement.

The comfort and beauty of the passenger trains of the late thirties had disappeared completely, along with the Pullman and dining cars with white linen tablecloths, fine silver service, and finger bowls. Having experienced this service on several coast-to-coast trips plus several shorter trips in the East, I can only say that I had seen racehorses transported in better accommodations than the army was accorded. As a farm boy I had seen sheep and cattle being loaded for the markets in Chicago and Portland in better rolling stock than was being provided, but this was "wartime," an expression which excused every flaw in our society.

The coaches were eventually hooked to a slow-moving freight train which stopped at all milk stops and pulled off on every siding to allow the express trains to pass. The engine emitted a constant stream of black coal smoke as it labored its way along the rough tracks to the sidings to pick up more coal and water and eventually into the stations to discharge and pick up more freight. Occasionally we sat on country sidings for over an hour waiting for express and other traffic to clear the lines before we could move again.

The couples joined together to play a war game called "Battleship" while others played cards to pass the time, but eventually even these diversions lost their appeal. We were tired, dirty, and hungry; no provisions had been made for eating. The wives would have prepared picnic baskets had we known ahead of time the conditions we would face, but, as usual, the only information given was to board the train.

Almost thirty hours had passed when we finally pulled onto a siding in the outskirts of Denver. We could see the lights of a grocery store about a hundred yards in the distance. Four of the lieutenants jumped off and ran for the store where they hoped to buy bread, the makings for sandwiches, candy bars, or anything that was ready to eat. The wives had pooled some ration stamps for meat in case wieners or cold cuts were available.

Just as they disappeared into the store Old Smokey started to pant and labor its way back onto the main line. In several minutes the lights of the store disappeared. It was our shortest wait on a siding, just a little under four minutes.

Of the four lieutenants who jumped off, three were married. Sherry and I were kept busy consoling the newly widowed. Their main concerns were what would happen to their husbands since they had jumped train, how would they get together in Salt Lake, and so on. I wasn't much help, but all I could tell them was if their husbands could reach the base at Salt Lake City before midnight on the twenty-second nothing would happen to them since we were not required to travel by train anyway.

About halfway between Denver and Cheyenne in the pitch black of night we were again shuttled onto a siding in the bleak countryside where we waited an hour and a half for several trains to go by. Once again back on the main line we huffed and puffed our way into the station at Cheyenne.

As we came to a stop near the station, in the dim light, I could see our lost lieutenants standing on the platform with their arms full of grocery bags. They scrambled aboard the coach with cheers of the occupants ringing in their ears. As they doled out the goodies they explained that the stationmaster at Denver had placed them aboard an express train which passed us while we were on the siding and they had been waiting for us for over an hour and a half. We decided that the lieutenants had violated protocol by carrying the bags of groceries in public, so in the future only the wives would be allowed to make foraging trips.

The train finally pulled into Salt Lake City and again the search for housing became the order of the day. Sherry and I were extremely fortunate to find a room at the Milner Hotel within the hour.

Checking in at the Replacement Center we found that forming crews would be delayed briefly since there was a shortage of air crew members. The brouhaha at Roswell over the extra three days required for the fly-over faded into oblivion as this brief delay lasted two months. Our only duty was to report to the center for four hours on weekdays.

With the pressure of the rapid pace of training etched in our minds it seemed strange to have absolutely nothing to do but visit for hours. However, as copilots, bombardiers, navigators, engineers, and gunners reported in, the process of forming bomber crews began.

The crews were formed on the basis of psychological tests

which were given earlier. People were assigned in a manner designed to avoid personality clashes. One member of the crew must have Type O blood, a universal donor, and no more than two people from the same state could be on one crew.

The first to check in was the copilot, Second Lieutenant Myron D. Doxon (M.D. Doc) from Auburn, Washington. It was his first assignment after earning his wings at the twin-engine flying school at Douglas, Arizona. He was blessed with a fun loving, infectious personality and perpetual grin, and it was immediately obvious he was going to add humor and color to the life of the crew. Doc was also a licensed civilian pilot and railroad conductor before joining the cadet corps just two weeks short of his twenty-sixth birthday. Now twenty-eight, he had the distinction of being the oldest man on the crew. Doc and his wife Margaret had a two-year-old daughter, Kimmie.

The next crewman assigned was Staff Sergeant Edward W. Brown from Wier, Kansas, the flight engineer gunner. He was a very serious, sincere, dedicated young man who proposed to make the Army Air Force his lifetime career. Ed had been a staff sergeant since 1942 and was used to working with flying officers. He had crewed several different airplanes including the B-17. Ed was single with a rural background.

Then came the radio operator gunner, Corporal George W. Hinman from Pinckneyville, Illinois. George was small in stature, a feisty, talkative young man from the farm country. He was an expert in code and I knew he would make up for my own deficiencies in this area. With his expertise he was a welcome addition to the crew. He was also married. His wife Mary added a quiet, stable influence to his life.

Corporal Joseph J. Firszt from Chicago, Illinois, was assigned as waist gunner. Joe was single and in addition to being a gunner he was also qualified in radio code and trained as a flight engineer. Joe was very quiet and a dedicated crewman.

At the same time Private First Class Kenneth C. McQuitty from Ardmore, Oklahoma, was assigned as the ball turret gunner. Ken was single, light complexioned, and small enough to fit in the ball turret. He had a good education and an easy-going personality. It was apparent from our first meeting that this would be the individual that in jest everybody would play tricks on.

Corporal Robert L. Lynch from Muldrow, Oklahoma, was assigned as the armorer and waist gunner. As armorer, he would aid the bombardier in the loading and fusing of the bombs. Bob was eighteen, single, from a rural environment, and very shy and quiet, but he knew his job. His pleasant personality and slow southern drawl counteracted the hyperactive personality of some of the men and made him a good crew member.

Private First Class Robert C. Larsen from Montana was assigned as the tail gunner. Unfortunately he was hospitalized at our first duty station and was not able to fly with the crew. He was replaced by Sergeant Martin J. Smith from Milwaukee, Wisconsin. Smitty was married but was more of a loner so we did not know much of his background.

The last two to be assigned were the bombardier and navigator. The bombardier was Second Lieutenant Frank S. Dimit from Steubenville, Ohio. Frank was single, nineteen years old, and just out of bombardier school. The navigator, Second Lieutenant Robert C. Work from Urbana, Ohio, had graduated from college with a degree in accounting and had also just received his commission. He and Frank were ordered to report to us at Ardmore, Oklahoma, after completion of a ten-day delay en route which all cadets were given at commissioning.

We were not disappointed when these two men arrived. Their personalities were as different as day and night. Frank was very outgoing and quick to see the humor in every situation. He was a crack bombardier, and his infectious grin and pleasing personality soon endeared him to the crew. Bob Work (Roco), also single, was more serious and given to hiding his emotions. He was somewhat aloof, but he knew his job and there was no question he would hold up his end.

These were the men who were assigned to me as my first command. These were the men whose lives and fortunes were joined with mine, and with them the lives and dreams of their wives and families.

As I evaluated the crew members, we ranged in age from

eighteen to twenty-eight with at least four of us having our roots securely anchored on the farm. Brownie was the professional soldier. The rest of us had never served in the military except for our training. It was then I realized that I was going to need the ability to inspire and to teach because only the engineer and I had ever flown the B-17. The rest of the crew, including the copilot, had never been aboard a four-engine bomber. With a lot of help from some very dedicated instructors I had just nine weeks at our operational training base to train a combat crew.

We made a lot of mistakes in the beginning, some so bizarre they defied belief, others life threatening, and some just plain amusing. But we survived our mistakes and by our last few training missions I was extremely proud of my crew. I knew they could do the job, but could I rise to their level? I found out on our first mission as we battled for survival against the best that the Axis Powers had to offer.

I was flying formation by instinct when I heard the dreaded interphone transmission, "Tail gunner to pilot. I've just been hit." In spite of the chill that went up my spine, the sweat was pouring. I immediately ordered the waist gunner, Bob Lynch, to check on Smitty.

After what seemed to be an eternity, Lynch's Oklahoma drawl announced, "He's okay. He was hit in the chest and had the wind knocked out of him. He'll have a bruise, but it didn't break the skin. Thank God for the flak vest!"

The old ship was taking a beating when Frank called, "Bombs away." In the same instant the radio operator reported that only half of the load had dropped. Six bombs were still hanging in the left-hand racks. We started evasive action as the formation loosened up. Every ship was on its own until we reached the Rally Point.

"Gad, won't the bombardier ever close the bomb-bay doors?" The answer came promptly: "Bombardier to pilot, the bomb-bay doors won't close." Almost immediately the engineer reported the electric motor for the bomb-bay doors had shorted out and was smoking. The motor was located on the forward bulkhead in the bomb bay, approximately three feet down from the catwalk and close to the fuel transfer lines. A fire in this position could eventually burn through the fuel lines, setting the whole aircraft on fire or creating an explosion. The only way to prevent it was to unhook the hot lead to the motor.

I ordered the copilot to take charge of the emergency and directed the crew to help him in every way they could as I had my hands full trying to keep the ship under control and catch the formation. I was not aware of the drama that was being played out behind me as the bombardier and gunners attached the ropes that formed the safety support in the bomb bay onto the D-rings of Doc's parachute harness. The waist gunners snapped the other end of the ropes onto their parachute harness. Forming a human chain, anchored by the bombardier, the engineer grasped Doc's legs under his arms with his hands locked in an "Indian grip." Slowly they inched forward putting some slack in the safety ropes. With a fire axe in his hand, Doc was lowered head first into the open bomb bay. The roar of the engines and the noise of the wind rushing up through the bomb bay separated me from the action of the crew. When Doc knew he was in position he swung the axe, and after several blows was able to sever the hot line, disconnecting the motor. Our fire hazard was averted. Dimit inched his way along the bomb-bay catwalk, 15,000 feet above the English Channel, replacing the ropes, while the others returned to their positions. Doc had been given a view of the Channel which he was in no hurry to repeat.

The crew had solved their problem in a very dangerous but efficient manner. Now it was my turn to live up to their expectations. Could I land a B-17 still half loaded with bombs with the bomb-bay doors open? I knew that the open bomb-bay doors had plenty of clearance when the aircraft was at rest on the ground, but what would happen on the shock of landing? How much would the landing gear compress when it took the full weight of the aircraft? The dilemma was mine to solve as I ordered the crew to prepare for a crash landing.

The old queen of the skies, no stranger to adversity, filled the role of a protective mother hen as she gathered the young crew under her wings and clucked the sound of confidence inspiring a green pilot to use his capabilities to make the softest landing of his career. Filled with holes and groaning under the weight of the bombs, she responded to the controls as she settled onto the runway with her bomb-bay doors barely clearing the tarmac. Delivering her brood to safety she discharged her chicks, a group of scared young men who had beaten the odds.

The age of innocence was over. This was the first and last mission where we would leave the base in happy anticipation of a confrontation with the enemy. We had learned that the enemy played for keeps and this was a dangerous game. We were so naive we did not recognize that the actions of these crew members who saved our ship and our lives constituted "heroism," and they were not awarded the Distinguished Flying Cross. But we did know we had become that most admirable, complex, and proud entity: a unified heavy bomber crew.

How we forged ourselves into an efficient combat crew, and how we fulfilled our obligations to ourselves, to each other, and to our country is told in another book, *Fletcher's Gang*, which documents the experience of our thirty-five missions against the Third Reich.

Postscript

The first things in life are never forgotten. This is not confined to aviation but applies to all aspects of society which include the thrill or aversion of any significant event in life. The firsts always stay with you to become the measuring stick by which all subsequent activities are judged.

So it was with the wide-eyed, shaken crew that crawled out of the battered airplane on 6 July 1944. This was not our toughest mission by a long shot, nor was it our easiest.

All of the first pilots who reported into the Replacement Center at Salt Lake City eventually were assigned crews and reported to Operational Training Units in the United States for nine more weeks of training. Most eventually were transferred to England where they became a part of the many groups which made up the three Heavy Bombardment Divisions of the Eighth Air Force. These were replacement crews which were used as substitutes for lost crews. Some took the place of those being rotated back to the United States and others were used simply to expand the size of the group.

Most of the pilots from the Class of 43-J were never to see one another again. Not all survived, but those who did went their separate ways and it was only by chance that occasionally paths would cross.

A Boeing engineer once told me that over 60,000 pilots, including Army and Navy, received primary training in the

Boeing Stearman biplane. This was just one model of the primary trainer. There was also the Fairchild and Aeronca PT-19 series, the Ryan, Fleet, and DeHavilland PT-20 series, and several other manufacturers of trainers involved. But for me it was enough to record the personal, human side. Figures such as these I leave to the dedicated statistical historians.

Now to give an accounting of the few cadets and events which are known to me:

My first Primary roommate, who washed out and to whom I gave the name of Lester, eventually became a ball turret gunner and was assigned to a B-17 crew while I was at Salt Lake City.

After graduating from the Central Instructor School at Randolph Field, San Antonio, Texas, my brother-in-law, Cap, was assigned there to teach instrument flying to other instructor trainees. My sister was allowed to join him. He received two other assignments and at the war's end was flying B-24s.

Norment Foley completed a tour of duty with the Eighth Air Force and returned to a farm in Texas. Unfortunately not all of his crew survived as they flew some harrowing missions. In 1985 he told me that I did not know what work was until I had filled the gas tanks of a B-17 in an open field in France with a five-gallon Jerry can.

Cadet Gene Jones made the Air Force his career. He flew thirty-five combat missions in B-17s with the Ninety-sixth Bomb Group stationed in England, plus ninety-nine combat missions during the Korean Conflict. He gained nationwide recognition on August 18, 1960. While flying a specially modified Fairchild C-119 cargo airplane, he snagged the first data capsule recovered in flight from an orbiting *Discoverer 14* satellite. In fact, he personally flew the airplane that recovered two of the first three capsules. His unit was awarded the Mackay Trophy for the outstanding Air Force flights in 1960. Jones also was the aircraft commander of a C-130 that set a nonstop nonrefueling world's record of 3,800 miles in ten hours and fourteen minutes for turbine-powered aircraft.

Lieutenant Colonel Jones was assigned as Chief of the Air Force Flight Test Division at Lockheed-Georgia in Marietta. While there he personally flew every one of the C-141s that came off of the assembly line. With this experience he was assigned as Air Force Project Officer on the C-5A Galaxy and was also appointed Air Force Plant Representative. In this capacity he was chosen to be the military pilot for the first acceptance flight by the Air Force of the C-5A, the world's largest airplane. He retired from the service in 1969 with the rank of colonel.

At Santa Ana, after the war, a high-ranking officer and two master sergeants were court-martialed for charging the cadet corps for government issue physical training clothing.

From the countless thousands at the cessation of hostilities, a number of air crew members chose to remain on active duty with the Army Air Force, but the major portion of this huge manpower pool elected to return to civilian life—many to either start or finish a college education, some to establish a business, and others to return to jobs in the cities or on the farm. A minuscule number of the flying officers who received the temporary Army of the United States commissions received Regular Army commissions, but over a five-year period as the Air Force became a separate branch of the armed service, most were offered the opportunity to accept or reject a reserve commission. Those of us who accepted, along with others who joined the National Air Guard, combined to form a civilian pool of flyers available to the armed forces in the event of a national emergency.

On June 26, 1948, the first pilots from this reserve were accepted as volunteers to help man the Berlin Airlift as supplies were flown to the beleaguered city whose land access had been cut off by Russian troops. Then on June 25, 1950, the North Korean Forces crossed the Thirty-Eighth Parallel into South Korea. Many of us from the Reserve and Guard Forces responded to provide additional air crew members for a limited time for participation in the Korean Conflict. Some of this group chose to remain on active duty and saw service during the Vietnam War, but for me the call of the farm was overpowering and I elected to return to reserve status.

In 1941 the nation faced an emergency. The young men

responded *en masse* by enlisting in the Aviation Cadet Corps. The reader will have to judge the success of this tremendous program since those of us who participated are too prejudiced to make an honest assessment.

Notes on Sources

The sources of the information contained in this book were many and varied. There were the letters that I wrote to Sherry along with my personal recollections. The chronology is kept intact within the framework of army orders contained in my personal 201 file, a compilation of every order affecting an individual officer of the U.S. military. The flying experiences are documented by each flight as listed in the military and civilian pilot log books.

As we progressed through the training schools our actions were recorded in classbooks. Some information came from handouts that were presented to us upon entering these schools, and the Douglas, Arizona, statistics were provided in 1943 by the Chamber of Commerce.

Relevant information was provided by Colonel Gene Jones USAFRet, Lorraine Littleton McNew, Catherine Rawlings, and Leonard Patton.

In addition to my personal photographs, pictures were furnished by Jack Nelson, senior engineer, Boeing Company, Wichita, Kansas, and my brother-in-law, Leonard Patton.

FLETCHER'S GANG

*Dedicated to those who anxiously waited,
and especially to Alice and Sherry,
the former who thought it should be
recorded and the latter who made it possible*

Contents

Foreword

Written while the author was in combat crew training in the United States and later flying combat missions in Europe, Eugene Fletcher's letters to his beloved wife, Sherry, capture faithfully the joys and sorrows of a typical bomber crew during World War II. With varied backgrounds and interests, from different sectors of the country, Fletch's crew of four officers and six enlisted men were thrust together for only two months of training before being sent to England to engage in air combat just after D-Day.

On the other hand, Fletch documents the challenge and seriousness of his task in molding an effective team of young men; on the other, he reveals his sense of humor in writing about such incidents as their goof when they became lost on a training mission.

As one of their instructors at Ardmore, Oklahoma, and later as their squadron commander in England, I well remember Fletcher's crew as one of the most dedicated and professional of those I had the pleasure to lead. He and his crew served their country exceptionally well under the stress of repeated missions over Germany in a high threat environment, knowing that each time they took the risk of being shot out of the sky. Reading Fletch's letters covering that combat period, one detects his realistic acceptance of such hazards while at the same time one notes his attempts to reassure Sherry that all would be O.K.

For those who would like an insightful documentation of what it was like to be on a U.S. bomber crew in World War II, this is well worth reading. My compliments to Fletch for having written the letters and to Sherry for having preserved them for history.

James O. Frankosky
Maj. Gen. USAF Ret.

Author's Note

This narrative is not intended to be a saga of the Battle of the Air during World War II. Many authors have already documented the thrilling air battles and the heroism and danger inherent therein. It is a study of the mood of the times, and what went on in the minds of the people who were caught up in this crucial struggle. Some stories of combat must be told to provide a setting for the documents, and to justify and explain certain references in the letters.

It is well to point out that on any base in the combat area there were two dirrerent groups of people. The Permanent Personnel were there for the duration. If they were extremely lucky, they might get a furlough home for thirty days and then return, or they might be transferred to Higher Headquarters. But most would remain on the same field until the war was over. These people had their own living area, their own mess halls, and their own circle of friends.

This narrative is about the men of the replacement flight crews. They were assigned to a group, flew a tour, and left, if they survived. These were temporary people, "Pipeline Personnel." They had their own living area and combat mess halls, but they shared the clubs, post exchange, and theater. The two groups lived in two different worlds, and their worlds were not of their own making.

If you find people and their thoughts as interesting as deeds and battles, perhaps you will find this chronicle to your liking. The events that are detailed are true. The letters are authentic, but they have been edited for spelling and punctuation, as well as deletion of personal messages and other extraneous and repetitious material. Deletions are marked with ellipses.

Our crew was reunited in late July 1985 at Boeing Field in Seattle, Washington. The nine living members of the ten-man crew were present along with their instructor from Ardmore, Oklahoma, who later became their squadron commander in England. They were privileged to meet Ed Wells, the man who designed their airplane, *Knock Out Baby.* The crew and commander flew one "Last Mission" for KING-TV in Seattle. This documentary has been aired several times.

The reunion coincided with the fiftieth anniversary of the Boeing B-17 Flying Fortress, and the reunion of the 95th Bomb Group, plus numerous other groups of the Eighth Air Force. The occasion gave impetus to the recording of the life and thoughts of this crew in accordance with the time in which these happenings occurred. Thus it was that the idea for the book began.

In regard to the participants: their biographies will unfold as the story goes along. The one exception who needs a special introduction is the recipient of the letters. They were written to my wife, Evelyn. Her sorority sisters of Alpha Chi Omega gave her the nickname of Sherry, which was derived from her maiden name of Sherrod. We met on a blind date while attending Whitman College in Walla Walla, Washington. Sherry was an honor student, a music major studying piano, with plans of being a professional accompanist. She was a lovely young lady with a bubbling personality and a host of friends. I felt extremely lucky and fortunate that the dates were continued, even though many of them were study sessions.

My college and working life was interrupted when I received a notice that I would be drafted into military service on July 1, 1942. Since I was a licensed pilot and desired to choose the branch of service in which I would serve, I enlisted as an aviation cadet in the Army Air Corps on June 22. With the war dominating our lives and our desire to be together growing we were married August 25. Sherry was able to accompany me through my flight training as we moved from field to field. However, when I received orders in March 1944 to report to Ardmore, Oklahoma, for combat crew training, a task which would require all of my time, we decided that Sherry would return to live with her parents in Tekoa, Washington, until we could be reunited.

The crew consisted of the following members:

Pilot	Eugene R. Fletcher	1st Lt.	Dayton, Wash.
Copilot	Myron D. Doxon	1st Lt.	Enumclaw, Wash.
*Copilot	Billy Bob Layl	1st Lt.	Piggott, Ark.
Navigator	Robert C. Work	1st Lt.	Urbana, Ohio
Bombardier	Frank S. Dimit	1st Lt.	Steubenville, Ohio
Engineer	Edward W. Brown	T/Sgt.	Weir, Kan.
Radio Operator	George W. Hinman	T/Sgt.	Pinkneyville, Ill.
Ball Turret	Kenneth C. McQuitty	S/Sgt.	Ardmore, Okla.
Waist Gunner	Robert L. Lynch	S/Sgt.	Muldrow, Okla.
Waist Gunner	Joseph J. Firszt	S/Sgt.	Chicago, Ill.
Tail Gunner	Martin J. Smith	S/Sgt.	Milwaukee, Wis.

Bear in mind that these were young men, ranging in age from eighteen to twenty-eight years. Some were still college students or just out of high school. Others were working, and two had just finished college. To me they were men who had been trained to do a special job, and what they did in the future was of more concern than what they had done in the past. What I knew of them will be revealed in the letters.

While this is the story of my crew and associates, it could have been any heavy bomber crew, on any base, of any group, of the Eighth Air Force.

* Copilot for last fifteen missions.

Acknowledgments

The author would like to express sincere thanks and gratitude to Professors Tom Pressly and Maclyn Burg of the University of Washington History Department and Glen Adams, printer from Fairfield, Washington, for their timely advice and encouragement to keep going with the project. May they know that their support and critique were truly appreciated. To Paul Andrews of Vienna, Virgina, for information provided from the archives of the 95th Group, a very warm thank you. A note of appreciation to Roland Byers, Professor Emeritus of General Engineering, University of Idaho, for his continued interest and helpful advice. And a very special thanks to Lane Morgan for her editing expertise.

Although my name appears as the author, this book could not have been written without the material supplied by the crew members: Robert Work, Myron Doxon, Frank Dimit, and Robert Lynch.

Fletch

Prologue

Operational Training Unit
Ardmore, Oklahoma

March 8, 1944

Dear Sherry,

Well, here we are at Ardmore. I don't know where to begin, so I'll just start out rambling. We have just about settled down. After reporting in, processing, and assigning crew positions aboard the ship, I gave the boys the old pep talk to get them on the ball. We sure have had our hands full.

Here's what we're doing now: going to school eight hours a day for two weeks. After that we will fly for four weeks, two more weeks of classes, four more of flying. Then our little stay here will be over.

We could live off the post but the field is eighteen miles from town and with no more time than we have off it pretty much discourages that. Those who are trying it are finding that it isn't so good. Besides, they are neglecting a lot of little things in order to have time off. I know we were right in having you not come.

Cap and Sis wrote me a letter and I think they are coming down soon to visit for a little while. It will be swell if they do. Now about my crew: they're really a swell bunch of fellows and I'm proud of them, my flight engineer in particular. His name is Brown and he's a staff sergeant, an old Army man. He has been Staff since '42. You can tell him something and you don't have to worry about it again because you know he'll do it and it will be done right. Right now he's my right arm and worth his weight in gold. As time goes on I'll tell you about the rest of the crew as I get to know them better.

P.S. I almost forgot to tell you that I'm now a flight commander— pretty fancy name for just a go-between.

Leonard Patton, nickname "Cap," brother-in-law, married to my sister, Leora. He enlisted in the Army Air Corps for glider training. When this unit was disbanded he was transferred to the Aviation Cadet Corps. Upon graduation he was assigned for training at Central Instructor School, Randolph Field, Texas, while I received B-17 Transition Training at Roswell, New Mexico. Cap and I received our wings and were commissioned second lieutenants on the same day, but in different flying training commands.

When I was at Ardmore, Cap was teaching cadets to fly in basic trainers at Coffeyville, Kansas. Before I left he was transferred back to Randolph as an instructor at the Central Instructor School. Before the war's end he was flying B-24s.

March 12, 1944

Here it is Sunday evening about 9:30. Being Sunday I took the evening off and enjoyed a show here at the Post Theater. It was The Uninvited Guest—not too bad.

By the way, if you can't read this it is because I'm trying to write on a stationery box which I am holding on my knee and it doesn't seem to be working out so good.

Sis and Cap came down Friday morning and stayed until this morning. We had a nice little visit. I went to classes all day but could see them at night. Cap went to a couple of classes with me Saturday. They were pretty dry and I had a hard time keeping him awake. Then we went out to look over the B-17. After we finished he decided the BT was big enough for him. . . .

It sure is lonesome here. Poor old Larry [Gassman] and me! When we get down in spirit we go look the other one up and moan together for awhile, then we get back in good spirits again. Larry called Izzie the other night so I had to get my two cents worth in. We are just about bosom pals here. Misery loves company they say. Since we're in the same boat we just hang together.

Oh yes, I almost forgot to tell you that Flores got a telegram yesterday. You remember that he's the guy from Alamagordo. Well, he's now the proud father of an eight-pound baby boy. Boy, is he swelled up and happy! We just about have to hog-tie him to keep him from going over the hill. Tonight he called the hospital where his wife is and they let him talk to her. Then they brought the baby out so he could hear it cry over the telephone. He just about went wild over that!

We have really been busy since arriving here—doing just routine things but they have sure kept us on the run. Oh yes, we have started P.T. [physical training] again. Everybody has more aches and pains than we ever thought possible. But I guess after a couple of weeks we'll get used to that again. . . .

March 14, 1944

Here it is Tuesday, my day off, so Larry and I are making full use of it by writing letters. Here's the setup: Larry has a table in his room and I have two chairs in mine so we got together on a little compromise. I bring my chairs over to his room; then we divide the desk in half and start writing letters. So far we've been doing good. I'm on my fifth letter of the day and Larry is on his fourth. We've been writing like mad all afternoon. You know me and my letter writing—one package of cigarettes and an hour and a half to each letter.

I made out an allowance of $225 which will be sent to you each month starting with April's pay. That should leave me my flight pay to have over and above the other allotments like board and insurance. I think I can get by here on $75 a month. If not I'll have you send me some occasionally. The reason I made it for that much is this: Allotments are paid every month regardless of whether I sign a payroll or not. This means that if something should happen that I can't sign the payroll you would still get the money. The pay would still continue indefinitely if I were missing in action or prisoner of war, or anything of that nature. Although I don't think I'll miss the pay formation it's just an added precaution. . . .

The Major explained the little article in **Bombs Away** *that I sent to you about a furlough when we finish here. Well, he says it doesn't apply to us so not to get our hopes up. He said it applies to those who are now graduating from cadet schools and pertains to their leave after graduation, like our ten-day delay-enroute. He also said our commitment date to the staging area is June 4. So about the only way we can get a leave is to finish here ahead of schedule and maybe get a delay-enroute. I don't know how it is going to work out—nobody does. But I'll sure be disappointed if I don't get one. . . .*

Here is a little verse I gave my copilot to make him feel better when the going gets rough.

You Lucky One You

For nine long months
  I've toiled in the sun
Just dreaming of flying
  A P-51.

Then came that great day
  Our sweat wasn't in vain
To think that now
  We would fly a hot plane.

But out of each group
  Some will get screwed
And just sure as hell
  I was one of those few.

My fighter pilot dreams
  Have gone up in steam
I'm now a co-pilot
  On a B-17.

The job is exciting
  Oh, the thrill that one feels
When the pilot says, Now,
  You may pull up the wheels.

I let down the flaps
And keep the cylinder heads cool
I call off his airspeed
But hell I'm no fool.

I'm now in my glory
In my highest esteem
I'm second in command
On a B-17.

Author Unknown

March 17, 1944

I haven't written for a couple of days so I hope you'll understand. Of late we've been having quite a few examinations. Consequently we have been studying a little of evenings, reading technical orders and what not. Last night I was going to write but I had a crew meeting instead which lasted until about nine. Lately that has been my bedtime so I turned in instead of writing. These classes sure wear me out. After eight hours of it I'm dead tired. I guess I just got so lazy in Salt Lake that it will take me a little while to get over it.

I sure get a kick out of my crew. I really lay the law down to them. They are a good bunch of boys and probably wouldn't get out of line anyway. But I just don't take any chances. You see, if one of them gets into any trouble the first pilot takes the blame and the disciplinary action from Headquarters. Then he, in turn, comes back and chews out the whole crew for the actions of one man. They are our whole responsibility. We give them their passes, their promotions, have the privilege of breaking them, and, in general, control all of their disciplinary action. But we, in turn, have to answer to Headquarters for the whole crew. So if one guy messes up it's a black mark on us. We suffer from Headquarters, so the rest of the crew suffers from us. That's just one reason for keeping them on the ball. There are lots of others which I'll tell you about some day.

Larry and Bud both said to tell you "hello." They always ask about you every time I get a letter. I always tell Bud it's none of his business how you are and any interest he might have in my wife he can confine elsewhere. But he knows I'm kidding and always has some wisecrack for an answer.

March 21, 1944

Yesterday was our last day of classes. We start flying tomorrow. It looks as if we'll get our eight hours in okay. But if it should weather in and we don't it will be all right because we will get paid for back flying time whenever we get the hours in, regardless of the three-month period. At least that's one thing in favor of Ardmore. I forgot to tell you we didn't draw any travel pay coming down here. We had to pay for our own meals on the way, but that didn't make any difference—we just got rooked.

Today was supposedly our day off but I ran around more, trying to straighten out a few things, than I would have on an ordinary day. I had to exchange some flying equipment, draw a new oxygen mask, exchange a Mae West, get helmets fixed for the new mask, and draw a bunch of books and notebooks, papers, pencils, maps, computers, and other incidentals. That was this morning.

Then this afternoon my copilot, engineer, and assistant engineer went down to the line with me and looked the ships over, going through procedures and locating things on board the ship. This was voluntary, just an idea of mine to get the boys acquainted with the airplane before we fly together. We have been doing that occasionally when we have had spare time. I think it's a good idea myself and they are willing to do it.

Then later on this afternoon our bombardier and navigator reported in. We now have a full crew and I've met all the fellows. The bombardier's name is Dimit and the navigator is Work, both are from Ohio. I'll let you know what I think of them later, as soon as we get better acquainted. Right now I think they're both pretty good fellows.

I don't like my navigator so much, though. I'll tell you why—he just left on a ten-day furlough along with all the other navigators. I guess I shouldn't be too bitter because he has just graduated from Cadets and this is his graduation leave. Besides, we can't use him here for a couple of weeks anyway. But I'd sure like to have a furlough too!! Incidentally, neither of these two is married.

March 24, 1944

I was checked out for day flying a couple of days ago. At first we used only a skeleton crew, but now all the enlisted men have been checked out. I checked out my copilot, too, so we are all flying together. We get along swell. It looks like everything will be okay.

I have been getting up at 6:30 and reporting at 7:30 for Link trainer [a training system for instrument flying]. Two hours of that, then bomb trainer at 9:30 for another two hours. That makes it 11:30 —we have forty minutes to eat, change clothes, and get to the line at 12:10 for briefing. After briefing we take off at about 1:30, landing at 7:30. Then we fill out all our required forms and have another briefing. About 9 or 9:30 we get back to the barracks, eat, and go to bed. So you can see they have really been rushing us. . . .

March 26, 1944

The last couple of days we have been flying nights. I received my final night check last night in time to get back and take the rest of the crew up for their first night ride. They enjoyed it no end.

Oh, yes, I was going to tell you about the boys. Starting first with the copilot: Myron Doxon is his name and he's from Tacoma [Washington]. He's twenty-eight years old, married, and has a daughter fifteen months old. His wife and daughter are coming down sometime next week, I believe. He is a little taller and a little heavier than I am— blond, blue eyes, and smiling all the time. He's quite a character, has a good sense of humor which keeps everybody laughing. But, at that, he has a wonderful sense of responsibility and can be trusted to do things, and do them right. He really likes the B-17 and is eager to learn how to fly it, so I don't have to worry about him. I know he can do his job and also do lots of things for me.

Now the bombardier and navigator: Well, the navigator is still on leave so I guess we'll have to skip him as I haven't had time to get acquainted with him. He's single, though, and a college graduate so I would imagine he's probably twenty-four or twenty-five years old. He is dark and would probably weigh about ninety-eight pounds soaking wet. At least he's smaller than I am so I know he won't cause me any trouble. If he can just navigate we will get along okay.

The bombardier is from Ohio, single, and quite a bit larger than I am. I imagine he weighs about 170 pounds, nineteen years old, fresh from Cadets and still glamorized by the gold bar on his shoulder—I know the feeling. He has a good personality and is easy to get along with—more than that he knows who the boss is so that's well taken care of.

Next comes the flight engineer, Brown. His home is in Kansas and I believe I have told you all about him, so will just say I still think as much of him as I did before, and pass on to the radio operator, Hinman.

I can't remember right now where his home is, but it's some place here in the West. He's married and has his wife here. I've met her and she seems very nice. Hinman jabbers at just about the same rate at which he takes code, which is twenty words a minute. I have quite a time keeping him quiet sometimes, but, nevertheless, he is a good radio operator and that's what counts.

Next is the assistant engineer or assistant radio operator. He is trained for both jobs and can take over either. His name is Firszt—brown hair, brown eyes, and fairly tall. His home is here in Muldrow, Oklahoma. Another good boy.

Then comes the armorer gunner, Lynch. Wait a minute—my mistake—Lynch is from Muldrow and Firszt is from Chicago. I don't want to get my farmer boy and city boy mixed up. Lynch is a slow easygoing Oklahoma farmer, a little slow to catch on, but once he catches on he doesn't forget. He is about 5 feet 6 and has blond hair and blue eyes, quite young, but very quiet, well-mannered, and knows his job.

Now comes the real character, the ball turret gunner and turret specialist, McQuitty. He's about my size and just as light as I am dark, always laughing or smiling at something. He's the one that somebody is always pulling jokes on. His home is Kansas City, Missouri. Every time I think of him I just have to laugh. He can screw up more things in the shortest length of time than any guy I've ever seen. He can listen to a lecture and come out with everything just backwards of what it should be. His mistakes aren't anything serious—just comical, that's all.

The tail gunner, Larson—I am not very well acquainted with him yet. He is still in the hospital with scarlet fever. But he's older than the rest of the boys. He's real quiet, never has anything to say, and is from

Baker, Montana. He's quite conscientious about his work, though, so I know he'll be all right.

All in all I think I have the best all-around crew on the field. Of course that's just my opinion, but they think I'm a pretty good guy— they don't know me yet—so I'll stand behind them all the way.

Last, but not least, is the pilot. His name is Fletcher and his home is almost anyplace in the State of Washington. He is short, dark, and deeply in love with his wife. His wife is a blonde whose home is in Tekoa. He surely does miss her—probably a lot more than she knows. Also, he's going to be a proud papa and he's all puffed up about that. So he really has a lot to work for, and believe me, he's doing his best.

Well, so much for the crew. I can't describe them very well, but that will give you an idea. You really have to see them, work with them, and know them before you can appreciate them.

We now have all our flying time in for flight pay and my pay vouchers have already been turned in. By the time you receive this I should have been paid.

I'll have to buy some new clothes this month. After the first of April suntans will be optional and after the fifteenth they will be compulsory uniforms. And me without a suntan to my name! So I guess I'll have to break down and buy some. It's okay, though, because right now I have only one pair of pants that I can wear. I broke the zipper on my greens the other day so all I have left is a pair of pinks. . . .

Now then, about my job as flight commander. You know how it was in Cadets—at all the formations the flight commander stood out front and issued commands, took the roll, informed the Group of anything new, and in general was a go-between between the Squadron and the Tactical Office. It's the same way here.

We have fifty-six crews in Section "A" and Section "A" is divided into five Flights with eleven crews to the Flight. I'm the first guy in Flight 4 so I think that's how I was picked. Anyway, within the Flight are three Elements: two four-crew Elements and one three-crew Element. Each Element has a leader and I had to pick the Element Leaders. Gassman is head of Element 2, Flores head of Element 1, and Gosewisch head of Element 3. All the fellows in my Flight are Roswell men and the same goes for Flights 3 and 5. That's all the dope on that. We don't do much except take the chewing out for the whole outfit.

March 28, 1944

There isn't really much to tell you. It's the same as usual—Link trainer, bomb trainer, and flying. Today we were caught out in an overcast and I thought for a while we would probably fly up to Tulsa to land, as that was the only clear spot. But they got us back to the field just in time to land before the ceiling dropped to the ground and the field was closed. We were anticipating the bad weather, however, so everyone was in fairly close—there was no trouble at all.

I'm becoming more attached to my crew every day. It's really a pleasure to fly with them—if flying can be a pleasure.

April 1, 1944

Yesterday I received a nice long letter from you and also a wonderful box of cookies. They sure are good! Gassman and Flores and I have been sitting around eating them and chewing the fat. They wanted me to be sure to tell you how good they were.

Today we got a break. "C" Section, that is, what is left of it, had some formation flying to do so they took all the airplanes. Consequently, we didn't have to fly. They told us last night we wouldn't have to, so I figured I would just sit down last night and catch up on all the letters I had to write.

I didn't even get started before Gassman came over to see if I would go to town with him since it had been over a week and a half since either of us had been off the post. I decided it might not be too bad an idea because I was getting pretty well fed up with the base myself. So we chased off to town. We met most of our crew in town—just walked around and shot the bull. It was about nine o'clock when we got there so it wasn't long until the last bus left for the base at twelve. We put our men on the last bus, went over to the hotel, got a room, and slept in a good bed all night. We got up this morning in time to catch the ten o'clock bus to the base. I guess I really should have stayed home and written my letters as I'd planned, but, doggone, it sure seemed good to get off the post and just forget things for the night.

My copilot's wife and baby arrived yesterday. I haven't met her as yet but talked with her on the telephone today. She seems nice, but why not, she's also a Washingtonian. I guess I didn't tell you there are seven fellows in my barracks who are from Washington and I don't know how many scattered around the Field. Our section commander on the flying line is also from Washington. We sure have a good representation here.

Yesterday was pay day but our vouchers won't come through until Monday. They had better hurry up and get here as I have to buy some clothes. The guys on the crew have been kidding me about having only one pair of pants to wear.

The payoff came yesterday afternoon when the radio operator, Hinman, came up to the B.O.Q. [Bachelor Officers' Quarters]. He said he wanted my green pants as his wife had already bought a zipper for them. She was just waiting for him to bring the pants in so she could fix them. I played it cagey—I argued with him a little, but he wound up with the pants, so it won't be too long before I'll have two pair again. The guys are sure on the ball and looking out for me all the time. I have a lot of little funny things to tell you when we are together again about my crew and the things they do.

The last few days I haven't felt any too good. One of my wisdom teeth has been hurting so yesterday I had the dentist look at it. He doctored it up and it is feeling a lot better now. As soon as I get time, after all the soreness is gone, I'm going back and he's going to yank it out.

My navigator is supposed to get back either today or tomorrow. Most of the others are back now, but mine hasn't arrived yet. He's probably stretching the time just as long as he can, for which I don't blame him.

Oh yes, you wanted to know if the last class here had leaves. I don't know whether they did or not, but I do know that they now have five missions over Germany to their credit. That was of a week or so ago—probably have a few more by now. We'll know more about the leave deal when "B" Section leaves here. We should get a fair idea of what will happen to us by seeing what happens to them. I can assure you I have my fingers crossed. Maybe it will work out so we can get a short leave anyway.

April 4, 1944

I mailed you a little Easter package today which I hope you'll receive by Sunday. Sure had a lot of fun looking around for it. The wrap job was

Eugene Fletcher, November 1943

Sherry Fletcher's photo that Fletch carried with him

Crew photo taken at Ardmore, Oklahoma. Back row, left to right: Kenneth McQuitty, Robert Lynch, Martin Smith, Joseph Firszt, Edward Brown, George Hinman; front row: Eugene Fletcher, Myron Doxon, Robert Work, Frank Dimit

"Cap" and "Sis"—Leonard and
Leora Patton

Myron, Margaret, and Kim Doxon

George and Mary Hinman

Ed and Mary Brown on their
wedding day

Pathfinder radar ship. Mickey radar unit mounted in ball turret position. *(Boeing Archives)*

Front view of Operations 412th Bomb Squadron, bulletin board and bicycles, crew quarters in the rear

Frank Dimit raising the red Mission Alert flag, occasionally referred to as "Maggie's Drawers"

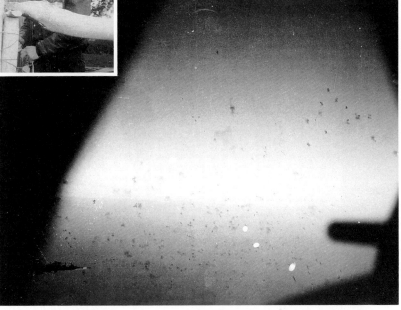

Flak and more flak

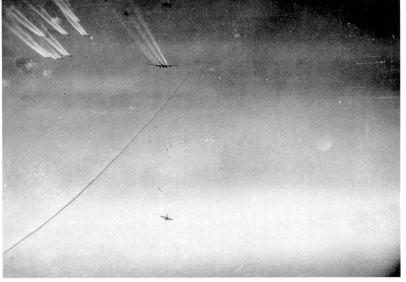

Plane shot down with tail trailing. Some stared death in the eye that day, but death blinked and chose another. *(95th B.G. Photo)*

Myron "Doc" Doxon, copilot, seated on an aircraft towing tug

(Left) Robert Work, navigator.
(Right) Frank Dimıt, bombardier

Billy Bob Layl, copilot for the last fifteen missions. Two good friends—the P-51, our little friend, and Layl

(Left) Edward Brown, aerial engineer and top turret gunner. *(Right)* George Hinman, radio operator, hanging on to antenna

(Left) Robert Lynch, armorer and left waist gunner. *(Right)* Joseph Firszt, right waist gunner

(Left) Kenneth McQuitty, ball turret gunner. *(Right)* Martin Smith, tail gunner

Lake Geneva was a jewel in the distance. *(95th B.G. photo)*

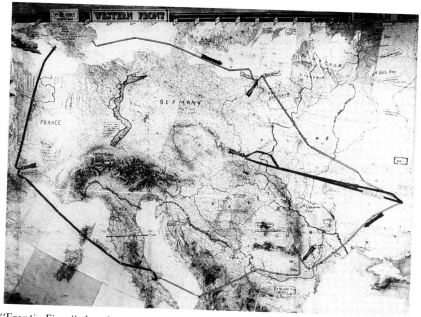

"Frantic Five," the shuttle raid *(95th B.G. photo)*

Lt. Florian, official interpreter and cameraman for the 95th Bomb Group, with Russian soldiers *(95th B.G. photo)*

Paul Fiess with Russian dignitaries; *I Dood It*, also known as *Berlin Bessie*, in the background *(Paul Fiess photo)*

Wheat field, Poltava. Standing, left to right: Dwight Stevens; Russian commander (with wings on cap); commander's executive assistant; Russian woman interpreter; Paul Fiess, wearing the cap he had exchanged for Fletch's at the evening festivities. Kneeling, left to right: Russian woman; Russel Williams *(Paul Fiess photo)*

Briefing room and theater, Poltava, Russia; housing and mess tents in background. Poltava was totally destroyed during the course of the war. *(95th B.G. photo)*

A government building in Poltava. All that was standing was this front wall; the rest of the building had been completely destroyed by bombs. *(95th B.G. photo)*

Mess and housing tents, Poltava *(95th B.G. photo)*

Bargaining for melons with Italian boys in Foggia *(95th B.G. photo)*

Main Street, Foggia, Italy, 1944 *(95th B.G. photo)*

The shell-pocked buildings of Foggia show the ravages of war.
(95th B.G. photo)

Bomb damage, Foggia *(95th B.G. photo)*

The enemy didn't fare too well either. Junkers 88 (Ju-88) destroyed on the ground at Foggia, Italy *(Paul Fiess photo)*

Piccadilly Circus, London, with the statue of Eros encased in a concrete shelter for protection against bombing. *(95th B.G. photo)*

Smitty modeling the dangerous 45-caliber pistol. From left to right: Smith, Lynch, Brown; kneeling, Hinman

(Left) David Eugene Fletcher. *(Right)* Leora and Michael Patton, Sherry and David Fletcher

done by my radio operator's wife. She works in the place where I bought it. She spent almost the whole morning showing Gassman and me the contents of the baby department. We prospective fathers have quite a time. . . .

Yesterday I had to stand retreat (formal retreat) with all the enlisted men in my Flight. Boy, did I look sharp dragging that bunch around behind the band. It would be nice if I could just remember which one is my left foot! Oh well, we got through it and didn't encounter any serious difficulties.

I went to town first thing this morning so I could have breakfast off the post and not get in a rut. Besides, I wanted to get some Easter cards, and Doxon, my copilot, wanted me to meet his wife and baby. So I paid my duty call there.

Then Brown, my engineer, has his girlfriend here and he wanted me to meet her this afternoon and place my stamp of approval. So I spent most of the afternoon with them. They want to get married and wanted to know whether I thought it best they should—and all about it. So Old Pop Fletch took care of that little detail. I gave them the real lowdown. After all, why should he be single and happy when the rest of us are married! Now she's going home to quit her job, tell her folks, and live happily ever after. In the meantime Doxon and I got stuck with the check for dinner for the whole crew!

I'm really finding out what troubles are. I used to think I had enough of my own, but now any time one of the fellows has anything happen, wants some advice, or wants to do something he comes to me and we hash it out together. Just call me the Chaplain!

As soon as my tail gunner gets out of the hospital we're all going to have a picture made of the whole crew so you can see what they look like.

April 12, 1944

It has been quite some time since you've heard from me and I hope you haven't been worrying. Everything is okay. I have just finished about the busiest nine days I've ever put in since being in the Army.

About a week ago we had some bad weather and that, coupled with a lack of airplanes and being assigned some that weren't flyable, re-sulted in our getting behind on our flying hours and number of mis-

sions completed. Consequently, we have been going night and day to catch up. We aren't entirely caught up yet, but have made a good gain. The ceiling has been low most of the week and, as a result, we're behind on bombing missions. But with a couple of days of good weather we might very easily catch up.

We have done all types of flying the past week, including formation, instrument, low altitude bombing, instrument calibration, and air-to-ground gunnery. My gunners get a kick out of that! They're pretty good at it too. I would surely hate to be anywhere in range and have them pumping away at me!

The box of cookies you sent came the day before Easter. Needless to say, they're all gone. . . . Any time you want to send some more just go right ahead. . . . You don't have to wait for holidays—just send them anytime. Sis also sent me a box of cookies for Easter but they're all gone too.

Your Mother said they had a padlock for me and wondered about the size. Tell them it's okay. I can use it.

April 13, 1944

Went to a show here on the post this evening. First one I've been to for a week and a half, I guess. The name was Up In Arms—*slapstick comedy all the way through so I enjoyed it immensely.*

This is our day off so I'm holding down the barracks alone. Most of the fellows have gone to Fort Worth, Dallas, or someplace. But not this kid. I decided now was a good time to catch up on a lot of things which I have been letting go. I have been filling out a bunch of forms which I want you to have. I haven't finished them yet, but when I do I'll send them along with a few other papers which I should have given you when we were in Salt Lake. By now you should have received a power of attorney form and a will which I filled out. If not, let me know and I'll see what is holding them up.

I haven't been back to see the dentist yet about my wisdom teeth— have been just too busy to make it. I hope I have time before we leave here but it looks dubious. I don't expect to be here as long as I told you at first. Could be wrong, but have good reason to believe that within the next five weeks Ardmore will be a thing of the past as far as I'm concerned. . . .

Cap didn't come down last weekend as the weather was bad at both ends of the line—and it was Easter Sunday. I'm sure he had a better time in Coffeyville. He intends to fly down, though, one of these weekends before I leave. We'll probably have quite a time when he comes. I hope to take him on a regular mission in the B-17. I know he would enjoy it because it is quite interesting to those who don't see it every day.

In my last letter I asked about the padlock. Well, it came this morning so now I'll have you thank your folks for me. It will work okay—just the thing I've been looking for. Another thing I could use if you can find one—I can't—is a flashlight. . . . Have been looking for a good steel hunting knife too, but, as yet, have not found one that is worth anything. I did find a good Boy Scout knife. It wasn't worth the price but it will do okay.

It's hard to be apart but if we're just brave enough to see it through I know we'll be repaid for it in the near future. It won't be long until we'll be back together and all this will be just a dream of the past pushed into the dusk by happiness and joy that will light up our lives forever. As I look outside I can see only a short distance along the ground because of the darkness of night. But as I look upward I can see the stars and the moon, a distance immeasurable. So it is with our lives. If we look only a few days ahead we see nothing but emptiness and loneliness. But if we look upward to the stars and the moon we can see clear to eternity showing us our life ahead and the pathway of happiness we'll walk together.

April 15, 1944

Here we go for the daily report: We flew from 6:10 p.m. last night until 2:30 a.m. this morning after our day off. I finally got to bed about 4:30, but that was cut short by the fact that the dentist wanted to pull my wisdom tooth at 7:45 this morning. He was quite definite about it so I didn't argue. Besides, I was so sleepy I didn't know what was going on until the novocain started wearing off. I spent most of the morning with the dentist, with him taking x-rays and picking out splinters. From 12 until 2 this afternoon I had Link trainer and bomb trainer from 2 till 4. We were supposed to fly again at 6:10 this evening but the flight surgeon grounded me for lack of sleep and the fact that I had a sore jaw, and was still full of dope. Good thing he did because I sure didn't feel like flying.

I had some real fun last night. My navigator went with another crew on a cross-country and I, supposedly, on a bombing mission. Well, we missed the target and got miserably lost. When I finally located myself we were over Shreveport, Louisiana. So in the long run I guess I took a longer cross-country than the navigator! Everything worked out okay, though, as we had enough gas to get home. This is nothing unusual for we have no radio beam here or anything to locate the field. Usually one or two get lost every night. Some have to lay over and refuel and get into all kinds of trouble. I guess it was just my turn and I was lucky at that.

I received two letters from you today and also the box of fudge. It would come on the day I had my tooth pulled! I have it hidden, though, where the vultures can't find it and I intend to enjoy it when my jaw is better. . . .

The truth is that we took off at 6:10 p.m. for a practice night-bombing mission. Our briefing hadn't indicated any particularly bad weather, but the wind was blowing pretty hard at the time. We were airborne after dark and started out to find the bombing range, which was supposed to be marked by flare pots. They were to be placed in a cross, the center of the cross being the actual target.

After approximately an hour of flying time we still hadn't found the bombing area. About that time we received a message from the base telling us to return as the mission had been called off. The weather had turned bad—a front was moving through—and the flare pots at the target had all been blown out, or were never ignited, which was probably the reason we didn't find them. It was also possible we didn't have enough wind correction in and would have missed the target anyway, since the winds were far in excess of what we had been told.

I was on the tower frequency and received the message to return. I tapped my copilot on the shoulder and told him on the interphone that we were heading back to the base: "If it appears on your side of the ship let me know." He nodded his head a couple of times, although he didn't say anything. I assumed he had received the message because the copilot was supposed to remain in interphone contact with the crew.

We made a 180 degree turn plus a correction for what I thought the cross-wind might be, which, in retrospect, was not nearly enough. We flew for about an hour and fifteen minutes. Then Doc motioned to me to switch to interphone and said, "What's going on? Where are we going?"

I said, "We're returning to the base. I called you on the interphone and asked you to tell me if you saw the base. Up to now I haven't spotted it."

"Oh," he said, "we passed the base quite a little while ago. It was on my side of the ship."

"Why didn't you let me know?"

"I didn't receive your message."

To which I replied, "Yes, you did. I tapped you on the shoulder and when I finished you nodded your head 'yes.'" He said, "When you saw me nodding my head I had Jan Garber on the radio—on commercial radio—and I was listening to his program. I was keeping time to the music."

At this point the copilot's job was to monitor the interphone system and my job was to monitor the tower frequency. But it was also my job to make sure the message had been received, which it hadn't.

We made another 180 degree turn and started back. Unbeknownst to us we were drifting farther east because of the severe winds and our lack of sufficient correction. There was no problem—we had been out before at night not knowing where we were. You just tune in a commercial radio station or a military beacon, identify them, turn on the radio direction finder (RDF), and get a bearing to the station. With two stations you can get a fix. Your approximate location is where the two lines of position cross when plotted on a map. There are all kinds of ways to locate yourself with these aids. Another procedure would be to start a "square search." In this you fly in a square and each time you come around you lengthen the leg a little bit and eventually you're going to get back to your home base—providing you have enough fuel. A square search takes a long time as you have to fly these elongated legs to eventually get back around.

We kept searching for something that would give us an indication of where we were. The static was so bad on the radios
they were absolutely useless—we couldn't get a bearing on
anything. I finally called the radio operator and told him to
check in at the NET at our base. NET was a radio receiver and
transmitter that was kept open so the radio operators could
gain experience in their job. If anyone was out and having
trouble he could call the NET. It was done through the radio
operator's equipment in code and it had long-range capability.
It gave him practice, but in this particular instance, I felt we
really needed help, not practice, because the lights on the
ground had long since disappeared. We apparently were over
the top of an overcast and there were several thunderheads in
the area which were causing a lot of electrical interference.

After probably a half hour the radio operator contacted me
again and said, "I can't get into the NET. I think they must be
shut down for the night. No one will answer me and we're
certainly well within range."

We hadn't been able to reach anyone. We couldn't even pick
up a commercial station. We had set up a square search, but
this wasn't helping anything because of the undercast. Even if
we had flown over our base we wouldn't have seen any lights.
There were no radio beacons. Actually, there was a light line
leading to the base that came from the Gulf Coast—through
Fort Worth, Dallas, and on up to Ardmore. With the lights on
and a clear sky it was no problem to fly up that line.

Realizing by now we were thoroughly lost, I called the radio
operator again and told him to send out an SOS signal. "Why
not let me send out PAM signals?" he asked, referring to an
international distress signal of a lower grade which did not
require a written report. "If I send out an SOS you will probably be filling out reports long after we leave here—if we ever
get out of here." So I said, "Roger. It really doesn't make any
difference." After all, a PAM signal was a good signal. It had
the next priority under an SOS—anyone responding to an
SOS would certainly respond to a PAM. So he sent out his
signals—no response.

In the meantime we set up a long-range cruise condition—
low manifold pressure and low rpm on the engines to con-

serve fuel. After a while we abandoned our square search. It wasn't doing us any good. I couldn't even make a guess as to where we were, but I knew we were someplace we shouldn't be!

After what seemed an eternity the radio operator called back and said, "I wasn't able to get a QDM [a code name for a bearing to the station] which you requested, but at least I did get an answer and a bearing away from the station at Shreveport, Louisiana." I grabbed the map and plotted the bearing on it, realizing then that we could be out over the Gulf of Mexico, depending on how far out we were on this line of position.

We turned around and started toward Shreveport, flying the reciprocal of the bearing they gave us, plus a correction factor for what we assumed the wind drift would be. Eventually we began to pick up a little bit on the radio. After what seemed like forever our radio direction finder indicated that we were passing over the station, so we started tuning in other radios heading west. It wasn't long until the sky broke clear— we could see the ground lights of Dallas and Fort Worth below us, and there was the light line heading north to Ardmore.

We'd located ourselves. We knew how to get to the base. We could fly the light line home, but another problem was starting to develop. Our fuel supply was almost depleted.

We knew we were getting close to the base but had not yet spotted the airport beacon when the red light came on for the #3 engine. This indicated we had roughly ten minutes of fuel left on that engine. So I called the engineer and said, "Brownie, can you transfer some fuel—it looks as if we're going to lose #3. Can you take some out of #1 or #2 tanks, come across the center line and into #3?" He answered, "Better yet, maybe I could pull a little out of #4 as it indicates more on the gauges." This meant he'd have to dump from #4 across the center line of the ship into either #1 or #2 and then back again. I said okay.

As soon as he started to pull a little out of #4 and put it into #2 the red light came on on #4. So then he turned around and transferred what little extra he had put in #2 back to #3, which turned the light out on #3. But about the same time the

#4 engine, starved for fuel, sputtered and quit. We feathered #4, and at this point I didn't have any desire to try to transfer any more fuel.

Just as we feathered the engine I told him that if we didn't see the field in a few minutes he should alert the boys for bailout. At this instant I saw the field lights, and as he looked out the window he said, "Isn't that the base up ahead?"

"Yes, it is, but we're short of fuel, as you well know, and I don't know if we can make it. It may be that we will still have to bail out, so let's be ready. But we're going to try to make it in."

I called the tower and was informed we were cleared to land, but to hurry up because we were the last ones out. Obviously they were irritated and tired of waiting for us. We left for a two- or three-hour flight and now we had utilized the full tanks on the B-17. By this time we had flown eight hours.

They told us to make a straight-in approach, which is what we were going to do anyway. I told Doc not to lower the landing gear until we were sure we could make the field. A belly landing would be preferable if we fell short. Just as we touched down on the runway we lost another engine. By this time we had red lights on all four—two engines out—but we were on the ground and still had two engines to taxi back to the line. People weren't—well, in a way, I guess they were overjoyed to see us—but they were rather put out that we had kept everybody up for so long. We went on home, as by now it was early in the morning.

At 7 a.m. I was ordered to come down to the Operations Office to make a report on why I was so late the night before. Of course we knew what we had done was wrong. The mistake on my part was that I should have received confirmation from the copilot that he understood my message that we were returning to the base. There was also the factor that he was on the wrong channel listening to commercial music when he should have been monitoring the crew efforts. But these boo-boos were not mentioned in my report. Be that as it may, the squadron commander and the operations officer wanted me to understand that they were unhappy with what had happened.

I wasn't happy either. My only defense was that here we were with an aircraft worth a considerable amount of money, we had a crew on board without a navigator, and we had bad weather, bad enough for them to cancel the mission. Yet when they canceled the mission they also closed the communication NET. I assume this is the only thing that saved me. I made a point of the fact that had they left the NET open after they contacted us to return, we could have been in.

Apparently they didn't really want to break up a bomber crew just to discipline me. It was just a stand-off.

"Have you learned a lesson?" they asked.

"Yes," I replied, "I've learned several lessons." I enumerated what they were and this seemed to satisfy everybody as nothing more was ever said.

Clearly, at this stage of our training, we were a greater danger to ourselves than we were to the enemy.

April 19, 1944

Things are running about the same as usual—they couldn't get any worse. We're still flying just as hard and long as we can and putting in all the ground school and trainer time possible. We haven't averaged six hours sleep a night for the past week. But we still have to keep at it or we won't be able to finish here by the 18th of May. All our days off have been canceled and we're on a straight schedule.

I can say one thing, though, we have really learned a lot since we've been here, both from books and experience. It seems as if every time we go up something goes haywire. We always have a malfunction somewhere. If possible we try to fix it. If we can't we improvise some way so we can do without it and keep on going. We get experience all right— if we could just separate the good from the bad everything would be okay.

I've sure been having a time. My tooth hasn't healed up yet. My cheek is still puffed out and my jaw sore. Every day we go to high altitude and you should see me when I try to poke my face into the oxygen mask!

That's enough gripes for now. I must get to bed and get all the sleep I can, for tomorrow I have to fly high altitude formation to Galveston, refuel, fly a gunnery mission over the Gulf, refuel again, and fly high altitude formation back. We'll probably be in the air at least twelve or thirteen hours. Allowing a couple of hours for refueling we'll have quite a day ahead.

We went out on a daylight mission. We were given ten bombs to drop, giving Dimit a little practice. This was no problem. It was broad daylight. We found the bombing range, we had the practice bombs in the bomb bay, on our first pass over Dimit made his drop, and he made a good drop. We were using the Automatic Flight Control Equipment (AFCE), auto-pilot. On the bomb run, when you are on AFCE, the bombardier actually assumes directional control of the aircraft through the Norden bomb sight. The pilot maintains the altitude and the airspeed as requested by the bombardier, and it has to be accurate, as he has preset this information into his sight. However, if you have a malfunction in the automatic pilot you can always disengage it and fly manually using the Pilot Direction Indicator (PDI) needle. Things were working fine and we were letting him control the aircraft from the IP (Initial Point at which the bomb run commences) to the target each time.

On our second pass around we set up another good run, and there was no doubt that Dimit was a good bombardier. He dropped this one and we came close to getting a bull's eye. But on our third bomb run the radio operator said the bomb did not release. Brownie checked the electric bomb release mechanism and found a fuse had blown. We had some extra fuses on board so I told him to put another one in and we would try again.

We then made another run and the bomb went away. Frank again made a good drop. At the same time the fuse blew again, so Brownie said he'd make the switch. In the meantime I called the tower at Ardmore and told them what our problems were. With our being lost in my mind from the time before, I decided this time we had better communicate with our people and get their okay on what we were doing. They asked if we were experiencing any difficulties other than blowing fuses. I said no, as near as I could tell there was no danger to anyone or to the aircraft. There was never any smoke. It was just that each time a bomb dropped we blew a fuse. If we replaced the fuse we could drop another bomb.

"How many fuses do you have left?" I answered, "Three." "Roger, drop three more bombs and come home."

That sounded good. On our next drop the bomb released. Again the fuse blew. This time Brownie called me and said that when the fuse blew it welded the end of the fuse into the fuse block. "I'll have to try to pry it out of there, but when I touch it with my screwdriver we get sparks everywhere. If you can pull the power off of the buss I'll go ahead and pry it out and put in a new one."

"Okay, there's a procedure for this and it'll take me a couple of minutes, but I'll get that system isolated for you."

Well, Doc was still pretty new to the airplane and its systems, but he was learning fast. Our copilots came direct from twin-engine flying schools. This was their first experience with the B-17, and at this point they had had very limited ground school. He said, "Oh, just a minute. I'll solve the problem for you." I started to say, "Wait, Doc"—but by that time his hand was already forward and he pulled the master switch.

Believe me, you can't imagine how quiet it is in the aircraft when all four engines quit! The props are still windmilling, but it is extremely quiet, and it does shake you up.

In this situation I needed to get the manifold pressure control turned down or else the engines and props would run away. Luckily, the aircraft had an electric system with a single knob for the manifold pressure on all four engines. Many of the aircraft had four manual levers. Each engine had to be adjusted individually, and this took time. But just as I reached to grab the manifold pressure knob and spin it back, Doc pushed the master switch back on. All four engines roared back to life as I was still hollering because I didn't want him to turn them on until I had the pressure turned down.

As luck would have it I got just enough twist on the knob and the batteries on the airplane activated the control. The props did not overspeed, and the waste gates which direct the exhaust gasses down through the superchargers held. It is possible to blow them out, and this was what I expected would happen. But we were lucky that day.

When an engine goes into overspeed it means a mandatory engine change, and even in those days that Wright Cyclone engine—not to mention the labor to install it—was not cheap. The thought of buying four of them just didn't appeal to me. Most people didn't realize that in those days damage to aircraft that was caused by pilot error or ignorance could be charged to the pilot, and it took a long time on the installment plan to get even. I had friends who were already paying for wing tips damaged in taxi accidents, but the tips were trivial compared to this. This type of thing was frowned upon during the training stage. A pilot could and would be "washed out" for using poor judgment.

But we were very fortunate. Brownie turned white and I know I turned two shades of white because we both expected all the problems that go with an overspeed condition. Needless to say, we had had enough. We didn't want to try to drop any more bombs. We felt we had got out of that one—our engines had been restarted, we did not exceed the manifold pressure, and the props didn't run away. Not desiring to push our luck any further, we headed back for the base.

Doc was quite embarrassed and felt bad. He said he really thought that the master switch turned off everything on the aircraft except the magnetos, which would keep the engines running. I said I was sorry I hadn't pointed that out to him before. The master switch kills everything on the plane, including the magnetos. In the event of a crash landing or a wheels-up landing, you pull the master switch just before touch-down and it kills everything electrical on the plane, reducing the fire hazard.

Again it appeared that we were our own worst enemies.

April 21, 1944

Here it is Saturday and I still haven't made the trip to Galveston. The weather has been so bad on the Gulf that even the ducks are grounded, but we have managed to keep on flying. We have been flying lots of big ship formation at high altitude. They're trying to get us in shape for the big contest we have coming up next Saturday. We have challenged the fellows taking OTU at Dyersburg, Tennessee, and those at Alexandria, Louisiana, to fly formation with us. We'll probably have twenty-four ships from each field. Our group has been chosen to lead. The idea is we'll have a formation the size that they use in combat, then we all fly to our objective, which will be some large town down there, and we'll camera bomb it. The Big Shots will be stationed along the way to judge the formation and the bombing films will be exchanged. So the competition is not only formation but the accuracy of the bombing. It might turn out to be fun but right now it looks like a lot of work. Oh yeah, they've also arranged with a Fighter Transition School to give us fighter escort, and other ships to be enemy fighters. We'll use blank ammunition in our guns and also cameras. It will, no doubt, be a harum-scarum affair with all kinds of shooting and noise and airplanes scattered all over the Southwest.

Thursday evening I had quite a pleasant surprise—Cap and Sis dropped in. They were on their way to Randolph Field, Texas, where Cap has now been stationed as an instructor. It was just by luck that they came by after I had just finished flying. They stayed overnight in Ardmore so I was able to visit with them four or five hours. I enjoyed their visit but was so tired I could hardly stay awake to talk. . . .

Boy, am I having troubles. First, I was fined five dollars yesterday because the ball turret slipped when we were coming in for a landing. It let the guns point straight down at the ground. If the tower hadn't notified us and we'd landed that way we would really have torn things up. Then bright and early this morning they tell us that there are only three first pilots out of fifty-six crews who will make 1st lieutenant while we're here. At first they said at least twenty-five percent would make it. So everybody has been working like the dickens to get in that class. Now we see that we have been disillusioned. Even that wouldn't be so bad, but no, I've taught my copilot too much, so now I think they're going to take him away from me and send him to Transition. If they send any copilots back at all he'll be among them because he heads the list. As you can see I'm slightly disgusted. Oh well, I have to tell my troubles to someone and you're the only one who will sympathize with me.

We have been working like hell to get someplace and it seems that the harder we work the more things go against us. If it weren't for all the old buddies here going through the same thing and the thoughts of what we are working for this place would be unbearable. We thought we were having a rough time coming through Cadets, but I'm convinced that was child's play compared to this. Several fellows have been dismissed from the service here already for some of the darnedest reasons, dishonorably, of course. None of them were from our outfit, however.

Ran into Gassman while at the chow house and he gave me some of the latest dope. It seems, according to him, that the Donkins and Gosewischs are expecting. It must be something in the Oklahoma air that did it because I don't think the fellows have had enough time off to do the job. That's just my opinion, though. . . .

Must close—we fly at 4:30 in the morning. Incidentally, we leave here May 18th.

The incident with the ball turret deserves further comment. We had been out on a combination air-to-ground practice gunnery and bombing mission. The gunnery phase was completed first and we were well into the bombing phase when I decided to let the ball turret gunner leave the ball turret. The ball turret is probably the most uncomfortable place in the airplane. Since the mission was about over it would be a good time to let him get out, stretch his legs, and get the blood circulating again.

For the ball turret gunner to leave the turret while in the air, he has to point the guns straight down toward the ground. In this position he has a small trap door above his head that opens up into the waist gunner's compartment. After he climbs up from the turret the normal procedure would be to close the door, rotate the ball until the guns point aft and parallel to the fuselage, and then lock the turret in this position. This decreases drag and is the normal landing position. A landing made with the guns pointing down could inflict serious damage to the aircraft and personnel.

In this instance—thinking he would later re-enter the ball—Mac left it in the guns-down position and went to the radio room where he could visit with the other gunners who had gathered there. Now this was also where the gunners were positioned during landing. They sat on the floor, facing toward the tail, with their backs to the forward bulkhead. This was the safest position for them in the event of trouble on landing.

In a matter of thirty minutes or so the mission was completed and we started home. I called the tower and received permission to land—"use runway 26, wind 10 mph with gusts, altimeter setting 28.92" and so on. We would be number one to land as there was no other air traffic in sight.

The copilot called for the crew landing check on the interphone. Every man on the ship had to acknowledge that his position was ready for landing. The bombardier reported that his guns were stowed, bomb-bay doors closed, and so on. The engineer reported the top turret stowed for landing, and he took his station between the pilot and the copilot to help monitor the gauges and do whatever was needed. The radio operator confirmed that his trailing wire antennae was retracted and the top window in the radio room was closed. The ball turret gunner was expected to report from the radio room that the ball turret was stowed, locked, and ready for landing. After everyone had checked his position the copilot notified me the aircraft was ready for landing and proceeded with the cockpit check.

I returned to tower frequency for any other instructions they might have, as well as reporting my position, turning final, gear down and locked, aircraft secured for landing. The tower acknowledged, "Roger, Able Fox 246, have you in sight, number one on final approach, clear to land." Good, we won't waste any time in the pattern today.

At 200 feet above the runway the tower called, "Able Fox 246, permission to land denied. Pull up and go around. Please acknowledge." Oh well, they probably had some trouble on the ground that I couldn't see. We wouldn't have to leave the pattern, just pour on the power—the props are already at high rpm—get the gear up, and come around again.

On the downwind leg of the pattern we completed the landing check again and the copilot notified me that all positions were checked and the aircraft was ready for landing. I called the tower again, reporting on the downwind leg, "Landing check complete. Request permission to land." They answer, "Roger, Able Fox 246, number one in the pattern cleared to land. Give call on final approach." Again at 200 feet over the runway the tower called. "Able Fox 246 permission denied. Pull up and go around."

"Roger, Tower. Able Fox 246 executing go-around procedure." Obviously they had more trouble than I thought, but they would get their problem solved eventually.

In the meantime we went through the landing check again and proceeded as before. The same thing happened on our third approach. Oh well, they would get their act together and we would get down. Besides, it is a beautiful day for flying, the crew needs practice on their go-around procedure, so we're all learning and logging more air time.

So we try for the fourth time. Again we followed the same procedures, but—pull up and go around. Well, you only need so much of this kind of experience, and I can take a hint. I began to suspect there was something wrong with the airplane. I asked the copilot to start the landing check again and again he reported that everything was secure and ready to land. Before starting our cockpit check I switched back to tower frequency and called, "Ardmore Tower, this is Able Fox 246 requesting landing instructions. I suspect there is something wrong with my airplane since we're not allowed to land. But my crew reports the aircraft is ready for landing. So if it is the aircraft just give me a clue and I can assure you that I will solve the problem." The Tower reported back, "Able Fox 246, when you stow your ball turret you will be allowed to land."

This is rather embarrassing to a first pilot because every ship within receiving range of Ardmore Tower now knows that we have committed a real goof. You could almost hear the laughter in the tower as we sheepishly flew away.

I switched back to the interphone and in a very quiet but firm voice stated, "Fellows, I don't mind flying in circles, but we are going to do so until somebody stows the ball turret instead of just *reporting* that it has been stowed." Believe me, there was some frantic activity on board that aircraft as every gunner checked his position before the next landing check.

When we re-entered the pattern we were real pros on landing procedure and there was no holdup this time. I also knew that the engineer, who was the ranking NCO and the crew leader, would do some chewing before the day was out. The pilot was fined $5 before the day was over too, to remind him that this was a mistake that could have been prevented. But these were small matters involving a potential disaster to an airplane and crew, or so one thinks at age twenty-two. These things wouldn't happen again.

April 24, 1944

Another day gone by and time grows shorter proportionately. We now have sixteen more days of flying left. Needless to say, we are still behind in our missions. The weather has been the main contributing factor. While we haven't been in the storm center of all the weather activity down this way, we have been on the edge of it and have been hampered by strong winds, low ceilings, thunderstorms, rain, hail, and blowing dust. Today was really the best day we've had here—blue sky, no winds, and a real warm spring day.

As far as any news from here there really isn't any. Things are just the same as usual. My bombardier and navigator have been quite concerned with me lately because they say I live like a hermit. Since my copilot has moved into town no one is in my room with me so I'm quite content to be alone to read and sleep any time we might have off. They have tried numerous times to get me to go to the show with them here on the post. Up until last night I've always refused. First, because I feel that I can't waste the time and secondly, I felt that if I wasn't working I should be sleeping.

Last night I finally gave in and went with them as we had a couple of extra hours off. Today they felt as if they had really done a good job. Don't get me wrong, I haven't really developed any habits or manners of a hermit. I have just been busy devising schemes and methods to make the crew function better, and brooding over a few responsibilities which have been placed on me which they do not fully realize. You see, they are concerned only with the worries and responsibilities which affect their own position. In my case I'm concerned with the worries and have the responsibility of all ten positions. I can't quite explain how it works, but here the pilot is held responsible for everything that affects his crew. He answers to the Squadron Commander and the crew answers to him. It's just the old Army chain-of-command. The Big Boys bite me so I bite the little ones.

Incidentally we have had a slight change in set-up. Four more crews were added to my Flight so now we're a Squadron and the official title is Squadron Leader.

April 25, 1944

. . . Life here is as usual. We're still flying lots of high altitude formation and high altitude camera bombing in formation. It's kind of fun but there's a lot of work and strain to it. My copilot is getting to the point where he can fly pretty good formation so that gives me a chance to rest occasionally and eases lots of the worry. I hope they don't take him away from me and send him to Transition because I've really worked with him to get him in shape. But if he gets the chance I won't stand in his way because he has lots of ability and is just an all-around good pilot. Besides, I like him well enough to want to do all I can for him. The rest of the fellows are doing all right in their positions and I still feel that I have the best crew on the field.

Incidentally, I have a new tail gunner as of day before yesterday. Larson is still in the hospital so he was taken off the crew. The new fellow seems like a very good fellow, maybe even better than Larson. His name is Martin J. Smith—a Buck Sergeant. I haven't had time yet to find out where he's from or anything else, but will find out all that tomorrow. . . .

I haven't any idea of what will happen when we leave here. I am sure of one thing, though, and that is that we won't get any leave while stationed here. I rather doubt if we get any after leaving either because I think we will go right to a staging area for overseas replacement. But that is only my opinion based on rumors, and you know Army rumors! I wish I could tell you one way or another about it, but I can't. All I can do is hope and pray that I will get to see you before then.

I would like to have you get me a small book of poems—one containing some of those that we like best. Also when you send it put in Elbert Hubbard's Scrapbook. I would kind of like to read some of them in my spare moments.

I am going to close for now. I have a few minutes left but Work and I have been working on letters to send to my crew's folks, so we want to *write a couple of them tonight. I should have written them long ago, but you know me and my letter writing. Work makes a good Executive Officer!*

April 28, 1944

Yesterday I was through in time to go down and pick up my package at the post office. The knife is swell—just what I wanted and the sheath will fit on my belt. It is recommended that we carry it in case of a bailout or other situation. Thanks a lot. I really like it.

We had quite a busy day yesterday. We flew from 4 a.m. till noon, or rather, we were on the line that long. We flew only five hours and forty minutes. My engineer wanted to get married last night so I got him out of flying and retreat so he had the whole day off. The rest of the enlisted men and myself stood retreat at five. Then we all got dressed for the big wedding. I even splurged for a haircut and barber shave! I went in and saw the Squadron Commander and got the whole crew off today. I knew that if we got him married it would be late and we wouldn't feel like getting up at four and flying. He didn't much want to give us today off because today is the big group formation with the other fields participating. I argued pretty strong, and he kind of likes our crew so he finally gave in.

Anyway, to proceed: The wedding was to be at eight so we went in town for dinner and were all ready, but then it was put off until nine-thirty. We finally got them married in the presence of the whole crew at the Baptist Church. Poor Brownie was so nervous I didn't think he was going to make it. Good thing the service was short. After the wedding we went over to a lady's house where my radio operator lives and had a gab fest. We broke up the party at eleven-thirty—left the newlyweds to themselves and we came home.

Brown is having his wedding pictures taken at one today so we're all going in and have a crew picture made. Just as soon as they are finished I'll send you one so you can see the fellows I'm working with.

April 29, 1944

Today I received two letters from you and also a box of cookies. I hope you realize how attached I'm becoming to your cooking. What a lucky guy I am! Dimit and Work agree with me and they watch my mail like a hawk so they won't miss out on any of the goodies. . . .

Incidentally, we have had a slight change of schedule—we are supposed to be all through flying by the 2nd of May. That means we have only three days of flying left. I am pretty sure we are going back to ground school. We can't possibly finish all of the flying we were supposed to have here, but, at least, we have done most of the important missions. So I guess we won't miss out on too much. Doggone, they sure keep us guessing. We don't know from one day to the next what is going on. There is only one thing fairly certain and that is that we will be leaving here by the 18th of May.

May 1, 1944

Here it is the first of May and another month gone by—just one more day of flying left. The last two days the weather has been so bad we haven't been able to get in the air. Consequently we can't possibly finish even our required missions in one more day. In my case I would have to have at least three good days. We still haven't been to Galveston. It's definite that we will quit flying, though, for a while. We are going back to ground school for a week, then those who still need more flying will go back to the line for a week or until they do complete their flying. That takes care of our last two weeks here at Ardmore.

Our proofs came back yesterday and the pictures were exceptionally good for a group. Of course I had a silly grin on my face in all of them, but the pictures of the rest of the fellows were really good. . . . They're not regular portrait pictures—they're like those squadron pictures I had when I was in Cadets. We should get the regular pictures in a couple of days and I'll send them right on to you. . . .

Guess what?! Today I found a billfold containing over three hundred dollars, but there would have to be an identification card in it! I didn't know the fellow but he was a navigator on one of my buddy's crew. Boy, he sure was a happy guy when I gave it to him—so happy, in fact, he tried to give me a twenty dollar bill for returning it. I refused, though, because he was a married man and I figured he could probably use it just as well as myself.

Oh yes, while we are on the subject of money, you can wire or send me fifty dollars anytime before the 18th of this month. I'll probably need it to move out of here. Later in Staging Area I'll probably need more but you can send that to me later when I see how much I need depending on where we're going.

I'm now going to tell you something about the more personal side of Army life. The reason I think to tell you now is that today I received your letter telling about our friend who is having trouble accepting Army life and facing a combat tour overseas. I've seen this start since I've been here and watched it grow. It's commonly called "combatitis" or "third phaseitis." The instructors say it happens in every class when they are about to finish up. As you know, we're the next class to leave here—don't know where we're going or why—but one thing is certain and that is combat. Outside of the pilots, I don't believe the rest of the men have thought much about it up until now. The pilots have been trained for this and told to watch for it from the beginning, and have looked forward—rather I should say, expected—this. But, for the rest of the crew, it has just now dawned upon them what they have gotten into. For the gunners, bombardiers, and navigators the Air Corps has suddenly lost a lot of glamor. Life has suddenly lost a lot of glamor. Life has suddenly become very dear, combat very close, and their imagination playing tricks on them. It leaves them tight-lipped and very much engrossed in thought, or rather, in idle dreaming, without which they would be better off.

Surrounding us is an atmosphere of nervousness and, in some cases, even making us antagonistic toward those who have relatively easy jobs, or who at least have security. In cases where their job is not done properly they assume an attitude of "who cares, it's me that's going overseas, not you." They give the Permanent Personnel a little trouble and no end of worry. Some would like to quit right now and would if a court martial didn't stare them in the face.

It's quite an odd thing. You can hardly describe it—in some cases you can't see it, but it's a feeling you know that's there. It's nothing to worry about because they are all good men. They can and will do their jobs. It's just something you have to put up with now until they get their minds in condition for what's coming ahead. These are all gener-

alities and do not necessarily apply to any one crew even though I write in first person.

P.S. I forgot to tell you that Work and I have all the letters written to my crew's folks.

May 4, 1944

Doggone, I sure have a time with my cookies! Fontana came over to get his one but wouldn't leave until he'd had about six or maybe more. Then Dimit, Work, and Doxon wanted a sample. I'd have been better off to have given them the box and kept the sample myself! . . .

As you have probably guessed we have quit flying and are in ground school, today being the second day of it. We are now scheduled for six days of ground school, then return to the flight line to pick up the rest of our missions. I still have to have at least three days of good weather to finish. Still have some high altitude bombs to drop and some high altitude formation plus the Galveston trip. Oh well, I refuse to worry about it now. If the weather holds I'll finish. If not, it probably won't make any difference anyway.

May 5, 1944

Nothing of interest here today—a routine schedule with hour after hour of lectures. Only three more days of it left. . . .

May 10, 1944

After so long a time here I am again. Same old story so I'll not bother you with it again. Instead I'll tell you what I did on my letter writing night. The evening that I had free I went to town to the picture show, The Memphis Belle. *I enjoyed it very much. It is a picture of actual combat, no Hollywood in it. That we know for sure because we have four of the first pilots who were on that raid here as instructors. Also the fellow who filmed most of the picture is our Group C.O. Well, it was very interesting to us to know these fellows, talk with them, work* with them, then go to a show and see just exactly what they went through and what they did. So much for that.

We are now back to flying. I didn't finish ground school—the weather looked as if we might be able to fly so we were pulled out of ground school only to sit on the line and watch the clouds go by. The last two days have been reasonably good, though, and we did get a lot done. All I need now is just one more good day. I'm still sweating out the Galveston mission—sure hope they have good weather there tomorrow.

Oh yes, I forgot to tell you how our big formation bombing contest came out with the other fields. We came out on top! No competition, they said, but I'm convinced we worked for it. . . .

I'm going to close for now as I have a thousand and one things to do and hardly enough time to get them done. With only eight more days left here we'll really have to hustle to get everything done. I'm pretty sure when we leave here we'll go to some place in Nebraska—Camp Kearney, Grand Island, or some such place. If we don't get a leave at our next station I would say that within four weeks from now we'll be in one of the theaters of operation. If that's the case I'll promise you I'll be home by Christmas. But I'll tell you more about that when the time comes.

May 14, 1944

We finally flew our big Galveston mission and it was a long, hard, grueling flight. But it was also very rewarding as far as experience and accomplishments went. All members of the crew had a good workout and I was very pleased with their performance. It far exceeded my expectations. I can truthfully say we now look and act like a real "bomber crew." We certainly pulled some real boners in the beginning, but the rough edges are now gone. I only hope they have the same trust in me as I have in them.

Our very last flight here was a dog-leg cross-country and we were allowed to choose our own route. I called Roco (rhymes with cocoa) [Work] in and told him to plan a route that would take us over the homes of as many crew members as he could work in with the amount of flying time we had. I wanted to give as many of our boys as I could one last look at home. Work plotted a good course and there were some *happy boys on that airplane. We didn't break any flying regulations but we sure bent some in our let-downs and pull-ups over the homes!*

Two "boners" come to mind at once. One involved us and the second involved another crew. Ours first:

When Doc first came aboard the aircraft he felt that it was an awfully big airplane, not too maneuverable, and not all that much fun to fly. He had his eye set, the same as every other pilot, on a nice single-engine fighter that you could loop and roll and do all kinds of aerobatic maneuvers. Or if not that, at least a B-25 or an A-20—something that was hot and highly maneuverable.

I tried to explain to him that while the B-17 was big you could still make some pretty sharp turns with it. You could stall the aircraft, do wing-overs, and other unusual positions that would produce some real flying sensations. I told him if he wanted to get familiar with it he could stall the plane and get the feel of what a stall was like in this big airplane. He could have the thrill of going over the top when she breaks away, but not to be too violent as the crew didn't have any safety belts, or if they had safety belts they wouldn't be fastened as they were working around the airplane. We did tell the crew we were going to stall the airplane and to be prepared for some unusual positions.

I assumed we would ease the power off gently, pull the nose up until the airplane stalled, then as it started to break over, catch it with full power on the engines. But Doc's idea was a little different. He wanted it to break clear away—which he did—but not on the first one. We made three or four stalls with each one progressively a little steeper and a little rougher than the one before. Of course when you are in the stall phase just as she breaks away you experience what the pilots of today and the space shuttle people feel with their weightlessness.

Although we didn't become completely gravity-free, things in the airplane had a tendency to float around. On the first or second one the flight manuals started floating around the cockpit. We had some extra fluorescent light bulbs that would be used in night flying to illuminate the instrument panel. These hadn't been installed but were lying on the console.

They were floating around too. We were having a good time laughing about that.

The boys back in the radio room noticed that their things were also floating around. They had the top hatch open and we had a camera on board. Our mission did not require a camera so it was still in the radio room in its storage box. Evidently it had not been turned in by the preceding crew. I don't know, but I imagine that box weighed close to twenty or thirty pounds. On the last stall Hinman called me and said, "Do you know the camera that was in the box is gone?" "What do you mean it's gone?" I answered. He said, "On that last maneuver it just floated up and out the top hatch." Of course my next thought was, "Did it hit the tail plane?" We hadn't felt anything. Hinman assured me it hadn't hit anything. It was just plain gone!

This sobered us up a little bit, and we decided we had done enough steep turns and stalls. By this time Doc had found out the airplane was much more maneuverable than he ever thought it would be. These were the most violent maneuvers we ever made in the B-17 until we reached combat. Then we did some really violent maneuvers!

Anyway we were all wondering how much one of those cameras costs, and if we would have to pay for it. All kinds of scenarios went through our minds.

When we landed at Ardmore a jeep pulled up to the aircraft and we were asked if we had a camera on board. We said we didn't, which wasn't an actual untruth. We might have had one when we left, but we sure didn't have one on landing! So the jeep proceeded on to the next aircraft and so on down the line. We didn't run into any problems over that because no one on the crew had signed for a camera.

But it also brings back to mind that on our way back from Galveston we had one B-17 in our unit return without the top gun turret. How that thing got out of the aircraft I'll never know. But Doc is of the opinion—and I suspect he's probably right—that after the formation had broken up this crew decided to loop the aircraft, and as Doc says, it was probably an awfully poor loop. They stayed on their back too long, and this was how they lost the turret. Our losing the camera looked pretty pale in comparison. Now there was a crew that was going to have to give a lot of answers!

May 18, 1944

Leaving immediately for Kearney Army Air Base, Nebraska. Will wire if possible from there.

Incidentally, there were no first pilot promotions. We are all leaving as 2nd lieutenants with the exception of Fontana, who has been a 1st lieutenant ever since we met back in flying school.

May 20, 1944

After another one of those enjoyable train rides we arrived here late yesterday afternoon. The ride wasn't nearly as bad as lots we have taken, but even at its best it was far from comfortable.

Before leaving Ardmore I sent you a note plus a letter from one of the fellows' sister. I thought perhaps you might enjoy reading it. I also had a letter from Brown's father and one from his mother. I want you to keep these letters for me. I had occasion just prior to leaving to meet some more of the fellows' parents. It was rather a touching time but, nevertheless, the duty of a pilot. They have all expressed trust and faith in my ability to bring their boys home. I can readily assure anyone that I too have the same confidence and that it's only a matter of time before we'll be home.

Now about the leave situation—it's very bad and it's definitely decided that there will be none except in cases of emergency, verified by the Red Cross.

You are probably wondering how, when, and what goes on here and in the future. Well, so am I. I'm sure you are thoroughly disgusted with the brevity and vagueness of my letters. I don't blame you, but I think you understand the restrictions we're under. The regulations don't mean so much in themselves, but our necks do. So you can see we have a good reason for squelching any rumors before they get started. At this point of the game there's not much to say. I promise I'll write you at every opportunity. I'll try to call you this evening if it's at all possible.

May 22, 1944

. . . *Right at the present things are kind of screwed up. We don't know as yet whether we'll fly or go by boat. Some of our fellows have already received new airplanes and they know for sure what the deal is. The rest of us are still hanging in the fire waiting for somebody to make up their minds. They can take just as long as they want as far as I'm concerned.*

I won't be able to wire or call you when I leave here, but will write so you'll know when I leave. You are the only one I'm writing to while I'm here so you'll have to let my folks know. I tried to wire them my new address like I did to you, but was refused by the telegraph office. They're kind of tough with us, but you know why. Incidentally, I received the money okay. Thanks a lot. I also received the last letter you sent to Ardmore today. The number of missions is now thirty, but I'll have them and be with you Christmas.

Above all, don't worry about me—I know you will, but don't let it get you down. You know me, I'll look out for myself, for I haven't spent all this time training without an eye to that. Besides, I know what I have to come home to so I just won't be taking any unnecessary chances. That's a promise!

May 23, 1944

I'm rather surprised at the fact that I'm still here. But as yet things are still all messed up and it seems as if nobody can get any orders on us. They manage to keep us busy, though, with a few classes and training films the whole day. The war of nerves is well underway. We are a little used to it, so in another day or so it should wear off—that is, if finger nails and shoe leather hold out. None of us are any too anxious to leave, but then in another way we'd like to get started so we can get it over. Boy, I sure want to get it over so I can get home to my wife and little one—that's paramount with me.

If we should get an airplane it wouldn't take us very long, probably a couple of days to get over. But if we go by boat it will probably slow us down, maybe two or three weeks. It makes little difference to me since I don't have any choice anyway. They say everything happens for the best so one way or the other will be okay.

That's just about all the news from here. There are no rumors. This is one time when everyone is content to keep his mouth shut and wait for orders.

May 28, 1944

Surprised to find out that I'm still at Kearney? Well, I am too! Our stay of over a week here has set a record at this field. They were beginning to refer to us as part of the Permanent Post Personnel. But I can safely say now that our stay has just about come to an end. I presume that you have already received my temporary APO number, but to be on the safe side I will include it at the end of the letter.

The orders have been received on us, but as yet we do not know their content, only the APO address. But this much is sure—we will not fly away from Kearney. We could possibly fly away from the POE [Port of Embarkation] which will be our next stop. If we did fly we would not receive our own plane. It would be via ATC [Air Transport Command.] There's a very strong chance that we might be ferried across that way because we are shipping out of here four crews at a time. I think I prefer that way to going by boat. After all, we are supposed to be fliers. Don't know what difference it would make except for probably a week's difference in travel time. In any event it looks as if we'll probably be on hand for D-Day.

Now to relate what I've been doing the past three or four days and why you haven't heard from me sooner. Let's start with Wednesday as that was the first day with nothing scheduled. Wednesday I slept the clock around for twenty-four straight hours and, believe me, it was wonderful. I got out of bed only long enough to eat two meals.

That brings us to Thursday. The setup here is that you're restricted to the post all day, but can go to town in the evenings. Of course now we are restricted all the time. To continue—Thursday my crew challenged another to a game of baseball, which, by the way, was Foster's crew. Needless to say, we beat them easily. That took care of all morning and the early part of the afternoon. At five o'clock we were able to get off the post so we all went to a riding academy, rented some horses, and had fun chasing jackrabbits all over the countryside. We rode until about 9 p.m. Then, as we were in the mood for more fun, we went to a roller-skating rink and stayed there long enough for everyone to have a good spill which, incidentally, didn't take long. After that we called it a day and went home to bed.

Next comes Friday in which we just about repeated the events of Thursday except that we played ball early in the morning with Flores' crew and chalked up another win. My boys haven't lost a game of baseball, volleyball, or basketball since we've been together. While none are exceptional players they just work together and we always come out on top.

Friday afternoon we spent washing all our dirty clothes, and believe me, we had enough of them. There's no laundry service here and we didn't care to carry any dirty ones with us so it left us just one choice. I sure miss you at times like that, but you know I miss you all the time, anyway. After putting out the laundry we went over to the stables and those of us who weren't too stiff from the day before went for another long ride. When that was finished we put in another hour on roller skates, then bowled for a while. Work says to tell you that I may lead the league in horseback riding but when it comes to bowling I'm not much competition. By the time we had bowled three games we were tired enough to start a "back to the sack movement."

Now for Saturday. All good things have to come to an end sometime so we had to quit playing and settle down to business. We went through a complete clothing process. We were issued lots of new equipment and turned in most of the old stuff. I even turned in my heavy leather pants. The new things they gave us are wonderful—I like them far better than the others. We also got a lot of junk which we'll probably never use, but regulations say we must have it so we have it! The rest of Saturday was spent trying to pack. Boy, what a job! You can take just so much and it has to be in the right bag in the right place. They have a baggage inspection just to make sure you have everything in the right place and also to see if you are taking all the required equipment. . . .

This morning was Sunday so we got up just in time to go to breakfast and then to church. First Sunday we've had a chance to go to church in quite some time. . . .

There are lots of things I'd like to tell you but it is almost impossible to put them on paper.

* * *

P.S. I can't promise how soon you'll hear from me again but will make it just as soon as possible. You can start writing any time to my new APO. . . .

Don't worry about me, I'll be okay, and don't forget we have a date for Christmas and I'll keep it. In the meantime keep your chin up.

May 30, 1944

This is it! If you don't hear from me for a while don't worry as it is all a part of the game. . . .

Feiss, Fletcher, Flores, and Fontana all say "so long" for now.

The day we left Kearney, Nebraska, for New York City the honor of being the Officer In Charge Of The Troops was conferred upon me. What this meant was I would be in charge of the troop movement and I would carry all official papers and the sealed orders for the crews. These papers were to be delivered to the Commander of the Station we were reporting to in New York City.

As I read my orders as troop commander, I saw that we were to change trains and train stations in Chicago, but there was no mention of what we were to use for transportation. Well, Army Air Corps crews should travel in good style. After all, we were the glamorous and the elite who would fly and die, if necessary, for our country.

With this thought in mind I asked the major who had presented me with the honor if buses would meet us at the train station. I would have four crews to transport—sixteen officers and twenty-four enlisted men. The major said, "No." So I scaled down my expectations somewhat and inquired, "Trucks?" At this the major looked at me and said, "Lieutenant, didn't they teach you how to march in Cadet School?" "Yes, Sir," I answered.

"And did they teach you how to give commands?"

"Yes, Sir."

"Then you will have no problem placing your troops in formation and marching them to the other station."

"Then, Sir, will there be a '6 by 6' to carry the baggage?"

"Lieutenant, you know eighty pounds is all the weight you are allowed to have with you. A good field pack for a soldier would weigh far more than that. You shouldn't have any problems."

After a very weak "Yes, Sir," I was stupid enough to ask if they had included a map with the directions on how to reach the other station. His reply was, "You're a commissioned officer. Surely you can figure out some way to perform your mission." I was very happy to say "Yes, Sir," and disappear. He didn't even wish me well.

Seven years earlier, at the tender age of fifteen, I had arrived in Chicago at the same station at which we would be arriving. I had spent one night in Chicago and left the next day. I had no idea where the other station was located. During the train ride it came to me in a flash that our waist gunner, Joe Firszt, was from Chicago. He was very familiar with the area and I had him write down the street names and directions we should go to change stations. I had him put this in writing just in case he decided to go AWOL when we reached his home town.

In reality the distance between stations was probably a good country mile. But there we were in formation at route step— all thirty-eight of us—the officers dragging their B-4 bags and the enlisted men with their barracks bags over their shoulders, bent double from the weight. The people on the streets at that early hour were indeed treated to a look at thirty-eight real sad sacks, the pride of the U.S. Army Air Corps, staggering down the streets of Chicago enroute to battle.

Since there should have been *forty* men staggering along those Chicago streets, the reader may wonder where the missing two had gone. Brownie and Joe Firszt believed in improvisation. They took a taxi and were waiting for us at the other station.

The Main Event

"Aye, 'tis a great contest going on over there. 'Tis a great contest."

European Theater of Operations
Eighth Air Force
Third Air Division
Thirteenth Combat Wing
Ninety-fifth Bombardment Group (H)
412th Squadron

June 18, 1944

Here is the letter you've been waiting for. It has been some time since you've heard from me. I only hope you received the cablegram and the last V-Mail change of address. My last address is for my permanent station.

I doubt very much if I'll receive the letters sent to my first APO. There was a mix-up some place and we are not where we thought we were going to be. Outside of the mail situation, though, it worked greatly to my advantage so I guess I can't kick. Maybe I'll get the letters sometime, but it won't be for a while.

I know you're very interested in where I am and what I am doing. I would sure like to tell you but the censors say "no," and I know you understand. I will say one thing, though, and that is that I'm with the best outfit in the ETO and I'm not just kidding. I feel very fortunate to be a part of the 95th Bomb Group, and more so to be in Squadron 412. When I get home I'll be able to tell you why.

I don't want you to worry about me. Things aren't bad over here. In fact, I kind of enjoy it. The people I'm working with are swell guys and they give you credit for what you do and treat you accordingly. That's something new for me after Cadets and Training Schools. I have finally found out where most of the good men in the Air Corps are— they're overseas! . . .

*We have a lot of fun over here and the food is exceptionally good—
even better than Cadets. Only recently I have procured the best bed in
the ETO. I got it on a midnight requisition and will tell you more
about it later.*

Since our identity was closely tied to our squadron and
groups, let me introduce you to ours.

The 95th Bomb Group was one of the older groups in the
Eighth Air Force. It was formed in September 1942 at Geiger
Field, Spokane, Washington, where I enlisted.

The 95th was the sixth heavy bomber group to arrive in
England. They flew their first mission May 13, 1943, with the
92nd Bomb Group, which was then located at Alconbury. After seven missions with the 92nd Bomb Group the 95th
moved to a new base at Framlingham. Within a month they
moved to their permanent home at Horham, Suffolk, and remained there until the end of the war in the European Theater.

During this time the group flew 321 combat missions, plus
eight supply missions to the Continent at the cessation of hostilities, and became the only group in the Eighth Air Force to
earn three Presidential Unit Citations. They led the raid on
Münster on October 10, 1943. On March 4, 1944, nineteen
aircraft from the 95th Bomb Group flew the Lead, with twelve
aircraft from the 100th Bomb Group, to become the first U.S.
heavy bombers to drop bombs on Berlin. The Eighth Air
Force heavy bomber gunner who held the record for the most
enemy aircraft shot down was from the 95th Bomb Group.

The 412th Squadron was commanded by a number of fine
men and contributed its share to the success of the group,
along with the 334th and 336th Squadrons.

The 335th Squadron of the 95th trained all PFF (Pathfinder) "Mickey Ship" lead crews for the Thirteenth Combat
Wing. These were primitive radar ships with the capability of
bombing through an undercast or a smoke screen, and were
officially known as H2X aircraft. The 335th also supplied
some lead crews for other groups outside the wing.

The 95th participated in three England-to-Russia-to-Italy
shuttle raids. They also flew a shuttle from England to bomb

Regensburg, landing in North Africa, and bombing in France on their return.

In the course of the war they lost over 1,700 men and 192 airplanes in action. The replacement crews did their best to uphold the motto "Justice With Victory," as well as to protect the group's reputation for honor and integrity, which had been established by the original crews.

June 21, 1944

Remember I told you I had procured the best bed in the ETO? Well, I don't have it any more. It seems that I had swiped the Colonel's bed! Needless to say, he was very unhappy about it so I had to give it back. Didn't even give me a chance to argue about it. Oh well, it was too soft to rest on anyway, I keep telling myself.

Another thing I almost forgot about telling you. I now have a bicycle. It cost me six pounds (i.e. 24 dollars and some odd cents). Boy, am I getting hot on it. If I don't get hurt on it there's nothing else to worry about. It really comes in handy, saves a lot of steps. Everyone has one and it's about the only mode of transportation available. . . .

Now something about this country. It isn't anything like home—all very different, kind of hard to explain—it is all so quaint and old. The villages are small and the people seem to be living in the eighteenth century, yet, at the same time, it's all very picturesque. The English countryside is about like I had pictured it from story books. Little cottages all over and very small grass and hay farms of an acre or two, sometimes less. Everything is green wherever you look and tiny black roads thread their way in among the cottages like a spider web. Everything is done on such a small scale. The farms are small, the houses small, the roads are very narrow, the cars are Austins, Fiats, and the like, and they all drive on the wrong side of the road!

London was somewhat of a disappointment to me, but only because I didn't understand their way of life when I was there. I might enjoy it now, but England is no substitute for Washington. I'm hoping I can remember all the little incidents that happen so you too can enjoy my experiences in the United Kingdom. Believe me, you'll laugh yourself sick at some of them.

Today I signed up to go to a stag Miami Triad. Looks as if we might

*rejuvenate memories of the good old days. One of my buddies here who
lives in our Nissen hut is a Sigma Chi from Northwestern. His tail
gunner is from Dayton [Washington] and his engineer and Brown are
old pals. So we now have quite a bond of friendship between the two
crews.*

*I have run into a lot of Washingtonians here—some from Walla
Walla, Seattle, Kennewick, and all around. One of them is saving the*
Walla Walla Union Bulletin *for me. That reminds me that I must go
pick them up shortly.*

We arrived in England—or rather, Valley, Wales—on D+1-Day
via ATC. The airport was just a runway in the Welsh farm
country. Upon deplaning, knowing the invasion was in progress and wanting some information about the war, I walked
over to a Welsh farmer not far from the runway, and asked if
there was any news from the Continent.

"Aye, 'tis a great contest going on over there. 'Tis a great
contest." These were the first words to greet my ears in the
ETO.

Our crew was assigned to the 412th Bomb Squadron on
June 16, 1944. Major Don Pomeroy was our squadron commander.

As crew housing was very short at this time, two crews of
officers were assigned quarters in Squadron Operations. A
bunch of wooden foot lockers approximately three deep in
width were stacked from floor to ceiling. Squadron Operations
thus had half of the Nissen hut and we had the other half.
This was not a very satisfactory arrangement for the squadron
or for us.

Lieutenant Gordon Braund's crew had reported in one day
ahead of us and were bunked in four single beds, with mattresses, no less. His crew consisted of Lieutenant Paul Baird,
copilot; Lieutenant Elmer Murray, navigator; and Lieutenant
Raymond Davis, bombardier. When we arrived there were
two old angle-iron double bunks for our crew of officers.
These monstrosities were so dilapidated and rickety that
Frank Dimit was prompted to say that it was the only bed he
ever saw that could lean in three directions at the same time!
These bunks were complete with "English biscuits"—the

straw-filled pillows. It took three of these "biscuits" to make a single mattress. Needless to say, the ones in the top bunk would wake up in the morning suffering from a form of motion sickness while those in the bottom bunk were losing sleep because of the creaking of the beds as the top man rolled over. As the biscuits would separate, with the top and bottom ones disappearing, you would wake up draped over the center one. This went on for several days. Luckily there were no casualties.

One morning as we were passing a building near the officers' club we saw some remodeling going on. We looked inside and here were four single beds complete with mattresses. Myron Doxon decided we could put those beds to better use, so he and Dimit worked all night carrying those beds down the hill to our crew quarters. The sorry-looking double bunks with the English biscuits were then carried up to the Club Area and set up in the room that was being renovated. What a sad sight it was, too—those old iron bunks leaning to the four winds in what was now a fairly attractive looking room. Little did we realize that this was Colonel Karl Truesdell's pet project, the beginning of a VIP quarters in anticipation of a visiting general!

It was said that when the good colonel looked in on his new project and was greeted with this sight, the smoke was blacker and heavier than usual from the perennial Truesdell cigar. An order was issued forthwith to all squadron adjutants that the beds must be found and returned within twenty-four hours, and that nothing would be said. However, if that deadline was not met some heads would roll and some hides would be nailed to the door of group headquarters.

There was quite a stir in all the squadrons as the search was launched. Captain Steve Stone was the adjutant for the 412th and no one will ever be able to describe the expression on his face when he looked in the back of squadron operations and saw the four beds that were missing. For a moment he was speechless—it was then that I realized that the Permanent Party people took these shenanigans much more seriously than flying personnel, who would fly for a while and then be gone, one way or another. Captain Stone, still suffering from apoplexy but partially regaining his composure, mumbled something about a court martial, and if it happened to him four officers would surely go with him.

Immediately three second lieutenants started dismantling and hauling the beds back to the VIP quarters in the squadron truck, which was readily made available. The fourth was busy administering first aid to Captain Stone and assuring him that everything would be okay because there were still three hours left on the twenty-four-hour deadline.

Thus it was that Fletch's crew became a well-known Nissen hut name throughout the group, and they had yet to fly their first combat mission!

This incident ended some time later when Colonel Truesdell, showing the "humanitarian" that he was, had four beds similar to the ones we had borrowed delivered to the rear of the 412th Squadron Operations. Later on at the club I received the admonition to the effect that enough was enough, and "I don't want to hear anything except good about you fellows again." He was heard to mutter as he walked away, "Hell, I wouldn't have slept in them either, but there should have been a better way!"

June 23, 1944

Our mail still hasn't arrived and no indication of when it will. We still have hopes of getting it—just takes time. I imagine there are things a lot more important which have to be done first. Because of censorship it really doesn't leave me much to write about, especially with no news from home.

June 26, 1944

Life is just the same here from one day to the next. Nothing unusual— nothing to write about—still no mail.

*   This is kind of personal and you don't have to answer it if you don't want to. The question: Am I a father yet? I've been pacing the floor*

every night and smoking cigarettes by the pack, but I can't tell whether
I'm having any luck or not.

In spite of a low-key letter this was really a red-letter day for
our crew. We flew our first full-scale practice mission in England. Gordon Braund, Paul Fiess, and Nelson Day, all first
pilots of the new crews who arrived when we did, were in the
formation for the first time also. All of us "Green Hands" were
mixed in with the veterans. We were all a little nervous, but we
knew we did a good job and were complimented on our formation flying by some of the veterans, along with the group
commander at our pilot's interrogation. We were also given
some good advice about how to react to certain life-threaten-
ing situations. We were really walking on air, but didn't dare
write about it, still not knowing, because of censorship, what
was permissible.

June 27, 1944

Had a hard day today—got up at eleven, had breakfast and dinner all
at the same time. Spent a couple of hours in the library reading all the
latest news reports. Then came home and read poetry to Doc and Dimit
until supper time. Later we took a bike ride for exercise, after which we
played ping pong until we were worn out. I must quit working so hard,
that's all there is to it! Some day when my grandchildren ask me what I
did in the last war I'll have to answer very meekly that I toured En-
gland on a bicycle!

Sure wish I had some news from home. It would make writing so
much easier besides boosting morale. One of these days Uncle Sam will
finally catch up with me and I'll probably have more mail than I'll
know what to do with. Oh happy day!

June 28, 1944

Guess what! I just got beat two games in a row pitching horseshoes!
Brown and Smith really worked Dimit and me over. But we'll show
them tomorrow—the grudge fight is on.

Dimit challenged me to a ping pong game which we'll play pretty soon. I'll let you know how I make out before I finish this letter. Today has been a repetition of yesterday except that I got up at nine o'clock this morning. What a life—too bad I'm not in the States so we could enjoy it.

Sherry, I have a confession to make. I've been hoarding!! Yes, every week bit by bit I've been hoarding my tobacco rations until I now have a whole box of fifty cigars. I'm all set just waiting for you to send the Cablegram that will make me the happiest guy in the ETO. When that news gets here and we get all these cigars lit up the smoke will be so thick the Germans will think the whole of England is on fire!

Back again—the game is over. Dimit just won three to two. Oh well, you have to let them win to keep up the teamwork and friendship of the crew. Same old story—pilot sacrifices ability for goodwill!

June 30, 1944

Doxon broke the ice today by receiving the first letter. Maybe business is picking up. Perhaps tomorrow will be my day.

Received a couple of Walla Walla Bulletins *today and have just about caught up on the April and May news of the old home town. When I started reading news of dear old Whitman College it almost got me down. We have a lot of fond memories centered around that institution. But our real joys of life are yet to come when we settle down in our own little home and raise the family we now have started.*

July 1, 1944

Here it is the first of July. The weather is cool, damp, and rainy practically all the time. Occasionally we have wind which reminds one of March weather at home. Sometimes you can see the sun, but the occasion is rare and never for more than a half hour at a time. This would be a very poor country for romance because the hours of darkness are short. At eleven o'clock at night you can read a newspaper with as much ease as at noon. At twelve darkness prevails and lasts until about 3 a.m. Then comes the dawn and another day in the ETO has started.

I can't make up my mind whether I welcome or dread the coming of a new day. About the only thing I would welcome now would be a trip home to you. It seems that about the only way I can get home will be to sweat out the dawns for the duration. So, in that case, I guess I'll have to concede the point and usher in each new day with the consolation that it's just one more day closer to when I will be home.

Bath day was yesterday. Today I washed all my dirty clothes. Boy, what a laundry I put out! You know I'm getting pretty good with these domestic duties. You can't afford to let me get away 'cause I'll probably make you the best little wife when I return. But me thinkest that I shall be very glad to turn the little duties over to you. . . .

Just had a talky-talk session with the rest of the boys on the crew. We were reminiscing, talking about what we were going to do when we returned to the States, and, of course, a few other various and sundry subjects. In the end we decided the crew would turn out en masse for church in the morning, this being Saturday evening.

Received my first pay in the ETO yesterday—twenty-three pounds, nine shillings, and two pence. In good old American money that would be ninety-four dollars and sixty-five cents. Living expenses are very reasonable here. After adding up all expenses it comes to twenty-nine dollars a month. Maybe a shilling more or less either way, but I can't kick about it. This is one place where we really get our money's worth. Twenty-one dollars for mess bill, club dues four dollars with a free snack bar at the club. Things aren't as nice as in the States, but dollar for dollar this is the real deal.

We were just getting settled in our Nissen hut home in the 412th Bomb Squadron when a young man, a crewman on another flight crew, came by and stopped in for a social call. He was curious about where we had trained in the States and whether we had been on any of the bases where he had received his training. As it turned out, we had been at different fields and could not provide him with any information about the friends he had left behind.

Had we flown a combat mission yet? The answer was no, and we didn't have any idea what combat would be like. His crew had over twenty missions. They had had some rough ones and he would be happy to explain what combat was like and what would be in store for us. We were all eyes and ears as he proceeded to crawl up on the top of one of the rickety bunks and dangle his legs over the side. He was carrying a small air pump—the kind you would use to inflate bicycle tires —and it had a holder which could be used to fasten it onto the bike. He had just purchased it, and he was enroute to work on his bicycle when he decided to stop and visit with us.

As he started to tell his combat tales we noticed he was very hyper. As the stories continued his eyes took on a rather glazed look and the bicycle pump was getting quite a workout as he twisted it around in his hands. The longer he talked the more agitated he became. The bicycle pump by now was rendered useless—it had been twisted and bent, the plunger with the handle looked like a pretzel.

As the stories became more violent his speech was starting to slur and by now his eyes had a very faraway look. His body movements had become jerky and appeared to be uncontrollable. In this state he jumped down from the bed and took his leave, completely oblivious to the condition of the bicycle pump which he still clutched in his hands.

We were glad to see him go, and as he left the room we were in complete awe. We looked at one another and questioned whether this was a performance designed to impress the new recruits, or was this "combatitis" in full bloom. Or, as Doc would remark, "have we just witnessed the performance of a man who is one-quarter brick short of carrying a full load?" In my opinion it wasn't an act. The performance was too genuine to be faked. What had we gotten ourselves into? Maybe we should go home now. But only time would tell. We too reached the point where we were under great stress, but physically and mentally we may have carried and hid it much better. However, we never adjusted to it. We had reason that day to stand in awe and wonder, but we were not yet smart enough to realize it.

July 2, 1944

Just sweated out another mail call. Still having the usual luck—no letters. I hope you are having better luck with my letters than I am with yours. About another week of this and I'm going to volunteer to go back to the States and investigate this postal system. I'm quite sure they would authorize this visit too. As you can readily see I have been here too long already!

There's not much to write about today. We went to church as we had planned, and have spent the rest of the day reading and sleeping. . . .

July 3, 1944

Happy days are here again! Today I received fourteen letters—two from my mother, two from Cap and Sis, one from your sister, Mildred, and nine from you. They run pretty much in sequence but a few are missing. I'll probably receive the others before too long. . . .

July 4, 1944

I'm getting so lazy doing nothing that one of these days they're going to ask me to do something and then I'll feel insulted. All I can say is that if we don't get started pretty quick the war will be over and I'll still be riding my bicycle along with a lot of other ETO happy fellows.

Incidentally, no one has been injured seriously yet on our biking tours although Dimit wore a little skin off his hands and scraped some off his leg. As yet I've lost no hide but have had several good spills. (Boy, he sure missed a bridge completely one day. M.D.D.) (Hand is healed—barbed wire fence will never be the same. F.S.D.) Sometimes these bicycles get a little tipsy!

Now that the boys have put their two cents worth in I'll continue. How do you like my new stationery? We're just about destitute for something to write on. That is just to prepare you for the shock should you receive some letters on stationery with perforations about every four inches!

July 5, 1944

Received a very nice letter from Mildred and have answered it already. There isn't much I can write that's of interest, or, at least, what people are most interested in. I could refer to my work more closely than I do and it would probably get by. But I look at it this way, why take a chance? The rules were made for my safety and the least I can do is try to live up to them.

When you have time please send me stationery. Forget the envelopes, but send the paper—also a scarf and any kind of candy bars available, if there are any.

July 6, 1944

Now for the events of the day—no mail but perhaps I'll have better luck tomorrow. I hope so. Now then, remember I said if they ever asked me to work I'd probably be insulted? Well, let me tell you tonight I'm very highly insulted! Oh well, I must get into the routine of things sometime, so it was just as well to be now as later. I'm more firmly convinced than ever now that I shall be home with you by Christmas.

Mission #1, *Abbeville, France, July 6*

Frank Dimit, Bombardier

Left coast of England over Bixhill—between Hastings and Eastbourne. Hit France at Bayeux. Our target was pilotless bomb or rocket installation.

Didn't see target—too damn busy trying to get rid of bombs. Load was hung up, and was only able to salvo half my load. Had trouble with bomb-bay doors. Finally solenoid jammed and motor in bay caught on fire. Doc and I finally cut wire and put out fire. More fun. Learned one lesson—always have axe handy.

Flak was light but plenty accurate. High squadron caught it all. Picked up 23 holes—no casualties.

Head up and locked this a.m. When I checked chin turret,

grabbed triggers when I reached for dead-man switches. Fired three rounds from each gun. Scared hell out of me, crew, and ground personnel. Guns were in full down position. No damage except two big holes in hardstand.

We were a spare ship today but one of the boys aborted and we took his place. *[End of mission notes by Frank Dimit]*

Robert "Roco" Work, Navigator

It wasn't long until the crew grew accustomed to seeing "Maggie's Drawers" flying in the breeze before a mission. For several nights these highly keyed men slept all too lightly, wakening frequently when RAF planes returned from night raids to the Ruhr. Or perhaps it was their early morning sleep which was disturbed by the unbelievable roar of the Eighth Air Force heavies forming for an attack on some continental target.

Then came the seemingly interminable days of practice missions as Fletch learned to fly the 95th way and Roco pondered over problems of navigation in England. But the training flights finally ended and the night before the first mission arrived with far too little fanfare. For several days they'd all been scanning "The List" to see when it would be. When the time came there were parched throats, pounding hearts, and throbbing pulses! Tomorrow was to be the culmination of nearly two years of training in the methods of waging war! Tomorrow, perhaps, there would be empty bunks where these young men tossed fitfully tonight.

As is the Army custom, the officers and enlisted men lived in different barracks so we don't know what they did that night. But, anticipating an early arising, the officers prepared to rest before the big test. Just before turning out the lights Fletch took out his Bible, by request, and read a few chapters. Each man had his own private religious beliefs, but that night they jointly turned to God for guidance. Fletch has a nice reading voice (he used to be a radio announcer before the war) so it was fine to hear him as he read. Then, when the lights went out, each man held his own communion with his Maker and sought solace for his tortured mind. Prayers were said in that hut in England—not prayers for safekeeping, but pleas for guidance. These men didn't seek safety; they sought strength —and He came to them!

Sleep was slow in coming on the eve of that first mission, and when it came it didn't bring rest. All sorts of pictures passed through their minds as they lay there: Would it be a rough mission? Do you suppose our ship will be disabled? Will *I* be injured or killed? Why didn't I get in the Finance Department? Muddled, selfish thoughts—they were "sweating it out."

It was around 0130 when the CQ roused them from their dreams chanting a ritual that would soon plague every startled awakening. "Lieutenant Fletcher, Lieutenant Doxon, Lieutenant Work, and Lieutenant Dimit—it's one-thirty, breakfast at two-fifteen, briefing at three o'clock." With that he was gone to spread his cheerful dirge throughout the squadron area and we were left to stretch before actually getting up. Suddenly the thought came: "Will I sleep here tonight?" And then we shook off our fears, literally as well, for it's pretty cool in the early morning in England. But it wasn't the temperature that rattled the teeth. It was fear!

At the mess hall a bedlam greeted us as we entered the door. The smoke of burning grease assailed our nostrils and smarted in our eyes as we filed in for our "real fresh eggs." Perhaps a slice or two of salty bacon also on the plate and to a table for the first problem: Can I get them down? After a drink of grapefruit or tomato juice it usually became easier, but it didn't take much to satiate our appetites that morning! Each mouthful became an additional lump of lead in the pit of our stomachs and we were soon ready to board the truck that would take us to briefing.

Here we found another riot of noise and haze of smoke stirred up by those who'd preceded us. Few of the fellows were flying their first mission and they weren't quite as obviously frightened. But a discerning eye could spot the haunted look in their eyes and the sharpness of tempers that would flare up in a flash if something went wrong. Ever so meekly we sought four seats together and tried to relax until the briefing officer arrived from the other briefing where he was preparing the gunners.

When he arrived the door was closed and everyone tensed up for the bad news which would come as soon as the roll had been called. With a true sense of the dramatic characteristic of all briefing officers, he whisked back the curtain which had covered the map and route for the day's mission. Gasps of dismay greeted this act when it became evident that Bremen was to feel the weight of our bombs. For Bremen rated near the top of the list of "roughies."

"Gentlemen, your target for today is the Rosenheim Oil Plant at Bremen. In keeping with the current attack on oil, the Eighth Air Force is going out in force again today, sending over a thousand bombers against synthetic and natural oil targets in Germany. The First Division is sending five groups of B-17s to Magdeburg, the Second is going to Hamburg with six groups of B-24s, and we in the Third Division are putting up five groups to Bremen." Then follows the technical details of assembly and departure, zero hour, fighter rendezvous, etc. "There are 280 heavy guns in the target area, of which 135 can be brought to bear on you if you follow the briefed course. A sharp right turn after bombs away will get you out of the flak the quickest."

Through our heads echo these substantial figures—280 heavy guns—yipe! Soon afterward navigators and bombardiers are dismissed for their separate briefings while the pilots remain behind for instructions pertaining to their duties. For the next three hours everyone will be in a hurry to climb into their flying clothes and attend to all the minute details that are so essential for a round-trip. But wait, something just came in —this target is scrubbed and there will be a new one ready in just a few minutes. Whew! At least it can't be much rougher. Finally the route is put up, and to our surprise it's a short trip to the Pas de Calais area. That's right, a flying bomb site on the coast of France—why, we'll be back before lunch! Then we go through another and shorter briefing, for takeoff time is rapidly approaching. Only twelve guns at this spot. It should be a milk run, and we're due back at 1115. Golly, we thought, perhaps this isn't such a tough war after all!

Later, filled with vital information, we climb into our ship, *Government Issue,* named for a characteristic tan roll found in all latrines. Our first incident of note occurred before the 1st pilot and navigator even got to the ship. Dimit was loading his chin turret and checking the solenoids when everyone was startled by a loud *brrrt* emanating from his direction. Someone had left the gun switch turned on and Frank tore two holes in the concrete hardstand about four inches deep when his gun cut loose. There were only about five rounds from each gun, but they did make the gravel fly! After that our preparations were completed without incident and we taxied out for the takeoff.

Naturally we were delegated a place far back in the formation because of our newness to the game—number six in the high squadron. With the engines roaring in our ears as Fletch and Doc completed their check, the rest of us fiddled with this and that to make doubly sure that everything was as it should be. Eventually, it was our turn to take off so Fletch locked the brakes and ran up the engines to maximum power before releasing them. With a lurch of acceleration we gathered speed and those who could watched the airspeed meter, knowing we'd need at least 110 and preferably 130 or 135 mph before he could lift her off the runway. Flickering slightly as we zoomed down the runway the needle crept slowly upward past 60, 70, 80, 100, and we crossed the yellow line indicating one-third of the runway was left; 110, 120, and at long last 130 mph when Fletch eased back on the stick. The ship vibrated when Doc kicked the brakes to stop the spinning wheels before he flicked the retraction switch, and then climbed smoothly upward as our airspeed neared the normal.

That part of the day's drama was a success. Let's hope the rest goes off as well. We continued to climb and circle the field to join the formation leader who was already at assembly altitude and firing red-green flares. When things still went okay, so that we were sure we wouldn't be forced to abort because of mechanical trouble, Dimit went back to the bomb bays to remove the safety pins from the bombs. By the time he had returned to the nose we were in position and about ready to leave the field. The next thing we knew England was dropping away in the rear and we were over the Channel.

None of us will ever forget the first view of France, which was then still occupied territory. The sky was cloudless, the water was a deeper blue even than the heavens, and there were the rocky shores of Calais. Other groups ahead of us were opening their bomb-bay doors for the bomb run. But that was before those twelve guns began sending their death-dealing shells our way. I guess the flak is always closer on the first and last missions every crew flies (or so it seems) but that day we figured we were the only plane that those damned flak gunners could see in the sky. Twelve guns—there must be twelve hundred! Not yet convinced of the danger of flak, the navigator was standing up behind the bombardier trying to pick up the target when a near burst brought home the fact that he was being shot at, and damn it, he wasn't being missed by much. Then it was that terror set in. Stamping his foot to accent his words, Roco proclaimed long and loud that no one would ever get him to fly another mission any place under any circumstances whatsoever! "I won't, I won't, I won't," he kept crying out. "You can't get me to do this again!" Suddenly it dawned on him that he hadn't turned the mike switch on while he was screaming out his fears.

Every heart in the ship stopped momentarily when Smitty frantically called out, "Tail gunner to pilot, tail gunner to pilot, I'm hit, I'm hit!" Sending Lynch back to check on him, Fletch sweat blood for a few minutes until Lynch's easy drawl came over the interphone. "He's all right. A piece of flak just bounced off his chute harness!" That episode had hardly let us breathe a deep breath before Dimit called out, "Bombs away!" and Fletch swung into some evasive action on the way to the rally point. And before we knew it we were turning back toward England and starting to let down from altitude as we crossed the Channel. As soon as he could make himself heard over the sighs of relief, Fletch asked Mac to look under the wings for oil or gas leaks. Upon receiving a negative report he said something about, "That was close," and went back to the interplane frequency to learn landing instructions. Already we could see England below us and Roco ventured a guess at the Estimated Time of Return to the base.

After five hours and ten minutes that seemed more like five years and ten months we settled none too gently onto the runway and proceeded to our hardstand. Swiftly gathering up his equipment, the navigator barely waited for the props to stop turning before he jumped to the ground, where only a large oil spot prevented him from kissing the earth. Anyway he patted it very affectionately and climbed back in to remove his guns. By the time everyone had gotten his equipment in the truck the ground crew had counted the holes in various parts of the ship. Twenty-three was the sum and you can imagine our surprise upon returning to interrogation to find that we were the only crew of the day to suffer any battle damage at all. Just like we thought, every one of those twelve guns had been shooting at *us! [End of mission account by Roco Work]*

Our first combat mission was to Abbeville, France, a second-choice target. We were to attack sites which were launching areas for the V-1 buzz bomb which had plagued London and a lot of England. When the target was changed the "old timers" heaved a sigh of relief and let it be known that we were going on a milk run (a very easy mission), since most of the targets would have very few antiaircraft guns.

It had been the practice up until then to break up a crew for the first mission so they could see what combat was like, and have a chance to gain some knowledge while flying with an experienced crew. Or if that wasn't possible, at least the pilot would be sent as copilot along with a crew who had already received their baptism of fire.

We did not want to start our tour that way and requested that we be allowed to begin our tour on our own as a complete crew. We had confidence in our abilities, and besides, we had survived all of our training mistakes. What could possibly be worse? Surely not the Germans. We were completely ignorant of the ways of combat, but we would learn. When we made this request our squadron commander, Major Don Pomeroy, was noncommittal. It was possible that he knew much more than we. But here we were, on our own, unsupervised, in a war-weary airplane headed for battle.

We had looked forward to this day for months. Now we would find out what all our training had been about. We were off the ground with only a few minor mishaps due to nervousness, with an embarrassed crew member and a rather nervous ground crew left behind. Only twelve flak guns were expected at our target, and this news had caused a round of cheers from the old hands at our briefing. We easily found our place in the formation. We would be the last ship in the high squadron.

Before long it appeared that all twelve guns were firing right at us. The glamor was rapidly disappearing—then the one message I never wanted to hear was coming over the interphone. In spite of the chill that went up my spine the sweat was pouring. "Tail gunner to pilot—I've just been hit." Why would anybody volunteer to do this? My next message was, "Hang on, Smitty. Lynch, check him out."

After what seemed to be an eternity, Lynch's Oklahoma drawl announced, "He's okay. He was hit in the chest and had the wind knocked out of him. He'll have a bruise, but it didn't break the skin." Thank God!

We were taking a beating. When Frank called, "Bombs away," we immediately started evasive action. The formation loosened up and everyone was on his own until we reached the Rally Point. We then formed a tight formation and headed for home.

"Gad, won't he ever close the bomb-bay doors?" The answer came immediately: "Bombardier to pilot, the bomb-bay doors won't close." Almost immediately the engineer reported the electric motor for the bomb-bay doors had shorted out and was smoking like crazy. The only way to stop a certain fire was to unhook the hot lead to the motor. The motor is located on the forward bulkhead in the bomb bay, approximately three feet down from the catwalk and close to the fuel transfer lines. A fire in this position could eventually burn through the fuel lines, setting the whole aircraft on fire or creating an explosion.

The copilot left his seat and joined the engineer, along with the bombardier. The gunners and radio operator left their positions and came through the open bomb bay on a very narrow catwalk, bringing with them the two ropes which formed the safety support in the bomb bay. I was notified that they had a plan to disconnect the hot line to the motor. I told them to go ahead as something had to be done quickly. There was no time for a conference—these were trained people and I was confident they would do their best. I would fly the aircraft in formation until they solved the problem, or until they felt it was necessary to abandon ship.

Unbeknownst to me their plan was to lower the copilot headfirst down into the open bomb bay. They intended to accomplish this by hooking the two ropes onto the D-rings of Doc's parachute harness. The waist gunners would snap the other end of the ropes into the rings on their parachute harness. The radio operator and the bombardier planned to grasp the gunners around the waist, thus anchoring them. The engineer planned to crouch down at the bulkhead opening into the bomb bay, taking Doc's legs under his armpits, locking his own arms around Doc's legs, with his fingers interlocked in an "Indian grip." As the waist gunners slowly inched forward with their anchormen, putting some slack in the safety ropes, Doc was lowered into the bomb bay with a fire axe in his hand. When he felt he was in position he swung the axe, and after several blows was able to sever the hot line, disconnecting the motor. Our fire hazard had now been averted. Dimit inched his way along the catwalk, 15,000 feet above the Channel, replacing the ropes, while the others returned to their positions. Doc had been given a view of the English Channel which he was in no hurry to repeat.

Our next problem was, "Can you land a B-17 with the bomb-bay doors open?" We knew the stalling speed would increase but we could solve that by coming in a little hotter than usual. We knew also that the open bomb-bay doors have plenty of clearance when the aircraft is at rest on the ground, but what will happen on the shock of landing? How much will our landing gear compress when it takes the full weight of the aircraft? Let's be on the safe side and put the crew in a crash landing procedure.

The aircraft touches down; this crew now knows that you

can land a B-17 with the bomb-bay doors open with relative security. When we reached the hardstand and crawled out we found we had twenty-three holes in the aircraft—and this was a milk run? What would a toughie be like? At interrogation we learned that we were the only plane in the formation to have battle damage. The age of innocence was over. This was the last mission where we left the base in happy anticipation of a tangle with Jerry. We had learned that Jerry played for keeps and that this was a dangerous game.

We were so green that we did not realize that the actions of these men, who saved our ship and our lives, constituted "heroism," and it is sad to report that none of them received the Distinguished Flying Cross. This in a day and age when these medals were awarded for completing a combat tour. Rules could change, but heroism would not.

July 7, 1944

There was a wonderful letter from you awaiting me when I returned today. Today's letter was dated the twenty-third of June. So now I'll wait for the gap from the seventeenth to the twenty-second to fill in. In this letter there was no mention as to whether you had ever heard from me. I hope you have because I know my letters mean as much to you as yours to me.

I have written to everyone at least once, but now I'm back in my usual routine of writing only to you. Gosh it has only been a week since I was griping that I had more time than anything else. Time has changed things slightly, though, and I don't know when I'll get around to write them again.

In case you're worrying about me, don't. Things aren't bad. Not good, but I know it could be worse. Don't worry one bit, though, Sherry, because I know your prayers will be answered. In that much I'm confident. Our whole life is still to be lived and I know that the joy the future will bring will completely overshadow any sorrows that this separation has caused us to bear.

The fellows always ask about you and how you're getting along. Believe me you're a pretty popular gal with ten men. They all send their regards and hope you're getting along fine.

Mission #2, Merseburg, Germany, July 7

Frank Dimit, Bombardier

Briefed at 2:30 a.m. for a target in Germany. Synthetic oil refineries (Leuna Oil Refinery) at Merseburg, near Leipzig.

95th led the big show today. We flew a wing formation with the 390th and 100th. We were flying #3 in second element of low squadron—tail-end Charlie in purple heart corner.

Tail gunner's, radio, and left waist's oxygen system went out just after we hit the coast of Holland just west of Zuider Zee. So we aborted.

It was a rough mission. Gordy Braund's crew came back alone with #4 engine out. Maybe Someone upstairs is looking after us.

Saw no flak and no fighters except ours. Golly, those fighters of ours sure looked good.

Fingers getting worn out from putting pins back in bombs. Carried 20 250-pound G.P. [General Purpose bombs].

P.S. *July 9.* Sun is shining today—we received credit for the abortion. Chalk up #2 for us. We believe we received credit for this one because we brought back some "hot news" about some ships off coast of Holland. The next day we saw in the paper where Beauforts had sunk six merchant vessels in that vicinity. *[End of mission notes by Frank Dimit]*

Roco Work, Navigator

Without even having a day to think over what they had just been through, our heroes found themselves alerted anew on the evening of their first trip against the Hun. This time they were almost too tired to bother about worrying over where they might have to go. For even though the flight had been a short one, the strain on their nerves had been almost more than they could bear, so they went to bed early in the evening, within an hour of learning that they'd probably fly again on the next day.

Sure enough, 0300 found the CQ rattling at their door with

a slightly different chant, the essence of which was the same. . . . Hurriedly donning their clothes and downing their breakfasts with little more zeal than they had displayed on the previous day, these four young worthies again presented themselves for briefing. Sacre bleu! Listen to the old timers moan this time. It was Merseburg, undeniably the roughest target that can be found on this earth! There were between 350 and 400 guns in the target area, 120 of which would be unable to bother those groups which followed the briefed route from the Initial Point of the bomb run (IP) to the target to the Rally Point (RP). Because undercast conditions were expected, the IP was quite a way from the target so the special instruments could be used to their best advantage in picking up the target. And the RP was picked with great care as well, to give the maximum possible time for the formations to regain their proper spacings.

Being as yet frank novices at the game, Fletcher's crew were not as frightened as might be expected because they didn't know enough to realize what was before them. This day they were assigned to a ship which was beginning to be known as a "battle weary" because of the large number of missions that had already been flown in it, and also because of the many patches covering former flak and bullet holes in the metal skin. The name of that notable craft was *Roaring Bill,* and no one quite recalls what inspired such a cognomen. Taking its idiosyncracies in their stride, the crew scrambled to their places when the time came and began the ritualistic last-minute check of oxygen regulators, gun belts, etc. So takeoff time found them, if not eager, at least resigned and ready to go.

As on the previous day our boys were delegated to be fill-ins in case some one had to leave the formation going across the Channel. And again they quickly found a spot: number six in the low squadron. So when the time came to depart from the shores of England they were all settled back for the long ride in. Mac began to crawl into his ball turret before they were out of sight of land, because, he said, "It's warmer in there." As they approached Holland at an altitude of 18,000 feet, Frank and Roco were engaged in the process of determining that they were on course. Everything seemed to check as they crossed the narrow strip of land that separates the Zuider Zee from the North Sea.

Suddenly George came on the interphone inquiring of Mac and Smitty how much oxygen pressure they had left. Roco was amazed to hear them answer that their needles pointed at 125 pounds and were falling rapidly, and he called Fletch so he would know of the situation. A short conversation with George, who'd gone back to look at the ball from inside the ship, led Fletch to realize that if he chose to continue with the formation it would necessitate three men going the remainder of the distance on walk-around bottles which would have to be constantly replenished from the main system. Therefore he signaled the group leader by giving the proper response for leaving the formation, which was lower the gear and rock the wings. This way we could maintain radio silence.

By this time Mac had come out of the ball and was nursing a walk-around bottle in the radio room, while George had switched to an oxygen line on the opposite side of the ship, as had Smitty. Since he didn't as yet know the cause of the abrupt drop in pressure, Fletch couldn't be sure how soon the oxygen for the entire ship might give out. So he made a diving turn to the left, losing altitude as rapidly as possible without gaining too much speed. During the conversation, Roco had realized that a course home would be in order and had one ready when they had reached a safe altitude to remove their masks. With Frank's aid he pinpointed their position on the map so they could tell how far in they had gone before turning back. Just after leaving the Dutch coast Smitty called Roco to report that there were about eight medium-sized boats in the Channel, but scurrying toward the safety of the coast. Their position also went into the navigator's log for the interrogation.

By this time Brownie had gone back through the bomb bays to determine the cause of the trouble. A short inspection showed that the oxygen filler hose to the ball turret had become unfastened from its normal position. As a result when Mac twirled his ball around, the hose caught on something and eventually pulled loose from its connection, thereby allowing the precious, life-giving oxygen to escape. Since there are four systems which carry oxygen throughout the plane, only the positions fed off that line were affected. Accidents happen even on the best of ships, and this *Roaring Bill* had long since lost any claim to such flattering terminology.

Roco's course for home was correct and not many minutes elapsed before they were on the ground again. Four hours and fifteen minutes they had been in the air, all to no purpose it seemed at that time. Rather disgruntled over their misfortune in going through all the preparations and nervous plannings only to be forced to return early, but nonetheless rather happy that they hadn't had to fly over Merseburg, they gathered their equipment and changed their clothes. Then Fletch and Roco reported to the intelligence officer in charge and told all about what had happened.

When they told him about the ships Smitty had seen he grew much more interested and copied all the details, after which he telephoned them to the proper place for such information—hot flash. It must have been a good tip, for the next day's papers claimed that Coastal Command aircraft had attacked and sunk six out of eight enemy ships in the neighborhood of the Frisian Islands, where the observation had been made. Who knows, perhaps that's why our boys were given credit for a mission. At any rate, George's alertness in noticing the loss of pressure prevented what might have been a very embarrassing situation for Mac in the ball alone, to say nothing of the others who might not have caught on in time to make the necessary changeover! *[End of mission account by Roco Work]*

July 8, 1944

In a few days I'm going to start sending some newspapers home. Read them if you like, then save them for me so we can go over them together. Along this same line—anything we do here you can read in the papers at home just a few hours after it happens. If you like you can save clippings and dates, then we can have some fun with them later on when I get home.

July 9, 1944

Today was nothing out of the ordinary. We got up just in time to go to church. Afterwards we partook of dinner and breakfast all at the same time. This afternoon and evening has been devoted to sack time and reading. I read a whole pocket book this afternoon, don't even remember the name. It was some murder mystery thriller, pulp stuff, but it was the only thing I could find in the trash can. Reading material is at a premium.

July 10, 1944

Here's a tidbit of news that may be of interest to you. We now have to sweat out thirty-five missions!
The cartoons you've been sending are a godsend. Keep them coming. We get a big kick out of them as they always manage to make us laugh and cheer us up when we're pretty low in spirit.

July 10

Doc Doxon, Copilot

At noon today we had a really rugged practice mission—sixty ships. What a wreck to fly to put on a good show for the colonel. We flew aircraft #8140, *The Pregnant Goose.*

Mission #3, *Munich, Germany, July 11*

Frank Dimit, Bombardier

This was our first pathfinder mission. We flew over an undercast the entire distance. Was damn glad they couldn't see us—heavy flak. Threw out window [aluminum strips] to deflect radar. Aiming point was center of town.
    Climbed through 10,000 feet of overcast after takeoff to rendezvous. Sweating that out was worse than the mission. Plenty

dangerous when several hundred other planes are circling through the soup to get to altitude.

Had to crank up bomb-bay doors. Helluva job at 24,000 feet. Learned two lessons: put up hand rails in bomb bay and have crank and extension in front end of plane. Had to walk catwalk with doors open again to get extension.

Crew performed perfectly. Great bunch of guys. With only three missions we all feel like veterans. [End of mission notes by Frank Dimit]

Roco Work, Navigator

Four days after their failure to get to Merseburg, Fletcher's crew was again routed into the predawn grayness. This day's briefing pleased them only because there were only thirty-two more missions to be flown—if they made it both ways! The briefing officer spoke fluently about what a favor we would be doing the Londoners if we creamed the target. The aiming point was an assembly building for robot motors used in the buzz bombs which had been causing some trouble in "southeastern England" the past month.

The target area was on the outskirts of Munich, with approximately three hundred guns guarding the city. The route as briefed led across some 150-odd heavy guns with a sharp break to left after bombs away in order for least exposure to flak. All the facts given, everyone scattered to see about his particular pre-mission duties.

Munich, which lies far south in Germany and less than fifty miles from the Swiss border, promised to be a plenty rough target. The route, while essentially flak-free, was a tortuous one because of the planners' attempts to do many things.

The problems are essentially as follows: First, the route must avoid, if possible, all known ground defenses with the exception of the target itself. Since nearly every city of any size had a vital industry to be protected, antiaircraft defenses made it mandatory that all large towns be skirted by at least six miles (normal range of flak at 20,000 feet). Second, it was hoped that the target wouldn't become obvious because the bomber stream was headed for Munich from the very start. So a few additional turns had to be inserted to keep enemy fighters from being gathered for a concerted attack. Last, and of primary importance for this mission, the route with all its twists and turns must be short enough to ensure that all the bombers would have sufficient fuel for the return trip.

As a result of all these problems for the planners, this route to Munich zigzagged with many turns through the flak areas of Holland, Belgium, and France before settling down to a more direct route to the target. That promised a particularly difficult day for the navigators since a solid undercast was expected over most of the distance.

When Frank got out to the ship he called the crew together and announced what he'd learned at his briefing: "Remember the 'Beer-Hall Putsch' that was in Munich? Well, HQ seems to think there are a lot more Nazi big-dogs there today. Regardless of the rules of civilized warfare we're out to kill Germans with these incendiary bombs! Our aiming point if it's blind bombing—which it probably will be—is the center of the city. We're going after arms, legs, and elbows!"

After the usual amount of sweating the boys finally discovered it was time to crawl into the ship and begin the day's work in earnest. All preparations completed they took off, climbed through about 10,000 feet of clouds and came out on top without event. Dimit didn't have any pins to pull this trip because those 500-pound incendiary clusters go off on general principles when they get to a preset altitude. That is, the cluster of fire bombs scatters and each individual bomb starts a separate fire, which is mighty hard to extinguish. Soon they'd gotten into position and the long haul across most of southern Germany had begun.

During the penetration Roco marveled anew at the navigation instruments which enabled this huge striking force to make good a narrow corridor between flak batteries even though a solid undercast prevented visual navigation. In a few minutes, however, he was too busy trying to keep track of where they were to worry about such fine points. As the target drew ever nearer on his map Roco decided to warn the crew about putting on their flak suits when they were ten minutes from the IP. At the start of the mission there was the normal chatter over the interphone that comes from youth setting out on a great adventure, but the nearer they got to the target, the less anyone had to say. After their fighter support had been identified no one said a word except for short answers to Dimit's checking to make sure everyone was all right.

At last the time came and Roco gave the warning that the IP was near. Fletch and Doc put on their flak helmets that Brownie handed to them. Both were sensitive to the fact that flak comes up from the ground. Therefore, they sat on their flak suits. At first thought this sounds silly, but they'd already found them too heavy and cumbersome to fly formation. Brownie, of course, had no suit to wear because the upper turret doesn't leave the room, but he did wear that helmet. George had discovered on the first mission that it was nearly impossible to toss out "chaff" with his suit on, so he spread his on the floor and knelt on it while he threw his bundles out the chute. Lynch was never very trusting, so he wore his parachute and flak suit both when they went down the bomb run. Powerful man, that Lynch lad. And Smitty in the tail somehow felt better dressed for the occasion so he wore his properly, too. Once the ship got on course Dimit was anchored in the nose. Only the strangest of circumstances could get him off his seat and the bomb run wasn't strange enough. Not half strange enough! Frank would twist around to fasten the shoulder straps for Roco, then Roco would stagger to his feet and make Frank's suit secure.

By the time these details had been attended to on the Munich trip it was time for Dimit to open the bomb bays. There was that rumble one could hear even above the roar of the engines—even on a practice mission the sound of the bomb-bay doors coming open sent chills up their spines. As they turned onto the bomb run a barrage of flak appeared in the sky ahead. Seen from this distance, the black smoke looked like a huge cloud; individual bursts were not distinguishable. "Remember we make a sharp left turn after bombs away, Fletch," Roco said, and then all was silence over the interphone.

Seconds ticked by and became minutes. Little by little the

smoke pall broke up into small black smudges, and as the planes got nearer new bursts could be seen to appear over the target. Suddenly there was a mushrooming mass of flames in the middle of a preceding group of ships when some poor souls suffered a direct hit and the entire ship disappeared into thin air. All that remained was a larger smoke cloud and a few burning streamers floated earthward. At this distance the flak was fascinating to watch. They were close enough to be able to discern how each shell appeared as if by magic. Where there had been a clear space a second before there was a small puff of black smoke that rolled and spread before it eventually reached maximum size (about ten feet in diameter) and began to dissipate.

With each turn of the propellers the 95th sped nearer to what promised to be certain death, for it didn't seem possible that even one plane could penetrate the area, let alone thirty-six. And then they were under fire themselves. Sometimes near, sometimes far, the bursts appeared right among the ships. *Crump!* The plane lurched with the explosion as a shell burst somewhere near the left wing. In the space of a minute they flew through at least ten smoke clouds and the acrid odor of the powder became noticeable in the very oxygen they breathed. Lynch's eyes opened wide as he stared at a hole that appeared in the side of the waist. It missed him by at least two feet, but the suddenness of its appearance jerked him more vividly conscious of their danger.

Off to the left and slightly below them a plane wavered out from its position. Smitty watched with horrified eyes, expecting to see it blow up at any moment. But it returned to the formation almost immediately and he was somehow deliriously happy to see the recovery. As he watched the pilot feathered his left outboard engine, and Smitty could visualize him struggling to gain more power so the copilot who was flying could maintain position. Brownie had his turret facing forward so that he looked directly into the flak-filled skies before him. Even as he scanned the heavens for possible enemy fighters he saw a plane from another group begin to trail black smoke from a wing. Flames appeared, licking their way toward the fuselage, and Brownie could do nothing but watch as it became more and more evident that the crew of the plane above would have to bail out. And there they went, twisting and turning, one, two, three, four, five, before the ship slid out of formation and below his field of vision. Brownie closed his eyes to shut out the memory of what he'd seen, then murmured a prayer for them all.

"Bombs away!" That from Dimit when everyone had decided that the leader never would drop. George paused in his chaff throwing to make sure they'd all dropped out, then repeated, "Bombs away!" after which Frank started the doors closed. Already Fletch had pushed the throttles as far forward as they'd go and swerved to the left, following the leader who'd broken away toward the Rally Point. Everyone mentally got out and pushed to accelerate their progress toward the edge of the flak. And they were out of it in a few seconds, for the gunners below were more worried about the planes yet to bomb and let those who had already dropped proceed about their own business.

The Rally Point was reached and the 95th headed homeward. The air leader in the lead ship began calling the formation to tuck it in lest Jerry fighters continue the attack. None developed and soon the radio began to crackle out the bad news as men were heard telling about their troubles. Someone had a wounded navigator and two engines out. He needed fighter support to lead and protect him for he couldn't possibly keep up with his outfit. Another had a wing fire and the pilot was hoping to get over Switzerland before they had to bail out. At that precise moment Mac called Fletch to tell him there were several small holes in the bottom of the wing, and a little bit of gas seemed to be coming from one of them. "Okay, Mac, keep your eye on the leak and if it begins to look serious let me know," he answered. Then he gave the order that there would be no smoking on board the aircraft.

And so the long journey back to England had begun. The worst part of the trip was over (if fighters didn't attack, and it wasn't likely with the fine support those P-51s were giving) so the boys removed their flak suits and peered into out-of-the-way places for undiscovered holes. Roco announced that it would still be two hours before the Channel was reached and another forty-five minutes before they could get to their base. Even the long trip at altitude still to be undergone failed to dampen their spirits now, though, for they'd survived the flak and weren't much worried about anything for a while.

At short intervals more planes could be heard on the radio calling their formation leaders of their inability to keep up. One pilot reported that they had only fuel enough to reach the Channel so they'd have to jump. "This is Ozark P-Peter, will you attend to some personal items for us at the base?" "Go ahead, Ozark P-Peter, will do." "Ozark P-Peter. My navigator wishes you to destroy all letters and correspondence. Did you read?" "Roger, Ozark P-Peter, destroy all navigator's letters and correspondence." "Thank you. Ozark P-Peter, out!" And as coolly as that the pilot was telling everyone within range of his radio good-bye. If they were lucky they'd probably be German POWs; some might evade, but—

Finding his work pretty well caught up, Roco glanced out the window at the hundreds of airplanes around them. Suddenly struck by the size of the armada he started counting them. "Hey, you guys, I just counted better than 400 ships within sight right now. I'll bet Munich really took a clobbering today!" So it went. The time did pass by and finally he could tell them that the coast was only seven minutes away. Then across the Channel and back to their field and some chow. Wow, they'd been in the air nearly nine hours already! Time once again stood still in their minds, but eventually they could see their field ahead and preparations were made for the landing. In a few minutes they were on the ground. Interrogation, chow, read the *Stars and Stripes* and the new letters that had come during their absence, and then off to bed lest they be routed again in the morning.

Mission number three had been their first real toughie—lots of flak, with death on every side. The ship had over forty holes, but outside of a small leak in one tank, no damage worth worrying about had been done. Now the poor ground crew had a job to do, removing the wing and putting a new tank in the place of the punctured one. That ship wouldn't fly in the morning, but it would the day after! *[End of mission account by Roco Work]*

July 12, 1944

Life goes on around here the same as usual. Kinda in a rut, I guess. The sun comes up in the morning and sets late in the evening. The moon comes out for a couple of hours then gives way to the dawn—the endless cycle goes on. That's life in the ETO. Some days I work days and sleep nights and other times I work nights and sleep days. That, too, goes on in an endless cycle.

I'll give you a little tip. I'm not working for Uncle Sam any more. It's this way—I figure my training is paid for now. Any work they get from me from here on in they'll have to consider free gratis because no amount of money can compensate for what goes on.

Early July 12 we were briefed to go to Munich again, flying ship #7882, *Blues in the Reich.* The preflight went like clock-work, but at "start engine time" we couldn't get the #2 engine started. Both the ground crew and the flight crew became very frustrated. We tried everything possible, but it just wouldn't fire. In the end we watched the group take off without us. The one thing going through everyone's mind—was this a good or bad sign of things to come? But at least we had the whole day to reflect on this and the crew chief had a black mark on his record.

On every crew certain responsibilities were delegated to certain crew members. Not all crews used the same procedure we did, but as a result of our training experience and a couple of missions, I felt this to be the best for us. There would be some variation from time to time, but, basically, it followed this plan.

All crew members were considered to be observers. They were the eyes and ears of not only our airplane but also for the formation. If everyone was alert, collisions could be prevented and friendly and enemy fighters could be identified; in general, the whole welfare of the formation depended upon timely information from all observers.

The navigator, Robert ("Roco") Work, was the executive officer. His duties, in addition to his primary specialty of being responsible for where the aircraft was and where it was going, included keeping the ship's log. He noted everything that took place on the mission, plus time and location. This was a very comprehensive report and was used to verify everything at interrogation. Some examples from the log might include where did we encounter fighters: how many; what were their maneuvers? Where and when would we encounter flak: how much; how accurate; tracking or barrage? What happened in our formation: did we see aircraft go down; where; what time; were any chutes seen? And what did we see on the ground and in the Channel? And on ad infinitum until the complete happening was recorded. Roco was assisted in this by the bombardier. He also checked out and returned all escape kits for the crew, and was responsible for his guns and their cleaning. It was a busy and thankless task, and he was rewarded only by the esteem in his own mind for a job well done.

The bombardier, Frank Dimit, was responsible for the bombs, their fusing and arming. He was assisted in this by the armorer gunner and other volunteer help. He was responsible for his guns and giving aid to the navigator. During the mission, at altitude, he initiated the crew check at fifteen-minute intervals, making sure everyone was physically okay, for a lack of oxygen could cause severe problems within minutes, while the victim would have a sense of well-being and euphoria. But of course his main job was what the mission was all about: to put the bombs on the target and do maximum damage to the enemy. He also performed other functions as needed—first aid and so on.

The copilot, Myron ("Doc") Doxon, and later, Billy Bob Layl, was second in command and also served as coordinator. He monitored the VHF radio and served as our voice link with the other aircraft in the formation, and with the base while we were still in range. He would summon fighters for people in trouble. Only the lead ships carried radio crystals tuned to the frequency used by our fighter escort, so we could communicate where help was needed. He took his turn at flying. We would alternate this duty, flying either fifteen-minute or half-hour shifts depending upon the stress of the type of flying we were doing and the condition of our airplane. He would also be available for any type of help that was needed in the cockpit or elsewhere in the aircraft.

The engineer, Ed ("Brownie") Brown, was really a jack-of-all-trades. He was our systems specialist, and gunner, and the ranking NCO of the crew. His was a job that could make or break a crew, and he carried his responsibility well. His knowledge of the aircraft saved our necks more than once. The things that he was called upon to do are far too numerous to mention, but he would troubleshoot every emergency on the plane. On takeoff and landings he sat on a belt seat between the copilot and pilot to help monitor the gauges and keep all systems within required limits. When he was not needed in the top turret, he was free to roam the aircraft aft of the forward compartment to check on the efficiency of the other crew members and to help with any special problems they might encounter.

The radio operator, George Hinman, whose primary duty was long-range communication, also had many secondary duties among which was manning guns, and from the Initial Point to the target and Rally Point it was he who dispensed "chaff" or "window" through a chute located in the radio room to the outside of the airplane. Chaff was aluminum foil cut in very thin strips and in varying lengths. It very much resembled the tinsel that is used to decorate Christmas trees. This would be dropped out of the airplane to sink toward the ground in hopes it would give false readings on the enemy radar, that was being used to track our progress and to aim the antiaircraft flak guns. The heavier the flak barrage the faster the radio operator would dispense the material. He had a good incentive! He was the second ranking NCO on the airplane and supervised the radio room and the waist of the ship, particularly the bomb bay at drop time. We needed to know if all bombs had dropped or whether we had a hung bomb or a no-drop. In either event, these bombs were dropped manually.

The left waist gunner, Robert Lynch, was also the armorer gunner. In addition to firing and maintaining his guns, he was responsible to the bombardier for the loading, fusing, and the eventual removal of the safety pins arming the bombs for the drop. He had a good working knowledge of the electrical bomb release system and he and the bombardier were the

bomb and armorer specialists. All the people who were responsible for guns were required to be able to assemble them
blindfolded.

The right waist gunner, Joe Firszt, was also a trained radio
operator, and served as the assistant or back-up in case anything happened to Hinman. He was also trained as assistant
engineer, so he found no trouble keeping busy on our crew
since he could be assigned duties relating to three positions.

The ball turret gunner, Ken ("Mac") McQuitty, was our turret specialist. He was familiar with all turrets on the airplane,
but his primary responsibility was to be found in his duties as
gunner and observer. He had the only view directly under our
aircraft to warn us of fighters or whether any other aircraft
might drift under us on the bomb run. His was a lonely job as
his only contact with other crew members came through the
interphone system. In this respect he was like the tail gunner,
the only other position that was isolated from the other crew
members. In an emergency it would take time to get to either
of these two men.

The primary concern of the tail gunner, Martin ("Smitty")
Smith, was the tail turret and its two fifty-caliber machine
guns. It was he who saw what was happening behind our aircraft, but he was too remote while we were in the air to have
any additional duties. This isolated position had to be manned
at all times.

I served as 1st pilot and aircraft commander. In this position I was responsible for everything that happened aboard
this aircraft and its relationship to other aircraft in the formation. Only the 1st pilots attended four-engine specialized
training in the B-17. It was up to the 1st pilot to teach the
copilot all he knew about flying the aircraft and its systems. He
had to do the job well, for if the 1st pilot were incapacitated,
the aircraft with all its responsibilities would then fall on the
copilot's shoulders. All 1st pilots and copilots were given a
certain amount of gunnery training—not as much as the gunners, but enough to understand their problems and to fire a
gun if necessary. All pilots were given navigational training
and were very adept at some forms of navigation, particularly
radio navigation. But when it came to celestial, dead reckon-

ing, and other forms, we knew only enough to understand
what the navigator was doing. All pilots in Cadet School were
taught code and had to receive and send at least twenty words
a minute to be able to graduate. But this is one job we were
happy to leave to a man who was much more proficient, the
radio operator. The pilots also spent some time training on
the bomb trainer, but this was only enough to make us understand the problems of the bombardier and to make sure we
would provide him with a stable platform from which to do his
job, which, after all, was the whole point of the mission.

Flying the airplane should be routine for the two pilots.
This we should do by instinct and second nature from the
countless hours of practice in flying and emergency procedures. This left our minds free to grasp the "big picture" and
be concerned with all that was going on around us. Matters of
judgment involving split-second decisions had to be made,
and most of the time there would not be a second chance.

Thus it was that it took every one of us performing at our
best to fly a successful mission. A bomber crew truly was the
sum of its parts, and everyone strove to do his very best.

July 13

Doc Doxon, Copilot

We got stuck with a practice mission, drew ship #8140, *The
Pregnant Goose,* definitely not our choice. The crew was highly
POed. But Maggie's Drawers wave tonight. We have been assigned aircraft #7882 again—sure hope she starts in the
morning. The weather was far from perfect today.

July 14, 1944

*I will say we aren't recruits any longer in the true sense of the word.
We know what the score is!! We got the real McCoy from the start. We
all started together and we will all finish together.*

Now I'll let you in on a few secrets of the crew. You know they've been sweating out the addition to my family. Well, as soon as they see me over the hump we have to start sweating Hinman whose wife is expecting in November or December, I forget which. Then after we pull him through we'll go to work on Brown who has only recently received the glad news that he too will be a papa. It looks like all the married men on the crew are destined to be family men. Everybody's 100 percent except poor Smitty. He did his best, but his wife had the same misfortune Sis once had. But it won't be long until we'll have him home and he can try again.

You asked me to have fun and see all of England that I can. There's really no place to go except London. Transportation is very poor and food is scarce. I've already seen London and the English countryside. Off the post there is no means of entertainment or amusement. Things over here are very austere—there are shortages of everything. It very definitely is not like the U.S. where, in spite of rationing, most things are still available. Whenever we eat away from the post or share tea and crumpets with the local people on the train we have the feeling we are taking something away from them, of which they have very little. Nevertheless, we do accept some of their offerings because we have no desire to insult their generosity, and they are doing their best to be good hosts in some very trying times. The ones we have met have to be very brave souls to carry on the way they do after all they've been through and still have a sharing nature. Maybe you can see now why we are content to remain on the post to see a show, eat, and log sack time.

I have a pass coming in a few days, I hope, then I'm going to some other posts and try to look up some friends. Don't worry, by now I've seen more than just England and somehow sightseeing just doesn't appeal to me—maybe it's the hostile reception.

Mission #4, *Maquis, France, July 14*

Frank Dimit, Bombardier

Very secret mission. 95th Group made up the entire wing today of three groups. We dropped enough supplies to equip 10,000 men. (Free French Force of 50,000 men.)

This is one mission we won't forget, doing a little good for a change. Frenchmen seemed damn glad to get supplies the way they shouted and waved.

Saw no flak or enemy fighters. Fighter escort swell.

Hope we never have to take off at night again. Took off at 3:47 a.m. and it was pitch black. Climbing through that was worse than climbing to rendezvous through overcast. Really sweated it out, worst part of the mission. *[End of mission notes by Frank Dimit]*

Roco Work, Navigator

Our next trip out was the first one where we felt we'd really accomplished something. It was unique in that we were aroused earlier for the briefing than any other mission we ever flew—0030. At the briefing we learned what we'd hoped to be true, that our group had again been picked to drop supplies to the "maquis" by parachute. The canisters on the ships contained nearly everything up to the famous "jeep": pistols, rifles, bazookas, ammunition, medical supplies, etc. Our target was in far southern France, along the banks of the Dordogne River about sixty miles directly east of Bordeaux. It was planned that we'd cross into France, just skirting the bottleneck at Caen, at an altitude of 17,000 feet. Proceeding well beyond the advance units of our armies who were still struggling on the Cherbourg peninsula, we were to begin a descent in sufficient time that we'd be only a few hundred feet above the ground when we released the containers. This was so positive target identification could be managed and so the supplies would not be too badly scattered before the maquis got them collected.

Taking off at 0345 we chattered happily to one another over the interphone, overcome with delight that we could add another mission without undergoing dangerous flak. In a fairly short while all elements of the formation were in position and the time came for us to depart over the southern coast of England. As usual there was a pretty thick cloud layer over the Isles that day so we couldn't see a thing below us until we were well out over the Channel. Even then there were too many clouds for us to catch more than an occasional glimpse of what we had most wanted to see—the small portion of France that had been captured from the Germans.

But as the planes droned steadily onward the breaks below became more and more frequent until by the time we were two hours from the target it was CAVU [ceiling and visibility unlimited] from the ground up. The descent began as scheduled and every man stirred uncomfortably with the thought of what Jerry fighters could do to the outfit if they suddenly attacked at this lower altitude. Of course there were plenty of those "Little Friends" around, but it's always possible for a stray enemy fighter to sneak in when least expected. Down and down the formation went. Soon everyone had removed his oxygen mask and laid it aside for the time being. Soon the planes were so low that it became uncomfortably warm in our heavy flying suits, but there wasn't the time to change for the target was only twenty minutes away. At this altitude the war seemed far away and quite unreal. There were few military installations this far south in France and the weight of Allied bombs had not destroyed the beauty of the countryside.

Because of the nature of their underground work the maquis had to operate from out-of-the-way headquarters, as far from any German units as possible. Similarly, to avoid having the supplies fall into German hands they had to choose relatively inaccessible places for the drops. In case German spotters saw us flying at that low altitude it wouldn't take them long to decide that something of the sort was going on and they'd be sure to do everything in their power to intercept the canisters. Specific signals had been arranged and markers erected so we wouldn't have too much trouble finding the exact spot to drop.

In due time the IP was reached and we made a false run over the target area with bomb doors closed to make sure that the lead bombardiers had located where they were to drop. Sure enough, there were the bonfires and markers laid out on the plateau exactly where we'd been told they'd be. Circling to approach from the proper direction we opened the doors and tightened up the formations so the canisters wouldn't be too badly scattered. Frank hunched forward on his seat so he'd be sure to toggle our load at the same time as the leader. Everyone else scanned the skies at intervals to make sure no Jerries would catch us with our doors down. In between we eagerly scoured the countryside for glimpses of our secret allies below. French peasants ran from their homes as we roared overhead, cattle scattered, chickens ran this way and that, every living creature abruptly reacted to the unusual occasion.

On one farm we could see a farmer stop his plowing to shade his eyes from the sun and gaze at us. When we were near enough that he could see the insignia on our wings his arms went over his head in a wave. Soon we were so close we could actually recognize the fact that he was smiling and cheering us. Just as our plane passed over his head he removed his hat and the last glimpse I had of him brought tears to my eyes. This Frenchman, in far southern France, had crossed himself and stood with his hat over his heart as if he were saluting us, then his head bowed down, seemingly in prayer.

When Frank sang out his "Bombs away" over the interphone I jerked out of the reverie I'd slipped into when watching the farmer beneath us. The doors came closed and we circled once more to see where the canisters had fallen. Hundreds of men were running across the fields toward the dropping area and several trucks appeared from nowhere to move these supplies to a safer spot. By the time our formation had been regrouped for the return flight some of the trucks had already been filled and were driving off down the twisting trails to some hiding place even farther removed from prying Nazi eyes.

Nothing particularly eventful occurred on the climb to altitude, and even though we'd been flying for five hours already we weren't very tired. The interphone was buzzing with comments of the occasion just passed and time flew by as swiftly as the aircraft in which we were flying. Soon I realized how close we were to the invasion coast and prodded the boys to quiet down and get back on the job of watching for enemy action. There was always the possibility that there would be some activity near the lines. Our hopes of a clear view of the battle area were dampened considerably when clouds appeared ahead of and below us. Soon we were again over a solid cloud bank and started across the Channel to England.

As we neared our base there were a few breaks beneath so we didn't worry about having to let down through the clouds. Right over the field we flew and the peel-off began. In due time we were on the ground and back at our hardstand. Our spirits were high after this mission: no flak, no fighters, no trouble of any kind. The former missions were negative in our minds because we'd had to destroy something. On this particular trip we were lending aid to what later proved to be an extremely valuable band of allies. Every minute of sleep that had been lost the night before was gladly forgotten, and the fatigue from the long flight was as nothing. For on today's trip against the enemy we had done a real job and done it well. *[End of mission account by Roco Work]*

Mission #5, *Paris, France, July 17*

Frank Dimit, Bombardier

Briefed at 3:30 a.m. for target on Yonne River about 60 miles southeast of Paris. It was a three-track concrete railroad bridge. Takeoff was set back one hour to 7 a.m. because of light ground fog and our fighter escort could not leave ground.

Carried 2 2,000-pound bombs and flew #5 in the lead squadron of lead group. 95th put up an entire wing again. Target was creamed but good. Encountered moderate but inaccurate flak. Intelligence wasn't sure of flak gun emplacements, but we sure found them.

Saw no enemy fighters—had good escort.

Had rough time on letdown over England. Area covered by thick, low clouds. Ran into several traffic patterns of other fields getting back to our own base.

Swell day for intelligence observations. Boys picked up several interesting notes on marshalling yards, a truck convoy, and an airfield, besides flak gun emplacements.

Picked up some swing music on radio on way home. Listened to it over France and Belgium. Strange way to fight a war. *[End of mission notes by Frank Dimit]*

Roco Work, Navigator

Mission number 5 came up three days later in direct support of the ground troops, although this fact wasn't made clear until later in the summer when Patton's tanks made their drive across France. The target was a railroad bridge over the Yonne River about eighty miles southeast of Paris and forty miles southwest of Trayes. The nearest town of any size is Sens, France, a town of about 30,000 before the war.

Perhaps the outstanding feature of this mission as far as Fletcher's crew is concerned was the absence of any flak batteries in the target area. The usual prebriefing and postbriefing duties were performed with the same meticulous care that characterized the preparations for every mission. Guns were loaded, flak suits were counted, oxygen pressure verified, etc. All the innumerable small tasks were done.

Once aloft everyone kept an apprehensive lookout for other aircraft, for over England—America's largest aircraft carrier—there is an everpresent danger of collision. However rendezvous altitude was reached without any incident worse than an occasional jousting due to prop wash.

No one who hasn't spent many hours in the air can realize what a potent force this prop wash can be. It originates, of course, as a wind created by the rapidly turning propellers. The terrific thrust of the blades causes the air to swirl and twist in all directions, at a high velocity. If one tosses a matchstick upon surging water, he naturally expects it to be buffeted about by the changing currents on which it floats. That is precisely the same in the air. A plane's wings, which for all general purposes could be said to float on the air, are also tossed about by the unsettled air through which they pass. Severe downdrafts caused by whirling props will drop one wing of a B-17 like pulling the plug in a wash basin. This boiling, twisting air extends back of a propeller for a considerable distance until it eventually loses force. In the case of a B-17, the four propellers cause a terrific mass of turbulent air.

When flying into prop wash a wide-awake pilot can always prevent disaster. At the first brush with the wash, the wing tip trembles noticeably and gives a warning of what may come. The main lifting surface of the wing is in smooth air, but the tip has penetrated this surging air mass and flutters in response to the unsteady air. As soon as enough of the wing has gotten into the prop wash to cause instability in flight the pilot must make instantaneous corrections to return to level flight. Fletch was that sort of a pilot—it takes brains, not brawn, to fly a four-engine bomber. At the first hint of trouble Fletch and Doc coordinated beautifully to counteract the danger. No sooner would the left wing start to drop than they had full opposite aileron applied to lift it.

The greatest danger from prop wash lies in the possibility of midair collision while out of control. When flying close formation such as is used in the fight against Germany, a violent change of attitude caused by prop wash may put a bomber directly in the path of a nearby plane. Just split seconds could find two or more planes locked in collision.

To return to mission number 5—No troubles were experienced during rendezvous so Frank crawled back to remove the pins from the two 2,000-pound bombs we planned to drop on that bridge. Out over the Channel they proceeded, crossing the coast into Holland over an island at the mouth of the Rhine. South past Antwerp and Brussels they roared, drawing intermittent flak barrages from batteries just off course to either side.

On this mission our boys were flying *Full House,* so named because of the numbers 97797 on the tail. The route to the IP was short and quite soon that spine-chilling rumble caused by the open bomb-bay doors could be heard above the engines' thunder. The squadrons peeled off to make the run and George started tossing out his chaff in case some unexpected railroad guns were encountered.

Without a burst appearing in the sky the group made the run, Frank made his singing "Bombs away," and the squadron turned off to the Rally Point. From there the group swung

back over the target to more accurately assess the damage.
The bomb smoke had completely obscured the bridge from
sight so they knew the bombing had been a success.

Skirting the heavily defended area around Paris, the group
headed homeward and returned to its base without incident.
Once again Fletcher's crew had flown against the Hun—this
time for seven hours—and encountered no troubles. Now
there were but thirty to go; the tour was 14 percent completed. *[End of mission account by Roco Work]*

July 17, 1944

*You know the letter I promised you? Well, I'm really sorry but I'll have
to beg off again this evening. I have a delivery to make in the morning
so I should go to bed early. I hope you understand and will forgive me.
When I got home from today's work there were two more wonderful
letters waiting for me. They were dated June 3rd and June 5th.*

Mission #6 Hemmingstedt, Germany, July 18

Frank Dimit, Bombardier

Briefed at 2:15 a.m. for target in Germany. Target was an oil
refinery on eastern side of Denmark peninsula, about 40 miles
southeast of Kiel (Hemmingstedt). Carried 10 500-pound
demolition bombs.

Flew as a spare, but soon found a position in the formation
—ended up at #3 position in first element of low squadron.
Flight time was seven hours. . . .

Saw no enemy fighters and very little flak—not very accurate. Hinman threw out chaff. Had P-51 escort.

Listened to German symphony music on way back. Some
war—take music appreciation course and give Germans hell,
all at the same time. *[End of mission notes by Frank Dimit]*

Roco Work, Navigator

Next morning early we were routed out again and, after the usual egg breakfast, found our way to the briefing room. When the curtain was pulled back we greeted the target with sighs of satisfaction, for there was no flak evident during the entire mission. As the briefing officer began to give us the story of the day's attack, we grew slightly less elated, however. It seemed that the primary target to be hit by visual methods only was Hemmingstedt, a small town on the Danish peninsula. There we hoped our bombs would find some underground storage tanks for oil. And at that target there were no known flak guns.

The rub came on the secondary, which we were to attack in case the weather did not permit visual sightings. Instead of dropping on the primary target by PFF as we usually did, we were instructed to continue on to Kiel and bomb the dock area. The entire Kiel area contained about 150 heavy guns and we had no desire to test the accuracy of their radar. So naturally we all prayed for visual conditions over Hemmingstedt; the weather man, incidentally, forecast that there was a fifty-fifty chance of going in without cloud coverage.

After everyone had attended to his own particular postbriefing duties we gathered in the ground crew's tent to discuss our prospects for the day. Overhead there wasn't even a suggestion of a cloud and we hoped strongly that similar conditions would prevail on the Danish peninsula. Eventually takeoff time drew nearer and we piled into the ship for our last-minute checks. In a few minutes we taxied out on the perimeter in position. The usual gnawing in our stomachs caused by other reasons than hunger began to make itself known, and then everyone crossed his fingers as Fletch poured the coal on and we started down the runway.

As usual we were airborne without the slightest bit of difficulty and shortly found our place in the formation circling the field at 13,000 feet. Right on time we departed for wing and division assembly, and our coast out point, Great Yarmouth, was hit on the nose. Climbing over the North Sea we went to coordinates 5400-0500, 5415-0700, and proceeded toward the

RP at 5420-0837. Suddenly Doc came on the interphone to tell us that our air leader, Colonel McKnight, had established contact with the weather ship and had been informed that the primary was completely cloud-covered. At this time all of us began sweating, for we certainly didn't fancy the thought of going on to Kiel. Within ten minutes, though, Fletch came on to inform us that the decision had been reached to attack the primary on PFF instead of going on to Kiel. The reason for the change of plans didn't matter in the least, so long as it was true.

By DR (dead reckoning) I could tell we were quite near the IP and I decided not to trust the information given to our briefing officer. Maybe HQ didn't think there were any guns at Hemmingstedt, but I, personally, wasn't going to place too much credence on it. So I announced over the interphone that I was putting on my flak suit and everyone seemed to think the suggestion worthwhile. When Frank opened the bomb-bay doors there wasn't a hint of flak ahead, and below there was nothing but a sea of white clouds. For all we could tell looking down we might have been over the North Sea yet.

At the turn on the bomb run we all tensed up as always and debated with ourselves our judgment in joining the Air Corps. Nothing happened to back up our momentary indecision, though, and Frank sang out that welcome "Bombs away!" without our even seeing a burst of flak off in the distance. We made the RP good and headed westward on the way home, congratulating ourselves on not being shot at for the third straight time when Smitty announced none too calmly that where we had just been there was now a large cloud of smoke in the sky. Flak had suddenly started coming up and we felt quite happy that we had been the first ones over the target and were not just now bombing. Sometimes a group is lucky that way; the gunners on the ground are a little slow in starting to fire and the run can be made without a bit of flak. Then, just as the turn off the bomb run is made, the bursts begin to appear.

Evidently we had caught the flak gunners napping this morning. At our tender altitude of 18,000 feet, we'd have been pretty easy marks, too.

Then Smitty came back on the interphone to tell us that dense clouds of black smoke were rising through the clouds where we had bombed. Evidently our PFF attack had been accurate, for there was little doubt that the smoke was caused by burning oil. Rising to approximately 10,000 feet, the heavy smoke made us even happier than before. Now we not only had credit for another mission in the bag without going through any dangerous flak, but also all indications pointed toward success in the bombing.

On toward England we flew and below us the clouds began to dissipate in direct contrast to the way they had acted a couple of days before. Instead of clear weather over the Continent and messy stuff hovering over the Isles, we were amazed to see better conditions over Great Britain than we had seen in the vicinity of northern Germany. There's no accounting for the oddities that occur in Europe!

And so we returned safely to the base with the knowledge that there was now one less mission to be flown. Upon finishing interrogation and having a bite to eat at the mess hall we wandered back to the squadron area where we learned that we had finally earned a pass. For the next forty-eight hours our time would be our own. Plans were formulated in a hurry; we would all go to London together and any deviations from the party would take place there. But this is a story of combat in the air. The battling with "Piccadilly Commandoes" is an entirely different story! *[End of mission notes by Roco Work]*

July 22, 1944

Here I am back again. As you've probably guessed I did get my pass. We took off for London and had quite a time. Met a lot of fellows whom I knew and had been wondering about. . . . We had lots of fun discussing our present situation and swapping bits of combat news— where and what we'd been doing. Each knew where some other buddy was and what had happened to him, although all the news wasn't good. It was good to find out what goes on some place besides your own. I will again say that I'm darned glad I'm with the outfit I am.

Now getting back to London—we saw the Changing of the Guard

*at Buckingham Palace and lots of points of interest including Picca-
dilly. We found a place where we could get a steak. It's called the
Athens Cafe. We all suspect that it was horse meat but no one mentions
it because, after all, a steak is a steak! I've never seen anything quite
like this here and hope not to see it again—you have your life in your
hands with Jerry overhead.*

*I think I've just made my last trip to London. No, I take it back. I'll
have to go once more to pick up a battle jacket which I'm having made.
What I started to say was that I'm too allergic to Doodle Bugs [buzz
bombs] to spend much more time there. Now let me tell you about our
battle jackets which the four of us are having made. First, we bought
new blouses so we could have the material. . . . The tailor says we
can get them in about three weeks. All four are the same. Boy, wait
until you see them, they'll knock your eyes out! The cost is a little over
ten pounds ten shillings, or about forty-two dollars American. This
includes wings, patches, bars, and combat ribbons all embroidered on.*

*Last night when we got back there were eight letters waiting for me
and today I received five more. Maybe you think I haven't been having
a field day reading all my mail!*

While we were in London we stayed at the Regents Palace
Hotel, and during the night the top two floors were heavily
damaged during a raid, giving us all a good scare. Consequently, London lost a lot of its glamor. Now about our Ike
jackets—we had them lined with fiery red silk. This was not
visible from the outside, but was flashy when the jackets were
removed. Besides, we knew it was there when we wore them,
and this was our way of expressing pride and loyalty to the
95th Bomb Group, whose radio call sign was "Fireball Red."
That name always sent a tingle down our spines when we
heard it used on the radio on our way home from the target.
Absolute radio silence was maintained on the way to the target, but coming home emergency transmissions were permissible to summon fighter protection for those returning home
alone, or to effect a rendezvous of cripples so they might travel
home together for mutual protection. There was a time coming home on three engines when Doc and I put together a
formation of ten cripples from different groups, complete with

fighter protection and flying along at 130 mph with old "Fireball Red Leader" bringing them home.

Mission #7 St. Lo, France, July 24

Frank Dimit, Bombardier

Rather unusual mission all the way round. Briefed at 8:00 a.m. We were to bomb inside our own lines. Our troops had withdrawn 1,500 yards in order to give us a chance to blast an opening in the German lines. This direct support of ground forces by the heavies had worked around Caen and we were hoping it would work here. The group carried 100-pound demos and 20-pound frags. Our ship carried 38 clusters of 6 20-pound fragmentation bombs.

Had to climb through overcast again today. Target was clouded over so we didn't drop the bombs. We looked for target of opportunity, but no go. Had to bring bombs back. We flew #6 in lead squadron of the high group of the wing. Were supposed to fill in diamond of high squadron, but after an abort, we filled in this spot.

Had trouble with bomb-bay doors again.

Saw first ship go down in flames. First wing over caught hellish flak after dropping bombs. Plane evidently caught direct hit. Hard to explain feeling it gives you, but you wish to hell you were back at the base.

Work didn't fly with us. Lead ships were the only ones to carry navigators. *[End of mission notes by Frank Dimit]*

July 25, 1944

It has been a busy two days in the ETO. Some new deal—they're making me earn my money now. I don't think it's here to stay, though, should pass in a few days.

I can't tell you what I did this morning, but this evening we were presented the Air Medal, which was recently earned by the crew. As soon as time permits I will mail it on to you. . . .

Mission #8, St. Lo, France, July 25

Frank Dimit, Bombardier

Same mission today as yesterday. Briefed at 5:00 a.m. Same target, same load. We flew in #2 position of low squadron of the high group of wing.

We went in at 12,000 feet—plenty of haze and fog. Tried to go in at 16,000 feet but couldn't see the target. Don't know how much damage we did, but we'll find out soon. No write-up about this support in papers. Guess they want to keep it quiet.

Bob Work didn't fly again so I had to double in navigation.

Bomb-bay door motor burned out before we took off so had to crank doors both ways.

Fiess flew on the left wing in #3 slot. They picked up a little flak (25 holes). We didn't get a scratch. Flak was light and accurate.

Sgt. Wilson just came in and we are to receive our Air Medals tonight at 6:30. So I guess we'd better clean up for the Colonel. *[End of mission notes by Frank Dimit]*

On July 24 the Eighth Air Force was called upon to act as forward artillery for the ground troops trying to break out at St. Lo. When we reached the target area we had a solid undercast. Since we couldn't see we didn't bomb. The bomb-bay doors were closed and we brought our bombs home. The base was a beehive of activity—planes to be serviced, repaired, refueled, and made ready—for we would try again tomorrow.

On July 25 we were given the same briefing as the day before which was essentially this: "Since you are bombing in close proximity to the front lines every precaution must be taken to protect our own ground troops. Your bombs must not be released until you are sure you have passed across our own troops. The distance will be measured not in miles, but in yards."

With the equipment we had—and some common sense—we could protect our own people and still inflict heavy damage on the enemy, as well as demoralize those who would survive. This would be a shining hour for the Eighth, and we would prove that heavy bombers could be used in close support of ground troops.

On our base the briefing people were thorough and the law was laid down, "If you don't know where you are, don't bomb. Bring them back the same as yesterday. There will be no mistakes. Everything must be on the safe side or you will endanger the lives of our own troops. There is an absolute safeguard built in—this will involve your ILAS equipment in the aircraft."

The ILAS (Instrument Landing Approach System) is a radio beam which normally would be sent down the middle of a runway for the pilots to line up on for the final approach to a landing. This system is very accurate and can pinpoint the center of a runway. Today the narrow radio signal would be transmitted down no-man's-land between the opposing forces.

In the aircraft the pilot has a radio receiver connected to a round gauge with a needle in the center. The needle is hinged at the bottom. The gauge is divided in two—one half is yellow and one half is blue. When you are exactly on course to the runway the needle is centered between the two halves. If you stray only a few feet right or left the needle will move into the corresponding quadrant and you must make immediate correction to center the needle.

But this day instead of flying down the beam we would fly across it, which means that the needle would stay in one quadrant, gradually moving closer to the center. When the plane crossed the beam the needle would cross the center line and be in the opposite quadrant. You then would know positively that you had crossed the line, or the beam, that separates the two forces.

"There may be broken clouds over the front lines, so all bombing will be done by group lead aircraft using PFF, Mickey Radar ships," the briefing officers told us. "All other ships will toggle their bombs out when they see the lead ship bomb. The lead ship will follow the normal practice of dropping two smoke bombs. When you see the two smoke bombs and your ILAS needle is in the proper quadrant then drop.

Don't guess. Drop only if all things check out. It is very simple, all you have to do is follow the directions.

"You will not take your navigators with you as this is a short run and all navigation will be done by the lead ships. Fly a tight formation so the bomb patterns will be precise. Bombing will be done at 16,000 feet. There will be very little if any enemy resistance. You will be over enemy territory no more than a half hour or so."

Our group was in the first third of the task force, so we were able to see whether we would encounter serious enemy opposition before we reached the target.

Everything went as scheduled—all rendezvous were made on time. There were breaks in the undercast just as we made landfall on the French coast. As we started on the bomb run, with the bomb-bay doors open, the task force's lead groups were already heading home. The opposition was very light.

We were beginning to fly past the smoke trails of the preceding lead groups—long plumes in groups of two starting from bombing altitude and arcing toward the ground for several thousand feet. This could give the false impression that you were past where someone else had already bombed, if you forgot about drift.

The bombardier called and asked which quadrant our ILAS needle was pointing to. We replied that we still showed over friendly troops, but it was gradually moving to center. He pointed out that we must have a slight head wind because some of the smoke trails were now rather far behind us. Within a couple of minutes the needle moved into the enemy quadrant and we notified our bombardier that everything was "go" as soon as he got the signal from the lead ship. In less than a minute the lead ship, with two smoke bombs arching out, dropped its bomb load. Our bombardier dropped on the smoke signal, closed the bomb-bay doors, and the group headed for home.

We could now see the following groups coming in as we were going out. It was a tremendous sight—both the incoming and the outgoing groups stretching for miles. The heavens roared with 3,000 aircraft: bombers, medium and heavy, fighters, reconnaissance, and ships of every description. For the people on the ground, with the engine noise from the constant bomber stream overhead and the bombs exploding in close proximity of the lines, the shock of the noise alone had to be terrific and terrifying.

We had to feel good because everything had gone perfectly. Jerry was catching hell. We had achieved the purpose of our mission. When we landed everyone was tired but happy.

Toward evening we learned that a tragedy of mind-boggling proportions had occurred. Some errant group of a later task force of the Eighth or Ninth Air Force had dropped their bombs while still over the forward lines of the assaulting American troops. A general was killed along with many other American troops. An Associated Press cameraman from Detroit also became a casualty. The picture from his camera later was published in *Yank* showing this "Hell on Earth" in action. Ernie Pyle, the famous war correspondent, wrote a very touching story of the agony on the ground and the probable feelings of the air crews in England that night as they learned of the tragedy that had been left in their wake. Since what he wrote in conjecture was, in essence, the true feelings of the air crews, I only hope he learned the truth of his writing before his own demise.

We were sick. Everyone shared in the anguish along with those who were derelict. We had never seen a malfunction where a lead ship would drop early. A malfunction occasionally caused a "no drop." It was very hard to imagine any case where equipment failure could do this without human error present. But in battle nothing is impossible.

I do not know the official version of what happened, but I do know that a rumor immediately surfaced in which a lead bombardier was supposedly influenced while flying through the drifting smoke trails from other lead ships to conclude that he was now over enemy territory, and dropped his bombs in spite of the fierce opposition from his fellow crew members. When the bombs from this lead ship dropped, the others in the unit did likewise.

This was a rumor, but it was plausible. Equipment malfunction, human error, guilt or innocence, rumor or fact—these were out of our province and in the hands of those in the higher echelons.

For us it was saddening that it had to happen, and we would not know how or why. But such is war. Not all things are reasonable or even explainable. But, grief aside, viewed in the light of expendability which applied to all of us, the casualties were far less than if air power—even though fallible—hadn't been used.

July 27, 1944

Life here the last two days has been no different than usual—very peaceful, very quiet, and definitely no excitement to speak of. Back in the same old rut with plenty of sack time. I'm getting to the point where I can sleep for fifteen hours straight without once being interrupted. Not bad, huh! . . .

July 27

Doc Doxon, Copilot

Alerted again. This time we had the engines started before the mission was scrubbed. Must have been weather. Lightning struck the outhouse with Baird in it.

Mission #9, *Merseburg, Germany (Leuna Oil Refinery), July 28*

Frank Dimit, Bombardier

Fiess's crew flew in the formation with us today. Overcast all the way in and out. Navigating damn difficult. Thank goodness weather information was right on the money.

Hit intense and very accurate flak at Kassel, Germany. Damn near got us. Someone had to be looking after us. Flak bursts were so close to nose I thought it would blow it off. Bob Work did wonderful job of navigating. Entire crew was great.

Fighters looked damn good on way out. Had three P-51s escorting us. I'd like to spend my next pass buying drinks for our little friends. Great bunch.

Skies of Germany are a mighty lonesome place for one B-17. Have never been so lonesome and scared before. Nine men against the Third Reich isn't good.

Group came back from target shot to hell and with several wounded on board. Some never got back. It was a rough mission. Hope they creamed target and we don't have to go back again. Needless to say, our crew is very happy to get back. *[End of mission notes by Frank Dimit]*

July 28

Doc Doxon, Copilot

We almost made it to Stalag Luft today—three hours out of Germany alone. Boy what a lonesome sky. Those 51s are sure pretty when you are alone.

Roco Work, Navigator

Upon our return to operations ten days later we felt pretty good about this business of fighting a war. Shucks, hadn't we just completed six comparatively easy missions? What is there to worry about? At briefing we found out. Merseburg was the order for the day. By now we had a healthy respect for the place even though we had never reached the target. Enough of our friends had returned from that devastating flak and told us about it so that we shivered in our boots at the mere thought. Nevertheless, that's how things stood and the regular preliminaries done with we found ourselves at 20,000 feet over Cromer, departing England on course and on time.

Flying number five in the high squadron of the high group made us feel no better than if we were "tail-end Charlie."

When Merseburg is the target one might as well be sick in the hospital! At any rate, with many uncomfortable thoughts running through our heads we proceeded on into Germany and gave thanks for the solid undercast beneath. It's true the navigation would be more difficult, but everyone knew the Jerry flak gunners weren't nearly as accurate, either, and that seemed more important. One hundred ninety guns were all we were briefed on, but past battle damage suffered at Merseburg led us to strongly doubt the correctness of the report.

Suddenly, when still about fifteen minutes from the IP, Dimit tapped me on the shoulder to arouse me from trying to figure our ground speed and pointed at a formation which was fast disappearing in the distance. Grumpily I asked him, "So what?" His reply shocked me considerably, "So that's our group!" Looking out the right window I could see the reason. Number four engine was feathered and then I knew Fletch couldn't keep up on the three engines remaining. Group after group passed us in short order and finally Fletch was forced to give up his efforts to stay even faintly near our outfit or to join another. Doc was already calling for fighter protection over VHF when Fletch told Dimit to salvo the bombs. His answer will be always remembered as one of the most bloodthirsty utterances ever to pass through the lips of our noble bombardier: "But, Fletch, can't I toggle them out one at a time? They'll do more damage that way!"

So saying, Frank opened the bomb bays and sent ten 500-pounders—one at a time—screaming down into the undercast. Doc cut in to tell us three P-51s had been dispatched from the escorting force to give support on the way home. I couldn't be sure of our position because of the clouds below, but approximated it to be 5111-1010 and planned my course accordingly. "Better make a 180 to the right, Fletch," I said, and was startled to see that we were already in a turn to the left. Pilots seem to be reluctant to turn into a dead engine.

"The chances are that we'll come out of this turn right over Kassel, old boy," I warned him, but our course had already been committed. "The fighters asked me to turn to the left," he said, and I muttered a disparaging remark about our being the ones who'd have to tool through the flak and not them.

However, everything seemed all right for a couple of minutes until Frank suddenly yelled out that we were approaching a large town and would pass right over it. At that precise moment all hell broke loose!

Huge puffs of smoke gave evidence to our nearness to several flak bursts. We went into violent evasive action as Fletch attempted to throw the plane clear of the danger by sheer strength. Heeding my plea to end up on a 180 degree heading he continued to wrench the controls until our B-17 groaned in protest. That flak was really close, and the flame of the explosions could be seen easily. Our "little friends" had scattered at the first indication of what was to come and they were now riding comfortably out of range on our left. Finally we got out of range, but our nerves were a wreck. No one had been hurt, miraculously enough, but we could see several holes in the wings and fuselage.

The flak served one good purpose, however. Now there was no doubt in my mind where we were. So I immediately set to work from that point while Doc, who'd taken over the controls, flew the heading I'd given before our "incident." Feverishly I figured and plotted, interspersing my efforts with longing glances out of the window hoping to see the ground long enough to get a visual checkpoint to verify my work. None appeared, though, and we kept on at a slow 130 mph due to the feathered prop. After checking and rechecking my work I told Doc that we should turn northwest to go through the flak corridor between Liège and Brussels in about five minutes.

Just afterwards Frank informed me that there were some sizable openings in the clouds up ahead and I immediately began scouring the ground for some recognizable point. Right when I had about given up in despair the clouds opened wider and I could see a junction of a railroad and a highway near a small town with a stream running off to the south. I asked Frank if he thought it was the same place I'd previously marked on my map as our turning point. After considerable scrutiny of the map and countryside below he nodded his assent and I glanced at my watch as I was calling Doc to take up the new heading. Not bad, I thought, only a minute and a half off my calculations. The credit wasn't too much on my work, though. If the winds we were given at briefing hadn't been accurate, even the best of navigation couldn't have gotten us there on the money.

Warning Fletch, who had taken over again, to be ready for immediate evasive action if we were fired upon going through that narrow space between the ground defenses at Liège and Brussels, I again set to work and started working out an ETA for the Dutch coast and our base. Suddenly Frank called out flak off to the right. I noted that it was considerably out of range and went back to my work, only to be interrupted again by Brownie, who had spotted a strange fighter on the horizon up ahead. If it was a Jerry he didn't feel like tangling with our escort, though, and he disappeared in the same direction we were going. About then those P-51 pilots amazed me once anew by asking if we knew where we were. In answer to Doc's relaying what I thought to be our position they allowed as how that was about right, and no more was said. To this day I haven't found out how they could tell so accurately. Maybe they had obtained their location through radio contact with England. I don't know, but it was a good trick at any rate.

At last I was able to tell Fletch to head west, and we saw the ground drop away to the rear through some more openings in the clouds. As we started to descend he wisely cut back on the throttles, saying that he didn't want to exceed 130 mph because too much air speed would cause the feathered prop to windmill. He then left the pilot's seat to check the damage to the aircraft. Doc allowed the airspeed to build up to 150 mph and the vibration caused the prop to unfeather and start to windmill. Waiting only long enough for the rotation to pump up sufficient oil pressure, Doc refeathered it. Fletch returned to his seat with the admonition "Do not exceed 130 mph," and all went well once again.

To our immense relief the shores of England appeared in view and we crossed the coast just as Fletch was calling the tower for landing instructions. These received in good order, he nosed the ship down again and we entered the pattern. In no time we were on the ground and each of us heaved a big sigh of relief. Mission number seven [#7 for Work, but #9 for the crew] had proved to be the toughest one yet and the strain on our nerves was terrific! After we were out of the ship a crew chief showed us where a chunk of flak from Kassel had cut one of the main engine mounts and left it fastened only by the slightest of connections. Then the thought struck home about what might have taken place during that violent twisting and dodging we'd gone through, to say nothing of the vibration caused by the prop's windmilling as we started back across the Channel. It was truly a miracle that the whole engine hadn't fallen off from the strain.

Thinking that my navigation was one of the big factors in our safe return, and seemingly forgetful of the fact that that was what I'd been trained for the same as they had been trained to man their guns, the boys shook my hand and mumbled their thanks to me for guiding them home. I felt proud that I hadn't let them down, of course, but after all, I only did my job the same as they would do theirs when the time came. *[End of mission account by Roco Work]*

July 29, 1944

Yesterday was a busy one, one I probably won't forget for a long time. Some day I'll be able to tell you all about it. Guess I forgot to tell you this, but I've been keeping a little day-by-day report of what goes on so we can read it together. It'll bring back all these instances to mind so I'll be able to tell you all about it. Also I've been keeping all important dates—like when I got here and when I leave—in my little green book. This way you'll know where your wandering husband has been spending all his time since he left you.

You asked once if the letterhead on the stationery pertained to my outfit. Yes, it does. I might add that there isn't a better Air Force in existence than the Eighth. Of course, the fact that I'm in it doesn't sway my judgment a bit. But when you see it in action it makes you feel plenty proud to be a part of it.

This series of events had its origin in Roswell, New Mexico, where I underwent specialized four-engine training in the B-17. During the course of this instruction I had an instructor who had returned from combat in the ETO. His name was Captain Johnson and he knew his job well.

One day he said, "I want to show you a maneuver for evasive action. It will not be usable in a formation, but sometime when you're returning from a mission alone and on your own —and you will be at some point in your career—this maneuver could possibly save your life by outsmarting the German flak gunners and their radar. For the flak gunners' tracking-radar to be accurate some things have to be constant—a steady airspeed, a consistent heading, and a stable altitude. With these conditions you are a sitting duck. Now what I want to show you is how to keep all these things variable and yet make good the heading you have chosen.

"At the first sign of hostilities, which will be indicated by someone shooting at you, immediately lower the nose, ease back a little on the throttle, and start a turn to the left. Hold the turn until 90 degrees from your chosen heading. Let the air speed keep accelerating and lose approximately 500 feet of altitude, or whatever it takes to complete the turn. Then immediately pull the nose up and start a turn to the right. Increase the throttle setting and continue to climb until you've reached a point slightly above stalling speed—hopefully your turn has brought you back 180 degrees from the last heading. Each time you are overshooting your original heading by 90 degrees. The number of degrees does not have to be exact. In fact, if it varies some, all the better. The main object is to keep everything variable and to keep the radar shooting at where you were, rather than where you are going. By keeping your turns somewhere within the 180 degree frame you will eventually work your way out of the danger area, although you will be exposed longer to enemy action. But the advantage is that your direction of flight is always changing, your airspeed is either increasing or decreasing, and the altitude never remains the same. This can be a very violent series of maneuvers, but it is effective."

When I saw the first burst of four shells off the right wing tip and felt the concussion I automatically jammed the nose down and started a left turn. Obviously the instruction I had received was still lurking somewhere in the back of my head.

My first thought was, "Jerry, you missed, but just barely, when we were straight and level and a sitting duck. But if you get us now you're going to have to work for it."

Then it dawned on me that I had been so taken by surprise that I had forgotten my original heading. I called the navigator and said, "Give me a heading to get us out of here." His reply was, "The one you had was fine." I then had to say that I'm sure it was, but I had no idea what it was. Scared? No, just absentminded would have to be my excuse. Immediately I was given the original heading.

At least I now knew where we were going, and the show we were going to give was nothing short of fantastic as we dove and turned and climbed and turned with the aircraft first gaining and then losing airspeed. The burst of shells, in clusters of four, were first to the right and above us, then to the left and below us. They were bracketing us, but they couldn't hit us. The system was working and eventually we were out of range.

In the meantime, the crew was taking a real beating. There was no chance to warn them. All they could do was grab something and hang on. There was one exception. The ball turret gunner, snug in the ball with his safety belt fastened, was obviously enjoying himself because I heard him sing out, "Ride 'em cowboy!" How I wished I had his confidence!

About eight months later when we were eventually returned to the States and stationed at Hobbs, New Mexico, I called the Base Personnel Locator in Roswell—this base had now been converted to a B-29 Transition School. My purpose was to locate Captain Johnson. I wanted to fly up and thank him personally for showing me the maneuver that had been used to save the lives of our crew. I was informed that he had perished in the explosion of a B-29.

Oh, the ironies of war and fate! This man had taken all the enemy could dish out in a combat theater, only to give his life in a training situation, still trying to impart his knowledge into the minds of his students. It was a sad commentary, but in the Army Air Force there would be no havens of security.

July 30, 1944

*Here it is the end of another Sunday in the ETO. Today was spent the
same as the others—church, dinner, this afternoon in the Link trainer
and the show house. The show was* Once Upon A Time, *starring
Cary Grant. It was a four-reeler affair with no sense at all to it. It
brought on a few good laughs, though, so it wasn't entirely a waste of
time.*

*You would get a kick out of the shows here. They just tossed a bunch
of benches and boxes into an empty Nissen hut and we have a picture
house. The projector is an antiquated job suspended in a box from the
ceiling and the loudspeakers are tossed around any place where somebody is apt to sit. Now for the show—the lights are put out and the
machine is started. The next five minutes are spent trying to focus on
the screen. Finally the job is accomplished and you've missed the introduction of the movie. Things run along pretty smooth now for three or
four minutes, then the picture doesn't appear on the screen but the talk
goes on anyway. The operator immediately remedies this. The picture
comes back and the sound track quits. So the operator makes a few
more adjustments. Everything is all set now. Then what happens? The
first reel is finished and now we have to rewind and set up the second
reel. Then the whole process is continued until the last reel has been
shown. By that time you are completely worn out mentally and physically for the benches are very hard and your neck is so stiff from
bobbing your head around to see that you welcome the chance to get up
and go home. Each time I swear it's my last but I always wind up
going back. Ah! Such is the weakness of human nature!*

July 31, 1944

*Happy Birthday—and many happy returns of the day. Did you have a
cake with candles? I should think that would have been in order, and I
would have to be over here where I couldn't have any!*

*What did I do today? The same as usual, absolutely nothing. No, I
take it back as I spent an hour and a half in the barber shop trying to
get a five-minute clip. Finally got it too.*

*This morning was also payday. Wound up with twenty-two pounds,
six shillings, and four pence. In good old U.S. currency that amounts*

to ninety dollars and five cents. Here's the low down: My base pay is $165.00, flying pay $82.50, subsistence for this month $43.40, rental $60.00, which makes a total of $350.90. Now for the deductions: Bond $18.75, Allotment $225.00, Insurance $6.60, Rations $10.50. That totals $260.85. By the mathematical process of subtraction I wind up with $90.05. Not bad! I can get along very easily on that and have all kinds of fun while still affording the necessities of life. Next month I may take out another bond for the little one. I think it would be a good idea, don't you? That way we could start a little schooling fund and keep adding to it from time to time. Then when college time comes around the money will be there and we'll never have missed it. Along about then I should have a raise in pay. If so, that's what I intend to do. Let me know what you think about this.

The mail situation was not much improved today. There is no reason or regularity in the way the letters come. Some seem to come by boat and some by airplane. Right now your letters mean everything to me as I'm anxiously waiting to hear how you are and what the latest developments are. This surely can't go on much longer. I've just decided that after this one you're not to have any more until after I get home! Right now I'd give almost anything to know that everything is okay and that you're feeling fine. Then I'll be happy again with no worries in the world.

You asked how the people here find time for romancing with only three hours of darkness. I'll give you a little tip—they do it in broad daylight with no questions asked, and no one thinks anything about it. Piccadilly is a mess. The "commandos" carry a card which exempts them from war work and they also carry a health card, which they are very happy to show while making their pitch. They don't want to be confused with "amateurs." Don't worry, we wouldn't fit in over here so we'll just stay up in the good old Northwest.

Mission #10, *Mont Blanc, France, August 1*

Frank Dimit, Bombardier

Mission was similar to #4. Dropped supplies to Free French. Briefed at 7:30 a.m. Target area was about three miles north of

Annecy. Our course took us within a few miles of Geneva, Switzerland.

We carried 12 para-packs of supplies which included machine guns, medical supplies, and bazookas.

We flew #3 in the lead squadron of low group of our wing. 95th led the task force. No flak or fighters, except our own friends. Good mission, but long—flew 9 hours and 40 minutes.

Our division dropped enough supplies to equip 5,500 men today. Free French are doing a helluva lot of good. Have two panzer divisions tied up. Have been blowing up trains and bridges.

Saw some of the invasion coast on way back. Fiess and crew flew in the wing with us. *[End of mission notes by Frank Dimit]*

Roco Work, Navigator

Veterans of several missions by this time, some easy and some rough, we listened avidly to rumors that yet another maquis mission was due to come off soon. Some pointed questions put to individuals in the bomb dump brought the answers we wanted. Yes, there are supplies on the field—when they're to be dropped is still another question along with the chance that Fletcher's crew might not be scheduled to fly.

Late one evening the list was posted and we were delighted in two discoveries. The first one was that several people who flew only on milk runs were up to fly next day—that was a good indication of the type of mission coming up. The other interesting discovery was Fletcher's name. We felt positive that we were to fly on another "supply mission."

Going to bed we discussed the possibilities and decided we were strongly in favor of a repeat, remembering our previous joy over having no flak nor fighters to bother us. When we awakened next morning the same thoughts ran through our minds and we continued to hope through breakfast and on to briefing. The presence of more brass than usual made us certain that something unusual was scheduled.

Then the briefing officer drew back the curtain and received a lusty cheer from the crews. Sure enough, the route made it plain even before he began his speech.

"Due in large part to the overwhelming success of your past trips to aid the French Underground, the 95th is to lead the Air Force today on another relief mission. The supplies are to be dropped in the foothills of the Alps southeast of Lake Geneva."

He went on to say that messages of appreciation for past aid were being received from the French by SHAEF [Supreme Headquarters, Allied Expeditionary Force] constantly, along with urgent pleas for even more supplies. Most of his eloquence was lost on our ears, however, for we were practically glowing over the near certainty that there would be no enemy opposition. The greatest danger would be in flying formation at a low altitude in this mountainous area.

Climbing in our plane we were still extremely happy over the prospect for the day. Therefore the drudgery of the preflight checks on equipment seemed almost a pleasure. After takeoff there was considerably more than the usual amount of chatter on the interphone, due in the main to our shining outlook on life. Even as we climbed to rendezvous altitude (12,000 feet) where we had to plug in our heated suits and don our oxygen masks, joy was obvious in everyone.

When we headed south across the Channel the altimeter finally settled on 18,000 feet, the thermometer on –15 degrees C. At this height we were safe from any possible light ground fire when we crossed the enemy lines, yet we weren't high enough to be very uncomfortable. From the coast southward everything went according to plan. Exactly as briefed the lead ship started a descent in plenty of time so that we'd be near enough to easily identify the target area. As we went southeastward Lake D'Annecy appeared ahead and on our right soon after Lake Geneva came into view on the left. *[End of mission account by Roco Work]*

This is the end of Roco's narrative, which was written in January 1945. The pressures of living interrupted its completion and denied us the vivid description of the final twenty-five missions. We do appreciate that which was recorded as it reveals the sterling, warm character of a dedicated navigator.

While it has been forty-two years since we flew this mission, I still remember it like yesterday. We were in the French Alps, as Work said, in the vicinity of Mont Blanc. This area is bordered by both Switzerland and Italy. The country was very rugged and by now we had descended to the level of the mountain top. We were busy looking for the valley that would lead to the drop area. Evidently the leaders were having some trouble identifying the right valley because we made several large circles, but that was understandable as this was a very isolated, rough country and every valley looked alike. But if we didn't find the right area the mission would be for naught.

Finally contact was made and we descended into a very narrow canyon. My first impression was that this canyon was too narrow and rough for a formation of B-17s—that was also my last impression as we continued deeper. This mission, from a piloting standpoint, was one of the roughest and most dangerous, from physical hazard, that we were to fly. It was the tightest formation we ever experienced. We wanted to live, and the canyon became even more confining. We knew the lead was sweating because he had to be responsible for all of us, and that the "tail enders" were really playing crack the whip. The canyon had several sharp turns and very steep side walls. Only a pilot could appreciate the real danger of this situation with no room to maneuver—tuck in real tight, and pray!

Around another sharp bend a larger opening appeared with several bonfires. The bomb-bay doors popped open and in a matter of minutes the valley was filled with parachutes, each lowering a canister of much needed food, ammunition, guns, and medical supplies. I was told it was the most beautiful sight anyone would ever see—the panorama of beautiful green mountains, a small stream, the partisans, and the gaily colored parachutes. But my eyes, for the most part, saw only the silver wing of the aircraft I was trying to fly formation with. I heaved a big sigh of relief when the bomb-bay doors started to close so I could call for high rpm and open the throttles for the climb on up the canyon and out over the top.

We were just starting to breathe easy as we gained altitude

and could see Lake Geneva way off in the distance when Doc called and asked me to switch over to VHF on the command frequency. As I made the switch we could hear a pilot who insisted that he was low on fuel and was going to Switzerland. The commander demanded that he read off the amounts that registered as he flipped from tank to tank. Doc was doing the same thing on our ship. When the readings were complete, the commander requested that the ship remain in formation and try for home, but the pilot had made his decision and he left the formation. With good luck we might see him when the war was over.

We switched back to interphone and Doc informed me that we had far less fuel than the pilot who had deserted. All of a sudden the countryside looked beautiful. Lake Geneva was a jewel far off in the distance and the sun was shimmering off the snow on the mountain peaks. Switzerland could be a very tranquil and beautiful place to spend the rest of the war. Who said it wouldn't be tempting!

I looked at Doc and said, "Let's try for home." His reply was, "England's not that bad. I'll lean out the engines, cut down on the rpms, lower the manifold pressure and you can coast her home." It would have been a lonesome year because we didn't know anyone in Switzerland!

August 2, 1944

Sure would like to see Cap now—bet he's really in his prime! Eight-pound baby boy! I didn't know Cap was that good a man! Don't mind me, I'm just in unusually good spirits. Just call me Uncle Gene. Believe me, he had better send me at least a twenty-five-cent cigar! Be sure and let me know what they name the baby. Michael Ray is good if they like those names. . . .

August 3, 1944

No, I haven't received any of the Reader's Digest *yet, and very few people here receive a* life subscription *to a magazine! But that's okay since up to now we have been able to get them at the P.X., something that is very unusual. I haven't received the* Chronicle Dispatch *either. That stuff all comes fourth-class mail and it usually is a month or two behind when it gets here. . . .*

Now then, where have I been in my travels? I can't tell you any exact places, but I can tell you the countries I've been over, so hang on, here we go: England, Ireland, Wales, Scotland, France, Belgium, The Netherlands, Germany, Italy, Denmark, and Luxembourg. Switzerland and Italy I wasn't over but have seen them. Who knows, someday I may add more to that group. I'll say one thing, the European countryside is really beautiful, but it will never take the place of the good old USA.

I can't tell you how many missions I have in, but when I first arrived I figured out a schedule and how many a month I would have to fly in order to keep my date with you. I have even moved the date up a little. So now just let me say that I'm running ahead of schedule. Looks as if everything will work out okay, but I shan't make any rash promises because you never know what's going to happen now with the war news as it is.

We had now flown ten missions, and had experienced everything that could happen to a combat crew. Experience has a way of giving you confidence. But the unexpected also has a way of destroying this same confidence when accompanied by an element of surprise.

This was to be one of those days. Formal briefing for the mission was completed and everyone was at the aircraft making the final ground checks, installing the guns, and performing all necessary preflight duties in preparation for the upcoming mission, number 11.

I was in the pilot's seat making some minor adjustments and the crew was scattered throughout the airplane pursuing their duties in the usual fashion. The low-key background sounds of their preparation were suddenly shattered by the staccato firing of a 50 caliber machine gun. Were we being attacked on the ground?

Glancing out the window I saw the right waist gun of the

aircraft parked directly across from us swinging around and spewing fire, much like a loose fire hose under pressure.

With the scream of 50 caliber bullets whistling by, I hollered at the crew to hit the deck and lay flat on the floor, hoping to present as small a target as possible. In a matter of seconds, which to us seemed an eternity, the firing ceased.

Upon ascertaining that none of our crew was hit we jumped out of the airplane and could see several holes in the tail section, and a couple in the fuselage. The crew chief came running up to survey the damage.

In the meantime our gunners cautiously approached the B-17 with the runaway gun. In a few minutes they returned saying that the waist gunner had armed his gun and decided to stow it. The gun was stowed by a leather strap hanging from the ceiling which passed through the trigger guard, then was hooked to the fuselage and allowed to hang in this position. He was following a normal procedure, but had forgotten to shut off the power to the gun when he put the strap through the trigger guard and fastened it. As soon as he let go of the gun the weight pulled the strap against the trigger and wild firing commenced.

By the time the gunner could catch up with the gun and kill the power, we had become the recipient of some extra unwanted lead. The young gunner was not only embarrassed but was suffering shock because he thought he might have hit someone. Gunners have a way of understanding how these things can happen and they tried to console him with statements like, "Hey, this can happen to anybody. Forget it—no one's hurt. You just scared the hell out of us and shot down an airplane. Congratulations, but only the Germans will give you credit for it!" I'm sure they provided a lot of psychological help!

The crew chief said that he would need a couple of hours to inspect the damage, and then additional time for repairs and patching. I told him not to hurry—we only had forty minutes till start-engine time and we had already signaled for a truck to transport us to the spare aircraft. We were sorry to leave him with a battle-damaged aircraft without even starting the engines.

With a lot of hurrying we managed to get off the ground in our briefed position in the spare aircraft. What normally would have been a rather exciting and scary mission turned out to be rather uneventful, an anticlimax compared to what had happened on the ground. After all, the Germans were firing from over five miles away!

We concluded that we had not yet seen everything. This was the first and last time we were to be shot down before takeoff. War can be hell, but sometimes the preparation can be just as bad.

Mission #11, *Hamburg, Germany, August 4*

Frank Dimit, Bombardier

Briefed at 6:00 a.m. for target between Hamburg and Harburg. Target was one of the largest oil refineries in Germany.

It was a long over-water hop. Saw no flak until we hit the target area and then it hit us. Believe they have stopped throwing up flak in shells—it comes up in a blanket. 388th Group carried some new anti-radar equipment, and it seemed to work fine. But our group didn't get any benefit from it.

Number 3 engine gave us a bad time over target, but Fletch and Doc got it straightened out and we came back with the formation.

We flew #3 in lead squadron of lead group of wing. We led the entire 8th Air Force into Germany. Carried 20 250-pound General Purpose bombs. Didn't see the results of the bombing. Target was clouded over when we arrived.

Some of the planes didn't get back. It was definitely a rough mission. The old man himself, Col. Truesdell, flew command pilot. Logged 7 hours and 15 minutes form time.

There were some enemy fighters in the area but plenty of good fighter escort.

Glad to be back. Twenty-four more to go. Everybody OK.

[End of mission notes by Frank Dimit]

The results were good—all twenty aircraft bombed, but we lost one aircraft and nine men. They ditched in the Channel. Fiess flew in the group with us.

August 5, 1944

I don't know when I'll be able to write again. So don't think anything about it if you don't hear from me for a couple of weeks. Everything will be okay so don't worry a bit. In all probability you should hear from me before that long, but I'm saying this just in case it should be that way. Anyway, I know you understand.

On July 28 we flew the mission to Merseburg. The aircraft that we flew was *Knock Out Baby*, #7257. We lost an engine and had a pretty rough trip that day, but she brought us home and we became quite attached to her. Since the aircraft sustained major battle damage it was not available for flying on our next two missions.

August 1 and 4 we flew two different aircraft while *Knock Out Baby* was being repaired. On August 5 I was called to the flight line to test fly her, a procedure that was required after an engine change or major repairs.

That morning on takeoff the airplane exhibited a tendency to settle back to the runway immediately after becoming airborne. This was not a dangerous condition but just something to know and be prepared to cope with. Her flying characteristics had changed since our last flight. This was not unusual, for no two airplanes fly alike. At the end of the flight I pronounced her combat ready, and the ground crew called her back into service.

August 6 we were briefed to go on a shuttle raid called "Frantic Five." First phase of this journey was over the Danish peninsula where we hit a Focke-Wulf 190 plant. Others hit a "heavy water" plant in the vicinity and some highly secret engine plants for V-2 rockets. We were assigned to fly *Knock Out Baby*.

Doc and I had a little pact. In order for him to become a

good pilot I had agreed to let him make every other takeoff and landing. This was his day to make the takeoff. While we were at general briefing I tried to talk him out of it. He kept saying that we had made the agreement and he wanted to take his turn. I told him, "We have a particular problem today. When I flew this aircraft yesterday it had a tendency to settle back to the ground. Now the takeoff that you like to make is that the instant we are airborne you want to pull up the gear. I want this aircraft to be well airborne and have at least fifty feet of altitude before the wheels come up." Doc said, "Okay, I'll follow that procedure."

Later at specialized briefing I found out we had a rather unusual load. We had only half the usual complement of bombs plus two extra men and extra fuel in the Tokyo Tanks. The waist part of the ship was completely filled with all types of recreational equipment which was to be given to the Americans stationed at Poltava, Russia. They were the ground support people. I don't know how long they had been there, but apparently they were going to be there quite a while longer. I was briefed that I had an aircraft that, as far as weights and balances go, was within its normal weight configuration but probably out of trim in regard to where the weight was located. Having been forewarned I felt I would have no problem getting the aircraft off the ground. Caution with me had now become a virtue.

When I reached the airplane the bombardier was fit to be tied. He was really carrying on so I asked what was wrong. He came out the rear door of the fuselage carrying a baseball bat and said, "Where are my bombs? What the hell do they expect me to do, go down and club the enemy over the head with these damn bats?"

"I understand how you feel. I know you have only half a bomb load, but actually all the recreational equipment is for our people in Russia. Apparently the brass feels they need this equipment and it's our job to take it."

"Well, I'd much rather be carrying bombs—something you can do damage with."

"I'm sure you would, but there's a reason for everything, so we just go along."

I cornered Doc again and told him, "Doc, I'm going to re-nege on this deal we've made. I'm going to make the takeoff today, then I'll let you make two more later on to make up for it." "No," he said. "I'll do just exactly what you tell me." Doc has a way of being a good salesman so I finally agreed, but only under one condition—the gear was not to come up until I was ready, and I would operate the gear switch. Normally that's the copilot's job—brake the wheels to a stop and pull the gear up on signal from the pilot.

When we completed our ground checks and taxi time came, we taxied out, and lined up on the runway in our takeoff position. We were pretty well forward in the formation be-cause we were going to fly in the lead squadron of the 95th Bomb Group, which was being led by Colonel Karl Truesdell.

We started roaring down the runway and as the aircraft finally reached 130 mph Doc eased back on the yoke and she lifted off the ground. At this same instant he hollered "Gear up," but I did not respond. At the same time his feet went up on the brakes to stop the wheels from rolling. At that moment the aircraft settled back onto the runway with the brakes locked, the gear still down. When she hit there was a cloud of smoke and screeching of tires. He immediately got off the brakes. She bounced back into the air and started to fly.

After we were about fifty feet in the air I pulled the gear up and was sure we had some tires that were ready to blow out. When it became safe enough to put McQuitty in the ball turret I requested that he spin around and look at the wheels to see if he could detect any damage. He said, "I can see long strings of rubber that have been pulled off the tires. It looks to me as if I can see the cord in some places. The tread seems to be gone."

At this point we had to make a decision. Do we want to go to Russia and land with two tires that are apt to blow out? Or do we want to abort the mission, go out over the Channel, drop the bombs, burn up some of the gas load, and then come back and land? We still don't know the full extent of the damage. But we're in the air; the most dangerous part of this mission is past. We might as well go on as we have to burn the gas and drop the bombs anyway, and if the recreational equipment will help the morale of the group in Russia we had better go.

We went on to Russia and at this point I told Doc, "There is no way you're going to get your landing this time. I have no idea what kind of runways we will have when we get there, but *I'll make the landing*. We're in an emergency condition. We have tires that could possibly blow out, and since I'm the one who will be held responsible, I'll do it. Now prepare the crew and the ship for a crash landing." This time Doc readily agreed.

When we reached Poltava there wasn't a runway in the sense of blacktop or concrete. There was a bunch of perforated steel mats hooked together. So actually we were landing right on the ground with these steel mats placed on top of it— no foundation, just mats laid on the native grass. The mats were full of round holes to make them light enough to carry. It also helped to hold them in place. The holes were approximately four to six inches in diameter—the mats looked like a giant sieve spread out flat on the ground.

The landing at Poltava was one of my better ones. We set her down just as gently as we possibly could. When we reached the place where we were to park we commenced to wonder, "What do we do now?" Here we were thousands of miles from home. Both tires would have to be replaced and we suspected the service station probably wouldn't have too many spare tires on hand.

We were carrying some of our ground crew with us, but there was also the ground support crew stationed in Poltava who would help in servicing the aircraft. These were the people who were going to get the recreational equipment. In talking with some of them we found out that on the preceding raid forty-seven aircraft had been destroyed on the ground, so they had a good-sized bone yard to pick through. By now they had already spotted our ruined tires and said there was no problem as they had lots of wheels and tires. They all expressed amazement that the tires had not blown out. Sometimes you are lucky and it makes up for the bad times.

They then asked us if several Russians who were present could go aboard our airplane. We said okay. We still had a large supply of 50 caliber ammunition on board and they wondered why we still had ammunition left after crossing enemy territory. We tried to explain that we had the mission coming to Russia and we would have several more missions before we would have a chance to replenish our ammo. It was necessary not to expend our ammunition but to use it only to protect ourselves. The Russians didn't quite buy this theory. They felt any time you passed over enemy territory you should fire everything you had. We thought this was interesting because on our raids our bombs were our offense, the 50 caliber ammunition was strictly for our own protection. It was fired only at enemy aircraft and not used to shoot up targets on the ground.

That evening the ground crew busied themselves replacing the wheels and tires on our aircraft. By the next morning it was repaired. They thought it a fair exchange—tires for baseball bats. But Frank still wasn't happy—he wanted bombs. Some days you just can't please anybody—copilots, bombardiers, or Russians.

Mission #12, Rahmel (Gydnia), Germany, August 6

Frank Dimit, Bombardier

Briefed this morning for target in Poland, near Gydnia, which is close to the city of Danzig. Target was a FW-190 factory. We were to hit this target and then go on to a base in Russia.

We flew #3 in high squadron of lead group. Major General Kissner and Colonel Truesdell flew in the lead ships. We carried 6 500-pound general purpose bombs. Think we gave target a good pasting.

We are all excited about this trip. It's the second shuttle run from the U.K.

Shortly after hitting target, we were hit by FW-190s. Didn't get in a shot. Only saw one, but his yellow spinner and cowling looked as big as a barn. I've seen the Luftwaffe. P-51 escort took pretty good care of us. No ships down.

We brought a crew chief for our plane and a crew chief for a

P-51 fighter with us. They liked the ride, and it was a long one —10 hours and 25 minutes.

Saw light and very inaccurate barrage flak over target. Was a good target to hit, but it's too far from home. That sack will really feel good tonight. *[End of mission notes by Frank Dimit]*

The 95th and the 390th made up the entire task force of seventy-eight aircraft. Two fighter groups escorted us to the target where we ran into a group of Focke Wulf-190s. They were the famed Goering yellow-noses. The 190s made a frontal assault on our group, but instead of breaking off the attack and going over or under us, they came right through our formation. This was a very unusual maneuver, but each one had a P-51 on his tail. It was impossible to fire on them. All we could do was hold our position and watch them fly through, praying that there wouldn't be a collision. It was a very hair-raising experience. The encounter was all over in a flash, and the fighter escort headed back to the U.K. with nine enemy aircraft destroyed. We then made rendezvous with the 357th fighter group, who had sixty-four P-51s. This group escorted us on into Poltava. Twenty-three of our B-17s were damaged. One plane ran out of gas and landed short.

A rather humorous mixup occurred while we were in Poltava. General August W. Kissner, Chief of Staff of the Third Air Division, was the Division Lead for the mission. Also in our formation that day was Lieutenant Paul Fiess of the 336th Squadron.

Just a few days before this raid word had come down from Headquarters that the pilots would now be referred to as aircraft commanders and the copilots would be referred to as pilots. This order partly contributed to the subsequent confusion.

All of the 95th aircraft were B-17Gs and were aluminum in color with one exception. Paul Fiess was flying an olive-drab camouflaged plane since his regular aircraft was out of commission. He flew a war-weary B-17, #1410, named *I Dood It,* one of the older aircraft still in use on the base. She was almost covered with mission bombs and with several Bs painted on the bombs to denote missions to Berlin. In other words, she stood out like a sore thumb.

When we landed on the steel mats at Poltava we were directed where to park. Fiess pulled in right beside us and it was then that I noticed several Russian jeeps following him. As soon as the engines were cut and the props came to a standstill the Russians surrounded his airplane. When the crew emerged from the aircraft there was a lot of handshaking and frivolity going on. A Russian gal in uniform appeared to act as an interpreter. They pointed to the Bs on the bombs and I heard Fiess say, "Berlin . . . Boom," with appropriate gestures. The Russians were delighted and they all had to hug him and kiss his cheek. I am sure they assumed he had flown all of the missions painted on *I Dood It*. They loaded his crew into the jeeps and away they went. I remember thinking it was nice to see him receive such a cordial welcome since it couldn't have been that much fun flying that old airplane. I had flown her a couple of times before, on practice missions, and she wallowed rather than flew. It was hard work.

After about fifteen or twenty minutes a "6 by 6" came by and our crew was loaded in with several others. We headed for the housing and mess tents where we were informed that after chow we should change our flying suits and be in dress uniform because entertainment would be provided in a bombed-out building nearby.

That evening as we sat in chairs under the sky I noticed General Kissner and all of our ranking people seated in a line on the back of the stage along with the ranking Russians. The Russians were on the audience's left and the Americans on the right. There was a vacant chair between the Russian Commander and General Kissner.

Fiess and I were visiting back and forth, waiting for the entertainment to begin. A young Russian girl in uniform came by and she appeared to be somewhat agitated. In perfect English she said to him, "Oh, there you are. We have been waiting for you."

Fiess was a tall, good-looking young man but quite bashful and at this instant he was as red as a beet. He turned to me and said, "Give me your cap." I was wearing a Service cap, and Fiess was wearing his Garrison or Overseas cap with a lieutenant bar on it. I could have sworn that bar was also blushing. I said to him, "What for? My cap won't make you look any better." He roughly whispered, "They think I'm the Commander. Just trade me your cap." I said, "That's okay. I thought I was Napoleon once but I got over it. You'll be all right. Just ask her if she has a girlfriend and I'll go with you."

In the meantime the girl was gently tugging at his elbow. Fiess grabbed my cap, tossed his in my lap and said, "Shut up, this is no joking matter." I was astonished as I watched the girl lead him to the stage corner on the audience's right. As he mounted the stairs leading to the stage all of the dignitaries rose to attention. The Russian general greeted him heartily and signaled for him to sit in the vacant chair. All were seated and the entertainment commenced. The folk dancing was all performed by men and it was a spectacular display. The singing and dancing went on for over an hour, and the enthusiasm and exuberance was almost unbelievable. We were given a command performance.

When the festivities were over and we were back in our tent I said to Paul, "What happened? I know you were whisked away from your airplane in grand style but there must be more to it than that." He said that when the Russians pulled up to his airplane they asked one of the gunners, "Where is the Commander?" They meant General Kissner. The gunner, trying to become familiar with the order to use the term Aircraft Commander, said, "The Commander will be down in just a minute." Fiess unwittingly became a task force commander and was embarrassed no end. He didn't really realize what was going on until he got to that evening's entertainment and the show was being held up. He said they had invited him to participate in some activities after landing but he begged off, saying he was tired and since we were going to fly in the morning he would have to be up early. But he told them he would attend the evening performance and that seemed to satisfy them.

The next morning as we went through the chow line a young lady in uniform motioned to Fiess. It was apparent she did not speak English. We were then escorted into a special mess tent with two tables. One was already occupied by several dignitaries from our Force. We took the empty table.

While we were eating the young lady appeared with a coffee pot and refilled our cups. Then she left the coffee pot on our table, ignoring the other table as she left the tent. One of the group came over to our table; it could have been General Kissner, I'm not sure because we were not acquainted. But whoever it was had sufficient rank to make some lieutenants quake even though we all were in flying gear with no rank showing. His statement, while not verbatim, carried this meaning: "Regardless of what these people think we still serve by rank and not good looks in this man's army," whereupon he took the coffee pot and started back to the other table.

As he turned with the coffee pot I said, "Fiess, won't this make one helluva good story when we get back to our base!" Before Fiess could answer this gentleman turned back to us and said, "This story stops right now. There has been a mistake here that could be very embarrassing to these people if they find out what happened. Since they are our allies it goes no further. Now we have played along with it, but the play-acting is over. Only a few people really know what happened and you are among them. If word of this ever leaks out we will know it came from you, and I will have your hides nailed to the wall as an example for all to see. Do you understand me?" There was a second of stunned silence and then a chorus of "Yes, Sirs!" "Good," he said. "Now that we understand one another, let's go fly."

But this did not end the incident for Paul Fiess. When he reached his airplane the Russian commander was waiting and ready to fly with him. Through the interpreter he let Paul know that he would like to ride in the copilot's seat on the raid to Trzebinia. Paul refused, saying that he needed the help of his copilot, Dwight Stevens—it would be a long mission with over ten hours in the air. But the Russian commander, who was a rated pilot, was determined to go, so he stood between the two pilots with his arms draped over their shoulders, enjoying every minute of the ride. He did express displeasure that, after hitting the target with the bombs, Paul would not descend and allow the gunners to shoot up the ground targets. These Americans were crazy—bringing ammo home while there were still Germans to be killed and targets to shoot up!

Lieutenant Fiess was a division commander for two days, and true to his word, it was never mentioned again where anyone could hear. We valued our hides and had no wish to risk a court martial or cause trouble.

Mission #13, Trzebinia, Poland, August 7

Frank Dimit, Bombardier

Briefed at 5:00 a.m. for target in Poland about 10–15 miles west of Cracow. Target was large oil refinery at Trzebinia.

Carried 16 250-pound General Purpose bombs. Flew #4 in lead squadron of low group.

We were part of a first today. This was first mission to take off and return to a Russian base.

Creamed the target. Smoke up to 8,000 feet and flames up to 2,000 feet.

Light flak over target. Not very accurate. These boys don't get the practice that they do in Germany.

Logged 10 hours and 10 minutes form time. Only in enemy territory about an hour and a half. Poltava is long way behind lines now. Saw Russian front today. Saw several towns in flames. This country has had the hell kicked out of it.

Saw dogfight today. Had ringside seat. One FW-190 went down. Pilot jumped out. Enemy fighters made no passes at us. P-51s took care of them. *[End of mission notes by Frank Dimit]*

Our bombing results were good. Fifty-five aircraft out of our task force of seventy-eight were capable of flying. We received minor damage. Spooked by a wing fire, Lieutenant Dancisin's bombardier and navigator bailed out near Zhitomir, Russia. The next day we left for Italy.

Mission #14, Buzau, Romania, August 8

Frank Dimit, Bombardier

Briefed at 4:00 a.m. for our third leg of the shuttle run. Target was airfield at Buzau, 30 to 35 miles east of Ploesti, Romania.

Carried 16 250-pound G.P. bombs. Flew #3 in high squadron of lead group. Creamed target.

Flak—pathetic. Expected terrific fighter opposition, but P-51s took damn good care of us. Our group hit one airfield and the other group hit another. When a picture was taken of these two fields last month there were 230 aircraft on them. That's why we expected so much opposition. But the P-51 pilots reported that when the airborne Germans saw us coming they took off like scared rabbits. They saw about 60 ME-109s. If they had hit us we would have been pretty well beaten up.

Landed at Foggia Air Base—base of 463rd Bomb Group of the 15th Air Force. *[End of mission notes by Frank Dimit]*

By the following day our twenty-three damaged airplanes had been repaired and our B-17s were back in the air headed for Foggia, Italy. We were again flying in the formation led by Colonel Truesdell.

When we were a few minutes from the Initial Point the gunners spotted a large formation of airplanes along with a few stragglers. These planes were at 10 o'clock and about level with our formation, but they were so far in the distance they could not be identified. But we all knew they had to be the enemy because this was a very remote area, far removed from everyday battle. If they were fighters we would have our hands full.

Almost immediately these planes changed their course and flew away from us. We judged this force to be over sixty planes. Obviously they didn't want to fight. It appeared that they were running away from us. That would suit us fine. It was always better to see Jerry's tail than his nose.

All of a sudden we were making the turn at the IP and

starting the bombing run on the Airdrome. Our bombardier had a little free time today. He set his bomb-sight on the target, but he would drop our bombs manually on a signal from the colonel's ship. Since we were in formation we flew the plane manually. About half way down the bomb run the bombardier called and said that there was something unusual on the runways. I suggested that maybe they were aircraft ready to take off—at 28,000 feet they would be hard to identify. But he said, "No, I am looking with field glasses and they aren't airplanes. It's something very unusual, almost like men in formation, but I really can't tell just what it is."

At this point our conversation ended because we were now receiving some light, inaccurate tracking flak. It is always inaccurate if it doesn't hit you. That's the criterion. We continued the bomb run and soon the bombardier called "Bombs away." It was a report that was always good to hear, even though it was not necessary because the plane would literally jump about fifty feet in the air simultaneously with the release of the bomb load.

We immediately headed for the Rally Point and soon realized that the colonel's plane was on fire. We were flying in a position where we could observe the colonel's ship. We kept reporting to him what we could see of the fire, which was under the left wing. His situation was not improving and soon it appeared that he had made a decision to abort the formation. He wiggled his wings and lowered his gear, which was the signal he was leaving. His two wingmen, not understanding, left with him. We immediately notified them to get back up because if the ship blew up we would lose three ships instead of one. They then returned to the formation, and we soon lost track of the colonel's airplane.

After we landed at Foggia we kept scanning the skies looking for our leader. Our search was rewarded as the colonel's airplane appeared in the distance. The fire had gone out and with the crew intact they settled down on the runway with memories of some very harrowing moments.

We later learned that for some special occasion there had, indeed, been several formations of men on the runway. The aircraft we had seen were to be used in a massive flyover. Since this was a special occasion they either were not armed or did not want to fight. Anyway, the flyover they received was not only larger than planned, but carried a big bang which was not expected or even appreciated. The bombing results were termed excellent, but we would not know how well the personnel had fared.

Italy, August 10, 1944

Surprise! I have a chance to write a little sooner than I thought. Have really been having a time of late—picking up a little suntan too in this sun. Yesterday we went swimming in the Adriatic Sea, then rented a boat and sailed around for a while. Boy, what a time! . . .

I won't get to see Hallie—haven't the time, but I sure wanted to. They built the airfield here—but I guess I can't do everything—after all, I'm still in the Army.

August 10

Doc Doxon, Copilot

Swimming and sailing at Manfredonia again. Ate cantaloupes and watermelon. Went into Foggia at night—no black-out. The town is filthy, has been bombed to small bits.

August 11

Doc Doxon, Copilot

We laid around camp and rested. Traded for some whiskey, cognac, and cantaloupes. Supposed to leave for England tomorrow.

Just before leaving for Russia I received the following letter from Hallie:

Corsica, July 25, 1944

Hello Gene,

Got your letter last night. Sure wish I could tell you something about your wife but you probably know by now. Wish you the best of luck in the world and hope it is a boy. Several of the boys here have had to sweat out the same thing—all would like to have been with their wives, but couldn't. All babies were born ok—so take it for granted yours will be too—I hope so with all my heart. We have been over eighteen months now so when one's wife just has a baby we suspect a rat in the woodpile.

Hope you like your group—I am quite sure that it is an old and experienced outfit—but be darn careful, Gene—don't ever get careless, but you are not of the careless nature.

Don't think Jerry will last long now. Just wrote to Blake Knox—he was wounded in or near Rome the day it fell. I've just returned from the Rome rest camp—had the finest time since I've been in the Army— sure lots of things to see.

We might meet up some day some place, but think this part will end soon. . . . The last time I saw you was at Geiger Field. How about dumping a load on Jerry for me! . . .

Wilma is fine. . . . It has been 19 months since I've seen her—that is a long, long time. Sure would like to go home and see her. A good wife to back a man up goes a long ways over here. Some of the boys have not had as good luck with their wives, but time heals all wounds. . . .

How are the women in England? They are really beautiful in Rome —but maybe they just look that way after 18 months. Rome is just like the States—so clean and nice.

Write soon. . . .

All the luck in the world to you,

Hallie

Hallie Fletcher is my first cousin, although our relationship is more like brothers. He was drafted into military service, and saw service with the Aviation Engineers. His unit was stationed at Geiger Field, Spokane, Washington, when, on June 22, 1942, I traveled to Geiger to enlist in the Aviation Cadet Corps. This was our last visit together until the end of the war.

Hallie's unit later shipped out to Africa where they built airfields, following the battle lines up through Italy, Corsica, and into France.

When we were at Foggia Main I was hoping for a surprise reunion, but the distance proved to be too great. Hallie was on Corsica building an airfield which we flew across on August 12 on our way to bomb France in support of the southern invasion. Unknown to me, Hallie saw the large formation pass overhead and later learned that this was our group, and that *Knock Out Baby* was carrying a bomb load which was dropped on the enemy airfield at Toulouse. Inscribed on one bomb in chalk was the message, "From Hallie via the Flying 95th." This was in response to the request to "someday drop a load on Jerry for me."

In France, at the war's end, he had the opportunity of returning to the USA in a war-weary B-17 whose days of reliability had long since passed—a fact that was proven when they made a three-engine landing in Brazil.

Mission #15, *Toulouse, France, August 12*

Frank Dimit, Bombardier

Briefed in Italy this morning at 4:00 a.m. for our last leg of the shuttle run. Our target was an airfield at Toulouse in southern France near the Spanish border.

We carried 10 500-pound G.P. bombs and flew the same position as usual, #3 in high squadron of lead group. Target was creamed but good. Was one of the best bomb patterns I've seen.

Flak was pathetic, but the low group caught a little. Think the gunners must have been asleep when we went over. Didn't see any enemy fighters, but expected to. Our own escort was fine.

Saw the Anzio beachhead and it's in pretty bad shape.

Would like to have had a closer look at the Russian battle front to compare them. Don't see how it could have been any worse.

Logged 10 more hours today. That's a total of 39 hours and 45 minutes for the last four missions. That's a lot of time.

Fletch found out today he is a papa—9-pound baby boy. A big celebration is now in progress.

Was damned glad to get back. England looks better at the end of each mission. *[End of mission notes by Frank Dimit]*

August 13, 1944

Tonight you've made me the happiest fellow in the world! Nine-pound baby boy!! Honey, that was really worth waiting for. I've been running around on clouds ever since I got the news, which was late yesterday. I had just returned from a little sightseeing tour of Europe, Russia, Italy, and then back here to eleven letters and a package from you and the news that I was a proud papa. We were all dead tired but the news was what I'd been waiting for. Great clouds of cigar smoke rolled up as the celebration got under way with the uncorking of the sparkling vino we picked up in Italy! I wanted to write you last night but that was impossible as the fellows wouldn't leave me alone long enough. Just call me "Pop"! The boys are bound and determined the name will stick. The joys the baby will bring us will far exceed anything we've ever imagined. This was all we needed to make our life complete.

Now to answer a few of your questions which have accumulated in my absence. First, about the missions and when I'll be home. I have good reason to believe that I can come home after thirty-five missions. It's not a promise, but the deal supposedly works that after thirty-five we go home for a thirty-day furlough, then do another tour in another theater. That last part doesn't exactly appeal to me, for when I come home I intend to stay in the States. By the time I'm finished that can probably be arranged. Things are running smooth and I'm still ahead of schedule—the sum total is now fifteen. I'll feel like I've done something when the eighteenth rolls around and I'm over the hump!

Now for another list of countries that I've seen—hang on 'cause here we go again—I'm sort of like a traveling salesman: Sweden, Poland, East Prussia, Russia, Romania, Bulgaria, Yugoslavia, Albania, Czechoslovakia, Corsica, Italy, and Spain. Want some bodies of water? Okay: Atlantic Ocean, English Channel, North Sea, Baltic Sea, Black Sea, Adriatic Sea, Tyrrhenian Sea, and the Mediterranean. If you add this list to the other you'll have all of them. . . .

August 14, 1944

I've been wondering if you ever received my Air Medal. It says here on a little piece of paper: "Awards and Decorations—an Oak Leaf Cluster is awarded for wear with the Air Medal previously awarded to the following named Officer, Organization as indicated, Army Air Forces, United States Army. Eugene R. Fletcher 2nd Lt." The citation was the same as with the Air Medal. You know, meritorious achievement, courage, coolness, skill, and all that malarkey which makes good propaganda. Of course, they forget to tell how many MPs it takes to get me aboard my ship before takeoff time. It isn't bad, though, so don't worry about me. The crew really makes a good team and we're always looking out for one another.

Had a V-Mail from Mother today and she said you and the baby are getting along fine, just exactly what I wanted to hear. . . . The fellows are looking for a pair of boxing gloves now. Hope he doesn't meet the crew 'cause they'll make a roughneck out of him in no time. No man ever had more to come home to and look forward to than I have. We'll finish this job over here before too long and before you know it we'll all be home. . . .

The fellows are getting a kick out of me because I don't even know my son's name for sure. By the way, which name did you choose?

August 15, 1944

You say I haven't said too much about Mac and Lynch. Let me tell you they are two real good, likable guys. Lynch is the armorer gunner— helps Dimit with loading the eggs, arming, and all the stuff that goes with that job. He is very quiet but he is thinking all of the time— stability is probably his middle name. He has a great smile and is a good old farm boy, the kind I'm used to. Whether I'm slopping the hogs or on a mission I'm glad he's with us.

Mac has an engaging grin on his face all the time and a twinkle in his eye. He is also quiet but comes up with a jewel now and then. He has his teaching certificate if I remember right. You'd think with this much education he would have more sense than to ride in the ball turret. I guess he's a braver man than I am. I wouldn't crawl into that thing on the ground, let alone in the air. Good thing somebody is willing.

Brownie is in charge of the enlisted men and with his experience and personality they have a real leader. Sometimes I don't think they even realize that he is leading—such is his way.

August 18, 1944

The past couple of days were spent in London. We were fortunate enough to land another pass so we went to the big city to pick up our battle jackets.

When we came home this evening there were eight letters waiting for me. Your letters were all written before little David arrived. Thank your mother for all the letters she has sent me. I'll try to write to her tomorrow. Things happened so fast I'm still running around in a daze. Gosh, it'll probably be weeks before I settle down to a normal way of life. But that's okay 'cause it's a great feeling being a father!

You wanted to know if we had ever got our own plane. No, we haven't been assigned one as yet. We've just about given up hope for one—it really doesn't make any difference, though. Some day I'll be able to tell you lots of things and you will be able to understand how things work over here. How often do we fly? There's no regular order. You never know from one day to the next what's going on. You just wait until someone comes in and wakes you up—then you know you're going out. But don't worry, we get plenty of rest. Uncle Sam does a good job of looking out for his men.

Many of the officers visiting in London or passing through would be assigned messing privileges at Grosvenor House at 44 Grosvenor Square. Grosvenor House was a "mess" operated by the military for Americans stationed in London. It was the only place where you could receive a decent meal, but we would rather take pot-luck at the local English eateries at that time of shortages and rationing—it was the challenge.

We liked to stay at the Regents Palace Hotel where you could have white sheets and breakfast in bed, albeit the breakfast consisted only of coffee, dry toast, and orange marmalade.

The management there loved to put the Americans on the top floors, and in the buzz bomb season you could spend the night jumping up, pulling on your pants on the run while descending several floors for safety. When the danger had passed we would trudge back up the stairs to the uppermost floors and sack out again.

This was a bare bones hotel that tolerated Americans, and the price was right. Besides, it was close to Piccadilly, which was the entertainment section of London, and would be the most obvious place to meet a buddy from another group.

A strange phenomenon developed as we moved along in our flying career. We remained close friends with our roommates and the crews who joined the 95th with us. We visited with others and worked with them, but we did not come to know them or to associate with them socially. They were names on whose wings we flew, and later on names who flew on our wings. Unconsciously they were blocked out. If they did not return the hurt would be less.

I thought this might be just a peculiarity of our crew, but I later learned that this was widespread throughout the combat Air Force. On our trips to London much of our time was spent trying to find out what was happening to the people we had trained with and who were our close friends in another life far removed from here. They were our family—we had to know.

August 19, 1944

Received a letter from you today. It came through in record time—only 32 days!

Yesterday I received a few pictures which were taken on our most recent escapade. They were censored at the Base Photo Office but they asked us not to send them home by mail. It would be okay, though, to take them with us when we leave. Some of them are quite good and I know you'll enjoy them.

We took a bunch of pictures today of the crew. We might get the film developed but won't be able to get pictures reproduced. There's quite a shortage here of anything to do with pictures. The reason we took these is because Joe is being transferred to another outfit and we wanted to get the pictures while the whole crew was still together. . . .

August 19

Doc Doxon, Copilot

Wandered around today trying to get some pictures of our Russia-Italy trip. Weather is very bad—top of clouds above 30,000 feet as reported by the weather ship. The bombardier and navigator that bailed out in Russia returned today. Saw buzz bombs hitting tonight.

August 20, 1944

Today I registered David's birth with the proper authorities so that's all taken care of. . . . I'll increase your allotment and you can buy a bond a month for him.

Here are a few figures you might want. Base pay and overseas pay $183.33, Flying pay $91.67, Subsistence $43.40, Rental $75.00. Those statistics are for a married flying 1st lieutenant with one son. Hey, come to think of it that's me! The silver bars have been in vogue since the fifteenth. I found out this morning. Totaling the figures up makes a tidy sum of $393.40.

Brown and Hinman both made tech sergeant and the rest of the boys made staff sergeant. They're probably making more than I am now. I was sure glad their ratings came through because I've had quite a time trying to get them. The adjutant just heaved a sigh of relief and says he hopes I'll quit bothering him for a while now. But he's due for a surprise because I have a copilot, a navigator, and a bombardier who ought to be 1st lieutenants. And they will be in due time or the adjutant and I will go at it again.

We have been having some typical English weather lately—fog and rain almost every day. I guess winter time isn't far off. Hope I can finish before it gets too bad. The war news is quite encouraging so maybe it won't be too much longer.

Upon arrival at our permanent home in England we were all issued a weapon—a bright, shiny, blue-black 45 caliber automatic with several clips of ammunition. We were ordered to wear this weapon at all times because we were now considered to be in a Theater of War. Who knows—maybe the Germans would invade England.

But the guns saw their first use as a means of putting out the light on a night when someone was slightly inebriated, lazy, or unhappy with a response upon asking for "lights out." Our crew was not involved in these shenanigans, but we were present to see or hear some of them.

Frankly, the gun scared me to death. I had grown up in the West with real cowboys and Indians, and they had long since lost the need for a revolver. It would continue to be alien to my way of life. We were to carry this gun on our missions. In the event we went down this weapon could be used offensively or defensively. I could picture myself on the ground surrounded by a bunch of German farmers with pitch forks in their hands and me standing in the middle of a circle with my "45" drawn, requesting them to surrender in the name of our Fearless Leader!

But, in reality, I carried it on board the plane and strapped it to the pilot's seat. At least I wouldn't blow my own leg off or injure someone else if it went off accidentally. It was the last thing I wanted on my person in the event I was forced down in enemy territory. That gun made a lot of noise and I knew I could never fight my way out of enemy territory with it. In all likelihood it would get you killed. I was quite content to carry only my hunting knife. This would be my offensive weapon. It would not intimidate or scare some person whose home or city had just been bombed into seeking retaliation by shooting an American armed with a "45."

The order to carry this weapon at all times was changed, but not until it had created a situation that could have had some very dire consequences.

In the dark of night a captain left the Officers Club and was heading down the foot trail to his quarters when a shot rang out and the captain fell to the ground. A lusty, happy voice cried out, "I got one of the Sons of B———!" A young enlisted man suffering from delusions and alcohol was taken to the guard house and the captain was taken to the base hospital, where it was determined that he had only a leg wound.

Everyone knew flight crews were expendable—losses and wounded were to be expected. But this was a non-rated staff officer. They were not considered expendable. Therefore, all guns were turned in. From then on they were issued to each crew member after briefing and turned in after each mission. Thank goodness somebody got the message before a real tragedy occurred!

August 22, 1944

Today was another lazy day but the chance to rest was quite welcome. This morning was spent in bed, the afternoon in classes, and the evening at the movie. The show was The Sensations of 1944. *We got quite a kick out of it, namely the jive. It sure has been a long time since we've heard any music. At the present we have a deal on to get a radio—hope we swing it. They certainly are hard to get ahold of. It would be nice to listen to newscasts and radio programs again. . . . Right now our only contact with the outside world is through the* Stars and Stripes. *. . .*

August 23, 1944

Another quiet day. This is getting monotonous. We've been lying around so long that everybody is getting nervous and jumpy. One rough day, though, will sure put a stop to that. . . .

I spent all morning censoring mail. I read so many letters that I was getting "letter happy" when I quit. This afternoon was spent at the barber shop trying to get a three-minute clip job. While I was there the boys found some tin foil and a bottle of paste. When I returned I found I had silver bars on everything, including my underwear! Now I'm trying to think up some good counter measures for retaliation. I'll get even if I have to lie awake nights dreaming up something.

Work just returned with the news that we get a chance to earn our board again tomorrow. That's good. We'll get this over and get back home where we belong.

Mission #16, *Ruhland, Germany, August 24*

Frank Dimit, Bombardier

Briefed at 5:00 a.m. for target at Ruhland, a small town 65 miles east of Leipzig. Target was an oil refinery.

We flew the diamond in high squadron of high group. Carried 10 500-pound G.P. bombs. They contained a new explosive (B-2), supposed to be an improvement over RDX.

Saw Berlin for first time today. Had a good look at it—flew just out of range of their flak. That's as close as I want to get.

Flak was terrific at target area—most intense barrage I have ever seen. We were lucky—didn't pick up any holes until after we left target. Lead ship goofed up and took us into another flak area and they nailed us there. Picked up several holes.

Expected to be hit by the Jerries' new jet propulsion planes in Holland, going and coming, but never saw an enemy plane. Lucky us. Damn good escort—P-51s. Our wing was the last into Germany and last out, that's why we expected trouble.

Logged 9 hours and 10 minutes. Too damn long. One of the new crews didn't get back.

Most of the oil targets in Germany were hit today, judging from the fires we saw on the way back. *[End of mission notes by Frank Dimit]*

August 25, 1944

*Happy Anniversary!! Today marks two years of happily married life—
the two happiest years of my life. The little trials we've had to face are
only temporary and will all be solved when we're together again.*

*Surely hope the pictures of David turned out okay for I'm anxiously
awaiting a look at our little man. . . .*

*Things have been moving pretty fast over here lately. Maybe the end
is in sight. They can't end this thing too soon to suit all of us over here.
But it doesn't pay to be optimistic and then disappointed, so we just let
things go and not make any predictions. We are beginning to wonder
what they'll do with us if this should end over here before we finish.*

August 27, 1944

*Guess what? They made me work for a living today. Some new deal
after this long rest. I thought they had forgotten I was over here—that
was my mistake, though!*

Mission #17, *Berlin, Germany, August 27*

Frank Dimit, Bombardier

Briefed at 6:30 a.m. for our target—in Berlin. Our target was a
tank depot at Spandau, just 5 miles northwest of the center of
Berlin. 500 flak guns in target area.

But we didn't get there. We hit weather just as we tried to
cross the Danish peninsula between Flensburg and Kiel. The
weather ship reported clouds up to 30,000 feet. We hit the
first clouds and our group scattered like birds. We got through
that bank and had begun to form again when we hit the next
bank. We never did get out of that stuff until after we had
turned around.

This was the Group's 200th mission and Lt. Col. McKnight
really wanted to go in but we had to turn back. We hit a little
flak over Flensburg on the way out. We came back alone—the

same as everybody else. We really got split up when we hit the clouds.

We flew #2 in the high squadron of the low group of the wing. The 95th led the 8th Air Force today. It was to be our show all the way, but it didn't pan out. We carried 10 500-pound aimable cluster incendiaries. Our fighter escort was its usual superb quality going in.

It was some mission—we hope to get credit for it. *[End of mission notes by Frank Dimit]*

The 95th, along with twelve aircraft from the 100th Bomb Group, had led the first successful raid on Berlin March 4, 1944, becoming the first U.S. Heavy Bombers to bomb the city. So what better way to let them celebrate their 200th mission than to return again to the capital of the Third Reich leading the Eighth Air Force. This was the reason for the "go for broke, derring do" attitude on the part of our leaders. Nine of our aircraft aborted and bombed a target of opportunity at Husum. For those of us, including Paul Fiess, who stayed with the leaders until we were completely immersed in the second cloud bank, it was one heck of a nightmare.

It was only after a high-flying Mosquito weather ship informed us that we would not break out of the overcast until after we had passed the target that the mission was aborted. Following a standardized procedure we made our 180 degree turn around in the soup. We were very fortunate that we didn't have a midair collision as we were not too well organized at this point. We all returned home alone without fighter escort. But it wasn't necessary because even the German fighters were too smart to fly in this weather. . . .

While we were on the mission the ground and flight crews, who were still at the base, posed for a picture to celebrate this event. They posed around and on aircraft #8283. One week later this aircraft was assigned to Fiess, and was the one in which he completed his tour on November 21.

Upon our return we were too tired to participate in that day's activities, but we were told that the next time the group received a "stand down" (a phrase that meant the group

95th Bomb Group trying to reach Berlin for the group's 200th mission, but stopped by the cloud bank *(95th B.G. photo)*

200th mission of the 95th Bomb Group; Aircraft assigned to Paul Fiess on the right; "200" formed with 100-pound bombs *(95th B.G. photo)*

A perfect target for visual bombing but the joker closed the doors
(95th B.G. photo)

Crew assembled in front of their first assigned aircraft, *Knock Out Baby*

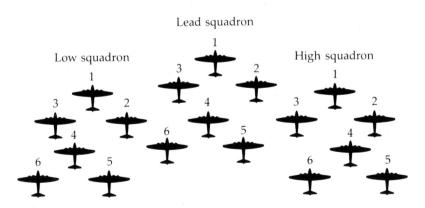

Top view of a group formation. The lead ship of a lead squadron was the group lead and was a PFF Mickey Radar ship. As a lead crew we flew squadron lead, leading either the high or low squadron as a backup or deputy visual lead to the group leader.

Side view of a group formation: three squadrons, eighteen ships, 850 feet in depth

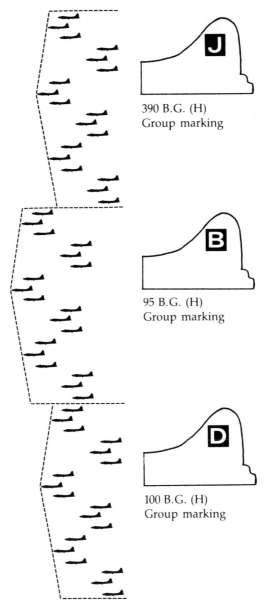

390 B.G. (H)
Group marking

95 B.G. (H)
Group marking

100 B.G. (H)
Group marking

Side view of the 13th Combat Wing formation comprised of the 390th, 95th, and 100th groups, showing the 95th as lead group; 3,000 feet in depth. Three groups constituted a wing and consisted of a lead group, a high group, and a low group stacked very similar to the squadrons within a group. We now had a formation of 54 aircraft.

Perfect formation as the 95th heads for battle over greater Germany *(Boeing Archives)*

Wingman flying perfect formation for protection against enemy fighters. "Tuck it in tight!"

On the bomb run *(Boeing Archives)*

Billy Bob Layl's airplane crash

Work, Dimit, and Fletcher in front of their new home, the Quacks' Shack, awaiting assignment of a new copilot. Notice the coke-stealing shovel, which sometimes doubled as a broom.

Doc in the cockpit of *Kimmie Kar*

The *Blue Streak*, based in Sudbury, Suffolk, with the 486th Bomb Group, piloted by Lt. David Paris and his crew; went down November 2, 1944, on the raid to Merseburg, Germany *(8th Air Force photo, from Ian Hawkins)*

A classic bomb drop, the bombs falling in trail *(95th B.G. photo)*

Crew of *Lucky Sherry* with new copilot Billy Bob Layl, after returning home from a mission. Layl: back row, second from left, wearing service cap

Russians following progress of the war (*Paul Fiess photo*)

Russian soldiers. The women had front-line duty for one week alternating with one week of KP duty behind the lines. *(95th B.G. photo)*

Pin-up girl, Russian style, Poltava, Russia *(95th B.G. photo)*

A ride through Flak Alley

The group sandwiched between two layers of clouds—the sun breaking through the top layer and Jerry's calling card through the bottom layer *(95th B.G. photo)*

Bombs exploding on the target at Bad Munster, Germany. Strike photo taken from ship #7783, *Lucky Sherry*, Christmas Day, 1944 *(95th B.G. photo)*

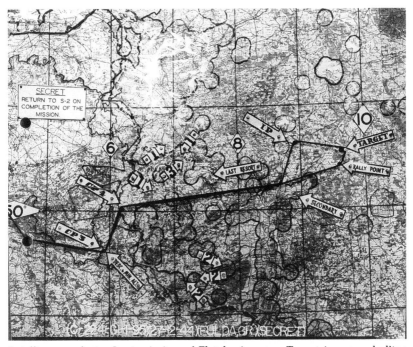

Intelligence photo. Last mission of Fletcher's crew. Target is a marshalling yard at Fulda, Germany. Photo shows route in, primary target, secondary target, and target of last resort, December 27, 1944. *(95th B.G. photo)*

The nine living members of "Fletcher's Gang," 41 years later. Back row, left to right: McQuitty, Lynch, Firszt, Brown, Hinman; front row: Fletcher, Doxon, Work, Dimit. "We miss you, Smitty."

Picture taken from *Lucky Sherry*, March 17, 1945 *(Boeing Archives)*

would not have to supply combat crews and aircraft for a specified period of time—usually twenty-four, thirty-six, or forty-eight hours) there would be a big party for everyone.

August 28, 1944

. . . That was really some newspaper clipping you sent. I don't object to my middle initial being "J," and I don't think Dad cares how they spell his name, but I'm quite sure Major General Partridge would object if he knew he was referred to as just plain "Major." I take it the clipping came from the new Tekoa Gazette.

I got up at eleven forty-five this morning. If that hadn't been the time they serve dinner I wouldn't have been up that early. A couple of hours this afternoon were spent in class—then the rest of the time up to now has been spent reading age-old magazines and some short stories by Kipling. This rough life is beginning to tell on me—I'm getting so lazy that I even hate to walk up to the shower to take a bath.

An instructor I had in Ardmore just came in. He's a Captain now, a West Point grad. He just got over here and is still full of hot news about Ardmore and the friends we had. We've talked about two hours and finally have things under control—really enjoyed talking to him. Of course I told him so many tales about combat that I think he's just about ready to book passage back. Oh well, he'll find out in due time that I was merely kidding and he'll probably have a good laugh out of it. By the way, his name is [James] Frankosky.

September 1, 1944

Had six letters from you today—not in sequence—but that's due to the fact that some come by boat and some by plane. . . . Also received a letter from Mrs. Doxon congratulating us on our son, and one from a cousin of mine you've never met, Virgil [Winnett]. . . . He has been in Italy, or rather I should say overseas, for twenty-seven months. Hallie gave him my address so he wrote to find out all about my little family and wondered if I had an extra snapshot of my lovely wife—or, as he puts it, "the poor unfortunate girl that got stuck with me." I hate to disappoint him so send along a snapshot that I can send to him. He was pretty happy—two years ago he was a buck private, finally worked up to staff sergeant and then a few weeks ago received a battlefield promotion to 2nd lieutenant. He's with a tough outfit and I know that he really worked to get that. Good deal, says I. . . .

You asked about the food situation. That's a touchy subject around here. It's definitely bad—it's nourishing enough but always looks and tastes the same. No one is losing weight so it can't be too bad, I guess, but the poor mess officer is about as popular as a German flak gunner!

Virgil Winnett is a distant cousin of the author, but they retained a close relationship. Virgil had won a football scholarship to the University of Idaho where he played tackle. He was a towering man compared to the author, who was 5 feet 6 inches, weighed 125 pounds, and required a waiver of physical standards to enlist in the Army Air Corps.

When the draft was instituted, in the very beginning, local communities had a lottery drawing of all people classified 1-A. Those whose names were drawn were the first to be drafted. Virgil won the lottery and was one of, if not the first, to enter compulsory military service from the community of Dayton, Washington. He saw service with a tank division in North Africa and Italy, where, after a very tough battle with many casualties, he received a battlefield commission. He fought a long, tough war.

September 2, 1944

Today was not out of the ordinary. We spent the afternoon flying all over England just for practice. Today was Work's day. First it is formation so Doc and I won't get rusty. Then it's Dimit's day to practice dropping a few bombs just to keep in shape. Finally a navigational mission to keep Work on the ball. When the cycle has been completed we start all over again. It is getting somewhat monotonous. Not long ago we were enjoying sack time days on end. Those were the happy days when we were wingmen with not a care in the world. Sure tough when they make you start working for a living.

We have seventeen missions in now so you can see we've slowed

*down. As yet we're not behind schedule, but have lost all that we were
ahead. We should get our own ship sometime next week. They'll probably give us the one we've been flying lately. We're sure attached to it
and all of us hope we'll get it. It has already been named, though.
Someone christened it* **Knock Out Baby.** *Its nose is graced by a lovely
little blonde in boxing shorts and sweater, wearing gloves and standing in the corner of a boxing ring. We all wanted to name our own
plane, but it's like I say, we just have a deep feeling for this one and I
think we'll get it. . . .*

We were scheduled to fly a solo practice mission. This was to
ensure that lead crews had plenty of experience, and was primarily a navigation mission. The navigator would have a
chance to sharpen his skills—he would do work with his Gee
Box as well as flying over and identifying the different
"bunchers" and "splashers," which were radio aids used in
forming the formation and joining the task forces. This would
be a relatively low-level mission, around 10,000 feet or below,
and for the rest of the crew just a fun trip. This mission could
have been performed in our ordinary clothes—A-2 jackets,
100 mission caps, and maybe long johns.

After we had completed our briefing and Roco had outlined
his course, which was only over land and about four hours in
duration, I changed my mind about our flight clothes. The
English weather is never to be trusted, so I informed the crew
to bring their mission clothes—heated suits and oxygen masks.
Probably won't need them, but just in case of an emergency
have them with you.

By the time Roco and I finished our errands and reached
the plane the crew reported that all preflight checks had been
made. All we had to do was pull the props through by hand to
check for liquid locks in the lower cylinders. If you could pull
them through by hand you knew there wasn't any problem, so
you could board the aircraft and start the engines. This we
did. Everything went like clockwork—we were soon airborne
and on our first heading, which we had received from Roco.
Doc set up the autopilot. This would be a fun day for us. Let

the autopilot fly and do the physical work, and we would enjoy the countryside while fiddling with the knobs.

We were making good progress and were about halfway through the mission when we saw a large cloud bank moving in. The base of the clouds appeared to be between 4,000 and 5,000 feet. We were flying at 8,000. I called Roco and he concluded we would have a better mission if we climbed over the clouds rather than going through underneath. We set up a climb condition and let the autopilot function, breaking out about 14,000 feet. It was beautiful above the clouds. The navigation was all by instruments anyway, so let Roco work.

It was starting to get a little chilly so I plugged in my heated suit and turned up the rheostat. I was glad I had changed the order and requested heated suits because this was the emergency that was always present while flying in England.

Doc suggested that while we weren't busy and everything was going smooth maybe he would go back through the aircraft and check on everyone. This would be a good chance to stretch his legs. I readily agreed but requested that Brownie occupy his seat and be my eyes on that side of the ship. This was fine with Brownie because the pilots' seats were the most comfortable place on the airplane and afforded a very good view.

Doc was gone about ten minutes when he called on the interphone and wanted to know if they could open the emergency bag, which was in the radio room. Each aircraft was equipped with an emergency kit. This was an olive-drab, heavy canvas bag about three feet long, eighteen inches high, and about the same width. It was closed with a heavy zipper running down the top, and the zipper end was sealed with a light metal seal. The bag contained all sorts of things that could be used in an emergency—extra oxygen masks, heated suits, medical kits, anything a crew might need if any of their personal equipment failed, and a lot of other things. The reason for the seal was to tell if the bag had been opened and anything had been removed. Since everything in the bag was inventoried it would have to be repacked any time the seal was broken. This would insure that the bag was complete, and was for our own protection. No one would want a bag with something missing—it might be the very thing you would need. In other words, you didn't open the bag frivolously.

When I asked what they needed, the answer was, "We need a heated suit and maybe an oxygen mask." "Okay, whose suit has burned out, and who has oxygen problems?" "Well, no one's suit has malfunctioned. We have an extra passenger on board and he's getting cold. If we get the suit we might just as well play it safe and put an oxygen mask on him in case we have to go higher."

There was something obviously amiss here as I hadn't authorized any extra personnel and had not been informed that operations had either. Somebody better fill me in on what's going on. "Well, we've got a cook on board." *"We've what?!"* "The cook from the combat mess hall is with us. We promised him a ride and this seemed like a good time for it—a low-level overland sightseeing mission without any danger attached."

The last thing we would want or need would be a casualty on board—and especially a cook—a cook whose presence would be missed one way or another come supper time.

"Break open the kit and make your passenger comfortable. We'll discuss this when we land." This was a "no-no" of major proportions, something that just was not done. How would I explain a cook on board a combat aircraft, even though it was only a practice mission?

A thousand scenarios went through my head. The best seemed to be "keep it quiet." Don't say anything—plead the Fifth, or drink it. Apparently the only ones who knew were the members of the ground crew and my flight crew. The ground crew wouldn't say anything, and with good luck no one would meet the ship except a truck driver to provide transportation back to the Ready Room.

The only problem was to explain logically the opening of the emergency kit. I let it be known that by the time we landed someone on board that aircraft better have a malfunctioning flight suit, and be prepared to justify the use of the emergency equipment. Doc readily agreed to do this, which seemed no more than right since he had been the perpetrator of the whole affair and had sworn the others to silence.

I then dropped the matter and let the cook enjoy the ride.

It was my policy never to discipline people in the presence of others, or when I was mad. This clearly called for a "woodshed" tactic hidden from the view of others. But this would take place only after my blood pressure went down and my temper had cooled.

When this time arrived, the cook had been smuggled off, but not before he shook my hand and thanked me for the wonderful ride and for the highlight that broke up a monotonous life of eighteen months overseas. It would have served no purpose to put a damper on such enthusiasm.

For my crew it would be a different story. During the course of our little discussion it came out that the cook was a paying passenger. A wheel of cheese, two loaves of bread, and a gallon of strawberry jam—all of which would be generously shared with the 1st pilot if he could overlook the slight indiscretions of his fellow man. These people knew that a man could be tempted—maybe we knew one another too well!

September 3, 1944

. . . Just had some good news a few minutes ago. We are authorized to go on pass tomorrow. The fellows are now eagerly getting off their last-minute letters, shining shoes, and all that goes with a pass. We will undoubtedly go to London again and see if we can find some of the old buddies. There isn't much you can do on a pass, but the idea is just to get away from the post awhile and enjoy a change of scenery. It also relieves the anxiety of the mind for a while. But then again, when the pass is over you hate to go back to it all. . . .

September 7, 1944

Here I am back with my nose to the grindstone again. The pass went entirely too fast and we really had fun. Can you imagine breakfast in bed at eleven-thirty? Believe me we really caught up on our sack time —as if we were behind. . . .

Riding on the English trains is really an experience—a rather pleasant one I might add. The trains are smaller than ours and they look rather antiquated, but they are cleaner and much more comfortable to ride. They have two shock absorbers on each end of the cars. This keeps the slack out of the connecting links between the cars—consequently, they don't jerk and bang on starting and stopping like American trains. They are actually very smooth riding. I have never seen anything like a Pullman car here. Maybe the country is small enough that they are not needed. . . .

Our closest contact with the civilian and military population comes on these train rides. I find it very difficult to understand their speech, but we do communicate. Since these rides to London take some time we are generally offered tea by the other occupants of the compartment. Now the English like sugar and cream in their tea and it is already mixed in their thermos so there is no choice of "with or without." A time or two I have tried to refuse because I knew they did not have very much—everything being rationed or nonexistent. But you also have the feeling that if you refuse you will hurt their feelings, so, in the end, you compromise and accept on the second firm generous offer. . . .

September 8, 1944

Today was quite a day. Received three letters from you including the one which contained the pictures of David. I don't think I need to tell you how happy I was to get them—really have some little man, haven't we? Be sure to take more pictures with you holding him 'cause I like to see my two loved ones together. . . .

Now about the papers I sent—yes, those are the ones which describe what we have been doing. They're pretty sketchy and you won't get much out of them until I get home to explain them. Yes, the candy came through okay and was devoured almost immediately. No, there's nothing special I want or need. Don't ever send over anything of value because things get lost too easily. Should be home by Christmas so don't go out of the way to send anything.

September 11, 1944

Back again after a three day layoff from letter writing. We had a day and a half off for a big celebration. There were USO troops, several guest orchestras, both G.I. and top English—even Glenn Miller and his band. It was quite a show—all took place on the post and a good time seemed to be had by all. I would like to tell you the reason for the big time but it'll have to wait. Also flew a couple more practice missions over the English countryside, just for the heck of it.

On September 9 and 10 the 95th Group was "stood down" and the 200th Mission Party commenced. On the evening of the ninth I was ordered to report to Group Operations, with a skeleton crew, at 6:30 Sunday morning. When we reported in we were told that we were flying up to Birmingham to pick up some VIPs who would participate in our big party. We were to fly aircraft #0235, *The Zoot Suiter*. This had been Bill ("Catfish") Lindley's airplane, the one in which he flew as lead pilot on the Münster raid, a mission which brought the group a Presidential Unit Citation. Lindley had at one time also been squadron commander of the 412th Bomb Squadron. Both the airplane and Lindley were already legends in our group, and we felt honored.

When we took off that morning the weather was poor, a very low ceiling with visibility about one mile. Work gave me a heading, but to follow it meant going on instruments, then having to let down over Birmingham and not knowing but what the ceiling could be zero. This could be very dangerous, so I decided to remain in visual contact with the ground and fly around the low clouds when it appeared they were too low to fly under.

After a while Work came on the interphone and said that I had made so many turns in such a short period of time that he had not been able to keep track of all of them. By now we had him thoroughly confused as to where we were. All I knew was we could see the ground so we must still be over England. Well, to a navigator this is not much help. About this time Doc came on the interphone and asked if the "Gee Box" was working. This was a navigating device which was developed for use in the U.K. It was possible to get an instantaneous fix of position accurate enough to be able to line up on a runway, and it was possible to keep a running fix going. Work immediately responded, "*The Gee Box.* I had completely forgotten about it. I'll turn it on and get it warmed up." Within a few minutes he said that he had our position and we were only a few miles from Birmingham.

Soon we were on the ground and had our VIPs loaded. On the way back to the base at Horham I was told they were members of the Glenn Miller orchestra and they would be entertaining us in the afternoon at our big party. This would be the highlight of the social activities while we were a part of the group.

September 12, 1944

Hello again. Yesterday I received your letter of August 27 and today received one dated September 2. In a day or so the ones that fill the gap will probably come in. I think that I get all of them, it just takes a little time. . . . So far I guess I'm about the only one in the barracks whose mail hasn't been spot checked by the Theatre Censor. Most of the other guys have had one or two censored. You don't have to worry about your letters as the Army doesn't touch civilian mail. So feel free to write anything you care to.

I get a kick out of the pictures of David. I'm always looking at them, admiring our little man. I've shown them to practically everyone on the Post. The guys think I'm worse now than when he was born—I don't brag any more than then, it's just that I have pictures now to back up my comments. They're all pretty envious that they don't have a son to go home and play with. Guess I'm just lucky! . . .

Incidentally, we are over the hump so now we're on the down grade. Chalk off number eighteen. Maybe we'll finish yet—never can tell.

Mission #18, *Ruhland, Germany, September 11*

Frank Dimit, Bombardier

Briefed at 5:30 a.m. for target at Ruhland. It was the same oil refinery we hit on our 16th mission, 65 miles east of Leipzig.

It was the most screwed up mess I have ever had the misfortune to encounter. Through good luck and the grace of God, the lead navigator had his head out. He was the only one in the lead ship that knew what was up.

We failed to hit our primary for some unknown reason, so we headed for the last resort target. I thought the lead bombardier was making for a small town with a fair-sized marshalling yard. He wasn't. About time for "bombs away," he closed the doors. The same thing happened at an average-sized town north of Frankfurt with a beautiful railroad yard, waiting to be creamed. But the joker closed the doors. We ended up bringing our 10 500-pound G.P. bombs back to the base. I never thought I would see the day when we would bring back a full load from the middle of Germany. There was positively no excuse for not dropping them someplace.

The lead bombardier passed up any number of targets of opportunity between the two bomb runs. Strictly a head up and locked affair. The command pilot and lead bombardier weren't worth a damn.

We started out leading the low squadron of lead group. Lost our wingmen because of mechanical difficulties. Next position was #5 in lead squadron and after crossing the coast on the way back, we flew #2 in the lead. Next stop would have been lead. I know we couldn't have done a worse job.

Fighter support was good, but some enemy fighters got into our formation. Smitty and Brownie got in some shots at a fighter attacking from 6 o'clock. The fighter knocked down one of the boys from the 95th. He was in the low group of our wing.

The wing ahead of us was hit bad by fighters. Saw no flak today while we were monkeying around over greater Germany.

Damn glad to be back. *[End of mission notes by Frank Dimit]*

We were inbound to "somewhere" and were now flying the #5 spot in the lead squadron when someone called on the interphone and asked if anyone knew what the strange looking little bursts were about 2 o'clock level and about 100 feet out. The thought went through my mind that they looked like firecrackers exploding, but this wasn't the Fourth of July. Before anyone could answer, Brownie called out, "Bandits in the area 6 o'clock high and closing fast." At that moment the tail guns and the top turret started firing. We were being fired on and not being missed by very much.

The initial attack went right over us and the second wave went under us, hitting the low group. The battle for us was over in a matter of seconds. The enemy fighters descended on the low group of the wing ahead of us. This was a part of the 100th Bomb Group. Mac called on the interphone and in a quivering voice stated that the entire formation of twelve B-17s had completely disappeared. Horrified, I couldn't believe my ears and asked Mac to repeat. He stated again that the complete formation was gone. As the fighters went through, the B-17s were just wiped out—twelve aircraft and 108 men gone in just seconds. It was the first and only time we ever saw a complete unit wiped out. Our loss was pale in comparison.

At interrogation we reported the funny firecrackers and were told that the Germans were now experimenting with proximity exploding 20 millimeter shells, and we had just had a demonstration.

Eleven aircraft from our group hit the primary and their results were good. We should have been following them. As it turned out this was a day in which the Eighth Air Force fighters broke all previous single day records by shooting down 116 enemy planes. We later learned that the 100th lost only eleven aircraft instead of twelve.

September 14, 1944

It's now the end of another perfect day—received four letters from you. Also received a letter from Cap which I answered a while ago. I got quite a kick out of his student instructor problems. So to make him feel good I let him in on a few of my little problems. They aren't many, but doggone it, I can't quite seem to get used to having people shooting at me. Makes me nervous at times. . . .

What a life we lead! About the only fun we have is enjoying one another's company and for amusement kidding and playing jokes on one another. It's a good thing we all get along together so well. Instead of arguing and quarreling amongst ourselves like a lot of the crews we're always laughing and joking. Most people think we've been here too long. We thoroughly agree with them. We figure that maybe if we act crazy enough they'll send us home. So far no luck! . . .

I spoke to the C.O. of the squadron about a discharge so I could take that radio job in La Grande, but he told me if I didn't stop pestering him he was going to give me a job. I took him at his word for the only job he can give me is where people take pot shots at you. He thinks I'm crazy anyway—wanting to leave here and go back to the States where you have to eat steaks, drink milkshakes and cokes, live with your wife, go fishing, and wear civilian clothes. Me thinks he's been here too long too!

September 15, 1944

. . . Dimit received a newspaper from home the other day and we ran across this article. Dimit knows the fellow well and we have been getting quite a kick out of it. After reading it you'll see why, so here we go: "Captain John W. Preble Jr., Stanton Blvd., has been highly commended by Lt. Col. T. Q. Graft, Air Corps Commander, Mediterranean Theatre of War, for the difficult task of preparing citations for proposed awards for various members of his organization. Attached to the Air Corps Intelligence Capt. Preble has served in the Mediterranean Theatre of Operation for fifteen months."

We have just come to the conclusion that if our flying around and earning these awards is causing the ground personnel that much trouble and work perhaps we should quit. "For the difficult task"—I'll never get over that. It must have been rough typing those citations. Flak all over the sky, completely surrounded by enemy fighters, two engines out, part of the control cables gone, gas leaking out of the tanks, airplanes going down like flies—then the keys probably jammed on the typewriter. Some day when this is over some joker like that is going to try to tell me how he won the war and I'm going to blow my top. Yes sir, that poor fellow beating that typewriter must have had a rough time. Too bad he can't take time out and go for a ride with us. Gosh, I must be getting bitter so I'll get off the subject!

September 17, 1944

Not much to report from this side of the Atlantic today. It was a very quiet Sunday spent in the usual Sunday manner of church, sleeping, and reading. This afternoon, though, we got up enough ambition to build an aerial for the radio which was just recently fixed. We had the aerial all fixed and hooked up and music just poured out of the little box—so far so good—but then we decided to change a few things. After we did this the radio quit altogether and wouldn't even give out with static. We drew straws to see who was to tear the radio down and fix it. I lost. I tore it all to pieces and worked about two hours on it. Finally the fruits of my hard labor began to ripen as the static increased and finally dinner music became recognizable. Deciding to leave well enough alone, I quit monkeying with it. The fact that that was the only station we could tune in had nothing to do with it. Everything went fine until the program was over and the announcer came on. Doggone, if I didn't have a German station tuned in! The fellows became very violent and insisted that I work on it until I got an English station. I tried to argue that it would be much simpler if we would just study German—then we could understand the newscasts and programs. They didn't quite see my point but, anyway, I refused to work on it any more. Somebody else fooled with it the rest of the afternoon and right now it isn't playing anything. The general consensus is that there isn't anything wrong with it that a new radio wouldn't help! . . .

We finally got an airplane—#257 Knock Out Baby. We were all very happy to be able to call it our own. We're pretty proud of it and we have some pictures which I'll send home in a few days. Someday I'll tell you just why we are so attached to that airplane. The ground crew that looks after it thinks we're pretty swell guys—don't know us very well, do they? They have fixed up lots of little extra things on it for us.

I don't know how you manage to read these letters of mine. I must be getting stupid. Can't spell, sentence structure going from bad to worse, writing becoming more illegible, words left out, and what's worse the same sentence or word written twice. I'm sure glad I don't have to read them. Guess I'm about due for a trip to the States to recuperate. Don't know what I would recuperate from seeing as how I haven't done anything, but it makes a good excuse for the state of the letters.

September 18, 1944

I have some good news for you this evening. In the continuing saga of the radio—it is working perfectly! We talked one of the fellows with radio maintenance into working on it for us. Now it works just like a charm and doesn't give us any trouble. It seems good to lie in the sack and listen to good old American jive. What a life! It comes in handy too to listen to the newscasts, and right now we're all very much interested in what is going on over the Channel.

Today was spent flying around all over the English countryside again. Cap has nothing on me as I'm getting to be quite an instructor myself. Lately we have been spending about three-fourths of our time breaking in new crews, getting them used to flying formation again and how to navigate in a combat theater. It does them a lot of good and also gives me practice leading. All in all it isn't bad but it slows down my missions. But I have learned one thing—"take things as they come and don't volunteer for anything," also "that everything happens for the best." That's the outlook we take on everything, good or bad.

No mail today for anyone in the hut. That's the first day we've had a complete shut-out for a long time. But that makes our chances better for a big haul tomorrow. Oh yes, today we were awarded another Oak Leaf Cluster for wear with the Air Medal. Same citation and all such stuff as goes with the Air Medal. I'll enclose the cluster in the letter so you may have it too.

September 20, 1944   ·

. . . We have initiated a new regime—no more lying in the sack until noon. We decided that we were getting lazy and, besides, it is a bad habit. So now everyone gets up before nine, or if you can't make it then, at least by eleven fifty-nine! No kidding, since we've been getting up earlier on our days of leisure we've been feeling better. Maybe it's because we're getting more exercise by volunteering for the little odds and ends jobs around the Group. At least we're happier when our minds are occupied. Yesterday we took a short hop in the morning— kind of a weather check—then went to a show in the afternoon. It was one of those Peter Lorre mystery thrillers entitled The Mask of Dimi-

trius. *It was a waste of time and money when they produced it, but it didn't cost me anything so why should I gripe about it? . . .*

Here's the payoff—this is one for "Can You Beat This." Since our radio speaks German better than any other language we find ourselves listening most of the time to German stations. Last night they were playing "Don't Sit Under The Apple Tree With Anyone Else But Me" —German words and all! That beats me! Can you imagine them playing our victory songs to their troops? Oh well, I guess they have to have some good music occasionally.

If it weren't for you and David I couldn't do the job I'm asked to do here. I'm not here because of patriotism to any ideals. I'm here to do what's expected of me only because I feel that in some way I'm aiding and protecting my little family. That feeling alone gives me the courage to keep on trying to do my part and just a little more. We all want to come home but we'll do our best before we do. Sometimes we get pretty discouraged, but that's only human nature, and usually comes as a result of loneliness for our loved ones. In the face of things here dreams of the past and future are about all that keep you going.

September 24

Doc Doxon, Copilot

Came back from London on a very crowded train. Buzz bomb went very close over the barracks. Fletcher really went under the bed.

It was after dark and the eight officers were gathered in Nissen hut #10 along with two visitors. A lively bull session was underway when we heard a buzz bomb coming our way.

The buzz bomb (or V-1 or Doodle Bug) was a strange instrument of war, somewhat like a small airplane. Buzz bombs were powered by a rocket engine mounted high on the tail and the fuselage was filled with high explosives. They were launched from ramps in Germany and France and headed in the direction of England. Their range varied by the amount of fuel the Germans pumped into them. When the fuel supply was exhausted the motor would stop. There would be absolute silence as the rocket plunged approximately 1,000 feet to the ground. A tremendous explosion would occur as these were strictly flying bombs.

The V-1s had short stubby wings and weren't particularly fast. In fact, the Spitfires and other fighters would, sometimes, try to intercept and shoot them down over the English Channel. Once they made landfall this process became more difficult because of the low altitude at which they flew. But the fighters would try to shoot them down over the farm country before they reached the major cities.

Since our airfield was located in East Anglia in the heart of the farm country we were not generally considered a prime target, although there were airfields located about ten miles apart all over the countryside. The buzz bombs didn't pose any particular problem to us unless they happened to run out of fuel while they were in our vicinity.

We had learned to respect them on our previous trips to London where we had seen the demolition even one could cause. We were all very conscious of them, and as long as we heard the engine running we didn't take any particular precautions. By this time a lot of people were smart enough to head for shelter when they heard the things coming. But this meant running outside in the rain, fog, or snow. You wouldn't have your coat on, and you'd have to go down and stand in the shelter—even wondering whether the thing would fall before you got to the shelter. So finally we just stayed in our Nissen hut and took our chances.

On this particular evening we stopped our visiting when we heard the bomb coming and, of course, everyone had the same idea in mind—"please keep that engine running!" When it sounded as if it were very close to us, all of a sudden there was dead silence. This meant you had better seek whatever cover you could—it was too late to head for the bomb shelter.

The beds we had in the quonset at this time were all singles and on one level, so the safest place would be under the bed. At least you'd have the mattress and bed covers over the top of you. If the building should blow in you'd have a certain amount of protection. When the engine stopped my immediate thought was to crawl under my bed, and since I had a friend there visiting me he also looked around for a place. But that was his problem—I had solved mine. When he saw me under the bed the first thing he did was grab the mattress and all the blankets from off my bed. He flopped down on the floor and pulled them over him. It left me wide-eyed staring up through the springs on the bed with absolutely no protection. You can well imagine the thoughts going through my mind and what I thought of my friend.

When the big explosion came the building rattled and shook, but luckily there was no damage to our Nissen hut, and when we got our wits gathered about, everyone was laughing at my predicament because they had seen my protection disappear over the top of my buddy.

As Doc tells the story, there was a WAC in the barracks with us who was visiting the navigator on the other crew. And, as his story goes, all the rest of them jumped under the bed where the WAC was seeking protection.

Anyway, the moral of the story is: If you are going to seek protection from the buzz bombs, don't have company in your room at the same time.

The buzz bomb landed just a few hundred yards from our barracks and, as good luck would have it, it was in a farmer's field and did not cause any damage on the base. These little incidents made you want to strike back even harder. Fear has a way of making you mad.

September 25

Doc Doxon, Copilot

Flying practice mission—high squadron lead. Lots of new ships on the field. They left plenty of B-17s in Russia.

September 26

Doc Doxon, Copilot

Another practice day—2 practice missions, one at night, and on the list for tomorrow. Looks like we've had it.

September 27, 1944

You haven't had a letter from me for six days. The first three days were spent in London on pass—saw a lot of the old buddies and did some traveling on the London subway, affectionately known as "the tube."

London has an extensive subway system. It is very modern and clean. Many of the underground stations are finished in white ceramic tile. In some of the cars there is a map of the system. The routes are a line of light tubes. You push a button of where you are and a button for where you want to go and the route lights up on the map. The stations are round circles of light with names like Charing Cross, Marble Arch, etc. These will indicate whether you need to change cars at a particular station. It is all very simple and you can go almost any place in London without having to ask directions. Just pick out the station nearest to where you want to go, go to that station, get off, climb the stairs to street level and start walking. If you are lucky you might find a cab, but don't count on it.

There is one thing that is very important—you want to know when the last car runs because you could be stranded. These cars or trains do not run all night, so don't miss the last one. It's probably a good thing that they stop running because many of the stations are filled with people who are trying to sleep. These are people who are using these stations for bomb shelters and are seeking safety from the buzz bombs, the V-2 rockets, or an occasional bombing. When you see people actually living in stations, whole families of them, with no privacy, you just have to feel sorry for them, this world, and the state it is in. The people at home have no idea at all of what it is to have a war fought over or on your own country. There are a lot of things that I don't understand about the English people, but I do know one thing, from the privations they have suffered they are a brave lot!

These last three days I have really been running in circles—more work than I've ever had to do. Guess I'm about caught up now, or will be just as soon as I put in the sack time which I'm behind on. Have managed to get four hours in the sack in the last thirty-six. But in just a few minutes I intend to average that out.

Yesterday marked the ninth straight day with no mail from the States, but today I had ten letters from you. We found out only a few days ago why our mail was being held up. We should have pretty good service from now on.

Incidentally, number nineteen is over with so you can chalk that one off. I may have some good news for you tomorrow when I write. At the present I'm not quite sure about it but will double check in the morning.

Mission #19, Mainz, Germany, September 27

Frank Dimit, Bombardier

Due to a night practice mission after 2 hours sleep we briefed at 3:15 a.m. for our target at Mainz, Germany, just a few miles west of Frankfurt. Our target was the marshalling yards. The ground forces wanted it K.O.'d because reinforcements for the Siegfried Line were being brought through there.

We flew lead in the high squadron of the low group of the 13th combat wing. Was our first mission as deputy group lead. We carried 10 500-pound aimable cluster incendiaries. Bombing was PFF so we didn't see the results. Somebody goofed up because the wing lead PFF ship was not carrying smoke bombs, and we didn't know when to dump our load.

Also raised hell when we came back, because upper and lower turrets of every ship in the group were stowed most of the time. If fighters had hit us, we would still be over in the Fatherland. Maj. Fitzgerald and Lt. Schwartz promised to raise hell about it.

Our wing was last one in and last out of Germany. So we caught plenty of prop wash. Caught flak several places besides target area. None of it accurate and most of it light. Saw no enemy fighters—glad of it. Escort not as good as usual. Think we missed rendezvous.

Chalk up another one for us. *[End of mission notes by Frank Dimit]*

September 28, 1944

The good news that I was going to tell you about was that if I make good as a Squadron Lead I probably won't have to fly over thirty-one. I'm not positive about this yet so as soon as I get some time off I will get some confirmation on this rumor. It's positive on Group Leads, but we're in slight doubt on Squadron Leads.

In the meantime you can check off number twenty as another one gone by.

Mission #20, *Merseburg, Germany, September 28*

Frank Dimit, Bombardier

Today was a pistol. Briefed at 5:15 a.m. for a target at our old friend(?) Merseburg, Germany. It was the third time we have been briefed for this target, but we didn't get there the other two times. We did today. Target was an oil refinery, and they wanted the thing K.O.'d. The entire 3rd Division (9 Combat Wings) hit the same target. We were the sixth wing in.

We flew lead of low squadron of lead group, and had the hell shot right out of us. Carried 10 500-pound G.P. bombs. Bombing was PFF—results unobserved.

No enemy fighters—damn good support. Flak worst I've ever seen or hope to see. Our ship looked like a sieve with between 45-50 holes. Nobody was injured, but I almost stopped a slug. A small hunk of flak came through the plex-iglass panel just above my seat. It clipped the back of my head, but it didn't hurt me. I didn't have my flak helmet on, but it didn't take me long to get it on. The extra radio man we carried collected two flak holes in his helmet, one going in, the other coming out. It scratched his skull but that was all. A hunk of flak knocked out our right waist gun. Fletch was saved

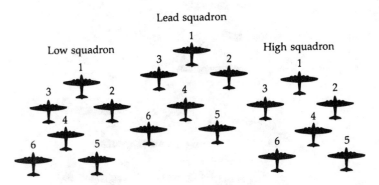

Top view of a group formation. The lead ship of a lead squadron was the group lead and was a PFF Mickey Radar Ship. As a lead crew we flew squadron lead, leading either the high or low squadron as a backup or deputy visual lead to the group leader.

from death or serious injury by the bullet-proof glass on his window. Number two engine was K.O.'d.

We came back alone again, but this time we followed a formation out and didn't have to sweat out the navigation. Work always does a damn good job, but when you come back over an overcast, the element of chance has a lot to do with it. Sometimes the weather information leaves a lot to be desired.

Our entire group was hit hard. Our right wingman had his copilot killed. Our left wingman lost an engine, and the prop and cowling flew off the damn thing over France. Major Pomeroy (Squadron C.O.) was in the wing lead ship and it was hit bad also. (Major Pomeroy was hit in the face.) Wounded at least one man, and #1 engine was smoking very badly. They crash landed near Brussels.

It was the roughest we've seen. Don't think we'll fly tomorrow—battle damage too great. *[End of mission notes by Frank Dimit]*

In a combat formation a normal group was made up of eighteen planes. These were divided into three squadrons of six ships. Each squadron had two three-ship elements. The first element had a lead ship and two wingmen. The second element had a lead ship in the diamond of the first element along

Side view of a group formation: three squadrons, eighteen ships, 850 feet in depth.

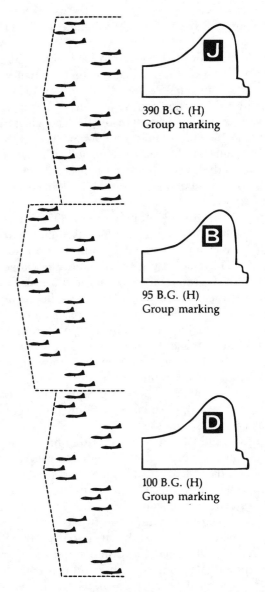

390 B.G. (H)
Group marking

95 B.G. (H)
Group marking

100 B.G. (H)
Group marking

Side view of the 13th Combat Wing formation comprised of the 390th, 95th, and 100th groups, showing the 95th as lead group; 3,000 feet in depth. Three groups constituted a wing and consisted of a lead group, a high group, and a low group stacked very similar to the squadrons within a group. We now had a formation of 54 aircraft.

with two wingmen. Each of the three squadrons had this same makeup.

The lead squadron had the group lead ship, a PFF Mickey Radar Ship, flying as the lead of the first element, with the second element in trail. The low squadron flew below, slightly behind, and left of the lead squadron with the lead ship slightly behind the left wingman of the lead element of the lead squadron. The high squadron flew above, slightly behind, and to the right of the lead squadron with the lead ship slightly behind the right wingman of the lead element of the lead squadron. From above the formation looked like the diagram on page 397.

In our case the three groups were the 95th Heavy Bombardment Group, the 390th Heavy Bombardment Group, and the 100th Heavy Bombardment Group. These three groups made up the Thirteenth Combat Wing and flew together. All wings going to the same target constituted a task force. This was the purist form and was used solely in the beginning.

As the groups continued to grow and received more aircraft and crews, it eventually became possible for a group to put up enough aircraft to make up two groups in a wing, or even a complete wing. As time went on even the number of aircraft in a group formation occasionally changed from eighteen to twelve, or any number in between. Squadrons became elements, groups became squadrons. But the eighteen-ship group was the most common.

The wings would fly in trail with a three-minute separation toward the Initial Point. At the IP the lead group of the wing would fire two flares five seconds apart and then turn for the target. The low group would continue on for twenty seconds, then turn in trail on the lead group and head for the target. The high group would continue on twenty seconds after the low group, then turn and start their run to the target in trail of the low group. This would put a maximum of eighteen aircraft over the target at any one time and was considered the maximum for a good bomb pattern, as all eighteen aircraft would drop simultaneously with the lead ship when his smoke bombs emerged from the bomb bay.

After "Bombs away" the lead group would fly straight ahead

for at least another twenty seconds, then start a descending right turn losing 1,000 feet of altitude to the Rally Point. The low group would then cross the target and bomb, continue ahead for about ten seconds, then start a descending right turn inside of the lead group, losing 1,000 feet, and wind up back in position under the lead group on the left side at the RP. The high group would cross the target and bomb, then start an immediate descending turn to the right, inside the low group. Upon losing 1,000 feet the high group would now reach the RP above and to the right of the lead group. The wing had now been re-formed for the best fighter protection and would head home.

The rest of the wings would complete this same maneuver until the entire task force had crossed the target.

General Curtis E. LeMay was the originator of this box-type formation, and it was considered a very formidable force, giving maximum firepower to ward off enemy fighter attacks.

Not all tactics are 100 percent effective and many casualties would result. But this was considered the very best that could be devised. The 100th Bomb Group was probably the best-known group in the Eighth Air Force for its many casualties, a rather dubious honor. There was one occasion in October 1943 when they sent out thirteen ships and only one returned!

On our twentieth mission our crew was leading the low squadron. Since the low squadron is always stacked below and left of the lead squadron it was much easier to fly this position from the right seat, which is the copilot's position. This was our third time to lead the low squadron. The first time I had found it difficult to see and maintain position for a long period of time from the left seat. I had a stiff neck from all the bobbing and weaving. So I requested that Doc fly from the left seat and I would fly from his position where I could have an uninterrupted view of the lead squadron. It would not only be easier on me but also on our wing and trail aircraft because in this position I could fly a more stable aircraft with fewer power changes. I could keep the lead ship in view at all times and detect any change in his position immediately.

The time before I had made this same switch and everything had worked fine, with the exception of a harmless case of vertigo on my part which was quickly pointed out by Doc, so it seemed logical to try again.

The bombardier had just called "Bombs away" when a loud explosion and shock wave rocked the ship violently. The huge shell had exploded on the right side of the ship just aft of the wing and beside the window of the right waist gunner. Instantly shrapnel from the burst filled the airplane. My windshield was like a spider web with lines radiating out from a hole near the top in the bulletproof glass. I immediately called for a damage report on the interphone. There was no answer. The interphone had to be dead. It was obvious that we had suffered major damage—we needed to communicate.

In this instant Doc grabbed the control column and patted the top of his head, indicating that he had control of the aircraft, and started his turn and 1,000-foot descent to the Rally Point.

Suddenly I was very mad—angry at the Germans—but more so at the lack of my ability to communicate with the crew, who at this time should need some leadership. In frustration I depressed what I thought to be a dead mike button and vented my emotion with a string of oaths. This was abruptly halted by the heat near my ankle and the smell of smoke. I looked down and saw that my flying suit on my right leg was smoldering and smoking, but there was no blaze. As I leaned over to grab the smoldering area and smother it with my gloved hands I heard two words—"Pilot hit," then after a couple of seconds, "Brownie." It was Doc's voice.

Immediately Brownie came out of the top turret. I knew then that some of the crew had communication. Brownie immediately grabbed me and pulled my head up from my bent-over position and was trying to find out where I was hit. I had squeezed out the glowing embers on my ankle and realized that the red-hot shrapnel had blown a hole in my flight suit, but had not hit my leg. It had also severed the wire in the cord leading to my headset, but it was still partly held together by the insulation around the wire. When I leaned over the broken wire made contact long enough for me to hear those few words. My string of oaths had been transmitted to the crew, then all was silent from my position since I assumed the inter-

phone to be inoperative. This in turn caused the crew to believe I had problems, even more so because I had a standing
order that no profanity would ever be used on the interphone.

In a theater of war the language would become somewhat
salty on occasion. Our communication system was vital and I
did not want it cluttered up with oaths or idle chatter. Up
until now this order had never been violated, so it must have
been quite a shock to the crew that the rule was violated by its
originator.

In the meantime Brownie was still trying to find my injury.
I, knowing that I had no physical problems, was trying to get
him to get back up in the top gun turret because we were now
at the Rally Point and could be subject to enemy fighter attacks at any moment.

In the course of our wrestling around in the copilot's seat
Brownie discovered the severed wire on the interphone and
quickly hooked up another to put me back into communication with the rest of the crew. It was then that I noticed that
the hose leading to Brownie's oxygen mask had been cut by
the flying shrapnel and he was receiving only a partial oxygen
supply. This was remedied immediately and the cockpit crew
was now back to normal. Thanks to Doc our low squadron was
back in tight group formation and we were headed home. The
#2 engine was losing oil pressure rapidly and had to be feath-
ered. We dropped out of the formation and started the long
journey home alone at 130 mph. Frank reported that there
was a hole in the plexiglass nose.

I was then told that the men in the radio room and waist
position had reported extensive damage and that it might be
wise to make a visual structural check. Grabbing a portable
oxygen bottle I went back to the radio room. It was almost like
walking into a giant sieve, but all damage was confined to the
skin and all structural members appeared to be okay.

Two days before this mission I had been contacted by a
"specialty" radio operator who had requested permission to
install his radio and recording equipment in our aircraft. I
asked him about his specialty. He said he spoke German fluently, that his radios were tuned to the German fighter frequencies, and he would monitor and record all fighter activity

from the time of their takeoff till their return to bases. He would record several different frequencies and return this information to Intelligence for whatever use they might be able to make of it. It sounded like a worthwhile project and one we would like to be associated with.

I asked him why he had picked our aircraft. He said Operations had told him we were a good, stable crew with plenty of experience. He also said that he knew Hinman, our radio operator, and George had assured him that this was the best crew on the field. Discounting individual prejudice, he had decided to go with us if I approved.

We had the ground crew install a table for him in the radio room at the forward bulkhead on the right side of the ship. Hinman was stationed just opposite on the left side.

While assessing the damage in the radio room, Hinman pointed to the other radio operator. Some of his equipment looked as if it had been hit by a hammer, and his eyes were as large as saucers. He handed me his steel flak helmet and I noticed two jagged holes near the top where flak had entered and exited. I looked at the top of his head. His leather flying helmet was split for about two inches with his white scalp showing and four little drops of blood interspersed along the crease. One look was all I wanted. Words weren't necessary—he knew how lucky he was. I gave him a pat on the shoulder and headed for the waist compartment where there was a rather large jagged hole in the right waist gunner's position. The right waist gun had been hit and rendered useless. This was Joe Firszt's position and he had just been dropped from the crew to comply with an order to change from ten-man to nine-man crews. I don't think anyone could have survived in that position—I gave thanks that Joe wasn't aboard.

Since we were flying the low squadron our left side was the one that was exposed to enemy fighter attack. For this reason Lynch was manning the left waist gun, which was staggered away from the right gun position. Flak had sprayed around him, but he hadn't been hit.

I called Smitty, the tail gunner, on the interphone from the waist compartment. He said his position was okay and that he was well wrapped in his cocoon of flak suits. I refilled the portable oxygen bottle and headed back to the copilot's seat, secure in the knowledge that the aircraft was structurally sound, maybe more so than its occupants.

On the way home it dawned on me that the crew had functioned perfectly during the time I was isolated—they could survive and continue without me. This is a terrible blow to one's ego, but it gave me a feeling of pride that these men knew their jobs and could perform them under any circumstances, with or without me.

What should have been a time of fear became a time of anger and sheer, cool determination to do the job and complete the mission. I had noticed many times that fear for some people sparked a very deliberate and deadly desire for survival. They functioned even beyond what was thought of as a brave or heroic capacity.

When we landed at the base the "specialty" radio operator had his equipment removed from our aircraft and never asked to go with us again. In fact, he never asked anyone else either. He decided flying was not his first desire and they could gather this information in some other way, such as automatic equipment which didn't require an operator.

For myself, I vowed never again to fly in the copilot's seat—that could be a dangerous place. From now on I would sit on the hallowed left side!

Then there still remained the matter of discipline for breaking the rule of profanity on the interphone. I thought about giving up the shot of whiskey which was provided each returning crew member just before interrogation. But that idea didn't sound too good—it should be a punishment more severe. So I decided to prudently ask for two shots and give up dessert at dinner that evening. I was sure the crew would understand and accept this as a reasonable sacrifice!

September 29, 1944

Have just finished logging fourteen hours of sack time and a couple hours of classes, so I'm back in pretty good humor.

I hardly know where to begin, but first I'll tell you more about my pass since that was the start of the non-letter days. We started out to go to Cambridge to look over the English colleges and universities. There are about twenty colleges there, I believe. We got our tickets, hopped on board a train and were to change trains in London. When we got there we loitered around the station for a while waiting for the other train to come in and who should show up but Geagan, remember him? He talked us into staying in London and spending our pass together. . . .

After we got back from our pass things were happening pretty fast so we got quite a little work out before we knew what was going on. When the rush was over and the smoke cleared we wound up with two missions. Now that we've had a good night's sleep everyone is happy and we're all sitting around catching up on back correspondence.

The pictures I promised you still haven't come back. The negatives were developed but there is a shortage of paper to print them on. We lost one complete roll due to the fact that the Limey filing system was screwed up. We may get them back but I doubt it. We returned the ones they gave us in place of ours. . . .

I'm not sure as yet but I'm becoming more convinced by the day that the thirty-one deal was pure rumor and pertained only to group leads. I was asked to become a group lead but I turned it down because I didn't want to break up the crew. Oh well, it was a good rumor anyway. Besides, when you have to do thirty-one, four more won't make any difference, I keep telling myself!

We will probably get a new airplane one of these days and get to name this one. Our good friend, Knock Out Baby *isn't with us any more.*

The radio is still working but I'm afraid we don't get to listen to any of the good radio programs. The German stations are so much more powerful than the English that they blanket the whole frequency band. Occasionally we get to hear an English station but the music they play isn't as good as the German. The Germans play most all of the hit tunes that were popular when I was home. We have a German condenser in the radio so we use that as the reason we can't get anything but German stations. . . .

On September 18 the 95th Bomb Group left on the third shuttle mission to Russia. This mission was called "Frantic Seven."

Our crew did not go because Doc had a wisdom tooth pulled and was DNIF (Duty Not Involving Flying). However, *Knock Out Baby* made the trip, and she was shot up on the ground at Poltava by the Luftwaffe during the night and could not return with the group.

September 29

Doc Doxon, Copilot

Rested today. Rumor has it I will get Layl's crew. Hate to think of leaving Fletcher's gang.

September 30

Doc Doxon, Copilot

Fletch checked out a new plane #7783. Guess it is my last flight with them—don't even want to tell them about it. They're sure a swell crew. They are going on Flak Pass.

October 2, 1944

This is a note to let you know that I'm at one of the rest homes for combat personnel. We were released to come down here a few days sooner than I had expected. A whole week with nothing to do but relax and enjoy life! So far today we've played tennis, badminton, ping pong, and walked all over town. The rest of the day will be spent taking a shower, eating dinner and hitting the sack. Fiess and Pipkin and their crews came down with us and we're all having a real time.

October 3, 1944

This morning was spent playing tennis—three solid hours of it. The afternoon was passed with several games of ping pong and then an afternoon matinee. The picture was The Song of Bernadette. *It was wonderful and I highly recommend it to be put on your "must see" list. To describe it would detract from the picture so I won't try.*

Doc didn't come to the rest home with us. We truly miss him. It looks as if he's going to get a crew of his own so he had to stay behind to look after his interests. His leaving the crew will be felt by all of us for he was a swell guy and a darn good copilot. I won't feel bad about it, though, because I told him in the beginning that if he had a chance to get ahead I wouldn't stand in his way, in fact, I would do all I could to help him. Like I say, I hate to lose him, but at the same time, it makes me feel good to think that he was picked for the job. Maybe the little things that I showed him and hollered at him about were okay after all. Incidentally, Joe got a very good job when he left the crew. We all did our best for him but, mainly, it was up to him. He was a darn good kid and I know now that I should never have let him go. But I guess we all make a few mistakes. . . .

Now let me tell you about a little incident that happened here today. We don't get very much fresh fruit so today as we were passing the grocery stores downtown we spotted some peaches, grapes, and a few scraggly looking apples. The peaches, though, were first-grade and really looked delicious. My mind was made up—I would have some peaches. Frank decided on the grapes. Fiess took a fancy to the apples. Now comes the part I don't expect you to believe. I bought $3.60 worth of peaches and ate all three of them myself. I'm not kidding or trying to exaggerate. The peaches cost me $1.20 apiece and that was the legitimate price. Frank paid eighteen shillings, or $3.60, for a pound of grapes so you know how many he got. Fiess got a bargain. He got four apples and a half pound of grapes for $4. As you can see, foodstuffs are not plentiful here and there is a slight trace of inflation. The average Englishman with wartime wages makes less than twenty dollars a week, so you can see how much fruit his family enjoys. . . .

October 4

Doc Doxon, Copilot

Fletch still on Flak Pass at Bournemouth. Our practice mission was called off so swung compass for him on his new aircraft, #7783. *Knock Out Baby*, #7257, came back from Russia today.

October 6, 1944

It is Friday so I'll pen my last letter to you from the rest home. We'll leave here early tomorrow morning. . . .

As you know we've been visiting the rest home on what is known as a "flak leave." Now we want to find out whether their sending us here was a matter of routine or whether they actually thought we were "flakky" enough to deserve it. Whichever the case, we've had a marvelous time and the rest has really been worthwhile. . . .

October 8, 1944

We got home late last night—didn't stay overnight in London as we had planned but came straight on home. The reason was that we were all anxious to get back and read the mail that had accumulated in our absence. And believe me, none of us were disappointed. Including today's mail I had sixteen letters! One was from my cousin in Italy that I wrote about. . . .

You know I told you about the Captain, who was one of my instructors in Ardmore, that came over here? He's now our Squadron Commander, and will probably be sporting shiny new oak leaves soon. That's good. We get along together swell so I'm glad he has the job.

Doc got his crew all right and they're flying together now. As yet I haven't been legally assigned a copilot, but the fellow I'll probably get is a swell fellow and was originally a first pilot. He has about the same number of missions that I have, so you can see that he's had plenty of experience and knows as much about his job as I do. So the crew hasn't suffered any by Doc's leaving except that we were good buddies.

There's a long story that goes with all this, but I can't tell you about it until I get home.

Braund has moved and the hut is a little dead with them not around. There are only about six of us old buddies left around—the rest have finished up. It's getting to the point where I hardly know anybody around the outfit anymore. Most everybody seems to know us and they refer to us as "Permanent Party"! . . .

Now about our quarters—there are two crews of officers to the hut and our enlisted men share a hut with two other crews. Since Braund has moved we have the whole place to ourselves. As for the hut itself, it was just a tin shed with a concrete floor when we moved in. But now with all the little things we've done it is fairly livable. We built shelves, got some linoleum for the floor, and fixed up all kinds of little things. It's just as comfortable as a barn can be made and we're quite proud of our shack, even if we are sharing it with a good-sized family of rats.

I'm trying to write with the hubbub of conversation going on and it was just mentioned that we have another Battle Star. I guess I have never mentioned them. It's this way—you know we are all entitled to the ETO ribbon. Well, we now wear four battle stars on it. To tell what the stars are for would involve military information so we won't go into that. In addition to this ribbon and stars plus the Air Medal and clusters, we also wear a Presidential Unit Citation ribbon plus a cluster. Every member of the crew has the same awards, which is as it should be—we're all in this together. Gosh, when we dress up we look just like a Gypsy wedding going some place to happen!

One of the fellows just came in and said we had to work tomorrow so I'll stop writing and start sacking it.

Battle Stars were awarded for participation in major battles or campaigns. Our crew participated in five major campaigns: Normandy, North France, Rhineland, Ardennes, Air Combat Balkans.

October 9, 1944

Have just finished with the day's work and feel in a retiring sort of mood but first will pen a few short lines. In the meantime, you can cross off number twenty-one—that's another we won't have to do again.

Bob Layl has been assigned as my new copilot and he flew with us today. He's a very good pilot and the fellows all like him so we'll get along swell. He was the fellow I was telling you about who used to be a first pilot. Personally I like him and like his flying technique so that's about all there is to say.

Mission #21, Mainz, Germany, October 9

Frank Dimit, Bombardier

Briefed at 9:00 a.m. for target at Mainz, Germany. Target was to be an ordnance depot if it was visual bombing, but it was PFF, so the "Mickey" tried to pick up the marshalling yards at Mainz. Don't know if we hit the target, it was a 10/10ths [total] undercast.

We led the low squadron of lead group of 13th combat wing. We were the last wing into Germany today. Carried 5 1000-pound G.P. bombs.

Fighter escort was good. Were supposed to have 3 groups of P-47s and one of P-38s. But didn't see any P-38s. Didn't see any flak in range. Saw about six bursts, 1,000 yards away. Were afraid we would be hit by fighters when we didn't see any flak, but they didn't show, thank goodness.

Would like to see several more missions like this one. . . . Doc was on the Leipzig trip last Saturday, his first mission as first pilot, when the group was hit by fighters. Was a rough go. Our group lost three planes, and the outfit flying the low group lost eight. They are definitely getting rougher.

The ship we took to Merseburg on our 20th mission is back on operations again. It has been out for ten days. The line chief says he never saw so many holes and so little blood.

This was our first mission without Doxon as copilot. He's got a crew of his own now. Our new copilot is Bob Layl. Fletch is well pleased with him. Seems like a good boy. He used to be a first pilot, but cracked up a ship. Doc has Layl's old crew.

We just got back from the flak shack, and are feeling in pretty good shape.

We fly again tomorrow. *[End of mission notes by Frank Dimit]*

October 9

Doc Doxon, Copilot

Fletch goes to Mainz—a milk run. Sure hate to see Fletch take off without me. He didn't even have 1 hole.

On September 9 Billy Bob Layl and crew took off on his tenth mission to Dusseldorf. Immediately upon becoming airborne they lost an engine. They left the area to let the rest of the group take off. When all of the takeoff activity was over with they came back to the base and attempted a three-engine landing with a full gas and bomb load, a procedure that was not unusual. During the flareout for landing another mechanical failure, real or imagined, was reported by a crew member. This caused Billy Bob to attempt a three-engine "go around." The attempt was unsuccessful because of the weight factor. The ship hit the runway with full power and the landing gear collapsed. The ship was completely destroyed, but the crew members walked away with only sprains and bruises. Thus Billy Bob became the victim of a system which required that the first pilot must accept full responsibility for everything that happens aboard his aircraft. He was removed from first pilot status and became our copilot.

October 10, 1944

I got up early this morning to work but for some reason didn't have to at the last minute. Instead, I spent practically the whole day flying around the countryside checking out an instructor, who used to be at Roswell when I was there, in the art of flying a lead squadron. Believe me I was in the height of my glory and I chewed on him just like he used to do on his students.

He's a good man, though, and realized that his students could teach him plenty about flying over here. We had a nice chat about life back in the good old days when we were in the States.

October 12, 1944

The events of the day were quite uninteresting. No practice—it was the real McCoy. So now chalk off number twenty-two as that's another one over. Things look brighter with the closing of each day.

Yes, our radio is working nicely these days, and it seems as if most of the music we hear are the tunes that were popular when I was home. We have some trouble picking up the good programs from the States because Jerry has a few stations with the same frequency and blocks them out. Give us a little time and we'll have Jerry blocked out in more ways than one.

Mission #22, Bremen, Germany, October 12

Frank Dimit, Bombardier

Briefed at 5:25 a.m. for a target at Bremen, Germany. Target was an aircraft components parts factory for FW-190s.

We flew the lead of the low squadron of the low group of our wing—really down in the cellar today. We carried 10 500-pound incendiary aimable clusters. Don't know how we hit today—cloud coverage of two to three tenths and a very effective smoke screen.

Escort was good. No enemy fighters and flak wasn't bad. There seemed to be a terrific barrage over the target. But when we got there, nobody was hit bad. The groups peeled off beautifully at the IP, and we hit the target at just the right intervals. Also think the chaff worked today. Anyhow, something had those flak gunners balled up. They didn't know where to shoot. But I'm not complaining—they can do that all the time.

With Fletch's O.K., Doc flew the lead of second element of our group today. That makes him 22 also. . . .

Heard that the missions have been lowered to thirty for all of us. I hope so. *[End of mission notes by Frank Dimit]*

Our twenty-second mission was to Bremen on October 12. The weather was good and we bombed visually. Our target was an aircraft factory that was also suspected of producing armored vehicles.

On this day the German Luftwaffe returned to the air in great numbers after a period of relatively little activity. Our gunners did not get a chance at the enemy fighters, nor did we receive their death-dealing massive attacks. Our escorting fighter squadrons gave us almost complete protection from the enemy guns.

When the dogfights in the sky were over our visual bombing showed good results. The cost to our task force was three bombers and six fighters, but eighteen enemy aircraft were shot down, with four being bagged by First Lieutenant Charles E. Yeager, a P-51 squadron leader from Hamlin, West Virginia. He was later credited with five to become an Ace in one day.

October 13, 1944

It's Friday the thirteenth and I've spent most of the day just puttering around the Squadron Area. Not that I'm superstitious, but just being cautious. With twenty-two missions chalked off I'm taking no chances at this stage of the game. It would have taken a whole company of MPs to have put me on board an airplane today!

Spent the whole afternoon cleaning up my end of the barracks, throwing away a lot of odds and ends that have collected and have my things ready to move. We're still staying in the squadron but tomorrow we move to a different barracks—just something to keep us from being contented. . . .

October 14, 1944

It's a beautiful Saturday night. The air is clear and crisp, thousands of little stars are winking at a great big red-faced moon. The wind is gently rustling through the branches of the trees breathing a sigh of contentment, and here I sit like a bottle of milk on somebody's front porch six thousand miles away from my loved ones, smoking my pipe and spinning idle dreams. . . .

October 15, 1944

. . . As of today we no longer have a radio. We gave it to Braund's boys. They had a stronger claim on it than we did, although the initial idea of obtaining it was ours. We're just about lost without it, but they were the same way so it's just rough on us. Maybe we can find another around someplace, but I rather doubt it because it took months to locate that one. Besides, we don't need a radio anyway—Frank can sing while Work whistles and I can M.C. the show! What we will miss will be the sultry voice of Axis Sally telling us what our wives and girlfriends are doing at home, and what the American fighting men are doing in England and over Germany. She can even tell us our losses by groups. The information is much too accurate to be all propaganda. She also dedicates certain songs to certain groups on certain occasions.

We haven't moved as yet but the papers have been served on us. We're waiting now for them to find us a shack to move into. Our minds are made up that we aren't going to like it wherever they put us be it shack or palace. Could be that we're getting slightly stubborn.

October 17, 1944

The events of yesterday were practically nil. We took a short hop during the afternoon over the wilds of England. Then last night when we should have been writing letters the crew got together for a little bull session which lasted way past our bed time. Today, however, was just a little different and you can now mark up number twenty-three. What a day! Remind me to tell you about it sometime when we have nothing else to do—by that time we'll probably be old folks and I'll have forgotten it, anyway.

There was no mail for me yesterday but did receive one from you today dated September 28th. It always happens—every time I work I get a letter from you. So the moral is if you want more letters you gotta do more work, and if you do more work the sooner you get home, and when you get home there's no need for letters. I have it all figured out and am turning into an eager beaver.

Mission #23, *Cologne, Germany, October 17*

Frank Dimit, Bombardier

Briefed at 3:20 a.m. for our target in Cologne—right in the middle of the Ruhr Valley. Target was a marshalling yard about a mile from the center of town.

It was a screwed up mission from the start with a night, overcast takeoff. We started out leading the high squadron of the low group of our wing. The 95th led the 3rd Division today and also the 8th A.F. Carried 34 100-pound G.P. bombs and 2 500-pound aimable cluster incendiaries.

Right after we departed on course the lead PFF Ship of our group aborted. We tried to re-form the group, take over the lead, and catch the lead and high groups of our wing. Our wingmen stuck with us but the rest of the group fell behind. We tried to catch our outfit and indicated 160–165 mph all the way, but no soap. Finally, we tacked onto the high squadron of another group (it turned out to be the 100th) at the IP and flew the 2nd element of the high squadron. Dropped our bombs and started back. Found out why the 100th loses so many planes. They damn near had a collision between two groups just after bombs away. Fletch had enough of that, and we tacked onto another group.

Shortly after that we found two more elements of our group wandering around over Germany so we picked them up and led them back home.

Enemy fighters—escorts good. Heavy flak barrage over target but not very accurate as far as we were concerned. Entire

8th A.F. hit the same target (PFF bombing through 10/10ths undercast) today. I think there were too many ships in the air for those flak gunners to shoot at. They must have been very sadly confused. Caught some very accurate flak over Koblenz coming out. But we didn't pick up one hole all day.

Maybe it was a good thing that our PFF lead had to abort. When we got back we learned that the other two groups had been badly shot up—our wing lost three ships. And neither of the groups had dropped their bombs. We were the only group to get rid of them.

Chalk up another one. *[End of mission notes by Frank Dimit]*

When making deep penetration into Germany we always flew north or south of the Ruhr Valley. The Ruhr Valley was truly Germany's industrial area—manufacturing and steel. It was an area to be avoided at all costs, unless the target was there. It was very heavily defended by anti-aircraft guns, many of which were mobile. If a target was known ahead of time more guns could be brought in. Consequently, our routes were altered. Additional turns and legs were added, not only to miss known anti-aircraft guns, but also to confuse the enemy, hoping that they might get their fighters airborne while we were flying a diversion leg.

German fighters were quite limited in their air time because of high fuel consumption—probably forty-five minutes to an hour at most—although they could refuel quickly and come back to hit other groups. They could fly much faster than the bombers, but the idea was to get them off the ground on a feint toward a target, then turn and head in a different direction, hoping they would expend a good part of their fuel before they could reach us. This could cut down the time they could actually spend fighting, but it also meant that we would spend more time over enemy territory, and be vulnerable for a longer period of time and from more places.

October 18, 1944

We had sort of a hard day today, which sends me to bed early. While I'm dreaming of you and little David you can cross off another one—number twenty-four is now behind us. Hope you don't mind these short notes but can't seem to do any better after a long day—know you understand.

Mission #24, *Kassel, Germany, October 18*

Frank Dimit, Bombardier

Briefed at 4:30 a.m. for target at Kassel, Germany. Target was an aero-engine factory about two miles south of town. The crew considered this a "grudge" target, because we figured we had a little score to settle with the flak gunners there, after the bad time they gave us when we were coming back from Merseburg alone on the 28th of July. So we went back today and took a few of our friends (the entire 3rd Division and part of the 1st). I don't think we made them very happy over in that part of Germany.

We flew lead of high squadron of low group of our wing. Carried 5 500-pound G.P. bombs and 5 500-pound aimable cluster incendiaries. Bombing was PFF.

Flak wasn't bad today. Used the new anti-radar equipment today for the first time—that may have been the reason. Escort was excellent and no enemy fighters seen.

Weather was our worst trouble today. Had to rendezvous at 24,000 feet this a.m. because of clouds. Then ran into the soup on the way back over France. Gave a bunch of Frenchmen the "willies," I imagine, because we were only about 500 feet off the ground. Thought for a while we were going to be weathered-in in France. Saw a little of France today when we were doing the buzzing. Gave us a chance to see the results of bombing at close range. Things have really been plastered over there. *[End of mission notes by Frank Dimit]*

We were inbound to the target at 25,000 feet and about thirty minutes from the Initial Point when I was alerted by the gunners that we had a strange B-17 flying along with us at nine o'clock—level and the same airspeed. This aircraft had come from behind us, and it was close enough that we could see that the gun stations were manned. They appeared to be watching us. I cautioned the gunners to watch this ship and move our guns so they could see that our guns also were manned. I could have saved my breath. These gunners were sharp and they watched that bird like a hawk trying to find out what he was up to. Immediately they flashed the "color of the day" with the Aldis lamp, but got no response.

After approximately five minutes the aircraft accelerated and I noticed that his trailing wire antenna was extended. The trailing wire antenna has a pear-shaped weight on the end and could extend out the back of the airplane a hundred feet or more. This would increase the range of transmission. In formation flying it was never extended because of the danger of someone flying into it. After the bomb run the task force commander used this system to relay to Eighth Air Force that a particular target had been bombed, and the time. The antenna was then retracted into the ship—this was its only use in formation. A ship returning home alone might use it, but the occasions would be limited.

After the aircraft accelerated he flew to the group ahead of us, but he still didn't join formation. He flew along for a while, then moved to another group. This seemed very strange to me. He obviously didn't have a bomb load because of the speed at which he could accelerate and move around from group to group. The group markings on the tail of the aircraft and the serial number appeared genuine, but it was not a group I was familiar with. Why would anybody leave the protection of a formation and go from one group to the other unless he was gathering data of heading, altitude, airspeed, and numbers, and passing it along to someone? It was a puzzle and the crew members kept watching and commenting on it.

I signaled the copilot to switch back to the interphone, and asked if he thought he could contact our fighter escort. He said that radio silence had already been broken—the leading groups had dropped and were heading home. It would be just a matter of calling and using the right call signs.

The fighters answered on the first call and we asked them to check out a suspicious-acting B-17. We gave the location, the group identification symbol, and the serial number. They replied that they would try to locate him.

We had now reached the Initial Point and the strange B-17 did not show any indication of going on the bomb run. After the bomb run when we were headed home, the fighters called and said they had located the B-17. His trailing wire antenna was still out. By now he was headed west and was still moving about the bomber stream. The guns were manned and were aimed at the "Little Friends" if they moved in too sharply. A friendly fighter would always fly parallel to you and slip over to you, keeping his nose away from you, and request identification. The gunners were apt to start shooting at any aircraft that came in nose first.

The fighters called again and said they could not make radio contact with the bird. But then, not all ships had fighter crystals so that didn't prove anything. This was our last wave of fighters for our unit and they were the ones to escort us home.

"What do you want us to do now?"

"We don't trust that airplane and we would like to see it cross the Channel."

"Roger, we have him in a box [a P-51 on each side and one behind]. Don't worry, he's going home or down—it's his choice."

"Roger, that's all we ask."

We never learned the ending to this aerial drama. But we do know that by this time the Germans had flyable B-17s pieced together from our many losses. It was later rumored that a German-manned B-17 landed in England. But this was only rumor. What happened to our bird was to remain a mystery to us. Only the Little Friends know the answer.

That mission saw another first for us. On October 9 we had been assigned a brand-new shiny airplane, a B-17G, every pilot's dream. After our second mission in her, while we were down on the line, the crew chief came to me and told me about a new device that had just come into the group. It was an electronic radar jamming device called "carpet." It consisted of a small black box and an antenna about eight inches long enclosed in a glass tube that would protrude through the underbelly of the ship. He said there was only one on the base, that he had access to it and could install it on the airplane for us if we would like it.

We asked him whether it was effective and he answered, "Who knows? It's an experimental device." He need say no more because in combat a man will clutch any straw that might provide hope, whether it be useful or not. The installation was completed in time for our mission on October 18.

Thus it was that *Lucky Sherry* was the first airplane in our group to be equipped with "carpet." I don't know whether it was ever installed on any other airplanes in the group, or whether it was really effective because, somehow, we still managed to attract enemy fire. But it was fun to see the expression on the faces of the other pilots and crewmen when we told them that our new aircraft had carpet installed. In fact, a few even went so far as to peek inside and comment on our color scheme. Who was kidding whom! But our presence was still tolerated and we were to be humored. After all, we had been around a long time. Maybe just too long.

October 19, 1944

While I said last night that I thought today would be one of rest, little did I realize that I would spend the whole day moving to another barracks. . . . It's just a little hut called the "Quacks' Shack," but room aplenty for four men, much warmer and more ideal than our old place. Things are still pretty much scattered around and there's a lot of work to be done, but when it's all over I'm sure we'll all be reasonably happy with our hut.

The mail situation is worse, that's for sure, because all the fellows have been commenting lately that their folks haven't heard from them for at least ten days or more. The situation probably won't improve because the boys on the Continent now have priority over us on the mail service, both coming and going. While our mail means everything in the world to us we also realize what it means to the boys in the foxholes on the front lines. That's the reason we've quit squawking when our mail is delayed. It used to be the mail came here and was then shipped over there. Now it all goes over there and ours comes back. This causes the incoming mail to be delayed, and also causes a transportation shortage on our outgoing mail.

Shortly after our twentieth mission we moved from Nissen hut #10 to the small Nissen hut which was our home for the rest of the time we were with the 412th. This was a little building that had formerly been occupied by the medics.

We spent considerable time fixing it up—building shelves, desks, etc. We even went so far as to acquire a portable wash basin which stood up on four legs. It would fold up like a camp stool that had a canvas seat. When you unfolded the legs you put the wash basin between the legs where the canvas top would be on a stool. Then the basin was held in place by installing two screws in the top. A drain at the bottom extended down only two or three inches from the bowl, but we had acquired some oxygen hose and some hose clamps so we made a drain. Then we cut a hole in the Nissen hut wall and shoved the hose outside. This was to be used only to wash your hands and face, or to shave. Since there was no heat whatsoever in the washrooms, shaving could be a rather cold event. So we were tickled to be able to heat a little water on top of our stove during the evenings when we were burning our coke rations—then we would use the hot water to shave.

When no one was looking we borrowed some aluminum and made some shelves plus some coat hangers so we could hang our clothes under these individual racks. We also cut into the wiring and ran a single wire down to each of the writing desks. You could have the individual light either over your desk or over your bed. The light was held in place in either position by hooking it to some wire we had attached to the building wall. All in all we were living, comparatively speaking, in the lap of luxury.

Most of the things we had came from salvage, but a few items couldn't be acquired from salvage so we just told people we'd like to have them and they'd turn their backs. This is how we got the oxygen hose to make the drain and a few other things.

Lo and behold, something was going to happen that hadn't happened before in all the time I had been on the base. We were going to have a stand-by inspection. The Group Commander would inspect the barracks of the 412th Squadron.

By this time Doc had his own crew, but he hadn't moved out of our barracks yet, so he was standing by with us. Each man was required to stand at the foot of his bed. There was a knock on the door. I opened the door, summoned the men to attention. The Group Commander, the Squadron Commander, and the First Sergeant entered. The First Sergeant was carrying a clipboard and paper, which in Cadets we called the "gig sheet." I don't know if they were actually going to give people demerits. Maybe they just wanted us to realize we were still in the Army.

The colonel became very interested in all the modifications he found in our room—the wires running to the individual lights, the wash basin, the shelves, the table desks, and all the other goodies. As he looked around the room it was hard to tell whether he was pleased or angry. Most colonels have a way of giving you a very noncommittal blank look. But he turned to me on his way out and said, "Lieutenant, I want the man who is responsible for the condition of this hut to report to my office within the hour."

"Well," I thought, "he obviously wants to know where we got all this stuff and by whose authority we had cut a hole in the building for the drain." The only thing I could visualize was that somebody had to be in trouble. It seemed to me that I was always before these people trying to explain our actions. Our encounters were always on a high plane, however, with mutual military respect. But I would not face them today. While I had contributed to the work, all the ideas were not necessarily mine. "So," I thought, "since most of these ideas were Doc's, if somebody is going to catch the devil for it, it might as well be him."

After the entourage had gone I told Doc, "You heard the order. You'll be the one to present yourself to the colonel's office." And Doc, with his usual big grin, said, "Fine. I'll go up and see what's on his mind." "Incidentally," I added, "you might prepare yourself for a good chewing out because many of the things we have in here are not necessarily contraband, but they haven't been assigned to us either."

He made his call on the colonel. When he came back to the barracks we were all anxiously waiting to hear what his reception was like and how long did we have to return these items—with good luck maybe the usual twenty-four hours. When he came in the door he still had a big grin on his face, but he didn't say anything. So I said, "Okay Doc, tell us about your experience." And he answered, "Well, frankly, the colonel had nothing but praise for our barracks and our ingenuity. The reason he wanted the man who was responsible for it was so he could congratulate him and have him make the same modifications in his living quarters."

The one time I could have been praised I turned it down. Anyway, we all wished Doc well on his new enterprise. None of us had courage enough to help him out, but as I understand it, he did a good job and now the colonel was able to have the same amenities that the former crew of *Knock Out Baby* were enjoying.

October 20, 1944

. . . *Our new copilot moved in with us today so now the four of us are all together. Brown and the rest of the boys pitched in both days and gave us a hand on the moving and building. A better bunch of fellows couldn't be found. As long as we've been together I've never heard one of them give the other a harsh word. I was certainly lucky when they passed out the fellows to make the crew.*

October 22, 1944

. . . *Didn't write yesterday—instead we held a big celebration for the crew in our new hut. In the morning they gave us a pass but our financial status was too low to take advantage of it, so we're spending it here on the post. We had some very good reasons for the celebration. First, we were on pass; Doc, Work, and Dimit made 1st lieutenants; it was my birthday #23 (and can you imagine being called "The Old Man"!); and with the new hut we had to have a housewarming. So we took care of all those things last evening.*

I'm anxiously awaiting a letter telling me all about your little trip to Dayton—who you saw—and what all you did. Hope you got to go to Walla Walla and up to the college. I don't imagine there are too many kids there now that we know, but hope you were able to see some. Would sure like to see the old campus on a clear, crisp fall night, see the big moon, and hear the clock strike twelve.

October 23, 1944

. . . We're really an antagonistic bunch tonight. We've been reading about the strikes in a few of the aircraft factories. Our thoughts and words, as you can guess, are not fit to write. How some people can quibble over a few dollars in times like these beats me. I only wish each and every one of them could be with us for a little while. I believe they would be content to go back and do a better job than they have ever done. But some people will cut off their nose to spite their face regardless. They have a point, though—the cost of living is high; it's pretty high here too, only we don't measure it in dollars and cents!

October 24, 1944

The fellows are always asking about you and David—wondering how you are getting along, and I sure puff up when I tell them how big he is. George is next to be a papa, the date sometime the first of January. Then Brown with the fifteenth of January. I sure give them a hard time with mine all over and a great big husky boy to brag about. They get quite a kick out of it, though, and know I'm only kidding. I have to get those guys home in time for the big event, that's for sure. It looks bad in a way but I think I can do it. I know what it's like to be away from your wife when that time comes and sure don't want it to happen to them. I may fail them, but if I do no one will feel any worse about it than myself. . . .

October 25, 1944

Here's some good news for you. You can mark up number twenty-five as water under the bridge. Things look better each day and with good weather I should be able to turn in some pretty good work for a while. I'm going to turn in for the sandman has me in his clutches.

Mission #25, *Hamburg, Germany, October 25*

Frank Dimit, Bombardier

Briefed at 6:30 a.m. for a target at Hamburg, Germany. Target was an oil refinery.

Flew lead of high squadron of high group. Carried 19 250-pound G.P. bombs. Bombing was PFF, but think we hit something. Two big clouds of black smoke were boiling up through the undercast when we left the target area. Entire 3rd Division hit the target and part of the 1st Division.

Was a little doubtful whether this anti-radar equipment was really working until today. When we hit Hamburg the last time, the group was shot to hell. Today we didn't have a feathered prop in the outfit. The outfit ahead of us really caught hell today, but when we hit the target, those flak gunners didn't have any idea where we were. They were just throwing it up and hoping to hit something. We came back without a hole.

Good fighter cover—no enemy fighters.

From now on we'll be working on Doolittle's missions. [Reference to extension of the missions from twenty-five to thirty to thirty-five.]

The PFF lead of our group aborted as soon as the bombs were dropped and we brought the group back. *[End of mission notes by Frank Dimit]*

October 26, 1944

I thought I was tired when I sent you that short note last night, but this evening I'm doubly so. I'll hit the sack in a very few minutes, but first just a few lines to let you know you can get out the pencil and chalk up another one. Number twenty-six is over!

Mission #26, *Hanover, Germany, October 26*

Frank Dimit, Bombardier

Briefed at 7:15 a.m. for our target at Misburg, Germany. It's a suburb of Hanover—one mile east of Hanover itself.

Target was an oil refinery if it was visual, but bombing was PFF, so the aiming point was the marshalling yards in Hanover.

Flew lead of the high squadron of lead group of our wing. Carried 20 250-pound G.P. bombs.

Target area had 150 guns, but the carpet and chaff were working and we brought our ship home without a hole again. Very little damage done to the group. Good escort and no enemy fighters.

Weather was our worst enemy today. That and prop wash. We followed an outfit (the 390th) into the target pretty close and some of the boys had a rough time. Had a bad time getting into the base. We went up and down through an overcast. The visibility was so poor after we got down through the clouds we could not find the field or anything else. And to top it off, the RAF and our Little Friends were in the area. We were damn near run over several times. But we got back. *[End of mission notes by Frank Dimit]*

October 28

Doc Doxon, Copilot

Group went on a mission. Fletch and I both stayed home. Gordon Braund had a wing fire and Futoma, his ball turret gunner, bailed out over Germany.

Periodically we had a pilot's meeting. During these sessions we discussed everyone's gripes and suggestions that would make us a better fighting force. This included all things from rendezvous, execution of the mission, to conclusion.

One thing that bothered our crew was the fact that many times we observed other aircraft in our formation with gun positions which were not manned. At these meetings we were informed that these guns were inoperable and they didn't feel it necessary to have a gunner in these cramped, cold positions when they were powerless to react to enemy action.

It was always my contention that these people were the eyes for all of the formation, and at least they could look and give information to the unit, whether it be enemy action or a mechanical emergency. If the guns were moving, even though unfirable, they still represented a deterrent.

These repeated violations were my pet peeve. My views were always reinforced and upheld by our squadron and group people, but I don't think I won any friends among the other pilots, who by now I thought were getting a little careless.

It wasn't too long before the wisdom of my contention was borne out as the enemy introduced airborne rockets into the fray. These rockets were fired from just outside the range of our fifty-caliber machine guns—they were crude but deadly. In the initial point of their flight they were quite slow and their trajectory somewhat erratic. But a watchful gunner could spot the release of the rocket and determine its flight accurately enough to have the pilot move the plane slightly up or down to avoid being hit.

From this point on it was no problem keeping the gunners

in their positions for it was now proven that a warning given in time could save their own lives. A better incentive would never be found!

October 29, 1944

Today being Sunday we got up and went to church as usual. Then this afternoon we ground swung the compass on our airplane. After that we just fiddled around, going over the ship fixing any little thing we found wrong, and in general, giving it a good once over. Incidentally, the airplane wasn't named Knock Out Baby. *Instead it was called* Lucky Sherry *and a picture is now in the process of being painted on the side which is quite apropos to the title. When the job is complete I will send you a picture of it and let you pass judgment. . . .*

October 30, 1944

Put in a good day's work today and it may turn out even better than I think. Destination Tokyo *was playing at the picture house so after supper I went up to see it. We saw it together, I believe, in Salt Lake City, but I enjoyed it again.*

Mission #27, Merseburg, Germany, October 30

Frank Dimit, Bombardier

Briefed at 6:15 a.m. for our old friend (?) Merseburg. Same oil refinery that we have been trying to knock out for so long. This was our fourth attempt at this target.

Didn't climb through any overcast during assembly for a change. But we ran into weather over the continent and we had to turn back. It was the same kind of soup we ran into on the way to Berlin. It was high cirrus above 20,000 feet. We got a little east of the Zuider Zee in Holland before the entire division turned around. And I was mighty glad to see them do that 180.

Found out later that Jerry fighters had already formed and were waiting for us. The radio man that monitors German frequencies could hear the ground stations giving the German fighters bearings on us. We were mighty lucky.

Were flying lead of high squadron of lead group. We were to be the last ones over the target. Carried 20 250-pound bombs and brought them back. Expected bombing to be PFF.

Don't know for sure if we get credit for this one. Sure hope so. *[End of mission notes by Frank Dimit]*

October 31, 1944

Here it is Halloween with no outhouses to push over and no pumpkins to make jack-o-lanterns. It would be a perfect night for fun-raising because it's just as black as coal outside.

It was also payday today and I collected my usual sum of twelve pounds. I paid back the four I had borrowed so I'm in pretty fair shape to start out the month. This should be a big month coming up and I don't figure on having too much time off to spend a few pounds.

Now I have some good news. Yesterday's work lived up to my best hopes so you can chalk up another one—make this number twenty-seven. Thought I was going to get another today but it didn't work out, which is very good. There are times to go and times not to go—this was definitely the latter!

October 31

Frank Dimit, Bombardier

Just got the good news we received credit for yesterday's mission.

Briefed this a.m. for the target at Politz, Germany, near Stettin. Target was oil refinery. 320 flak guns in target area. Last time the group hit it they lost 5 planes.

Mission scrubbed before we took off. Thank God.

November 1, 1944

. . . *It's beginning to get hard to write letters for I don't know what's
going on. I've had one letter in the last eight or nine days—drew a
blank again today—haven't heard from anyone. Could be that I've got
combatitis as the patience is worn kind of thin at times and I get rather
irritable over things here. The cigarettes go by the pack and nothing
seems to satisfy. Worries pop up everywhere about nothing. Well, it'll
all be over soon. Then I can sit down and figure everything out and
forget about it. This last part is the worst when so much hangs on so
little!*

November 2, 1944

*This is just a short note to let you know that I'm in a much better mood
this evening and am sorry for the bad humor last night. Could be that
I was sweating out a rough one. Anyway, it's all over with and I feel
like a new man. By the way, get out the pencil and mark up another
one—number twenty-eight is over!*

*Your letter of October 23rd was waiting for me when I finished. Was
glad to hear you enjoyed your visit to Dayton—only wish I could have
been there with you.*

Mission #28, *Merseburg, Germany, November 2*

Frank Dimit, Bombardier

Briefed at 5:15 a.m. for the same damn target—Merseburg.
We're getting mighty tired of this target. It was the same oil
refinery (Leuna) as always.

The 3rd Division and part of the 1st hit the same target. We
were the fifth outfit over the target. We led the 13th Combat
Wing. We were flying lead of high squadron of high group.
Carried 10 500-pound G.P. bombs. Bombing was PFF and
from 29,000 feet. But we weren't half high enough.

Flak was the worst I have ever seen. Saw more flak today
than on any other two missions. It was terrific. But thank

goodness for that carpet. The anti-radar equipment is definitely working. Flak was strictly barrage today and certainly not up to the true Merseburg accuracy. Battle damage was very slight compared to the last raid there. We came back with one small hole in the trailing edge of left wing. The group lost one plane. The Jerries were waiting for us with railroad guns and they threw up everything they had. It was terrible.

We expected to be hit by fighters, but we weren't. Some of the outfits were hit that went over the target after us. Our escort was excellent—never better. We even had a group of P-51s and P-38s from the 9th A.F. They were all over the sky.

One more for us. Not many more to go, I hope. *[End of mission notes by Frank Dimit]*

Forty heavy bombers were lost on this day, but the Eighth Air Force shot down a total of 130 enemy aircraft. This broke the record that was set back on September 11 when we went to Ruhland, a mission that cost us forty-four heavy bombers in exchange for 116 enemy fighters. Another twenty-five Nazi planes were destroyed on the ground.

The Mustang squadron led by Major George E. Preddy of Greensboro, North Carolina, who at this point was the top active Eighth fighter pilot in the ETO, shot down twenty-four Nazi craft to cop this day's squadron honors.

The 55th Fighter Group, a P-51 outfit, led by Major Eugene E. Ryan of Darien, Connecticut, tangled with over seventy-five single-engine Jerries which were "ganging up" on one bomber force over Merseburg. They claimed nineteen enemy planes shot down for the loss of one Mustang.

The heavies' gunners reported getting their share of additional "kills," shooting down fifty-three.

November 3, 1944

Had an easy day with nothing to do and that's exactly what I did—absolutely nothing. Got a haircut this morning and spent the rest of the day playing cards, reading, and participating in a bull session. The day of rest was welcomed, though, because yesterday's work really tired us out. It was a long, hard day. . . .

Doc got an airplane of his own awhile back and he has named it Kimmie Kar *after his daughter as her nickname is Kim. I'll send you a picture of it—it's very cute. . . .*

November 5, 1944

The mailman was good to me today for your letters written the 23rd and 24th and one from the folks were waiting for me when I finished work. Will answer your letter tomorrow, but in the meantime, you can chalk up another one—number twenty-nine is now in the list of has-beens. Nothing like making hay while the sun shines. Will enclose a few more negatives tonight and will continue to do so until you get them all.

Mission #29, Ludwigshafen, Germany, November 5

Frank Dimit, Bombardier

Briefed at 5:00 a.m. for a target that was northeast of Metz, France, and east of Thionville. Target was a German fort that has been giving our ground forces in that sector some trouble the last few weeks. The entire 3rd Division was hitting four fortifications in that area. But we had a 10/10ths undercast, so we had to go on to the secondary.

Secondary was at Ludwigshafen, across the river from Mannheim. Nobody knows what the target was. New buildings had shown up on some PRU [photo reconnaissance] photos. So somebody said let's blast them out of existence. That's what we did.

Briefed for 280 guns at Ludwigshafen and they have every one of them there. Bombing was visual through a smoke screen, so carpet didn't work so good. We had some of the closest flak today that we've had since our 20th mission. Picked up 10 or 12 holes—hardly bother to count any more.

Flew lead of high squadron of lead group of second wing

over target. The 100th led the Division today. Carried 6 1,000-pound G.P. bombs. Didn't see the results of our bombing, but we hit in the target area.

Had first serious damage to our new plane today. Some of the holes caused a wing change. One piece of flak hit the main spar of left wing. Piece of flak came in the left side of waist and went through ammo box of right gun. It hit a cap on one of the cartridges and it exploded. Tore up the case and projectile went out the right side of the waist. Bob Lynch has cases as a souvenir.

Enemy fighters—Bob Work saw a German jet-propelled job. Escort was good.

Had a helluva time getting into field tonight. Don't see how one country could have so much bad weather. They didn't expect us back tonight, thought we would be "weathered-in" in France when we left this a.m. But we beat the cold front back to the base. Damn near got killed in the traffic pattern several times. Getting so the weather we fly in is worse than the actual mission.

Not many more to go. Expect a pass soon. *[End of mission notes by Frank Dimit]*

We had just released our bombs at 27,000 feet but had not had time to close the bomb-bay doors. The formation had loosened up and was making the turn to the Rally Point when there was a tremendous explosion at the top of the bomb bay and then another off the left wing. The acrid stench of burning powder and smoke permeated the ship immediately. A shell had come up through the open, empty bomb bay and had exploded on contact as it was exiting through the top of the fuselage. Fortunately most of the force of the explosion was diverted upward. But in this instant the plane nosed over into a vertical dive. In an attempt to correct the nosing over I pulled back on the control column. The column came right back into my stomach—the elevator controls were gone and the aircraft was out of control. It was a time when you wanted to be on good terms with your Creator.

I called for the copilot to engage the autopilot, but it wasn't necessary for his hand had already reached the master bar which controlled all systems relating to elevators, ailerons, and rudders. As he engaged the master bar it was apparent that everyone on board had reached the same conclusion—short of a miracle we had had our last ride. In a few seconds, ever so slowly, the nose of the aircraft began its return to normal flight.

Our miracle came in the design of the aircraft. The manual control cables were mounted near the ceiling and the elevator control cables were completely cut in half. The electrical cables that supplied energy to the servo motors, which were located at each of the control surfaces, were positioned on each side of the ship in the walls at the bottom. This dispersion of the two systems saved the day for us. The backup system, which in our case was the AFCE (autopilot), now allowed us to control the aircraft.

Since we were flying the lead of the high squadron we were still able to maintain our position, albeit not with perfection, as our wingmen were working hard to stay in formation with us for maximum protection. We would be fine as long as we were airborne, but it would not be possible to land on autopilot. The manual controls would have to be fixed or else after bringing our squadron home to the base we would head the airplane back toward the Channel and bail out while still over land.

With all these things going through my mind, only a few minutes had elapsed when I was informed by the waist gunner that his ammo box had been hit by a piece of flak and several 50 caliber shells had exploded in the box, creating a weird fireworks display in his position. He had not been hit but I'm sure he had plenty of cause to worry about his life expectancy in all the excitement.

Immediately I called the engineer and asked if he thought it would be possible in some way to splice the cables together—although I had no idea of what he would use to do the job. He said it not only was possible but he was already working on it in conjunction with the radio operator. Everything he needed —cable, cable clamps, and a few tools—was in his emergency kit. All he would need was time, because at each movement of the control surface the broken cable ends would jerk fore and aft. It would not be easy, but he could do the job.

I had seen him carry his "goodie bag" aboard at every mission and it appeared to be a little heavier each time we flew as the ground crew cooperated and kept supplying him with more gear.

Long before the Channel was in sight I received a call that the cables had been reconnected, but they would not have the same tension as they would have had if the job had been performed on the ground with the proper instruments. No mind —let's unhook the autopilot and see what kind of control we have. It was sloppy, but we could control the aircraft and I felt comfortable that we could land it when we reached the base. The landing was sloppy, but the empty B-17 was a very forgiving aircraft.

We had a crew that had experienced some very terrifying moments, and knew it is of fear that heroes are born. But we also had an engineer who could take pride in the knowledge that he had saved an aircraft from certain destruction.

November 6, 1944

. . . There was no mail for me today so I'll read yesterday's letter again. . . . Even when your letters are behind schedule it is a small matter. The thing that counts is getting a letter. I live for the letters and the date makes little difference. Reading your letters is just like talking to you, and, believe me, I need those talks. They give me strength and courage where everything else fails. They keep my thinking straight and jar me back into reality when I get off on a tangent. . . .

November 7, 1944

I fixed the boys up last night so they could go on pass this morning. Much to my surprise only two of them left the post. The other fellows decided to spend their pass on the base too when they found out I wasn't going anyplace. We'll just spend the time chewing the fat, play-

ing some pinochle, and reading a few magazines which we've been lucky to get ahold of. . . .

Tonight is the night that the election returns come in. The election is kind of a minor thing over here. There are too many more issues of greater importance—I'm sure you know what I mean. I don't think the outcome of the election will have much to do with the outcome of the war. The main idea is to get the war over with. Then we'll argue over other things—one thing at a time is enough. I frankly hope Roosevelt beats Dewey by a wide majority, but that's only personally, of course. I have never liked Dewey or his campaign. He hasn't near the experience with foreign affairs, personalities, and policies as does Roosevelt, and we are definitely going to need a continuance of cooperation between nations when this is over. But that is not for me to say. Besides even Hitler wears a mustache.

November 8, 1944

. . . I'm glad to hear that you and Velda [Redfern, a Tekoa friend] enjoy each other's company so much. Friendship is a wonderful thing to pass the time and ease the moments of loneliness which pop up. It gives you someone to talk to who has the same problems you have.

Now we come to the favor you asked of me—"please don't ever change." I will admit that in some ways I have changed. First, my outlook on life has changed greatly due only to circumstances here. This is probably a temporary change only. We have to take into consideration that our life and our purpose here is different from anything we have ever experienced, so naturally our views are changed to meet the need of this existence, just as furniture is moved about the house. Never fear. The basic structure does not change a bit.

Your friends who are having difficulties are probably too weak to face the facts, or maybe they made a mistake in the first place. They quite possibly may have never had a deep understanding of one another, or a mutual love strong enough to carry them over long periods of separation. It isn't real love if it won't stand up under the test. You are the ray of sunshine in my life. It's you who gives me the courage and the determination to keep going. The thought of my little family at home waiting for me leaves me with a burning desire to keep going and not stop until we're together again.

Have I changed? Does that sound like a man who has lost everything that was dear to him and would return to his wife a total stranger, bearing only the physical looks of the man she had bid goodbye? I think not. Rest assured that I will come back just as I was when I left with the exception of a gray hair or two and a few minor things. Perhaps my letters have sounded to you as if I might be changing—I hope not. Before judging them too harshly remember that they are written in a world of nervous tension and sometimes the pen does not put the real meaning across the page.

I don't know whether I can keep our date by Christmas or not. I'll do my best, but if I fail it'll only be by a week or two. This evening brought our pass to an end so now we're back at the old grind of sweating the war again. We've been reading the election returns in the daily Stars and Stripes. *The election went as many of us thought it would, so it caused very little concern over here. Of course all the papers carried huge headlines, but other than that, there was no display. Could be that there are other things more important which occupy our minds.*

Now to tell you more about Billy Bob, our copilot. He is from Piggott, Arkansas, a very likable sort of person with a remarkable sense of humor. He isn't married and claims he has given up all hope, but judging from his correspondence, I would say he's still trying to make them all happy instead of concentrating a maximum effort on one. He's twenty-two years old and reminds me very much of my cousin, Hallie. He gets along very well with the rest of the fellows and they're quite attached to him, so everything is running smoothly and there is no lack of cooperation. In the negatives I sent were several pictures of him. Just look for the strange officer in our midst and you have him spotted. . . .

November 11, 1944

This is just a short note to let you know that everything goes well with me. It's past my sack time, that's my apology for the short letter. But wanted to let you know that you can now chalk up number thirty—it has come and gone.

Again the postman forgot to bring me any letters, but he compensated somewhat by bringing me a Christmas package from Cap and

Sis. It was a very nice package full of the little things we can't get here. You can imagine how it was appreciated.

Mission #30, *Koblenz, Germany, November 11*

Frank Dimit, Bombardier

Briefed at 5:45 a.m. for our target at a point about three miles south of Koblenz, Germany. It was a marshalling yard.

We used the new Micro-H [an improved radar bombing system supposedly better than H2X which we had been using] to bomb with today, and it looks as if we might have done some good. Bob Work got G-fixes all the way. At "bombs away" he got a fix that put us just short of the target.

Flew lead of high squadron of high group of our wing. Carried 12 500-pound G.P. bombs. Complete undercast—didn't see bombs hit.

Flak was light and inaccurate. No fighters seen. Close fighter escort. This could very easily be termed a "milk run" and hope we have two or three more just like it. Didn't pick up any holes.

Climbed through the usual overcast this a.m., but we had good weather when we got back to the base.

Our target was to be Politz today, but it was changed just before briefing. Thank goodness. Politz is going to come up one day, and I hope we're not on it. *[End of mission account by Frank Dimit]*

It was 7 in the morning and the crew was still sound asleep. We had finished a long, arduous, nerve-wracking mission the day before. Everyone was completely pooped out and had no intentions of getting up until 11, this being in plenty of time to reach the mess hall at 11:30 for dinner.

But here I was being shaken by the shoulder, and a voice was saying, "Fletch, wake up!" I opened my eyes to see my grinning ex-copilot standing over my bunk. "Why should I?" I asked. "Hey, I've got a big deal for us." "Go away," I said.

"We're all dead tired—we had a long, hard day yesterday."
"Ah, but today will make up for yesterday and give you a new
lease on life—no shooting, just a nice flight with lots of pleasant female company."

"What are you talking about?" I queried. "Well, this big war
bond drive that they're having on the base . . ." "Yeah," I
interrupted, "I heard about it. I know fighting a war isn't
enough now. They want us to buy bonds so we can pay for our
own airplanes."

"Naw, you've got it all wrong. They're bringing in a USO
troop or something for a big performance called *Petticoats* to
kick off the drive. They need two airplanes to fly down to one
of the bases near London and bring the troupe up for the
show. I told the squadron commander that you and I would
fly the airplanes down and bring them back. How about it?
Let's go!"

"Everyone around here is dragging. I don't think the boys
will want to fly." At this Work rolled over and mumbled,
"Count me out. I'm not going anywhere except back to sleep."
"Well, that ends that," I said. "I don't want to fly without a
navigator."

"Mine is flying," Doc countered, "so all you have to do is
take off, climb up on my wing and fly formation to the base."

At this Billy Bob roused up and said, "It sounds like fun." I
countered with, "We still don't know whether the radio operator or the engineer want to fly. They may have other plans—
like sleeping." "You guys get dressed and I'll go down to see
them," Doc said. "But hurry up because I have a truck and
driver standing by to take us out to the airplanes."

In a few minutes Doc reported, "Yeah, they will go, but they
weren't overjoyed. I promised them that you would let them
adjust the parachute harness for the girls and instruct them in
the use of the parachutes. That seemed to sell the deal."

With this we went out to the truck to await Brownie and
Hinman. Doc's skeleton crew was already on the truck.

The weather was typical for England—a real gray day, slight
mist, ceiling about 800 or 900 feet, visibility in the vicinity of
one mile.

Upon reaching the airplanes we made a hurried ground

check. With everything in order, and a lot of extra parachutes and harnesses in the waist position, we fired up the engines. When the last one sputtered to life Doc came taxiing by on the perimeter track. We fell in behind and taxied out to the runway. After the engine check Doc headed down the runway. We gave him a twenty-second head start and took off after him. As he headed back over the field we swung into position on his right wing and headed southwest at about 700 feet in poor visibility.

Billy Bob unfolded his map and asked the name of the base that was our destination. I had to confess that I didn't know. Doc hadn't said, so we would just have to stay on his wing until he landed. The weather didn't improve any and we would be right on top of an airfield by the time we could see it.

Finally after an hour and a half in the air, in which we seemed to be flying in circles since I had seen the same smokestack go by on three occasions, I asked Billy Bob to call Doc and see if he had a problem. He reported that they had been disoriented, but the navigator had the Gee Box working and now had a fix. In a few minutes we would be flying down the runway where we would peel off for a landing. This was good news because everyone was tired and grouchy—this was supposed to be a twenty-minute flight.

We finally settled down on a nice air base, not your usual bomber base with everything dispersed. We taxied up to Base Operations and cut the engines. I could hear Billy Bob, Brownie, and Hinman saying, "Bring on the girls!" as they were busy unloading the parachutes and harnesses in neat piles near the tail of the aircraft.

I thought, "Well, at least they will enjoy the flight back. This will compensate for dragging them out of bed when they were bushed."

Doc had already gone into Base Ops and I explained to Brownie if he happened to find a good-looking blonde it would be all right to put her in the engineer's seat between the pilots, because we would probably be crowded for space and I knew he would rather spend his time making everyone comfortable.

About this time I heard Billy Bob's slow Southern drawl

muttering something about Doc's ancestors—maybe there was something wrong. I turned around to see what appeared to be an endless line of GIs filing out the Operations door and lining up beside the two aircraft. There had to be a mistake!

Then Doc announced, "These GIs are members of the Thirteenth Service Company and they will be performing in the show *Petticoats* to kick off the Eighth Air Force War Bond Drive at the 95th. I'll take half, and Fletch, you get the rest."

I turned to Brownie and said, "Prepare the troops for boarding and if you need me I'll be up in the pilot's seat going through the checklist." I heard him say, "Men, this is a parachute harness and this is a parachute. Grab one of each and get on board. Don't worry about how to use it because we won't be above the tree tops anyway. Just hurry it up because the taxi driver is ready to head for home."

In about two minutes Brownie called on the interphone and said, "The troops are loaded, the hatches secure, ready to start engines." I gave Billy Bob the signal, he started winding them up, and we went taxiing toward the runway. Just as we lifted off Billy Bob reported that Doc wanted to know if we were going to circle the field until he could get off. "Tell him that we know a shortcut home, a single heading with no turns, and we will be there in thirty minutes. He can follow us if he can catch us. If not, he can fly in circles with his navigator." Billy Bob said, "Sounds good to me. I think we have been had. But by whom, Doc or the Squadron Commander?"

"I can assure you there is only one culprit and he is on our tail right now laughing away."

Hinman requested permission to go back and man the tail guns, but I suggested that he had better wait until we were on a regular combat mission. We would have a better excuse and not so many personnel would be involved.

As it turned out the show was pretty good—but I didn't buy any war bonds. My wife was already doing that at home.

November 13, 1944

*Thanks to Roco we attended church at ten yesterday as we do almost
every Sunday. Apparently he has more faith in Divine Guidance than
he does in his pilot! That boy likes to cover all bases, and we'll take help
wherever we can get it. It's a good insurance policy for all of us. . . .*

November 19, 1944

*I have neglected to write you for the past four days as I have been on
pass. As you can guess I didn't spend this one on the post. We went into
London again so we could sleep in a good bed with clean sheets and
have breakfast in the sack. The change was welcome. I didn't really
want this pass because it only slows me down, but I didn't have any
choice in the matter. When the Big Boys say you need a rest that's the
final word and no amount of argument will change their judgment.
The weather has been too bad for very much work lately. . . .*

*I'm in a good mood because when I got home there were three letters
from you. The box of Christmas cookies arrived and they came through
without a one being broken, not even the ones with David's footprints,
and just as fresh as if they had been baked yesterday. Boy, are they
good! We're all convinced that the design of trees and stars also add to
their flavor. Packing them in popcorn was a good idea. The fellows
join with me in thanking you for them, all hoping there are more
packages just like this on the way.*

*We got up early this morning in order to work, but nothing came of
it so we stayed up and went to church. Finished dinner just a few
minutes ago and am writing this while waiting for mail call. Now to
get back to answer a few of your questions. Yes, the picture is of a
Russian pin-up girl. Boy, those guys sure have a lot to go home to,
and I do mean a lot! I'm afraid I don't envy them in the least. The
reason I sent the picture home was because it gave me the jitters and
was shaking my faith in feminine delicateness. The soldiers were of the
same descent and are my prize pictures. . . .*

*Now then to answer your question about the missions. Yes, I've had
my share of the rough ones and also I've had my share of the easy ones.
There's no reason for me to believe that I won't have more of both.
Don't worry, though, we'll do all right. I much prefer not to write*

*about them, but will give you the highlights when we're together again.
I know some fellows do write home their experiences, but somehow, I
just don't see it that way. . . .*

*So our little man has already laughed out loud. He's learning fast.
Doggone, I sure would like to be home to see all these little things as
they happen, but I guess there will be plenty more when my time comes.*

November 22, 1944

*I have certainly been slipping on my letter writing. You no doubt are
wondering why. Each day I have started a letter to you, but somehow
they don't get finished and eventually wind up in the stove. I wish I
could explain it, but I can't understand it myself. When things are
going good and I have plenty of work to do and my mind is occupied
it's very easy to write. But when things aren't going so well, there's
nothing to do, and you can't do anything about it, that's when you get
so disgusted you can't write a decent letter. Things have been pretty
discouraging of late—maybe I had too many eggs in one basket. I'm
not complaining, but trying to give an explanation for my laxity in
letter writing.*

*When we lie around the war on nerves starts and fighting that is
worse than any job we've been called on to do. You get that started,
then get a few setbacks, and it leaves you pretty low. I've been fighting
a battle of time lately. At times everything looks pretty rosy like I might
come out on top. Then the picture changes—I start lying around, get
behind schedule, and realize I can't possibly win. I won't give up,
though. As long as there's a day left I'll keep trying, but, believe me, it's
discouraging. I can hardly bring myself to write when I haven't some
good news for you or am in a bad humor. I know how much you had
planned on my being home for Christmas and I realize how much I
had counted on being there. But, at the present, it looks as if that's one
dream that won't come true. I'm pretty morbid about the whole affair so
let's change the subject, besides, to explain it would involve a certain
amount of military information. . . .*

In the course of our thirty-five combat missions we received
three direct hits from German flak guns. One exploded while

exiting the top of the open bomb bay. Another was in the right wing, narrowly missing a fuel tank, but severing a part of the main spar. This one should have blown the wing off in a terrible explosion of fire, eliminating another bomber crew and making way for a new replacement crew in the barracks. But that did not happen. The shell entered the bottom of the wing and exited the top, leaving a jagged, ragged, expanded top edge surrounding a near-perfect round hole. The shell was a dud. We were very lucky and hoped that the Germans would not improve their quality control.

The third one came through the waist compartment—it also did not explode. Many other crews reported the same experience—a direct hit and no explosion. Was it just the nature of German mass production that so many shells were defective? Divine deliverance? Sloppy production? Who knows?

After the war another possibility was introduced. We began to read stories of the many workers who were pressed into slavery in German munition factories, and how they would occasionally, when not being watched, forget to put in powder or sabotage the fuse, or in any way they could hinder the German war effort.

So, to be on the safe side, we will credit and give thanks to all possibilities, knowing that someone or something sheltered us from certain death.

November 26, 1944

Why do I delay so in writing? I tried to explain part of it in my last letter. This time there were also two other reasons. First, I kept hoping each day that I might have some good news to write. In this I was wrong for each day brought more disappointment and less hope. Secondly, I kept hoping that each new day might bring me a letter from you which would give me something to grasp hold of and write about without boring you again with the problems of lonesomeness, blues, and homesickness of a fellow in my predicament. The postman has failed me in this respect, so now I've decided that I've let things go almost too far and regardless of the outside influences you must have a letter from me.

As you have gathered by now, this bum English weather hasn't let us work as much as we'd like. How long can a man stand idleness, away from everything he dearly loves, before cynicism will penetrate his character and outlook? The boys are fit to be tied. They sweat this thing far more than I do and I take it too seriously myself. The result is a bunch of nervous, agitated, and irritable individuals looking for one way or another to blow off the steam caused by the presence of this existence.

As usual, though, the crew is still one happy family and we air our thoughts freely with one another and depend more upon one another as time goes by. My part in this goes without saying—the man in charge, the guy who will lend a sympathetic ear to the most chronic of all gripes. Then give a little pep talk, keep your chin up and all that sort of thing, offer a few words of sound advice, then wind up with an assurance that everything goes well, be not short of patience, let nature take its course, and, in the end, our reward will be more than we had dared realize.

That brings a sort of satisfaction and they go off wondering whether I have any feelings at all. I'm the "Old Rock" they can cling to to keep their thinking straight while being unnerved by their existence here. Yet little do they realize that the guy who scoffs at their fears and finds humor when they are blue is probably more homesick and more lonesome than they ever thought of being. But it's my job, and since my neck depends on their actions they will never know my feelings. But I make no pretense with my wife—she will at least know the truth. While I'm endeavoring to keep my chin up, she will know that I haven't escaped the heartaches and the deep-down-inside hurt of being apart.

Now that we're discussing the future it's only fair to assume that sometime the day will come when Uncle Sam will no longer desire my services. Along with that goes a supposition that civilian clothes will be in vogue and a man will, no doubt, have to resort to work in some form of occupation to support a wife and family. Since you have told me that my future job will be one of my choosing, and in no way would you attempt to sway my judgment, I have given it considerable thought in order that my choice might be a wise one. Accordingly, I have sought some advice in this connection from those older and wiser than I. The words of wisdom which I have gathered when condensed down mean about this: for a man to succeed in any gainful occupation he must dearly love his work and put his heart and soul into it. I trust the judgment of that statement and thoroughly agree with it. Now it be-

comes only a simple matter to think of something which I'll love to do and can put my heart and soul into. At this point no real choices have been made, but a lot of possibilities have been eliminated! The good things in life come only after hard work and perseverance so if we will both be of good cheer I know our day will come soon.

November 27, 1944

We're on pass again. Yes, they decided that we should rest again, but I haven't done anything since the last pass! We can gripe all we want but it doesn't do any good. . . .

Our pass ends tomorrow night. Then with good weather maybe we can get a little work accomplished. I surely hope so because there's nothing more discouraging than just lying around. I've read more books, magazines, and newspapers this past month than I ever have before. My poetry books are all dog-eared from this siege of lonesomeness and inactivity. . . .

It's going to be hell spending Christmas over here but it can't be helped, so we'll just have to make the best of it. I hope we can finish operations by then—that will be the best Christmas present any of us could wish for. . . .

November 28, 1944

As the day comes to an end so does my pass. That puts me back in the old grind again taking my turn and my chances. Sure hope we can get a few good breaks during the next couple of weeks. Couldn't get any worse I don't think. We certainly have had plenty of weather both above and underfoot, and all of it has been bad. Did I tell you we had some snow here about a week ago? It did melt as soon as it fell, though. I have never seen such rain and mud in all my life. It rains twenty-four hours a day, seven days a week. Webs are beginning to grow between our toes—beats anything I've ever seen and I've seen six county fairs, a corn husking, an election, and a quilting bee! . . .

Fiess came over to bid me "so long"—the lucky guy! Well, in time that joyful day will come for all of us. . . .

November 30, 1944

It gives me great pleasure and satisfaction to send you this short note this evening. Why? Because it means that I have finally put in a good day's work. I'm really worn out because it has been a long, hard day, but, somehow, I feel much better than usual. I know I can hit the sack in a few minutes and rest well for a change, with a feeling that I have actually accomplished something. While I'm sleeping soundly you can chalk up another one. Number thirty-one has come and gone.

Mission #31, *Merseburg, Germany, November 30*

Frank Dimit, Bombardier

Briefed at 5:30 a.m. for the same damn target—oil refinery at Merseburg.

Flew lead of high squadron of high group. Carried 20 250-pound G.P. bombs. Bombed from 28,300 feet and it was a visual run. Very effective smoke screen at target; best I've seen, so can't say how much damage we did. Hope to hell we creamed it.

Flak was the usual terrific Merseburg variety. But we were lucky and only picked up one hole. They routed us in differently today and we were only in range of 270 guns. But every one of those were firing at us.

Fighter escort was splendid. Had little friends around us all day. Expected to be bounced by Luftwaffe, but didn't see any.

Felt pretty low when I went up to war room this a.m. and saw the target. I've had just about as much of this target as I can stand. Politz will probably be the next move. Was damn glad to get back.

The 1st Division went to Zeitz and Bohlen today. Half the 3rd Division hit an oil refinery just north of ours. They really caught hell. Saw about six planes down in flames. Convinced flak is wicked stuff. Gordy Braund's crew led the 13th Combat Wing today. Four more to go.

December 1

Strike photos show that we didn't hit Merseburg after all. Lead navigator goofed up and we unloaded them a couple miles north of Zeitz, which is south of Merseburg. Dumped them into a smoke screen and I think it was nothing but a potato patch, at most. *[End of mission notes by Frank Dimit]*

More than 1,250 Eighth Air Force heavy bombers and more than 1,000 Eighth and Ninth Air Force fighters made the attack against German oil plants at Bohlen, Zeitz, Merseburg, and Lutzendorf, all in the Leipzig area. Our group lost two aircraft—eighteen men. Initially the Eighth Air Force reported losses of fifty-six heavy bombers and thirty fighters. The heavy bomber losses were later revised as it was determined that some of these aircraft landed in occupied territory. Enemy flak was so heavy, according to some of the returning bomber crews, that they could hardly see the bomber formations in front of them.

December 1, 1944

Happy December 1st to you.

Since I worked late yesterday today was pay day for me, and that's always a happy day. I was paid early this morning so the rest of the day was spent settling up with my creditors. As the day comes to an end I find all debts paid and I, myself, am the proud possessor of a ten shilling note, which, believe it or not, I own outright. Oh well, I'll probably lose it in a card game and be broke as usual. But don't worry, the approximate value of a ten shilling note is only two dollars, so I can't do much heavy playing. Roco makes a pretty good banker. Someday me thinks he will make a good Shylock. At least he doesn't charge a pound of flesh—just a pound. . . .

Incidentally, I sent more newspapers to you today, but don't let the headlines worry you because I think we've seen our worst ones. It shouldn't be too long now—just a question of weather. Four more to go.

Late afternoon of December 2 the group was alerted for a mission the next morning. In the wee hours of the morning we were awakened by the "alert runner" and told to prepare for briefing. We headed for the ablution shack in the early morning chill to splash cold water on our faces to wake up and shave. We liked to fly clean-shaven because it made the oxygen mask fit better and was less irritating. We then went to the combat mess hall to get our special mission breakfast of "fresh" eggs. These eggs would probably cover eight inches of the grill when the shell was broken, but the cooks would do a good job of folding them back together in order to get them on a plate. The smell of burnt grease permeated the air, and the smoke from the grill, plus that from the cigarettes, created an eerie light.

There wouldn't be a lot of chatter in the mess hall on mission morning. People would usually speak only for a greeting or a nodding of the head. The crew would visit quietly, nothing boisterous. It was almost as if we were afraid we might wake up the enemy. Besides, it was a time when everyone wanted to be alone with his own thoughts.

After a light breakfast, which everyone picked at, and several cups of coffee, we headed for the briefing room. I always liked to have my crew there early—preferably in the front row, or at least in the first two or three rows. On this morning we were in time for the front row. The briefing room was rapidly filling up when the briefing officer from the Intelligence Section, Major Clyde Bingham, walked by. He stopped and inquired what in the world we were doing there. Well, it was pretty obvious we were going on a mission.

The major was a very low-key, likable man. His briefings were good and he was very sincere with a keen sense of fair play. If it was going to be rough he would tell you so—he didn't want anybody to be surprised. In this manner he commanded a lot of respect. Briefing for him was very serious and he would not be the one to tell a joke to lighten the tension— leave that to one of the other briefing officers. His business was Intelligence and this was serious. He would cover everything he could to help you.

After a short pause, during which he just looked at us, he

said, "I refuse to brief you to go on this mission." I became somewhat embarrassed. I didn't like to cause controversy and I didn't know what the problem was. At least by now most of the crews were assembled in the briefing room and there was enough visiting going on among several hundred men that our conversation was confined to our own area. So I cautiously asked, "What do you mean?" "Just what I said, 'I refuse to brief you for this mission.' "

At this time Colonel Jack Shuck, our Group Commander, came over and asked what the problem was. The mission curtains were still closed and we didn't know what the target was or where the group was going. Major Bingham turned to the colonel and said, "As you know the target is the Leuna Oil Refinery at Merseburg. I have briefed this same crew to go there six times already."

Merseburg, the most dreaded target in all of Germany—one of the very last oil refineries still operating. Every day more flak guns were being moved into the area. Every time we flew against it we had trouble—our bombing record against this target was poor. On October 30 our whole group had been shut out because of weather, but not until we were involved in enemy action and had flown around in clouds, which in itself presented a terrible hazard because of the number of planes involved.

"Now there are a lot of crews on this base who have never been to this target, and a lot of crews who have been there only one or two times, but this is a crew that has been briefed every time and I don't think it's fair." All of a sudden I was on Major Bingham's side. You don't ask to fly and you don't refuse to fly, but if someone is trying to help you, you don't turn him down either. Colonel Shuck said, "Well, let's check into this."

By this time our squadron commander, Major James Frankosky, could see that some controversy was going on and he came over to join our group. Subconsciously our minds were starting to revolt against this mission. I'm sure that we were not content to just put in our two cents worth—we felt we had better join the ranks of the big spenders and really unload. The colonel turned to the squadron commander and said, "You've heard a part of this controversy. Now why are these men here?"

Major Frankosky, not one to be flustered by controversy and a very sincere man with whom we had developed a good relationship, looked at the colonel and replied, "Sir, my orders were to supply the best crew I had. This is the ranking crew in number of missions flown in the 412th Squadron, and on that basis I have to assume they are the best." Somehow you just can't argue when you've been paid that kind of compliment, even if it only involves the number of missions you've flown.

At this the colonel turned to me and said, "We all have our jobs to do. You know why you have been chosen, and it's obviously too late to make any changes. But I promise you one thing—you fly this mission today and you'll never have to fly to Merseburg again. Agreed?" "Yes, Sir, but please be aware that I didn't start this controversy." (I hadn't done anything to stop it either.)

Major Bingham mounted the platform and pulled the curtain to reveal the mission board, then intoned, "Gentlemen, your target for today is the Leuna Oil Refinery at Merseburg, Germany." Immediately the room was filled with groans, oohs, aahs—obviously many of the others had been there too.

But I was not paying any attention to the groans. I was busy scanning the board to find our place in the formation. We had been flying visual deputy lead to the Pathfinders, but our usual slots were already filled. I couldn't find my name in the regular formation—what was all the controversy about anyway? Then way up in the corner of the board I saw my name —Fletcher (lead) with two wingmen and a diamond man. Radio call sign "Fireball Black." Somehow I thought that ominous call sign was very apropos because this mission would involve even more danger and responsibility than I had imagined.

The intelligence officer went on—the 95th would lead the task force for the groups bombing Merseburg for the Eighth Air Force, and so on. The rest would be a blur until he finally announced that Fireball Black would tack on to the lead squadron of the 95th Group. This way we could use the Pathfinder ship for navigation. But at five minutes before the IP we would break away from the group, increase our speed, and head for the target. We would not have any bombs. Our bomb bays would be loaded with chaff to confuse the radar that was aiming the flak guns. There would be approximately 300 in the area. We were to precede the group, and when over the target open the bomb-bay doors and allow the chaff to fall free.

I did not think that four aircraft could fly over that target. With four aircraft to shoot at, the flak gunners would use tracking flak, and they were good with this as we had found out over Kassel. They could save the barrage box firing for the main group. We would have one advantage; without the bomb load we could fly a little higher and a lot faster than the group. But not much higher because we wanted the chaff below the group where it would do some good for the whole task force, and they wouldn't have to fly through it.

The briefing went on and then it became time to break up for specialized briefing. I turned to my crew and probably told the biggest lie of my combat career. I don't know what the crew thought, but I suspected that like me they felt like men condemned to the gallows. But fear will feed on fear, and I was not going to let that happen. "Men, if there is a crew in the Eighth Air Force that can fly this mission then we're the ones that can do it. See you at the hardstand." The Squadron Commander was watching us and I don't know whether he heard what I said, but almost immediately he flashed the thumbs up sign. If he thought we could do it then we had better believe him.

After the specialized briefing when the airplane was ready to go, we gathered the flight crew in the ground crew's tent beside the airplane for our final preparation before boarding. The attitude was tense, a little more so than on most missions, but our thoughts were well concealed—*four aircraft with one hell of a backup!* We had no desire to be dead heroes or, for that matter, live cowards, but merely to fly the middle line between the two. It now appeared that circumstances were going to bounce us off the perimeters of each. We boarded the aircraft —our flight check complete. All eyes were on our watches counting the seconds to start-engine time.

Near each airplane was a loudspeaker mounted on a pole.
This system was called the "Tannoy." As the seconds were
counting down, the loudspeaker crackled to life and a single
word boomed out—"Boston"—a code word which meant the
mission had been scrubbed.

The weather had deteriorated over the Continent. We
crawled out of the airplane amidst shouts of joy. The cares of
the day were left behind. We could now start worrying about
tomorrow.

This crew would not fly to Merseburg again, and neither
would the 95th Bomb Group. We had a perfect record—six
for six. Over the years I've always wondered, "Could we have
really flown that mission and survived?" But maybe that was
the omen that neither the 95th nor we should return.

December 3, 1944

*. . . This evening has been taken up with a bull session. The main
topic was "What does tomorrow mean for us?" We argue back and
forth, never reaching a decision. The four of us have argued a point
all day long sometimes and the next morning started all over again.
You'd think we'd run ourselves down but we seem to have plenty of
wind and never at a loss for something to discuss. About an hour or so
each evening we get serious and discuss the possibilities of the next day.
It's a good idea and I've seen the time when a little pre-planning or
meditating, I should say, has come in handy.*

*I've just been informed that I have some little details to look after.
That's what I like about this job—you never know ten minutes ahead
of time what's cooking.*

Immediately after writing this letter I was alerted that we
would brief at midnight in order to fly a weather reconnaissance mission for the Third Air Division. This could be very
hazardous because a single aircraft flies the mission and there
wouldn't be any fighter escort. You were strictly on your own.

We were briefed to fly a course which would approximate
the one to be flown that day by the combat crews of the Eighth

Air Force. We would fly until we reached the enemy lines, then turn south and fly parallel to the lines, recording temperatures, winds aloft at various altitudes, cloud cover, icing conditions, and on through a whole weather checklist. This information would be transmitted back to headquarters in code at regular intervals. It would be given to the aircraft crews at their briefings, but its primary use would be in planning the mission—which targets could be hit visually, what the winds would be like, and so on.

We took off shortly after 2 a.m. with a full load of fuel. We felt very apprehensive, as this was to be our first time heading toward the enemy all by ourselves. We had returned home alone, but you could always see other aircraft. This was a big sky, and a long flight for a lone plane. The weather mission was flown before every combat mission and was rotated throughout the Air Force groups so that a crew would fly this mission only once. Because of the danger involved this would normally count as a combat mission, so if the tour was thirty-five the crews that flew the weather route would fly only thirty-four combat missions.

The night was especially black. There was no horizon—we made an instrument takeoff. The runway lights were turned on only when we were ready to take off and they were extinguished the minute we were airborne. Why advertise to Jerry where you are? On our way out we knew we would be a sitting duck for any night fighters that wanted to give chase. The four exhaust stacks were cherry red and they made a good target.

I was still fretting about these things when the navigator called and said we were getting close to the enemy lines and he would soon be giving me a new heading. I expressed amazement that we had covered so much ground so quickly. He replied that we had one heck of a tail wind, and at our altitude cruising at 150 mph indicated air speed, it was probably the fastest ground speed we would ever encounter.

I knew the radio operator would be monitoring his own frequency and would not be on the interphone so I asked the navigator, who was responsible along with the bombardier for gathering the weather data, if this information had been received at headquarters. He said the radio operator had been transmitting regularly. His messages had been received and each time they asked him to verify and repeat. So we knew they were getting through.

The navigator called again to give me the new heading. We now headed south and would hold this heading for about forty-five minutes. He told me we had made our turn a little late and were now a little ways over enemy territory. But he added that we had enough correction in the new heading to bring us back over our own lines and still make good the track that we had been briefed to fly. The thought of enemy action had now started to recede from my list of worries. If they hadn't hit us by now they probably wouldn't.

The winds were coming to the forefront as my number one worry—you have to keep your mind occupied. While I was still mulling this one around the navigator called and said it was time to turn to a northwesterly heading that would take us home. The whole crew heaved a sigh of relief. The journey home is always more pleasant.

After a time the sky was just starting to let a horizon form— in a few minutes I could barely make out the English Channel. Oh, happy day! The sky continued to lighten and I could see the outline of the coast of France. I checked my watch, scanned the instrument panel—the altimeter was on 27,000 feet, the heading was right on, and all engine instruments looked good. I fiddled with every knob in the cockpit that could be wiggled or jiggled, anything to pass the time. I looked out the window again. There was the coast, and there was the Channel. Nothing had changed. It was as though we were suspended in air and everything was at a standstill.

I called the navigator and asked him what was going on— we should be getting somewhere. His reply was that the tail wind we had going out was now a head wind. "We're still indicating 150 mph airspeed," I said. "Give me a true ground speed reading and ETA [estimated time of arrival] for the base so we can check it against the fuel supply." "I'll have it for you in a couple of minutes," he answered, "but it might interest you to know that in the past six minutes you have made a good five miles." Forget the ETA—even I can figure out that we have a head wind of approximately 100 mph, and at this altitude we can't get home on the fuel we have left.

I called the waist gunner and told him to tell the radio operator I wanted him on the interphone, but to make sure he didn't interrupt any communication he might be sending or receiving. In a few minutes the radio operator called. I asked, "Have you been getting all this weather information into headquarters?" He answered, "Yes, and every time I send the message they keep asking me to verify, which I do, so they know the score." "Okay, that's fine. Now please radio headquarters that we have to descend because we can't reach the base at this altitude and we will descend until we get a more favorable ground speed. But I want them to notify the Coastal Command that we are coming in under the assigned altitude and we don't particularly want to be shot at by our friends." To this he answered, "Roger. Will do. Shall I give them an altitude?" "Not in this first message because I don't know how far we will have to descend. We will descend at 2,000-foot intervals, allowing the navigator to get a ground speed at each altitude. When he finds one that looks as if it will get us home that's the one we will use. But I want the ground speed at each altitude radioed to headquarters." "Roger. Will code and start sending immediately."

By now it was broad daylight and we could see the first bomber groups starting to form into wings over the splashers and heading for Germany. "My God," I thought, "is somebody crazy? We have risked our necks to supply information and no one is paying any attention. They must know something we don't."

At 14,000 feet we were happy with the ground speed and headed on to our base where we made a quick landing. There wasn't any air traffic as our group had already taken off.

We headed immediately for interrogation and were very curious. Why would a mission be scheduled with the upper level winds reaching almost unheard of velocities? Our questions were soon answered. Headquarters had received our messages, and when decoded, they looked bizarre. Obviously such wind conditions did not exist. Consequently, we must be using the wrong code or we had something fouled up. This was the reason we had been asked to verify each time.

By now the lead crews on the mission were confirming our reports. The groups that were still on the ground were ordered to stand down. Those just taking off were recalled. The early birds would have to continue on—they were committed —but they could not return to England. After "Bombs away" they were diverted to tactical bases in France.

All of this was understandable because in that day and age not much was known about the jet streams. This was obviously an early encounter with the shifting winds. We were very irritated that no one saw fit to believe us. We felt we had the knowledge and the expertise to do our job and do it right— certainly we could read the "code of the day." We were gently reminded that our job was to "do"—the planning phase belonged to others.

We did not receive credit for this mission. It would be easier for all to just forget it and fly our thirty-five combat missions. We did, however, have the satisfaction of knowing that we had done our best.

December 5, 1944

Since I've had only five hours sleep in the last forty-eight and very little the day before that I deem it time I turned in. We'll probably sleep for the next twenty-four anyway. Get out the chalk now and mark up another one. Number thirty-two has joined the list of has-beens. Sure hope I don't get bogged down again. Can't make any predictions, but I can wish, hope, and dream, and I'm making an all out effort to finish as soon as is humanly possible. I know we can't make our holiday date, but I'll try not to be too late.

Mission #32, Berlin, Germany, December 5

Frank Dimit, Bombardier

Briefed at 4:15 a.m. for two targets. It was one of those Plan A
and Plan B jobs. "A" was an oil refinery at Politz. "B" was a
tank and flak gun factory at Berlin. We used B, thank goodness.

Had another one of those night takeoff and rendezvous.
Think my nerves and those of most of the crew are about shot.
Be glad when this tour is finished. We dived and climbed all
over the sky this a.m., like a P-51. Most of the time we were
dodging flares. The red-green jobs look just like the wing
lights of a B-17. Thought several times we were dead ducks
for sure. Looked like planes coming head-on. I haven't
stopped shaking yet.

Flew lead of high squadron of lead group and our group led
the wing. Carried 20 250-pound G.P. bombs. The load was
meant for Politz, but then we used B plan. Bombing was PFF.

Flak was pathetic. Really expected much more from Berlin.
They have moved a lot of their guns to Merseburg. Didn't pick
up a hole.

Expected to get a lot of trouble with fighters today, but we
didn't see any. Had splendid escort.

Smitty, our tail gunner, missed today's mission. Has been in
the hospital for several days. Out now, but not on flying duty.
E. J. Kolbush replaced Smitty. He taught me aircraft recognition at Kingman, Arizona.

Was colder than hell up there today. Damn near froze my
hands and feet. Trouble with bomb-bay doors. Brownie and I
cranked them open and closed.

Doc goes on flak pass tomorrow.

Three more to go.

Yesterday we flew weather ship for the Division. Up at 12
a.m., takeoff at 2:00 a.m. Flew to Rennes, France, and sent
back several weather reports. Landed about 9:30 a.m.
Thought we might get a mission for it. But no luck. *[End of
mission notes by Frank Dimit]*

The 357th fighter group, a P-51 outfit, led by Major Joseph E. Broadhead, of Rupert, Idaho, shot down twenty Nazi aircraft December 5.

If there was anything that struck fear in the hearts of the air crewmen, even more so than the enemy, it was the thought of a fire on board or a midair collision, mainly because you couldn't fight back. These two things resulted in many lost aircraft and claimed the lives of many crew members. These thoughts were never out of our minds and they preyed on us constantly—the pilots especially because they were responsible for the safety of the crew, not to mention their own necks. From a safety standpoint our flight procedures left a lot to be desired on our climb to altitude in the soup. To say it was a harrowing experience would be an understatement of gross proportion.

We took off at thirty-second intervals with fifty or sixty planes involved. This would require approximately thirty minutes to get everyone airborne. Each plane had to take off at the precise second in order to maintain our required flight separation. Sometimes our takeoffs were visual and we would have several hundred feet of altitude before entering the soup and going on instruments. But there were times when we made instrument takeoffs with one pilot totally on instruments and the other pilot trying to watch the edge of the runway. This resulted in both pilots making corrections and required complete cooperation.

On reaching 200 feet of altitude "takeoff power" was reduced to "climb power," and the pilot immediately started a left turn with 15 degrees of bank. This turn was held throughout the "climb-out." At the same time our airspeed was held constant at 150 mph, our rate of climb at 300 feet per minute. Our radio direction finder was tuned to the Base Radio Beacon frequency and the needle was kept on 270 degrees, which indicated that the field and beacon were always off of the left wing tip. Between this reading and our degree of bank, our position in relation to the field was held constant, and we were now spiraling counterclockwise up to altitude. Our flight pattern was a corkscrew with the air base being represented by the point on the screw. We held this position until we broke out of the clouds. This could mean anywhere from a few thousand feet to, at times, over 15,000 feet.

Now, visualize sixty aircraft from one field going up this corkscrew at thirty-second intervals and knowing that ten miles in either direction other groups were doing the same thing in clouds and pitch-black darkness. This system could and did work, but only if every pilot did precisely the same thing and held everything constant. There was no margin for error.

In the soup visibility was almost nil, but we used our red-green running lights on these "climb-outs," hoping they would be detected to avoid a collision if someone were out of position. We were young, but we were still subject to stress, and many a combat pilot will tell you that by the time we emerged from the cloud bank our flight gear would be soaked through with sweat.

Our crew never saw a collision in the overcast, but we did see several while trying to join up in formation after breaking out of the clouds. There are two that still stand out in my mind. On our July 28 mission we saw two ships from the 100th Bomb Group collide head-on in a clear sky well above the undercast. On October 26 we saw another midair collision during assembly.

On this particular day, as we were climbing through the overcast in the dark, we saw the red-green lights and I immediately lowered the nose to allow the lights to go over the top of us and then resumed normal climb. In a matter of a few minutes Billy Bob eased back on the yoke and in a nose-high attitude we allowed the lights to go below us. Then we made an immediate recovery to keep from stalling out for our aircraft was loaded to its maximum weight and our controls were sluggish. After this happened several more times it was hard to tell who was spooked the most, the crew, who could only watch, or the pilots, who were trying to react.

About this time Billy Bob and I put our heads together and pondered the problem. If we were this close to a midair collision so many times, why didn't we feel prop wash from the other aircraft? But in our agitated state we could probably have flown through a brick wall and never noticed. This was a conundrum that we think was solved when we broke out of the clouds. There was our lead ship flying in a circle above us firing red-green magnesium flares to identify his position so we could form on him. These were the colors that were assigned to us and he was doing his job, but did he have to do it so well? With tongue in cheek we told the crew that in all likelihood we had been dodging flares rather than airplanes, but who knows? We had already sweat blood, and no amount of explanation could erase what we had gone through.

I made a vow that if I returned from this mission somebody at group was going to hear about it. When we returned I was allowed to vent my steam, but there appeared to be no solution or alternative.

December 6, 1944

Just another short note before hitting the sack. I'm not a bit sleepy and I feel good—first time I've had such high spirits in a long time. Today I won a great moral victory on a matter which has been giving me trouble lately, so I have been quite jubilant since. Now I think things will go much better. It was the first time the crew had ever seen me mad. Little did they realize what I would do on their behalf if somebody started pushing them or us around. We really click together and we have an unbeatable team.

The reason for the elated spirits was that a problem had been resolved relating to our crew and the number of missions we would fly. There had been some talk of extending the number.

Our tail gunner had been in the hospital and had missed the December 5 mission. He was now one behind the rest of the crew. The group was now insisting that he fly a makeup mission by flying with a different crew. Since he was my tail gunner I didn't want him to fly with another crew and take a chance of losing him. Every crew had their own procedures and proven bond. (Our navigator had been two missions behind, but he had made these up by flying with other crews.) I was then reminded that Headquarters USAAF in Washington had recently said that crews would not be relieved from combat duty simply on the basis of number of missions or combat hours flown, but only after evidence of combat fatigue.

This meant that any crew could be asked to fly more than thirty-five missions. However, Headquarters of the Eighth Air Force knew that if the order were applied to everyone there would be some real serious morale problems. They knew that the flight crews had to have a goal to shoot for. So they initiated an order of their own which could be used to signify compliance with the order from Washington, but still give us a goal. The order simply stated that all flight crew members would be examined for combat fatigue by the group flight surgeons, and under no condition would this examination be put off beyond thirty-five missions. This meant that the group flight surgeons had the authority to set the actual number of missions flown. The flight surgeon and our group officers had no desire to see a crew fly more than thirty-five missions.

The discussion over the tail gunner became heated, but when I was dismissed I left knowing that all members of my crew, with the exception of the copilot, were fatigued enough to be able to finish upon the completion of *my* thirty-fifth mission.

December 7, 1944

How's my little family this dreary evening? Me? Oh, I'm in a pretty good mood for a change. No particular reason, just things in general. One of the reasons for our good spirits, I think, is because one of the fellows went to a rest home so he let us have his phonograph and collection of records to use while he was gone. It sure seems good to hear some good music. It kinda brightens up the day and puts a little atmosphere in our shack.

No mail for me yesterday, but today I received a letter from my cousin, Virgil, who is in Italy. He has been overseas 30 months and he's getting lonesome for the gal he left behind. I know just how he feels—today marks my six-month anniversary here. I know I could never stand it that long with the worries and trials of this life.

Received another Oak Leaf Cluster to go with the Air Medal this morning. This makes the fourth one—when I get them all on you can't see the ribbon. But they can take all their awards and decorations. All I want is a ticket home for a live passenger, and I may be getting that pretty soon. As you know, we have thirty-two in now. Not many more left, but it still seems like a long ways to go. This sweating every day in and out begins to get old after so long a time. . . .

December 10, 1944

. . . Want to buy me a couple of records? If you do here are the ones I would like—The Kerry Dance *featuring* Connie Boswell, *and* Don't Believe Everything You Dream *with the Ink Spots. Both are Brunswick records, and, of course, they are made in England. . . .*

We have had some cold weather lately. The temperature doesn't drop too low, although it is below freezing, but the air is so damp it goes right through you. I don't know how long it has been since there was a day when it didn't rain, sleet, snow, or something. It gets pretty chilly up where we work—many times around fifty below—that all adds to the comfort of flying. When I get home I'm going to buy a cat and just sit by the fireplace where it is warm. This flying racket is for the birds, and I don't have a feather on me.

Our rooms were heated by a little old stove which was probably twelve inches in diameter and maybe eighteen inches tall. We had a coke ration every three days, but if you had a fire for several hours a ration would last only for one evening. If your ration was used up, the minute you came in from the outside the logical thing to do was go to bed or else put on a lot of extra clothes because it always seemed colder inside the quonset than it was outside.

The English weather is very, very damp and all the time we were there I don't remember ever putting on clothes that were completely dry. Things would mildew fast; consequently, most of our clothing was wool. Wool could be wet and still keep you warm—the only thing wrong with it was that it would smell a little musty. This may have contributed to our reluctance to take a bath—we were never positive where the odor came from. Knowing that we had only a choice of being cold or staying in bed it seemed much more logical to make a midnight requisition to the coke pile and load a couple of shovelsful into an old wheelbarrow.

We used to draw lots to see who would go up and raid the coke pile. In the beginning, as the ranking officer on the crew, I refused to put my name in the list. But after a while this got old for the rest of them and, as I was enjoying the heat too, it seemed only fair that my name should be put in along with the rest of them. Sure enough my name was finally drawn.

The coke pile was located up a gently rolling hill probably 200 yards from our barracks. Some nights there were two sentries at the pile, but generally there was only one. In order to keep warm he spent his time walking around the perimeter of the coke pile, or maybe he'd walk back and forth, then stop and listen, light a cigarette, stomp his feet, and rub his hands. It was usually cold and very black.

On this particular night I took the old wheelbarrow up the hill and managed to get about three shovelsful in and was ready to start back. The sentry had his back to me and was 100 feet or so away. I thought, "Now is the time to get out of here." The sentry carried a flashlight, but he wouldn't turn it on unless it was absolutely necessary to locate somebody, because of blackout restrictions.

There was only one problem with this wheelbarrow. It had an old iron wheel with a bearing that hadn't been greased in all the time the group had been there. It let out a little high-pitched squeal every time it hit a certain spot on its rotation. Of course the noise was always louder once a little weight was added.

Now all the members on the crew, myself included, were somewhat mechanically inclined, but it had never dawned on us to bring some oil or grease from the flight line and grease the bearing. If there were two of us, we might carry the thing rather than push it.

After ascertaining that the guard wasn't paying any attention to me, I started back down the hill, pushing the wheelbarrow along with its squeaks and creaks. About this time I heard the guard say, "You know, I really don't mind turning my back while you filch the coke, but I certainly wish somebody would grease that damn wheel before we all get in trouble." Needless to say, that shook us up. Here we thought we had been executing a coup, and all these times we were being watched by the sentry.

In all the time we were there we wished that just one time we could have enough coke to start a fire, run it all day, and completely dry out our barracks and our clothes. But such was not to be the case. Even at that we probably had a larger ration than any of the civilian people, and maybe even more than some of the military personnel.

This wasn't a particularly big problem for our flight crew. They had converted their little stove into an oil burner. As the engines on the B-17 required an oil change occasionally this old oil would pile up at the dump. So with their friends amongst the ground crew, the boys could always figure out a way to get some used oil which would otherwise be thrown away. Their ground crew also supplied a few gallons of gasoline, which they would use to ignite the initial drips of oil going into the stove. Once the fire box was hot they could cut down on the gas and burn almost pure oil. So they didn't need to steal coke, but they were never completely warm either. At least their problems were different, because they had to spend their time figuring out a way to get oil and gas.

I can remember a couple of occasions when the boys invited me down to their barracks to get warm and it was rather pleasant to be next to an oil-fired stove. But it wasn't right or possible to do this every evening.

December 17, 1944

Another week gone by and a new one just beginning. Maybe this week will bear more fruit than the last. Last week was a pretty hard one, though, as we did quite a bit of work. None of it was the kind I wanted to do, but it was work that had to be done and someone had to do it. Lucky me, if there are any odd jobs lying around I get them. Asking the

Squadron Commander to keep us busy really paid off. There's one consolation; they can't keep this up much longer, I hope.

We missed church this morning. We were going to the evening service but changed our minds. They are having a choir come in and sing Christmas carols and no sermon. The reason we decided not to go was that the place will be crowded and I don't think any of us could stand to listen to the carols without getting a good solid case of the blues. We have them enough without bringing any atmosphere in it and asking for them. . . .

As you've probably guessed we're all pretty well disgusted with life over here. It's not because combat is unbearable, it's just because of certain events and happenings. Things have changed considerably since we first arrived. We're the "Old Timers" now—the "Remember When" boys!

In late November and December our crew had a pretty rough time. We were subconsciously suffering from stress and battle fatigue, but we were still very capable of doing our missions and any other job that was required of us. By now our experience had placed us at the very peak of our combat capabilities, but internal changes would now play a role.

We were a proud crew and we had extended the time of our tour by taking lead crew training. We felt we were making a real contribution to the welfare and success of our group. We had seen many crews finish, some of whom had spent much less time in the group than ourselves. We had been present at the awards ceremony when these men finished their tours and were awarded the Distinguished Flying Cross. It made us proud because we knew that you could not complete a tour of twenty-five, thirty, or thirty-five missions and not exhibit the outstanding heroism and exceptional performance to win this award—the old timers knew!

But we were to receive a new group commanding officer and this would no longer be the practice. A crew finishing their missions would not be recognized for what they had done in the past or would do in the future. Flying against the enemy would be just a job. Apparently the art of preparing citations had now become a far too *difficult task,* or simply too dangerous in the European Theater of Operations.

Previously when a crew finished their last mission they would depart from the formation after making landfall on England. They would pour on the coal and reach the base ahead of the formation, and fly down the runway at 200 feet firing flares in a victory celebration. There would be cause for joy both in the airplane and among the crews observing on the ground. This was tangible evidence that a crew could live to finish a tour and it was a real morale booster. This practice was ordered to cease.

Another honor accorded a crew when this big event arrived was the "Lucky Bastard Club" dinner. The whole crew would dress in Class A uniform and come to the Combat Officers Mess Hall, where they were seated at a table of honor with a white tablecloth and given a steak dinner with a bottle of wine. During their dinner they were given a standing ovation from the combat crew officers in the mess hall. It made them feel good and we felt good. Besides, it would be the only time a combat officer and crew would receive a steak at the 95th. The staff officers ate in a separate dining facility and I doubt if they knew what this little ceremony meant to the men who were to fly and go, *if* they survived.

They were also given a certificate stating that they had joined the Lucky Bastard Club. A 1st pilot who flew as a deputy lead or squadron lead, along with his crew members, was given a certificate signed by the group commanding officer and by the Third Air Division Commander, Major General Partridge, stating that they had been a crew leading combat formations.

It was all trivial in a sense, but it meant somebody cared. All of these practices would cease immediately—a new regime had come into being. I thought at first this was an Air Force–wide decision, but soon discovered that it pertained only to the 95th.

When these orders were given our crew still had four missions to fly, and we had just gone through the last scrubbed mission to Merseburg. There was even some talk of extending the tour. I would now have to relay all this information to my crew. The new C.O. obviously did not realize what impact these orders would have on the morale of the seasoned crews. The new ones wouldn't know any difference. A wise and fair man would have instituted a "grandfather clause," because the most important things in a combat group were morale and loyalty, but loyalty had to be a two-way street. All of a sudden the changes were coming so fast that we felt we were back in Cadet Training. We were no longer entitled to the respect and recognition that comes with having done your very best.

The day I told my crew of these new rules I played them down as best I could, and reminded them that I knew what they had done and I was proud of them even if they didn't get any goodies. In their hearts they knew they were good and had done their best—this would have to be their reward. The most important thing, with God willing, was that we would get home with something more meaningful—our lives!

I dismissed them in a hurry because I didn't want them to see how much it hurt to relay these orders. I wished the colonel could have seen the consequence of his orders mirrored in the eyes of all of us. Our crew had been let down by a man who would never know, or care, what we had contributed. I wouldn't be able to fly those last missions fast enough.

December 19, 1944

Happy Days! Only five more shoplifting days until Christmas! Why all the jubilation? Yesterday I had seven letters! Besides I was pretty busy most of the day, then went to bed early because I figured I would be routed out pretty early this morning. I wasn't disappointed, because I was awakened at four a.m. What an ungodly hour to get up. That's just the right time to be going to bed. Nothing like getting up early so you have a long day to loaf. That's our new policy.

I'm feeling halfway human and I don't think I'll ever get down in the dumps again like I was a short time back. I'm not saying that I won't have the blues—they're practically chronic. But morale will never slip as low again as then. That's a fact and a promise. Some mighty bleak and despairing days have passed, but I seem to have my thinking cap pretty well in hand now and have resolved my mind to a few things.

You may want to know what made me so irritable and hard to get along with awhile back. Well, I'll tell you. It was the culmination of a mistake I had started earlier. The mistake was trying to live each day as it comes. You just can't do that—it's impossible in the long run. Why? Because if you have bad luck every day for a period of time you gradually become dejected and finally destitute. No, you have to live more than each day as it comes. Life and happiness are more complex than the momentary elations of any one day. You must live each day as it comes and also live the treasured memories of the past as well as the exotic dreams of the future. Only in this way can you balance the mind over a continued length of time. That's the story.

Now to answer a few questions which appeared in your letters. Yes, you might say that Lucky Sherry *is a much better airplane than* Knock Out Baby. *It's our real pride and joy and we sure baby it along. The picture is quite unique and pretty hard to describe so I think I'll keep you waiting on this point until you can see the picture. We have quite a color scheme. The picture is painted on the back of all our leather jackets. Boy, are we flashy! I'll send you a picture of all of us with our dress battle dress on. The dress battle dress is what we wear when we want to impress the recruits. . . .*

We were awakened at 4 a.m., had breakfast, and attended briefing. Everyone was elated because we were finally going on a mission to aid the ground troops. But the weather didn't hold up and the mission was scrubbed at 9:30 a.m. It was a very disgruntled flight crew that piled out of the airplane to go back to the everyday grind.

December 20, 1944

. . . It has been pretty chilly here lately, and fog—I've never seen the like of it. It gets you soaking wet just walking in it. It's so thick you have to cut it before you can walk. At times you can see almost ten or fifteen feet in front of you, but most of the time you don't know whether you are walking on the trail or across the fields until you run into a

fence or fall in a ditch. Funny people these English. They dig a ditch instead of building a fence. But far be it from me to point out their mistakes.

Now comes the subject I've been wanting to talk over with you. I've been wondering how you felt about my flying. I don't mean my flying ability, technique, or anything like that because I think you know that I can pilot as safe an airplane as there is flying. No, I just wondered how you felt about my job here. There was a time when I loved flying in civilian life, but like everything else, the Army has taken all the joy out of it. Flying now is just a job and the worries and responsibilities are far too high for the compensation. It wouldn't necessarily have to be that way, but I think too highly of the men under me to endanger them through any shortcomings, fault, or ignorance on my part. . . .

Now let's do some supposing or wishing. Say my tour here was completed. In a couple of months I would be on a train looking forward to three wonderful weeks with my wife and son. At the end of that time I would find myself at a Reclassification Center being interviewed for reclassification.

One of the first things he would ask would be, "What are your objections or attitude toward another tour of combat?" I would say that I don't like it and I don't want to do another tour. Why? Because any man who has been in combat once is afraid of it and wouldn't ask for any more. It's a story he has heard a thousand times in his job. So he would say, "Other than that, what other objections do you have, physically or mentally?" To this I would have to answer none, for they haven't brought out the Army physical yet that I can't pass. And mentally I'm just as sane as I've ever been.

No, I know these two factors wouldn't keep me out of combat. At the end of this interview the verdict would probably be, "You've done a good job, but there is still a war to be won. With your experience you would be valuable in the South Pacific. We'll give you three or four months training here to rehabilitate you and get started with a new crew, then back to battle." To this I could probably refuse—then after the court martial I would undoubtedly find myself in the walking Army with the rating of Private. As you know that would never happen. First, because I have a sense of duty, and, secondly, there's a war to be won and somebody has to do the fighting. If one tour of combat were to exempt all from further combat there soon wouldn't be anyone left to fight on our side.

Now that you have that picture, let's say the reclassification officer had said, "Well, you've done your part in combat, so now we'll give you a job in the States. Let's look at your records and see what you are qualified for. Hmmmmmmm Pilot, specialized training only, good experience, would make a good flying instructor." He's right. There's no choice. The only thing I could qualify for would be duty involving flying. I'd be the low man on the totem pole, the guy who has to do the work. No administrative training and no chance of getting any in the States. It would mean flying day in and day out hoping you can catch a student's mistake before he smears you all over the runway. It's okay if you love flying and are content to remain a throttle jockey all your life. While I'm in the Army I would like to get above just being a pilot. I would like getting on the inside and help run things while somebody else does the actual flying.

Now let's see—I have the qualifications and experience of flying which are necessary for a job like that, but where can I get the administrative training? If you have enough rank you can get it in the States or anyplace. Everybody wants an administrative flying job so that puts it out of reach of the junior officers regardless of how much gray matter they might have. At this point it looks as if I'm stuck with flying even though I want to quit.

Now let's go further. What would happen if I stayed with this outfit when my tour was over. Of the several jobs that have been offered in the Group, what would they lead to? On one of them I could get a jump in rank, learn operational duty and at the same time fly a few more missions. Well, that's out! When this one's over I've had enough combat flying. There isn't anything that will force me to do any extra missions. Suppose I take one of the other jobs—fly as an instructor, no more combat, but plenty of flying. No thanks, if I have to fly as an instructor I'll take a chance of doing it in the States where I can be with my wife and family. Another job I could take here would be just monkeying around flying just enough to get flying pay, serve maybe six months or a year, and maybe make Captain with good luck. But yet I wouldn't learn anything that would benefit me or help me get the job I want. It would just delay my coming home and then when I did get there I would still be just a pilot and wouldn't have any better chance of staying in the States than I would right now. That's out. I can't get what I want by staying with this Group.

What I really want is to stop this everyday flying and come home.

But I can't realize both of those dreams right now and still help win the war, a little matter which I have to do. If I come home now I can be with you for at least six months chasing around the country, and with half a miracle I might get to be an instructor and remain indefinitely, wondering each day if I will be called back to combat duty. That was exactly what I was going to do and what I might still do. But when I come home I want to live the life we've always planned.

Here's what I'm getting at. I was interviewed yesterday by a Colonel from higher Headquarters offering me a chance to train and take a staff job. No more combat flying—just the four hours a month for flying pay, as the job requires a flying man with combat experience. This would be a chance to work toward a job which I've always wanted since coming in the Army—the planning end. I think I've had my share of the doing end. I would like to try to use my brain for a change and see how that works. If I make good at the job it would mean staying here at least another six months after my tour is over. If I don't make good or don't like the work I could quit and come home. If I do make good and come home my chances of staying in the States are greatly improved and the hazards of everyday flying are overcome.

I was very much impressed by Colonel Huglin. I felt that here was a man who would give me some responsibility and expect me to do my best. I had the feeling that I could learn a lot about administration by being on his staff. I have spoken with the Squadron Commander about this move and he thinks it is a wise choice. As you know, I have a lot of faith in his judgment. During the interview I kept seeing similarities between these two men. Of course, Colonel Huglin is much older, but both are real quiet, firm, sincere, and command respect. I wonder if this is what "The Point" does for you, but then, maybe it is just their nature. Anyway, I was pleased to be asked to be on his staff even in a junior capacity. Something tells me that Frankosky has had more to do with this than he is letting on. This man had to get my name from somewhere. Anyway, I am thankful to both and will be happy to get out of the pipeline and learn something different while still contributing to a just cause.

While you are reading all of this I'll be trying to finish this tour I'm on. I don't know how much longer it will drag on. With good luck and weather it wouldn't take long, but you see how things are going.

December 24, 1944

'Twas the night before Christmas and all through the house not a creature was stirring—everyone was just plain tuckered out. But there wasn't a man that wasn't thinking of home and his loved ones. It's pretty quiet tonight, only an occasional sage remark about this time last year. On close inspection you can see that the eyes glisten with a little water when home is mentioned. We'd give darn near anything to be home tonight, but since we can't we'll just make the best of it.

I hate to miss our son's first Christmas, but the best present I can give the two of you is that you can chalk off number thirty-three.

Mission #33, *Biblis, Germany, December 24*

Frank Dimit, Bombardier

Briefed at 5:45 a.m. for our target, an airfield on the Rhine River about 20 miles south and a little west of Frankfurt, or about 5–10 miles southwest of Darmstadt.

We flew high squadron lead of the lead group of our wing.

Carried 38 100-pound demolition bombs—used tail fuses only. Wanted to dig holes in their field. Had a bomb rack malfunction. Formation slid under us before I had a chance to salvo them. Got over Rhine River before I could get rid of them. Bombing was visual, but bad haze and we flew into the sun. Visibility was poor. Don't think bombing was so good.

Flak was very light and inaccurate over target. But we caught hell going over the front lines. Used to be a few corridors there, but they are definitely closed up. Picked up several holes.

This was a maximum effort for the 8th A.F. today. The 95th contributed 60 aircraft. Germans have been playing hell with our ground forces, so today we did a little playing. Everyone was hitting airfields or tactical targets.

Luftwaffe was probably up, but we didn't see it.

Two more to go. An alert on now, may fly tomorrow. *[End of mission notes by Frank Dimit]*

The month of December was hard on the nerves of the flying crews of the 95th Bomb Group. On December 16 the Germans staged a surprise counterattack, and troops of the 101st Airborne Division, a part of the First Army commanded by General McAuliffe, were caught and trapped in the forests of the Belgian Ardennes. Our group flew only one mission from December 12 to 24, to Stuttgart on December 16, the same day as the breakthrough.

Our crew did not fly from December 5 until the 24th. We had nineteen days of nonproductive work with our minds working overtime. The weather kept the group grounded and nerves were raw and on edge.

Meanwhile, the ground troops who were encircled at Bastogne and trapped in the Battle of the Bulge were hungry, tired, and cold. Their casualties were mounting. Their ammunition and supplies were running out. The supply depot at Antwerp was placed under intensive bombardment by German V-2 rockets. The First and Ninth U.S. Armies were attacking from the north, and the Third Army from the south. The snow and cold were making rescue difficult.

The weather was horrible. We couldn't get an airplane off the ground. This bothered us as we were helpless to do anything but worry. We were fighting men and we wanted to fight. We had flown in support of the ground troops before, both bombing and dropping supplies, and we wanted to again. But Mother Nature had us caught in her grasp. In a sense we were being held captive just as the troops were in the Bulge. Yet we were still warm with plenty to eat, in civilization, and this is what hurt. Our conscience was making life miserable for us.

But on December 24 the weather broke and we flew with a vengeance. That day we put over 2,000 heavy bombers in the air at one time in support of our people in the Ardennes. As our first echelons were bombing the enemy the last ones in the bomber stream were leaving England, a truly magnificent sight. Jerry caught it that day and he paid dearly for the misery that had been inflicted upon the ground troops. This was the largest bomber mission of the war to date, and it was supported by 900 fighters. Our frustrations eased, we could think clearly again. Our morale soared, we could now fight back!

December 25, 1944

Here it is Christmas Day come and almost gone. There wasn't too much time to think and really get homesick today. But I will admit that there was a more prominent loneliness today than usual. I sincerely hope I never spend another Christmas like this. When we finished our work we had a wonderful dinner, but everyone was almost too tired to enjoy it. We were so hungry we would have eaten the usual chow and pronounced it good. . . . Now then, get out the chalk and scoreboard and mark up number thirty-four while I sweat out the remaining one.

Explain to our little man that all Christmases aren't like his first and that it will be different when Santa Claus gets out of the Army.

Mission #34, *Bad Münster, Germany, December 25*

Frank Dimit, Bombardier

Briefed at 6:15 a.m. for our target. It was a marshalling yard at Bad Münster, a little town just south of Bad Kreuznach, which is about 20 miles southwest of Mainz.

Flew lead of high squadron of low group of our wing. Carried 10 500-pound G.P. bombs and 2 500-pound aimable cluster incendiaries. Bombing was visual and think our squadron did a damn good job. Other two squadrons hit the town of Bad Kreuznach. Four boys in our squadron goofed up a bit and dropped early, but still think we creamed it.

Our Division and the 2nd Division were the only ones to fly. 1st Division was stood down. The 2nd hit tactical targets and we hit marshalling yards. Fighter escort was good. Didn't see the Luftwaffe, but expect they were up.

Were not in range of any flak except coming home. Picked up a little in the Ludwigshaven-Mannheim area. No holes. Wasn't too accurate. Went across the front lines about 8 miles south of the place we did yesterday. Didn't get any flak today.

Was sweating out weather on return. Division said there was a 50–50 chance of having to land in France, because of fog at the base. Fletch didn't go much for landing away from our base and missing our Christmas dinner. Fog was just on the edge of the field when we came in. Finished our roll-out in zero visibility. We were the last plane to land. About two-thirds of the group got in, the others landed at another base in England.

Whatta way to spend Christmas!

Telegrams arrived from Generals Doolittle and Partridge congratulating us on our part in yesterday's big mission.

One more to go!! *[End of mission account by Frank Dimit]*

Lack of good judgment or mistakes in identification always seemed to result in tragedy whether it be bombs dropped on friendly troops or on friendly territory. There were occasions of our own fighters being fired on by bomber gunners. There were also instances of the ground troops firing on one another and creating chaos. Fighting in combat is a very fluid situation —identification and action have to be taken simultaneously or there will be no tomorrow for him who hesitates.

Christmas Day was one of those days—a flight of three low-flying P-51s were mistaken for ME 109s and were fired on by our own ground troops on the Continent. Two planes were shot down and the Eighth Air Force Fighter Command lost one of their top scoring aces and squadron leaders, Major George E. Preddy.

December 27, 1944

I have some good news for you! Now sit down and lay David in his crib because I wouldn't want you to drop him. Here it is. It's all over with now—I'm an ex-combat man!! You can chalk up number thirty-five, the last one, as of right now. Don't worry about me any more because the danger is over. Don't know as yet when I'm coming or what, but will get something definite within the next few days. But don't look for me home very soon.

Mission #35, Fulda, Germany, December 27

Frank Dimit, Bombardier

Briefed at 4:15 a.m. for our target—a marshalling yard at Fulda, Germany, a town about 30 miles northeast of Frankfurt.

Flew lead of high squadron of the lead group of our wing. Carried 12 500-pound G.P. bombs. Bombing was visual, and think we creamed it. Made two runs on the target. A squadron from the 390th flew a collision course with us on the bomb run. We were looking up at bombs and it was just about time to drop. We got out of there quick and came around again.

Didn't see much flak today. Caught a few bursts at several different places. Saw some at the front lines going in, but only meager coming out.

The Luftwaffe was up but we didn't see it, thank goodness. We were without fighter escort for a good while after that second pass at the target. Except for that, escort was good.

When we were awakened at 2:00 a.m. thought sure we were going to enjoy a night takeoff and a mission to Politz. But things worked out pretty good. We were going to take off in the dark, but they changed takeoff time.

FINISHED AT LAST!!!! *[End of mission notes by Frank Dimit]*

On our final mission there was more nervousness and trepidation than usual. It had appeared to all of us that more crews were lost on their first several missions and on the last two or three than at any other time during their tour. There were no statistics to reinforce this view, only a feeling which permeated all bomber crews in combat.

All of a sudden this feeling was brought home when on the bomb run to the target a squadron from the 390th came over the top of us on a collision course. As we stared up into the loaded bomb bays our normal breathing pattern quickly changed as we gulped for more oxygen to alleviate fear.

Our group lead immediately broke off of the bomb run and made a tight circle to get in behind the errant group. We were able to execute the turn and give the bombardiers the time they needed to synchronize on the target and still stay out of the way of the following groups of the task force. But, somehow, we couldn't pass it off as just another mixup in the target area. The mental jinx was working overtime, but we were fighting to overcome it and regain our composure.

As we flew through the flak at the target our nerves were ragged; the tension was building. One way or another, as a crew we were on our final ride. The flak bursts were not too close, but who knows where the next bursts will be. As Dimit called "Bombs away," some relief spread throughout the ship as we were now flying for ourselves. On the way in we flew for Uncle Sam, but going home was different, we'd done our job, we were now flying to save our own necks and to keep our group intact.

But the mission wasn't over yet. We still had about four hours of flying before we even dared to relax—almost two hours of it over hostile territory, not knowing when we might be hit by fighters or accidentally fly over some unknown flak batteries. There was always the possibility of mechanical failure which could spell disaster.

All the way back from the target I had a wrestling match with my conscience. The colonel's orders were still ringing in my ears: "No more DFC's on finishing a tour, no Lucky Bastard dinner, no more victory flyovers." *Obey the orders.* Don't violate the rules. This was ingrained in us from the first day we entered military service. My conscience was fighting hard and it appeared to be winning the battle. But my heart was revolting. What's a court martial compared to the dangers of what we had faced in flying thirty-five combat missions against the Third Reich, plus the countless training missions in poor weather over England?

I thought about my crew and the disappointment we had to face when these rule changes were made known to us—the misty eyes, the choked voices. I owed these men something. They had given me and the 95th Group their very best throughout some very trying times. No aircraft commander could ask and receive more from his crew.

We were leading the high squadron of the lead group and

the battle went on—conscience versus heart. While the wrath of a colonel is not to be taken lightly, a 105 millimeter shell exploding under your tail is no great pleasure either.

As we made landfall on the coast of England I called my right wingman, Lieutenant Metzinger, and requested he bring my formation home. He wiggled his wings and verified with a very happy "Roger." I switched back to interphone and asked Billy Bob to give me 2100 rpm and monitor the manifold pressure on the engines. My course had now become clear. My conscience and the military were thrust into the background as I shoved the throttles to the fire wall, lowered the nose, and called Roco to give me a heading that would take us straight down the runway at the base.

The crew now realized what was happening and each one let out a big "Yippee!!" We may be reprimanded, but orders or no orders—*we're going for it!* This was one thing they couldn't take away—I was in command of the aircraft. I told the crew that anyone who wanted to fire a flare should come on up to the flight deck and start firing when we reached the runway. I would make two passes to give everyone a chance, but cautioned them not to fire any red-red flares which indicated there were wounded on board.

Brownie immediately locked the Very pistol in the mounting bracket on the top of the fuselage on the flight deck and started breaking out the cartridges. As we went roaring down the runway on the victory flyover at full high rpm, *Lucky Sherry* looked like a giant roman candle gone mad, erupting the brightly colored magnesium flares—red-green, red-blue, red-white. Old "Fireball Red Leader" was coming home for the last time and our presence was being announced with great hilarity. I was sure I heard Billy Bob's drawl on the interphone, "Y'all be sure and fire one for the colonel, now."

In the middle of our second pass the group lead came over the field and requested permission to start their landing peel-off. The tower (code name Bezel) requested that they circle the field once as there was a ship in the pattern with wounded aboard. As the group went around we pulled up, made a real tight turn, and settled down on the runway where we made at least three good, hard bounces. It was a landing that Airplane

#7783, *Lucky Sherry,* and the crew would not forget. The Tower responded with "Good Show," and I with "Roger, Bezel, good to be back!"

Our tour had now been completed, and that was our "thank-you"—the only time I ever knowingly failed to heed an order. To this day I have a hard time forgiving the Group C.O. who denied my men the decoration they risked their lives to earn and so richly deserved!

As we cut the engines after taxiing to the hardstand we were congratulated by the seldom-praised and often forgotten true heroes of this war, the crew chief of the airplane and his ground crew. Without their dedicated service, many times twenty-four hours at a stretch in cold and inclement weather, these airplanes would not have flown. The flight crews were an extension of their aircraft, and the pride they exhibited toward both the crew and airplane made you feel like something special. It was good to report no battle damage today.

The hilarity now put behind us, we had to get on with the serious business of interrogation.

As the interrogating officer went through his checklist of questions, Roco mentioned that Smitty, our tail gunner, had reported flak while we were over Belgium—somewhat meager, about thirty bursts, pretty small stuff. They couldn't quite reach us, but they were trying. This was a surprise because we thought we were over territory that had already been liberated, yet as we flew across this little town someone was objecting.

The interrogation officer said the area was being held by the Germans, a small enemy pocket completely surrounded by U.S. forces. It was felt that they would realize the hopelessness of their position and surrender as they ran out of food and ammunition. This would be better than assaulting the area and having casualties on both sides.

At the close of interrogation the interrogating officer called out to others in the room to see if any of the other crews had seen enemy action in this area. Upon receiving a negative report he said that the position reported was a known area of enemy resistance. Hostile action had been reported by a crew who had now finished their missions and it would behoove them all to be more observant because this group of eyes would no longer be with them.

This is the type of statement that really endears you in the hearts and eyes of those who will carry on! It was time to go!

December 27, 1944   V-Mail

The good Lord has led us home for the thirty-fifth time today. May we all give thanks for the answer to our prayers. Letter will follow. NO MORE COMBAT!!!!!

Epilogue

December 30, 1944

How does it feel to receive a letter from your ground-pounding ex-combat husband? It sure seems good just to lie down and go to sleep with no worries to keep me tossing and rolling—most restful sleep I've had since my arrival here.

No, I won't be coming home for a while. I'm going to take a staff job with the Thirteenth Combat Wing. If I like the job and it pans out okay I'll remain here six months, that's maximum. The war isn't going so good right at the present and I would like to do just a little more than my part before departing here. Maybe I can make it a little easier for someone else. The good Lord knows I've had plenty of breaks and good luck during my tour. In fact, the whole crew came through well and happy without a scratch on them, even though they do feel as if they're living on borrowed time. Many of our buddies were not so fortunate, so I feel that I should do just a little more. All the boys except Work and myself are returning to the States. Layl has a few more to fly before he finishes up, but it won't take long. He'll get his old crew back when Doc finishes. Doc has several more to go but he'll come through okay.

Just got some good news. I've been picked to go to London to be on a broadcast Sunday afternoon. Must get started getting a few things in order. I think it's called "London Calling" and will be beamed to the U.S.

January 3, 1945

I got back from London just in time to go to work last night. They sure gave it to me. I was pretty tired after the trip, but when I finished a thirteen-hour tour of duty I was really dead.

Now about the broadcast. I didn't make it after all. My orders were incorrect and I got to the wrong place at the right time. By the time I found the right place it was the wrong time and the big show was over. Oh well, I had the satisfaction of seeing the New Year in London. Met some fellows who had been at Douglas, Arizona, with me so we had a big bull session.

The fellows have all started for home except Work and myself. Work is on a furlough and you know what I'm doing. I'm still living with the 95th, but will move to the 13th Wing tomorrow. So far I'm very much pleased with my new job. It's interesting and very vital—there's no room for mistakes. I think I can handle it okay but time will tell. Right now I'll have to put in long hours and work pretty hard to learn everything, but in a few weeks when I can handle things alone it will be okay. . . .

January 5, 1945

. . . If someone had told me that I had to stay here I would have been awfully unhappy, mad as hell, and probably griped about everything. But since I've done it on my own hook even the worst things have taken on a rosy appearance and life is much more bearable. After people quit shooting at you and the only danger you have to face is falling on icy sidewalks it takes quite a bit to get one in a bad humor.

I'm very well pleased with my new job. The training and experience are well worth my staying here a couple of extra months. It also gives me a chance to rehabilitate myself after combat in my own way.

It seems funny going to work in "Class A" uniform, blouse, tie, and all the trimmings. You, no doubt, wonder what the nature of my new job is and I'd like very much to tell you, but there are regulations which prevent it. As you can see, I'm with headquarters immediately higher than the Group I was with. We coordinate the groups within our command and see that they get the necessary info to carry on their operations. It's really interesting and at the present I'm very enthused about it. Maybe the novelty will wear off after a time. There's one thing about this job. It will occupy just as much of my time as I want it to. That is, I can live it all day, eat with it and sleep with it day in and day out, or I can forget about it any time and things will go on anyway.

I hope it is easier for you knowing that I am safe, that my combat is over, and all we have to do is wait a few more months before being together for good. . . .

There were times in combat when I wondered if I would see my wife again or ever see my son. That worry and that feeling are now gone. I know darn well I will and it's just a question of time. I realize that it was only through the grace of God that this was brought about, so I feel perhaps I should do just a little more in appreciation of our good fortune. We have more than either of us realize to be thankful for. I don't like being away from you, but I won't gripe about it now in the face of all our good luck.

January 9, 1945

. . . Darn near got injured this morning. The snow was packed hard on the sidewalk and was just like clear ice. I started walking down the hill with hands in my pockets, slipped, and before I could get my balance I had made a three-point landing and slid twenty feet on my undercarriage. It sure would be heck after finishing my missions without a scratch to slip and fall on the sidewalk and get hurt.

Here's something I'm very sorry about. I told you that I would get a picture of Lucky Sherry *just as soon as was possible since the last two bunches of pictures didn't turn out. Well, I've waited just a wee bit too long 'cause she isn't with us any more. But I'll say one thing . . . she was lucky all the way for everyone that flew her. . . .*

I received the fifth Oak Leaf Cluster to the Air Medal today so am sending it on. That's the last one I'll ever earn in this Theater and I hope it is the last one ever. I probably won't write again for a couple of days because I'm going to another field to attend to some duties. But I promise a long letter upon returning.

January 14, 1945

. . . *Here's what I've done so far today, and will do later. Being Sunday I got up at eight for breakfast and was ready for church at ten. After church I stopped and talked to Work and Billy Bob for about an hour and then it was dinner time. After dinner I worked an hour so another guy could go eat—I shouldn't say "work" as it was just a question of having a guy on duty in case the telephone should ring. This afternoon I have to go to one of the groups for interrogation of crews and find out what happened in today's operation. That will probably be over about six—then I'll have dinner and go to work at seven and get off at eight in the morning. You see when we get started we really put in the time and usually get something done. . . .*

January 15, 1945

In this new job I have a heck of a time trying to work out a sleeping schedule that will coincide with my working time. Did you ever stop to think that when you work twelve hours and take off twenty-four there isn't a plausible time to sleep? If I go to bed when I first get through work then I get up too soon and am tired before going to work again. But then I'm too tired to stay up after finishing work. Boy, I sure have problems to worry about. Notice how things have changed. Less than three weeks ago I was worrying about my neck. Now all I do is try to make my stay here just a little more comfortable. . . .

Had a letter from Smith today telling me all the news about the boys. They are still awaiting transportation home—hence are just lying around killing time and occasionally doing a few odd details. Sure hated to see them go, in a way. We had been through a lot together. I bid them good-bye in London, a rather touching ordeal. After all we've done it seemed kind of odd to see them with tears in their eyes—and in mine too—after everything was over and them with a train ticket home. A finer bunch of fellows will never be found again on one crew. I sure enjoyed having them with me. But every pilot thinks he has the best crew there is.

January 16, 1945

Here it is the middle of January and the way things look at the present I figure on tendering my resignation here the end of March. This is still subject to change one way or the other, but I think we're safe in planning on my leaving here in April.

Guess what happened this afternoon! Well, I won't keep you guessing any longer. They fell out the troops, had a big parade, band and all, and at the climax gave Work, myself, and a couple of other fellows the Distinguished Flying Cross. Are you interested in the citation? Okay, I'll copy it down for you since I have only one copy and it has to go in my 201 file. Don't believe any of it, though, just read it and forget it 'cause it does get flowery and all I was doing was saving my own neck.

"The Distinguished Flying Cross is awarded the following named Officers: Eugene R. Fletcher 0-759211 1st Lt. Army Air Forces, United States Army.

"For extraordinary achievements while serving as pilot on heavy bombardment missions to Cologne, Germany, 17 October 1944 and Hamburg, Germany, 25 October 1944. On both these occasions Lt. Fletcher demonstrated outstanding qualities of initiative and leadership by assuming lead responsibilities for his group when scheduled leaders were forced to leave formation because of mechanical difficulties. The superior airmanship, resourcefulness and devotion to duty displayed by Lt. Fletcher materially contributed to the success of these important operations and reflect highest credit upon himself and the Army Air Forces."

I'll send the medal on to you as soon as I can get something to wrap it in.

No mail for me today, but I didn't expect any for lately we have only been getting mail from the States about once a week. I hope by now you know my tour is over. I'm anxiously awaiting your reaction to my decision to remain here awhile. I believe you understand what I'm trying to do so I'm hoping you won't be too disappointed.

January 17 was a rough but happy day for Doc. He had engine trouble, but managed to get home on 3 engines from Hamburg for his final mission #35. Billy Bob was reinstated as

1st pilot and would now fly his remaining missions with his old crew.

January 18, 1945

. . . We have our working schedule all messed up again. Some day maybe we'll get it worked out. Last night I worked at the job which I'm trying to get. It's a good deal, but will take some time before I can handle it alone competently. The job I have been doing is very closely coordinated to it, but is the junior position which must be learned before doing this. I don't know how I'll make out. There are six of us all working for the same job and only two of us will get it. Naturally our work is very closely supervised and when a mistake is made it stands out like a sore thumb. So far most of us have displayed just about the same ability and willingness to learn, so it's just a question of waiting to see who will mess up the worst first, or if that doesn't happen then I don't know how they'll figure out who gets the job and who doesn't. I'll just do my best and if that isn't enough I'll take my leave of absence and head for my little family.

According to your letters right now you are reading my late November and early December letters. We're each just about a good month behind in the activities of the other. One of these days we won't have to put up with this pony express system. When we want to tell the other something we'll just be face to face, one of the advantages of close proximity.

I feel sorry for the ground pounders I work with here. Most of them haven't seen their families in well over two years. I don't see how they can stand it, and they know they can't get home until the end of the war. When I compare my predicament with theirs I really can't gripe because I know I can come home in a few months.

January 22, 1945

In my spare time I have been doing a little flying. We have an AT-17 here like I used to fly in Advanced Training, and I've been getting a kick out of flying it. But I guess I'm just a land lover at heart because now that I have my four hours in and just a little more I've lost the urge to sail in the blue.

February 1, 1945

. . . Things are going to change a little bit around here—don't know exactly how yet. But I suggest you stop writing me at this present address. I'll let you know before very long what to do. If you want you can start a letter and add to it each day, then when you find out what goes you can send it on. Don't misinterpret this as meaning I might be coming home because I don't want any hopes up. It's just a suggestion which will improve the mail situation for me a little later on.

February 4, 1944

Really had a time yesterday! It was a beautiful day with sunshine and all so I decided to go flying. Flew up to Edinburgh, then over Loch Lomond just so I could say that I have seen the "bonnie banks." It was a nice trip and I enjoyed myself. The weather probably had a lot to do with it because it has been cold and dreary up until then. . . .

We had some bad news on February 6, when we heard that Billy Bob had failed to return from a mission to Chemnitz. I went immediately to the 95th Group Operations and was informed that he was okay, having landed at Brussels.

February 24, 1945   Telegram

Arrived in New York last night will be home as soon as possible will wire again from Tacoma and let you know details with all my love
    Gene

Postscript

When the war in England ended I was serving in a staff capacity at the air base in Hobbs, New Mexico, and was one of the first released. I left the service knowing that I had proudly been a part of a massive struggle that would surely end all wars, and that totalitarianism had been dealt such a defeat that never again would greedy men seek to covet another nation's territory and its people. I felt we had truly brought peace to a world which in the past had known only war!

It was on this note that I dearly wanted to end this book for this was, in truth, my belief at the cessation of hostilities. But the passage of time showed nothing could have been farther from reality. It was obvious that again I was spinning "idle dreams."

Who could foresee that Brownie would participate in two more wars, that Doc would continue flying in the Air Force Reserve and retire a lieutenant colonel? Or, for that matter, that Frank and I would be called upon to serve our country in one more war? So now it seems only fair to the reader that we muster for interrogation one last time.

I am happy to report that all crew members have lived a full and rewarding life with their families.

Doc is still working full-time with his brother operating automobile dealerships in Tacoma and Auburn, Washington. He and Margaret live in Tacoma.

Billy Bob Layl is now Dr. B. B. Layl. He and his wife Emma Jean live in Piggott, Arkansas, where he is a practicing eye specialist.

Roco has retired after a career in accounting. In 1947 he came to Richland, Washington, to visit his brother who was a nuclear physicist at the Hanford project. He liked the state, and made it his home. He and his wife, Dottie, now live in Puyallup.

Frank Dimit has now retired from a management position of a subsidiary of a major steel company. He continues to serve on the Board of Trustees for a technical school. Peggy and Frank reside in Steubenville, Ohio.

Brownie was the only one of our group to make the military his career. After retiring from the Air Force he returned to Pittsburg, Kansas, where he purchased the farm which was his wife's family home. He has now retired and his son operates the farm. Mary passed away during the time this book was being written.

George Hinman has retired after a career with the United States Soil Conservation Service as a technician designing and overseeing conservation projects. Yorkville, Illinois, is home to George and Mary.

Ken McQuitty has retired from a life in the home building industry. Mac and Jane live in Columbia, Missouri.

Robert Lynch is working for an electrical company where he assembles motors. He will retire in January 1988. Muldrow, Oklahoma, is still home to Bob and Willie.

Joe Firszt operated his own dry cleaning business and has only recently retired after selling his business. He and his wife, Helen, live in Carpentersville, Illinois.

Martin Smith is the only deceased member of the crew, a fact which was learned when Doc attempted to locate the gang for our crew reunion in 1985. All we knew was his home was in Milwaukee, Wisconsin, in 1944. After many calls, a dedicated telephone company employee was able to locate his daughter. By strange coincidence she lived in Seattle and represented her father at the crew reunion.

Fletch, after a career in agriculture and many years of community service, retired in 1983 from the active management of the corporate family farm. This business is carried on by sons David and James. Sherry and Fletch live in Tekoa, Washington.

All members present or accounted for, Sir. Crew dismissed!

Eugene Fletcher
Major USAF Ret.

Appendixes

The Odyssey of Two Airplanes Plus Ten

We were assigned two aircraft during our tour—both were Boeing built. We were especially pleased to be assigned *Knock Out Baby*, #42-97257. This aircraft was originally named by Lieutenant Roy W. Gielen and his crew. Their first mission was to Berlin on April 18, 1944. This was a premier target for the group because the 95th and 100th had the honor of flying the first U.S. heavy bombers over Berlin on March 4, 1944. This Task Force was led by H. Griffin Mumford of the 95th Bomb Group. For this mission our group received another Presidential Unit Citation.

On September 18, 1944, *Knock Out Baby* took part in the third Russia-Italy-England Shuttle Raid. She was shot up on the ground during the night in Poltava, Russia, and was not able to return with the group. But she was repaired and ferried back to England and was returned to the 95th Bomb Group on October 4, 1944.

In the meantime, we were assigned #43-37783, a brand new B-17G, which we named *Lucky Sherry*. This was the aircraft in which we flew our last fifteen missions. She did not return from a mission to Frankfurt on January 5, 1945, and I assumed at the time that she had been shot down. In September 1986 I was informed by Paul Andrews from information he had gleaned from the archives of the 95th Bomb Group that she made an emergency landing at Lille, France. She was repaired and returned to the group on February 15, 1945. Sometime after that she was transferred to the 335th Squadron where she was renamed *Temptation*. The last personal record I have of her is a picture taken from a mission camera on board which indicated that she was still flying combat on March 17, 1945, when the group went to Ruhland. A recorded entry in the archives reported that she returned early from a mission to Berlin on March 18. The final entry in the archives showed her last operational sortie was May 20, 1945, returning POWs from the continent to England. During her lifetime she was dispatched on sixty-two combat missions plus eight mercy missions after the war ended.

On March 28, 1945, on a mission to Hanover, *Knock Out Baby* landed at Le Bourget, France, with the #1 engine feathered. The crew was not credited with a mission. That same day she was earmarked for salvage, but the order was cancelled—she was repaired and continued to fly.

Additional information provided by Paul Andrews and our own diaries makes it possible to record the destiny of the other ten aircraft we flew in combat.

On August 6, 1944, aircraft #231999, *Chicken Ship*, ran out of fuel and landed short of the base at Poltava, Russia, on our "Frantic Five" mission. She was left there and was assigned to the Eastern Command.

On August 16, on a mission to Zeitz, aircraft #297797, *Full House*, received a direct flak hit to the left wing. The aircraft disintegrated, killing six members of the crew. The other four became POWs. We lost four aircraft on this raid including #231514, also named *Full House* because of the card hand painted on her nose. She left the formation over the target with the #2 engine feathered and #3 on fire. All nine members of her crew became POWs.

November 2, on the mission to Merseburg, aircraft #2102678, *Ole Worrybird*, left the formation with the #2 and #3 engines feathered. At that time she was under the escort of a single P-51 fighter. One member of the crew was killed and eight became POWs.

On November 29, aircraft #231675, *Berlin Bessie*, after returning from a mission to Hamm, was declared beyond repair and joined the bone yard.

On our mission to Merseburg on November 30, aircraft #2102560, *The Thomper,* received a direct flak hit in the bomb bay. The aircraft left the formation on fire and broke in half at the radio compartment. Six members of the crew were killed and three became POWs.

On December 16 on a raid to Stuttgart aircraft #297232, *Government Issue,* was destroyed, killing all nine crew members. Aircraft #232066, *Silver Slipper,* crash landed on the base the same day. The aircraft was demolished but all crew members were safe.

On January 20, 1945, aircraft #231462, *Roaring Bill,* landed on the continent and was declared beyond repair. Two members of the crew bailed out over enemy territory and became POWs. The rest, including one wounded, stayed with the plane until they crossed the allied lines.

On April 16 aircraft #237882, *Blues in the Reich,* was declared beyond salvage and relegated to the bone pile.

And thus it was that our two assigned ships survived the war intact. *Knock Out Baby,* even though destined for the scrap pile, became a survivor in the tradition of the crews that flew her. At the end of hostilities she had been dispatched on 113 combat missions and on June 6, 1945, she arrived back in the United States.

The Missions

Target	A/C No.	Name	Date	Group Mission	Air Time
1. Abbeville	7232	*Government Issue*	July 6	168	5:10
2. Merseburg	1462	*Roaring Bill*	July 7	169	4:15
3. Munich	2560	*The Thomper*	July 11	171	9:45
4. Maquis	7882	*Blues in the Reich*	July 14	173	9:30
5. Paris (RR bridge SE)	97797	*Full House*	July 17	175	7:00
6. Hemmingstedt	1675	*Berlin Bessie*	July 18	177	7:00
7. St. Lo	1999	*Chicken Ship*	July 24	181	6:35
8. St. Lo	1514	*Full House*	July 25	183	6:05
9. Merseburg	7257	*Knock Out Baby*	July 28	183	8:35
10. Maquis	1675	*Berlin Bessie*	Aug. 1	185	9:40
11. Hamburg	7882	*Blues in the Reich*	Aug. 4	188	7:15
12. Rahmel (Gdynia)	7257	*Knock Out Baby*	Aug. 6	189	10:35
13. Trzebinia	7257	*Knock Out Baby*	Aug. 7	190	10:10
14. Buzau	7257	*Knock Out Baby*	Aug. 8	191	9:00
15. Toulouse	7257	*Knock Out Baby*	Aug. 12	192	10:00
16. Ruhland	7257	*Knock Out Baby*	Aug. 24	197	9:10
17. Berlin	2678	*Ole Worrybird*	Aug. 27	200	6:05
18. Ruhland	7257	*Knock Out Baby*	Sep. 11	207	8:40
19. Mainz	2066	*Silver Slipper*	Sep. 27	213	6:40
20. Merseburg	2066	*Silver Slipper*	Sep. 28	214	8:20

Target	A/C No.	Name	Date	Group Mission	Air Time
21. Mainz	7783	*Lucky Sherry*	Oct. 9	221	6:30
22. Bremen	7783	*Lucky Sherry*	Oct. 12	222	7:05
23. Cologne	7783	*Lucky Sherry*	Oct. 17	224	7:00
24. Kassel	7783	*Lucky Sherry*	Oct. 18	225	8:35
25. Hamburg	7783	*Lucky Sherry*	Oct. 25	228	7:20
26. Hanover	7783	*Lucky Sherry*	Oct. 26	229	7:15
27. Merseburg	7783	*Lucky Sherry*	Oct. 30	231	5:15
28. Merseburg	7783	*Lucky Sherry*	Nov. 2	232	7:50
29. Ludwigshafen	7783	*Lucky Sherry*	Nov. 5	234	7:50
30. Koblenz	7783	*Lucky Sherry*	Nov. 11	237	6:25
31. Merseburg	7783	*Lucky Sherry*	Nov. 30	242	8:20
32. Berlin	7783	*Lucky Sherry*	Dec. 5	245	8:35
33. Biblis	7783	*Lucky Sherry*	Dec. 24	250	8:45
34. Bad Münster	7783	*Lucky Sherry*	Dec. 25	251	7:05
35. Fulda	7783	*Lucky Sherry*	Dec. 27	252	7:50

Bombardier's Note

My notes were written immediately after each mission. Needless to say, they are not literary masterpieces—just notes as recorded while I was still scared.

As usual my hindsight is 100 percent, but my foresight leaves a lot to be desired. I wish now that I had written a more complete record. However, I can assure you that I'm not going to fly thirty-five more missions just for a better record.

Frank S. Dimit

Navigator's Note

My writing had its beginning during the waiting part of many nights between the end of our tour and the end of hostilities in Europe. For the same reasons Fletch chose to take a staff job with the Thirteenth Combat Wing, I became a group briefing officer reporting to Major Bingham (who became so upset about our being assigned to fly to Merseburg for the seventh time). My primary task was to prepare and present to combat crews an overview of bombing missions. Typically these briefings included targets being attacked by the Royal Air Force and the U.S. Fifteenth Air Force in Italy in addition to what the Eighth Air Force would be doing.

Each mission's specifications were received by teletype at intervals during the late afternoon and night before. Invariably the intervals allowed far more time than was needed to prepare the briefing, so I filled the waiting time by commencing a narrative of the missions our crew had flown. However, the time required for the writing exceeded the waiting time.

I briefed the 320th combat mission flown by the 95th Bomb Group on April 18, and was on duty May 7 when orders were received restricting all U.S. personnel to their bases for an indefinite period beginning early May 8 (V-E Day). Luckily there was enough lead time for me to arrange a pass, since I greatly preferred to celebrate that event in London.

In June 1945 I was surprised to be assigned to navigate *Knock Out Baby* on its return flight to the States. Through rare good fortune the payload consisted of personal gear for the flight crew and our passengers, *ten crew chiefs.*

In exchange for publications rights to what I have written, Fletch has opened himself to gratuitous remarks from this member of his crew. Somewhat arrogant and excessively competitive as I was in 1944 when our crew was formed, I was prepared to follow orders and salute by the book—period. Everything else would be "wait and see." What I saw was an aircraft commander not much taller than my own 5 foot 5, weighing perhaps 130 pounds in full flight gear. Look out, Hitler!

Having read this far, however, you already realize how capable Fletch was. He was admired and trusted by each of us. We knew he was loyal and would fight to protect our interests. The longer I live and the more people I observe, the more certain I become that Fletch was an exceptional leader; he is an extraordinary man!

Robert "Roco" Work

Note on Sources

The main sources of information for this book were the letters
I wrote to my wife, Sherry, and my diary. Also invaluable were
the personal notes of the copilot, navigator, bombardier, and
armorer gunner—along with information provided by Paul
Fiess. I have also consulted the following secondary sources:
the *Stars and Stripes, ETO edition,* and *Yank* magazine.

In all probability many of the facts and figures in our original diaries may have appeared in the *Stars and Stripes,* since
this was the official newspaper for the troops during World
War II.

In addition to our regular mission briefing, we had voluntary news briefings conducted once or twice a week which contained a lot of information. We were given facts and figures,
and followed the progress of the war. These plus our firsthand knowledge and experiences made up the bulk of our
diary entries. To differentiate one source from another after
forty-three years would be impossible.

If the reader should wish to verify that some of these incidents took place, three sources would be invaluable: *Contrails,*
the unofficial history of the 95th Bomb Group, published by
the 95th Bomb Group Photographic section under the supervision of Captain David B. Henderson; *Münster: The Way it
Was,* written by Ian Hawkins of Bacton, Stowmarket, England,
and published by Robinson Typographics of Anaheim, Califor-

nia; *Mighty Eighth War Diary*, by Roger Freeman of New Colchester, England, a foremost authority on the Eighth Air Force and the men who flew the planes. This last book was published by Jane's Publishing Company Limited, London.